COMPUTER SCIENCE, TECHNOLOGY AND APPLICATIONS



# ANT COLONIES: BEHAVIOR IN INSECTS AND COMPUTER APPLICATIONS

EMILY C. SUN
EDITOR

Nova Science Publishers, Inc.
*New York*

For permission to use material from this book please contact us:
Telephone 631-231-7269; Fax 631-231-8175
Web Site: http://www.novapublishers.com



**LIBRARY OF CONGRESS CATALOGING-IN-PUBLICATION DATA**

Ant colonies : behavior in insects and computer applications / editor, Emily C. Sun.
p. cm.
Includes bibliographical references and index.
ISBN 978-1-61122-023-0 (hardcover)
1. Swarm intelligence. 2. Ants--Nests. 3. Ants--Behavior. I. Sun, Emily C.
Q337.3.A565 2010
006.3--dc22
2010037893

*Published by Nova Science Publishers, Inc. † New York*

# CONTENTS

# PREFACE

Ant colony optimization is a population-based general-search technique that can be used for the solution of difficult combinatorial problems. Ant colony optimization uses the knowledge-reinforcing mechanism used by real-life ants while traversing possible paths in search of food, depositing a chemical substance (called pheromone), en-route and subsequently forming trails which can then be followed by other ants in the colony. With its strong mathematical foundation and its simplicity of use, ant colony optimization provides an alternative method to routing optimizations with a wide range of applications. This book presents topical research in the study of ant colonies, their behavior and application in computer technologies.

Chapter 1 - Progressive Organization of co-Operating Colonies/ Collections of Ants/Agents (POOCA) is introduced as a novel robot navigation and obstacle avoidance approach that is capable of efficiently as well as accurately operating in both stationary and dynamic unknown environments. POOCA follows the streak of existing pheromone-based co-operative foraging multi-agent models in its biological inspiration (colonies of ants foraging their environment in search of food) and the utilization of evolutionary computation for optimizing the various parameters involved, but differs from them in its simulation of minimal and uniformly applied ant-inspired notions. POOCA's main principles include: stigmetry; stereo-like sensors and a single type of pheromone; inertia to change in direction of motion; intensifying pheromone laying, constant-rate pheromone evaporation, diminishing pheromone diffusion. In addition, near-minimum ant/agent colony/collection sizes that allow speedy convergence to (near-) optimal trails are determined. Simulations demonstrate POOCA's potential as a competent robot navigation and obstacle avoidance approach that imitates minimal biological principles, while also putting it forward as a useful emerging paradigm in swarm robotics, ant colony optimization and co-operative multi-agent learning.

Chapter 2 - This chapter proposes a stochastic optimization method, based on ant colony optimization, for the optimal choice of transformer sizes to be installed in a distribution network. This method is properly introduced to the solution of the optimal transformer sizing problem, taking into account the constraints imposed by the load the transformer serves throughout its life time and the possible transformer thermal overloading. The possibility to upgrade the transformer size one or more times throughout the study period results to different sizing paths, and ant colony optimization is applied in order to determine the least cost path, taking into account the transformer capital cost as well as the energy loss cost during the study period. The method is expanded for the optimal choice of transformer efficiency to serve the loads of the considered network. For a given transformer capacity, the possibility to install transformers of different efficiency throughout the study period is investigated with the objective to minimize the total installation and loss cost. The results of the proposed method demonstrate the benefits of its application in distribution network planning.

Chapter 3 - Ant colonies have been used as model systems for the study of self-organisation. Viewing ants as identical agents following simple rules has led to many insights into the emergence of complex behaviours. However, real biological ants are far from identical in behaviour. New advances in radio-frequency identification (RFID) technology now allow the exploration of ant behaviour at the individual level, providing unprecedented insights into distributed decision-making. Two areas of decision-making have been addressed with this new technology: 1) Individual task decisions in a changing environment; 2) Collective decision-making during colony emigration. The first of these areas investigates how tasks are robustly distributed between members of a colony in the face of changing environmental conditions. The use of RFID tags on worker ants allows simultaneous monitoring of a range of factors which could affect decision-making, including age, experience, spatial location, social interactions and fat reserves. These multifactor studies have demonstrated that individual ants base some task decisions on their own physiological state, but also utilise social cues. For non-specialist tasks, self-organisation also contributes because movement patterns can cause emergent task allocation. The combination of these simple mechanisms provides the colony as a whole with a responsive work-force, appropriately allocated across tasks but flexible in response to changing environmental conditions. The second area of distributed decision-making which has benefitted from the use of RFID is the study of unanimous collective decision-making during colony emigration. RFID microtransponder tags are used to identify the ants involved in collecting information about the environment and to determine how their actions lead to the final colony-level decision. The studies using RFID technology demonstrate that ants use a very simple threshold rule to make their individual decisions; from these individual decisions emerges a sophisticated choice mechanism at the colony level. Inter-individual variation in thresholds is critical for this to be an effective decision mechanism in an unpredictable environment, so the collection of individual-level data is essential. This provides interesting insights for anyone trying to combine inputs from distributed sensors to determine a single computer action. In general, the decentralised robustness exemplified by both decision-making processes provides a benchmark for studying behaviour of other animal populations, as well having implications in designing decision-making algorithms.

Chapter 4 - Introduction of alien organisms is a major risk that follows international trade. Ants are among the most harmful groups of invasive organisms, with five species, including the Argentine ant *Linepithema humile*, listed among the world's 100 worst invasive species by the IUCN. The authors review the damage, ecology, and dispersal of invasive ants, with the Argentine ant as a representative. Invasive ants attain high population densities in the introduced range, and cause damage to ecosystems, agriculture, and human well-being by the sheer number. The high density may stem partly from formation of expansive 'supercolonies' (a supercolony is a large network of cooperative nests). In the Argentine ant, the high consistency of their supercolony identities makes them important units in inferring the dispersal history of this species. The authors highlight two topics in the dispersal history of the species: 1) formation of an unprecedented intercontinental supercolony by the 150 year international trade; 2) recent successive introductions to Pan-Pacific region seemingly in accordance with globalization.

Chapter 5 - Adaptive optics is the technology for correcting the static and dynamic aberrations of optical systems. Traditional adaptive optics systems employ wavefront sensors to measure the phase aberrations in order to implement feedback controls. In recent years adaptive optics systems without wavefront sensors have been developed with the benefit of reduced complexity, cost, and size. These systems use some optimization algorithms to directly optimize the system performance metrics. The authors show that it is possible to compensate for phase aberrations with ant colony algorithm as the optimization algorithm in a no wavefront sensor adaptive optics system, which iteratively adjusts the control voltages of a deformable mirror to optimize the system performance metrics of the far-field intensity distribution of the laser beam. Encircled energy and Strehl ratio is used as the system performance metric. The effectiveness of this approach is analyzed numerically by use of a 37-element piezoelectric deformable mirror to correct simple and combined phase aberrations. Results demonstrate that this approach could effectively compensate for the phase distortions of laser beams and significantly improve beam qualities. A comparison indicates that this approach is much faster than a genetic algorithm while achieving almost the same beam quality.

Chapter 6 - Ant Colony Optimization (ACO) is a population-based, arti_cial multi-agent, general-search technique for the solution of combinatorial problems with its roots based on the behavior of real-ant colonies. With its strong mathematical foundation and its simplicity of use, ACO provides an alternative method to routing optimizations with a wide range of applications. The chapter outlines ACO's mathematical background and describes a suggested possible implementation strategy for identifying shortest or longest paths in different types of networks. The ACO approach is initially applied to construction scheduling and resource-unconstrained network topologies, solving for the longest path in the network and utilized in performing critical-path calculations and evaluating a project's completion time. A second case study focuses on shortest-path calculations and on solving for minimum-impact paths in urban water distribution networks (UWDN) subjected to either unexpected or scheduled interruption of service. As with the scheduling paradigm, the application of ACO on piping networks provides the means to finding both shortest and longest paths between nodes of interest by imitating the natural selection processes utilized by real-life ants in search of the shortest path from an ant nest to a food source.

Chapter 7 - In this chapter the authors introduce a new ant-based method, named KANTS, that takes advantage of the cooperative self-organization of Ant Colony Systems to create a naturally inspired clustering and pattern recognition method. The approach considers each data item as an ant, which moves inside a grid, changing the cells it goes through, in a fashion similar to Kohonen's Self-Organizing Maps. The resulting algorithm is conceptually more simple, takes less free parameters than other ant-based clustering algorithms. In order to test it, some of the well-known benchmark classification problems have been solved using the authors' algorithm and some other methods. KANTS yields the best results after some parameter tuning.

Moreover, some experiments have been performed to assess the algorithm as a data clustering tool, concluding that KANTS is in addition a very promising clustering method.

Chapter 8 – The strategy of the swarm intelligence named Ant Colony has proved tobe an interesting way to solve difficult combinatorial problems. In this strategy, the learning of ants is built through the trail of pheromones left by the each ant in the colony on the problem space. The ants iteratively using the pheromone level of the each path of the solution problem to decide which way to follow. The problem is that this decision is often uncertain or inconsistent. Classical logic can not handle this kind of decision problem. In this sense we use the non-classical logic, named Paraconsistent Logic for increasing the power of decision to the ants colony. This hybrid system based on Paraconsistent Logic and Ant Colony proves to be an interesting approach and has been statistically demonstrated in this work that the hybrid system provides a result equal to or greater in relation implementation of the MAX - MIN Ant System (a classical Ant Colony Metaheuristic).

Chapter 9 - As instrumentation develops in industry and science, the authors frequently generate multi-dimension data sets that may involve input from a large number of factors or variables. Many parameters of these instrument systems may not be directly related with the core function of the systems, and some factor may even lead to noise contamination of output signals. The potential obscuring effects of these variables on the data set can make it difficult to determine which parts of the instrument data are the most meaningful. Therefore, feature selection within data sets is becoming a core technique to detect pertinent factors or variable for system characterization. This not only reduces the data dimension but also provides pertinent information for system mechanism studies, and can ultimately yield information about the underlying instrumentation function.

Chapter 10 - In recent days wireless communication plays a major role. The packets transmitted are vulnerable to Dos attacks caused by injecting forged packets. Authentication plays an important role in securing transfer of messages in wireless environment that are attractive to malicious attacks. In this chapter an Ant Colony Optimization (ACO) based method is proposed to reduce the computational and communication overhead while generating a mark for each packet. In this approach, the packets are represented in the form of a binary tree and are identified by a packet identifier ID. Each packet has a set of keys with which a mark is generated for the packet. The packets in a group are represented in the form of a truth table and a minimized boolean expression is obtained. The literals in the expression give the minimum number of keys for generating a mark. Sreelaja and Pai proposed an Ant Colony Optimization based Boolean Expression Evolver (ABXE) algorithm to obtain a minimized Boolean expression. The ABXE algorithm is judiciously employed in the proposed work to efficiently generate marks for each packet. The literals in the product term of the Boolean expression represent the auxiliary keys to generate the marks for the packets using the root key. The receiver receives the packets and the root key is recovered using the auxiliary keys. The recovered roots help the receiver to classify received packets into disjoint sets and hence authentic packets and forged packets are placed separately. While the Merkle Tree packet filtering approach requires (n.log n) hashes to authenticate the packets, the proposed method requires only (log n) keys which serve to reduce the computational overhead. Also, the proposed approach calls for only (log n) keys and n signatures to be sent to the receiver which serves to reduce its communication overhead. In comparison, the Merkle Tree packet filtering approach requires (n log n) hashes and n signatures to be sent to the receiver.

In: Ant Colonies
Editor: Emily C. Sun
ISBN: 978-1-61122-023-0


*Chapter 1*

# Progressive Organization of Co-Operating Colonies/Collections of Ants/Agents (POOCA) for Competent Pheromone-Based Navigation and Multi-Agent Learning

***Tatiana Tambouratzis*** *

Department of Industrial Management & Technology,
University of Piraeus, Greece
and Department of Nuclear Engineering,
Chalmers University of Technology, Göteborg, Sweden

## Abstract

Progressive Organization of co-Operating Colonies/Collections of Ants/Agents (POOCA) is introduced as a novel robot navigation and obstacle avoidance approach that is capable of efficiently as well as accurately operating in both stationary and dynamic unknown environments. POOCA follows the streak of existing pheromone-based co-operative foraging multi-agent models in its biological inspiration (colonies of ants foraging their environment in search of food) and the utilization of evolutionary computation for optimizing the various parameters involved, but differs from them in its simulation of minimal and uniformly applied ant-inspired notions. POOCA's main principles include: stigmetry; stereo-like sensors and a single type of pheromone; inertia to change in direction of motion; intensifying pheromone laying, constant-rate pheromone evaporation, diminishing pheromone diffusion. In addition, near-minimum ant/agent colony/collection sizes that allow speedy convergence to (near-) optimal trails are determined. Simulations demonstrate POOCA's potential as a competent robot navigation and obstacle avoidance approach that imitates minimal biological principles,

* Corresponding author: Department of Industrial Management & Technology, University of Piraeus, 107 Deligiorgi St, Piraeus 185 34, Greece, tel +30 210 41 42 423, fax +30 210 41 42 392, email tatiana@unipi.gr & *tatianatambouratzis@gmail.com*, url http://www.tex.unipi.gr/dep/tambouratzis/main.htm, Department of Nuclear Engineering, Chalmers University of Technology, SE-412 Göteborg, Sweden, url http://www.nephy.chalmers.se/staff/tatiana.html

while also putting it forward as a useful emerging paradigm in swarm robotics, ant colony optimization and co-operative multi-agent learning.

**Keywords:** robot navigation, swarm robotics, ant colony optimization, co-operative multi-agent learning, pheromone, optimal trail creation.

## 1. Introduction

Although navigation constitutes an action that is performed effortlessly by mobile living beings, the wide collection of robot navigation approaches appearing in the literature has not been as successful, irrespective of the methodology employed; recently, a number of navigation approaches inspired by ant colonies have been developed. Complementary to that line of research, simulations of the biological (especially ant colony based) principles underlying navigation have resulted in efficient multi-agent system and soft computing paradigms that provide interesting solutions to challenging optimization problems.

This piece of research aims at simulating ant-inspired principles that allow efficient and accurate navigation as well as obstacle avoidance in unknown stationary and dynamic environments. The resulting methodology is named POOCA, an acronym for Progressive Organization of co-Operating Colonies/Collections of Ants/Agents. Although POOCA follows the streak of existing pheromone-based co-operative foraging multi-agent systems in its biological inspiration (colonies of ants foraging their environment in search of food) and the utilization of evolutionary computation for optimizing the various parameters involved, it differs from these approaches in that it simulates minimal and uniformly applied ant-inspired notions. POOCA's main principles include:

- Stigmetry. In line with previous approaches, rather than using individual long-term memory or directly communicating with each other, the ants exchange information concerning their locations, recent trails and the environment indirectly via pheromone. The selection of the location towards which an ant moves is such that a location of high pheromone concentration is preferred over a location of low pheromone concentration; overall, the creation of each trail is influenced by the previous locations of all the ants in the colony, weighted by a decay factor.
- Inertia to change in motion-direction. Further to previous approaches, inertia is implemented as a bias towards straight-ahead motion, and progressively smaller biases for motion that deviates increasingly from straight-ahead motion. As a result, unrealistic and unnecessary directional changes are discouraged (the amount of discouragement being proportional to the change in direction) without the need to dictate a constant direction of motion.
- Pheromone laying. Unlike most previous approaches, a single type of positive pheromone is employed. Pheromone accumulation proceeds in the same manner for nest-to-foodsource and foodsource-to-nest trails, is uniformly applied to each location visited by an ant, is independent of the current pheromone concentration at the particular location, and depends only on the current feeding status of the ant (expressed by the number of trails so far completed by the ant).

- Pheromone evaporation. Once deposited, pheromone decays at a constant rate, i.e. by an amount that depends exclusively on the current pheromone concentration.
- Pheromone diffusion. Unlike previous approaches, pheromone spreads from each location where it is deposited to the entire environment, with the strength of diffusion decreasing progressively in space and in time. This formulation implements a stereo-like sensing of pheromone concentration which – in turn - promotes continuous pheromone concentrations at neighbouring locations and higher pheromone concentrations at bends of the trails as well as at narrow areas between trails. Combined with stigmetry, the creation of progressively straighter and shorter trails is encouraged.
- Competence. The minimum number of ants allowing speedy convergence upon an optimal or near-optimal trail is utilized.

Simulations demonstrate POOCA's potential as a competent biologically-inspired robot navigation and obstacle avoidance approach, while also putting it forward as a useful emerging paradigm in swarm robotics, ant colony optimization and co-operative multi-agent learning.

This chapter is organized as follows: section 2 reviews robot navigation, while section 3 presents ant navigation and its derivatives ant-colony optimization, co-operative multi-agent systems and swarm robotics; section 4 introduces POOCA problem representation and mode of operation as well as the application of evolutionary computation for optimizing the various POOCA parameters; POOCA performance is reported in section 5 for a variety of navigation problems, section 6 puts forward future extensions to POOCA and, finally, section 7 concludes the chapter.

## 2. Robot Navigation

The formal definition of navigation (Latin navis+agere, originally Greek ναύς+άγω= ship+drive) is to direct a ship to its destination. This entails determining the position of the ship (e.g. on a chart), relating it to the position of the destination (and, perhaps, also to other landmarks), and setting the appropriate course. In robot navigation (RN), these three steps are formally expressed as questions (a) "where am I?", (b) "where are other places with respect to me?", and (c) "how do I get to other places from here?" (Levitt & Lawton 1990; McKerrow 1991; Franz & Mallot 2000). In order to answer questions (a)-(c), two main RN methodologies have been developed:

- Path setting and following of automated guided vehicles (AGVs) to and from predetermined positions in known environments cluttered with obstacles. AGVs can follow pre-wired or otherwise set paths between start- and end-points; alternatively, they can have their paths planned in real-time according to the constraints and requirements of the navigation task. Complete path planning and partial path re-planning approaches include A* (Nilsson 1980; Lai et al. 2007) and D* (Barraquand & Latombe 1993; Stentz 1995; Hwang et al. 1998; Oriolo et al. 1998) search, potential fields (Khatib 1986; Borenstein & Koren 1989; Ge & Cui 2002), vector field histograms (Borenstein & Koren 1991), nearness diagrams (Minguez & Montano 2004) and path deformation algorithms (Lamiraux et al. 2004) to name but a few. Unfortunately, both path planning and path following constitute NP-complete problems[1] that are not directly graph-like translatable unless maze navigation, global communication and information exchange (radio-network or common evolving model of the environment) are employed; moreover, RN becomes even harder when the environment is dynamic, for instance when some of the obstacles appear/disappear/move, an end-point is relocated or becomes unusable etc.

- Pure sensor information exploitation and autonomous navigation in unknown - and perhaps dynamic - environments with sporadic or no human intervention. The gathered information is acquired by a variety of sensors and concerns both the robot's internal status (proprioception) and the environment (exteroception); it is encoded in absolute (idiothetic, e.g. via wheel-turn counting) and/or perceptual (allothetic, e.g. via sonar, laser or other range sensors) terms, and stored as an internal and progressively growing global representation of the environment. Best known as a cognitive map (Gallistel 1993), information representation is usually (geo)metric (Asada 1990; Gonzalez et al. 1994; Thrun et al. 1998), i.e. the locations of the environment are expressed via exact coordinates and distances/orientations[2]. The metric cognitive map is utilized for simultaneous localization and mapping (SLAM, Smith & Cheeseman 1986; Leonard & Durrant-Whyte 1991): during RN the robot answers questions (a)-(c); it matches the collected information against the map and estimates its current position in order to activate the appropriate motor actions and get to the location of current interest; at the same time, the collected information allows map verification, completion and updating. Unfortunately, SLAM is far from trivial as the acquired sensor information is susceptible to cumulative error and perceptual aliasing, whereby the same location may give rise to dissimilar sensor signals while distinct locations may give rise to identical sensor signals; this phenomenon becomes especially pronounced for outdoors as well as unconstrained environments, where a lack of robustness and stability is introduced even for the slightest changes in pose.

The aforementioned difficulties of RN have prompted research and simulation of the principles employed by biological systems.

[1] NP-completeness holds even for point robots navigating environments with simplified polyhedral obstacles (Canny 1988).

[2] Complementary to metric maps, (i) topographical (Kuipers & Byun 1987; Kuipers & Byun 1991; Choset & Nagatani 2001; Rajashekhara & Chaudhuri 2006), (ii) hybrid (Thrun & Bucken 1996; Poncela et al. 2002; Tomatis et al. 2003), and (iii) symbolic (Galindo et al. 2007) maps have been developed. In (i) the relations between objects are expressed in a qualitative graph-like manner; (ii) constitute a fusion of metric and topographical maps, while (iii) provide qualitative information via symbol graphs.

# 3. Real Ants Colonies - Ant-Inspired Navigation and Optimization

## 3.1. Ant Foraging - Stigmetry

The more than 12,000 species of ants inhabiting the Earth belong to the family of Formicidae and, together with wasps and bees, to the order of Hymenoptera. Although practically blind, ants live into highly organized colonies that occupy extensive foraging areas around their nests. Their superior adaptation capability has rendered them abundant, adding up to 15-25% of the total terrestrial animal biomass (Wilson 1963; Schultz 2000). The exact make-up and behavioural traits of each ant species depend on the environment, i.e. on the conditions for survival.

### *3.1.1. Independent navigation employing long-term memory*

In unforgiving (food-wise poor, dynamic and random) environments such as the Sahara and Namib deserts, the foodsources are not constant but – as a rule – consist of small insects that have succumbed to the extreme heat. Consequently, each ant (e.g. Cataglyphis fortis, Cataglyphis bicolor or Sahara desert, Ocymyrmex) is autonomous in its search for food. It estimates the direction and distance travelled away from the nest by taking periodic measurements of its angle of motion with respect to the sun (Sommer & Wehner 2004). It also remembers the encountered landmarks (Akesson & Wehner 2002) and does not go over ground already covered during the current trip (Wehner & Srinivasan 1981). As soon as a foodsource is found, the ant uses the sun like a compass and employs the previously memorized visual landmarks in order to establish the shortest straight trail back to the nest (Wehner & Menzel 1969; Fukushi 2001). When planning its next trip, the ant follows the previous foraging direction if this was successful in finding a foodsource, otherwise it randomly selects a novel direction; if more than one foodsource co-exist, ants split randomly and independently between them. Overall, minimal intra-colony communication, decentralized foraging and extensive long-term memory are employed, i.e. questions (a)-(c) are answered more or less independently by each ant.

### *3.1.2. Cooperative navigation and pheromone trail following*

In friendlier environments, where foodsources are numerous, plentiful and semi-permanent, the ants (e.g. Tetramorium caespitum, Iridomyrmex humilus or Argentine, Monomorium pharaonis or Pharaoh's) forage their environment with the collective aim of maximizing food collection over time (Denny et al. 2001). To this end, ants do not rely on individual long-term memory for answering questions (a)-(c) but rather employ the chemical substance pheromone (Wilson 1963; Jacobson 1972) for indirect intra-colony communication and information exchange concerning trails and foodsources[3]. Pheromone is secreted from the ant's posterior abdomen, flows down its sting and is deposited in small amounts on the ground as the ant

[3] Although these ants also evaluate angles and distances, their nest-pointing mechanism is error-prone (quantitative and rapidly decaying (Ziegler & Wehner 1997)) and, thus, does not allow the ants to calculate their exact position relative to the nest.

moves. Different kinds of pheromone are employed at different foraging situations[4], with the amount of deposited pheromone depending on both foraging conditions and foodsource quality[5].

At the beginning of navigation, ant movement is random, whereby a multitude of individual pheromone trails are formed to the various foodsources (in a manner similar to the topographical maps of footnote 2). Each ant senses the pheromone of all the ants in the same colony and uses its two antennae like binocular vision or stereophonic hearing in order to indirectly collect information about the different pheromone trails in its vicinity. It also prefers (in a probabilistic sense) to visit locations heavily marked with pheromone (Jacobson 1972) rather than novel (unvisited or weakly marked) parts of the environment. Shorter trails become richer in pheromone faster than longer trails (differential length effect) and their selection is further reinforced. This biased accumulation of pheromone at shorter trails eventually results into the entire ant colony converging upon a single shortest pheromone trail[6] between the nest and the best foodsource.

Pheromone evaporates as soon as it has been deposited and at highly divergent rates[7]. This causes trail dissipation once the best foodsource has been exhausted, whereby the processes of new best foodsource discovery and trail creation are re-initialized. It is in this manner that the ant colony adapts to changes in the environment (Wilson 1963) such as foodsource depletion, partial pheromone trail destruction/occlusion, obstacle appearance/ disappearance/movement, nest relocation etc.[8] In all, ants employ minimal individual memory but make maximum use of the knowledge concerning their environment (as this is represented by the collectively deposited pheromone) in order to optimize food collection without the need to explicitly answer questions (a)-(c): pheromone-mediated foraging occurs at a global scale in terms of the colony but locally in time and space, with communication being possible only in close proximity to the pheromone trail and before evaporation has occurred.

Although coined by Grasse (1959) for describing the nest building behaviour of termites, the term stigmetry is habitually employed for recounting the implicit communication and collective foraging behaviour of all hymenoptera including ants. In fact, stigmetry has been qualitatively demonstrated for the Linepithema humile ant via the "double bridge"

---

[4] For instance, marking the way either back to the nest after food has been found or to a new nest (Horn 1976); establishing a permanent foodsource of good quality while – at the same time – warding off ants from other colonies (chemical signposts and territorial pheromones (Holldobler & Lumsden 1980)); isolating a long and unrewarding trail (the Pharaoh's ants' repellent pheromone (Robinson et al. 2005)); alerting of imminent danger or threat (alarm pheromones); confusing enemy colonies and setting them off against each other (propaganda pheromones (d' Ettore & Heinze 2001)).

[5] Foodsource quality constitutes a combination of its distance from the nest and its benefit (food quantity and nutritional value) to the ant colony (Hangartner 1969; Breed et al. 1987; de Biseau et al. 1991; Beckers et al. 1992a; Sumpter & Beekman 2003).

[6] For many ant species (e.g. Pharaoh's), foraging resembles a network of branching pheromone trails, with fork-junctions appearing whenever a trail is divided into two branches. The branches diverge at symmetric angles of around 53° from each other when facing away from the nest (Jackson et al. 2004; Collett & Waxman 2005), whereby the angles help the ants determine, retain and regain their direction of motion (Holldobler & Wilson 1990; Fourcassie & Deneubourg 1994; Jackson et al. 2004). In this case, the shortest trail signifies the shortest combination of branches along the fork junctions rather than the shortest straight line between the nest and the foodsource (Goss et al. 1989).

[7] For the lasius Americanus ant, total evaporation occurs within two minutes, the time it takes to cover about 40cm (Wilson 1963). For other species - and depending on the environment -, pheromone decay occurs slowly, over hours or even months (Bonabeau et al., 1999).

[8] Kinesthetic and optical cues may also be employed in these cases.

experiments: when a colony is restricted to move along either of two branches connecting the nest and a single foodsource, the colony always convergences upon a single trail corresponding to one of the two branches (Fewell 1990). Convergence is consistent with positive feedback regulation, in other words it is determined by the initial random choices of the ants - concerning the branch to be traversed if the branches are of the same length (Deneugourg et al. 1990; Beckers et al. 1993), or by branch length if the branches are of unequal length (differential length effect, Goss et al. 1989). Monte Carlo simulations (Goss et al. 1989, Beckers et al. 1993) have further established the non-linearity of positive reinforcement in:

- branch selection: the probability with which an ant selects a given branch is a function of the square of the number of ants that have recently selected each branch, namely the square of the current pheromone levels at the tips of the two branches (Deneubourg et al. 1990);
- unconstrained navigation: the non-zero probability with which an ant chooses to leave a preferred trail and explore a novel (lightly marked, decayed or unmarked) part of the environment is inversely proportional to the amount of pheromone on the trail and directly proportional to its distance from the nest.

These findings have been extended to more than one foodsource (Beckers et al. 1993; Sumpter & Beekman 2003), with convergence occurring upon the best foodsource.

## 3.2. Ant-Inspired Navigation - Ant Colony Optimization – Multi-Agent Systems – Swarm Robotics

Owing to its effectiveness, stigmetry has been incorporated into a number of RN approaches implemented:

- traditionally (Trullier at al. 1997; Franz & Mallot 2000), e.g. vapour tunnel creation and chemical cue stereo-sensing (Sharpe & Webb 1998), optic flow stereoscopic vision (Coombs & Roberts 1993; Santos-Victor et al. 1995; Weber et al. 1997), phonotaxis (Webb 1995), view and view-graph matching (Nelson 1991; Franz at al. 1998a; Franz at al. 1998b);
- via soft computing techniques, e.g. back-propagation artificial neural networks (Rupe et al. 2003) and fuzzy/neuro-fuzzy modelling (Rozin & Margaliot 2006; Zhu & Yang 2007).

### *3.2.1. Swarm intelligence and ant colony optimization – Swarm robotics*

The cooperative characteristics of social insects including termites, ants, bees and wasps have also inspired the relatively novel soft computing paradigm of swarm intelligence (SI, Bonabeau et al. 1999), which is capable of providing adequately good solutions to NP-hard combinatorial optimization problems in a reasonable amount of time. Ant colony optimization (ACO (Dorigo & Stutzle 2004; Dorigo et al. 2006) - including the Ant System (Dorigo et al. 1996) and the ACO meta-heuristic (Dorigo et al. 1999) - is the branch of SI that draws directly from the foraging behaviour of real ant colonies described in section 3.1.2. In order to solve a combinatorially challenging task, ACO:

- transforms the problem into a graph-like structure (representing the environment as a network of branching pheromone trails),
- expresses the problem constraints as distances between connected nodes of the graph (encoding the differential length effect),
- constructs and updates potential solutions as sequences of nodes (pheromone trails) until convergence is accomplished upon one of the best solutions (shortest pheromone trail connecting the nest to the best foodsource)[9].

Owing to the fact that a multitude of combinatorial optimization problems can be appropriately adapted to path-length-based search, ACO has attracted significant interest (Blum 2005a; Dorigo & Blum 2005) and enjoys a steadily expanding range of successful applications, either as an independent methodology or in combination with genetic algorithms, TABU search, local search etc. Some of the most representative ACO implementations encompass (Dorigo et al. 2006):

- static problems including the symmetric and asymmetric travelling salesman problem (Dorigo et al. 1996; Dorigo & Gambardella 1997), quadratic assignment (Gambardella et al. 1999; Maniezzo & Colorni 1999; Stutzle & Dorigo 1999; Lopez-Ibanez et al. 2004), job-shop and other forms of scheduling (Colorni et al. 1994; Merkle et al. 2002; Blum 2005b; Silva et al. 2005; Gajpal & Rajendran 2006; Tseng & Chen 2006; Gutjahr & Rauner 2007), resource allocation (Lee & Lee 2005), communication, mobile/network assignment (di Caro & Dorigo 1998; Fournier & Pierre 2005), circuit design (Alupoaei & Katkoori 2004), sequential ordering (Gambardella & Dorigo 2000), graph colouring (Costa & Hertz 1997), maximum clique (Bui & Rizzo 2004), minimum spanning tree (Shyu et al. 2006), vehicle routing (Bullnheimer et al. 1999; Bell & McMullen 2004), bandwidth minimization (Lim et al. 2006), bioinformatics (Shygelska & Hoos 2005);
- dynamic problems such as connection-oriented and connection-less network routing (Schoonderwoerd et al. 1996; di Caro & Dorigo 1998; Heusse et al. 1998), learning automata and game playing (Verbeek & Nowe 2002), dynamic graph colouring (van Dyke Parunak et al. 2005) and data mining (Parpinelli et al. 2002).

ACO has also been utilized directly for AGV path following and planning (Borisov & Vasilyev 2002; Vaughan et al. 2002). Unlike real ant colony foraging however, communication is by no means local: either the information concerning locations of interest is broadcasted over a radio-network to all AGV's as soon as it is acquired by an AGV, or a partial – and common to all AGV's - model of the environment (in the form of a blackboard or joint utility table) is constructed to complement the individual ACO models.

Quite recently, and resulting from the combination of ant-inspired RN and ACO, swarm robotics (SR, Waldner (2007)) has emerged as a novel approach for co-ordinating multiple

[9] It is also necessary in ACO to determine the minimum number of ants and the values of various parameters (e.g. pheromone decay) that promote efficient convergence for the particular problem characteristics.

simple robots. Special emphasis is placed on the study of the minimal physical design of the robots, the large cardinality of the robot ensemble and the ant-inspired local communication, all of which characterise SR behaviour.

### *3.2.2. Co-Operative multi agent systems*

The "united we stand, divided we fall" quality of real ant colonies has further inspired the development of co-operative multi-agent systems (MAS's, Van Dyke Parunak 1996; Weiss 1997; Jennings et al. 1998; Huhns & Singh 1998; Weiss 1999; Stone & Veloso 2000). Like ants, each agent is simple (in the sense that it cannot individually tackle the task at hand), partially autonomous, has a local view of the task at any time, and although it does at no time control the other agents it can indirectly communicate its current knowledge to nearby agents. When considered collectively, the distributed processing and co-ordinated collaboration between the agents renders the MAS capable of self-organization as well as of robust and redundant operation such that (near-)optimal solutions to challenging optimization tasks are converged upon. Significant practical MAS applications have been reported to date in distributed vehicle monitoring (Dresner & Stone 2004; Nunes & Oliveira 2004), air traffic control (Steeb et al. 1998), electricity distribution (Varga et al. 1994; Schneider et al. 1999), supply chain management (Wooldridge et al. 1996; Brauer & Weiss 1998), meeting scheduling (Chalupsky et al. 2002) and industry (Van Dyke Parunak 1996) to name but a few.

A critical problem arising from the dense interconnections of populous MAS's is the steep escalation in operation complexity. Owing to the similarity between MAS's and ensembles of artificial systems (e.g. groups of robots) in terms of construction and operation characteristics, various machine learning approaches (Panait & Luke 2005) have been employed for tackling operation complexity. Such approaches include reinforcement learning (Sutton 1988; Kaebling et al. 1996), team learning (Sen & Sekaran 1996; Salustowicz et al. 1998) concurrent learning (Zhao & Schmidhuber 1996; Iba 1998) and credit assignment (Mataric 1994; Tangamchit et al. 2002). The indirect mode of communication of information between agents (Holldobler & Wilson 1990; Leerink et al. 1995; Monekosso & Remagnino 2001; Panait & Luke 2004a; Panait & Luke 2004b; Panait & Luke 2004c) is generally preferred over direct communication (e.g. Jim & Giles 2000). Indirect communication is inspired by the implicit information transfer and interaction between ants, as mediated by pheromone concentration, and is realized by the interrelated processes of environment modification[10] and subsequent decision making concerning the next transition. Accordingly, an assortment of pheromone-based co-operative learning techniques have been developed including fixed pheromone laying for implementing reinforcement learning (Leerink et al. 1995; Monekosso & Remagnino 2001), and single (Collins & Jefferson 1991; Collins & Jefferson 1992) as well as multiple (White et al. 1998; Sauter et al. 2001; Sauter at al. 2002) pheromones for accomplishing MAS optimization via evolutionary computation (EC, Holland 1975). These techniques have proved themselves on diverse benchmark problems such as foraging (Ostergaard et al. 2001), soccer playing (Kitano et al. 1997; Riley & Veloso 2000; Stone & Veloso 2000) and herding (Werner & Dyer 1993; Schultz et al. 1996; Potter et al. 2001).

---

[10] Modification may be implemented in a subtractive (e.g. following trails dug in the soil/snow), or additive (e.g. following trails piled with pheromone/crumbs) manner.

Pheromone-mediated ant communication has also directly inspired an assortment of pure co-operative learning MAS navigation approaches. AntFarm (Collins & Jefferson 1992) applies evolutionary computation and artificial neural network learning to multiple colonies in order to determine whether and under which conditions optimal co-operative foraging can be a result of evolution; navigation evolves on sets of 16x16 grids that are foraged independently each - and with variable success, depending on the parameter values - by 25 ants; two directional pheromones are employed, namely a variable-rate pheromone for nest-to-foodsource trails and a fixed compass-like pheromone for foodsource-to-nest trails guaranteeing speedy return to the nest. Along the same lines, Resnick (1994) and Nakamura & Kurumatani (1996) assume an ant-generated pheromone for nest-to-foodsource trails and a nest-generated distance pheromone (resembling the effect of a lighthouse on navigating ships) for foodsource-to-nest trails. Wodric & Bilchev (1997), Vaughan et al. (2000) and Panait & Luke (2004a-c) also employ pairs of directional and independently evolving pheromones, although they refrain from using any compass-like or sun-related information, as this is validly assumed to be beyond the present capabilities of RN.

The collective work of Panait & Luke, in particular, investigates pheromone-based foraging performance in obstacle-free environments as well as in environments cluttered with obstacles, both of which are represented by square grids. The navigation problems involve various combinations of dimensions of the navigating environment (10x10, 33x33 and 100x100), colony sizes (50, 100 and 500 ants) and numbers of foodsources. Biological characteristics are implemented, such as ant death, positive and negative variable pheromone laying, pheromone diffusion and precedence to transitions causing a change in direction of motion of not more than 45°. Additionally, two modes of ant motion are utilized, namely totally random and pheromone concentration-based transitions, while a blend of a "bored" mood and a pheromone gradient between the nest and the foodsource is used for directing the ants towards "interesting" parts of the environment.

# 4. Progressive Optimization of Organized Colonies of Ants (POOCA)

## 4.1. POOCA Principles

POOCA follows the streak of the aforementioned pheromone-based co-operative foraging MAS models in its biological inspiration and the utilization of EC for optimizing the various parameters involved. However, it differs from these approaches in that it simulates minimal and uniformly applied ant-inspired navigational principles that promote accurate as well as efficient navigation. POOCA is implemented as follows:

- Stigmetry - progressive knowledge of the environment – trail creation. The ants do not communicate directly with each other but exchange information concerning their locations, recent trails and the environment indirectly via pheromone. No long-term memory is employed by any given ant; instead, selection of the location towards which the ant moves is such that a location of high pheromone concentration (recently and/or frequently visited part of the environment) has a larger probability of being preferred over a location of low pheromone concentration (non-"interesting" part of the environment). Although all ants are equal in the sense that they employ identical procedures for trail creation and following, the randomness inherent in every transition compels each ant to create its personal trail that may vary from that of the other ants in terms of length, selected locations and time of arrival at any location of the environment. Knowledge of the environment is accomplished after repeated nest-to-foodsource and foodsource-to-nest trails by all the ants in the colony: only the nest is known at the beginning of navigation, with landmark (obstacle and foodsource) discovery being effectuated only once an ant of the colony bumps upon them; finally, any part of the environment never encountered by the ant colony remains undiscovered.

- Inertia to change in motion-direction. Practically all mobile (legged, winged etc.) beings with lateral anatomical symmetry move forward, unless they encounter a diversion. As confirmed by Wilson (1963) and Wehner & Srinivasan (1981), ants tend to follow a constant straight-ahead direction with small and infrequent directional changes while they do not go over ground already covered during the current trail. Similar to Panait & Luke (2004b)[11], inertia is implemented as a bias towards straight-ahead motion and progressively smaller biases towards transitions that deviate increasingly from straight-ahead motion. Such a formulation discourages unrealistic or unnecessary directional changes without, however, dictating a constant direction of motion (Bruckstein 1993).
- Pheromone laying. The location of transition is determined via straightforward roulette-wheel (Bäck, 1996), i.e. the more/less pheromone it contains the more/less likely it is to be visited. A single type of additive pheromone is used[12], with pheromone concentration incremented at each location visited by an ant and proceeding in an identical manner for nest-to-foodsource and foodsource-to-nest trails. Although independent of the current pheromone concentration at the particular location, the amount of pheromone deposited by each ant depends on its current feeding status and increases after each completed directional trail of the ant; this is inspired by the lasius Niger ant that leaves no pheromone during its first trail, but subsequently deposits amounts of pheromone that are inversely proportional to the length of the previously created trail.
- Pheromone evaporation. Once deposited, pheromone decays at a constant rate throughout POOCA operation, i.e. by an amount that depends exclusively on the current pheromone concentration.
- Pheromone diffusion. As in Panait & Luke (2004b), pheromone is not restricted to the location where it is deposited but spreads in the vicinity. Unlike Panait & Luke (2004b) however, the strength of pheromone diffusion does not remain fixed but decreases progressively in space (away from the location of pheromone laying) and

[11] In that model, precedence is given to transitions causing a change in direction of motion of no more than 45°, with the remaining five directions considered only if the preferred transitions correspond to non-traversable cells or cause excessive ant congestion.

[12] As detailed at the end of section 3.2.2, most previous approaches employ multiple pheromones, i.e. different pheromones (i) for nest-to-foodsource and foodsource-to-nest trails (e.g. Resnick (1994), Wodrich & Bilchev (1997), Vaughan et al. (2000), Panait & Luke (2004a)) and (ii) for distinct pheromone laying behaviours (e.g. Panait & Luke (2004c)).

in time (diminishing strength of diffusion as operation evolves): at the beginning of POOCA operation, the neighbourhood of diffusion encompasses the entire environment; the effective neighbourhood shrinks gradually and becomes virtually confined to the transition cell at the end of operation. This process bears a close resemblance to the training procedure of the self-organising map (SOM, Kohonen 2001), where weight modification is global at the beginning of training and becomes increasingly localized as training advances. Diffusion offers the advantages of (i) accurately depicting the natural phenomenon of pheromone laying, (ii) simulating the "stereoscopic" detection of the pheromone concentration at the candidate transition locations in a manner similar to the two antennae of real ants (section 3.1.2.) and the pairs of sensors of robots (beginning of section 3.2.), and (iii) smoothing the pheromone concentration of neighbouring cells so as to promote continuously varying pheromone concentrations at neighbouring locations as well as higher pheromone concentrations at bends of the trail and at narrow areas between trails. Combined with stigmetry, the creation of increasingly straight and short trails is encouraged.

- Competence. The combination of the minimum numbers of (i) ants and (ii) trails allowing speedy convergence upon (near-)optimal (short and smooth) trails is utilized. As will be detailed in section 4.4., this is realized via EC.

According to the aforementioned principles, POOCA stands somewhere between off- and on-line RN path planning (Undeger & Polat 2007); the path is known only once the optimal trail has been found and no change in the environment has occurred; otherwise, path planning is performed on-line.

## 4.2. POOCA Problem Representation

The environment, time and - consequently - ant motion are expressed in a discrete manner. A rectangular grid of square cells is used for representing the environment. Each cell stands for a location of the environment, which may be traversable (nest, foodsource, free space) or non-traversable (part of an obstacle). The nest and foodsource[13] occupy one cell each while the obstacles are composed of one or more adjacent cells; free space occupies the remaining cells. No maze-like environments are investigated, as the use of one-cell wide free-space corridors restricts motion along a single cell/direction (except for junctions, where a choice of more cells/directions exists) and renders corridor length the sole determining factor of trail optimality[14]. By using an unconstrained foraging area, the creation of a multitude of trails is possible and the potential of POOCA to create optimal trails can be better understood.

---

[13] Imitating AntFarm (Collins & Jefferson 1992), a single foodsource is used in this chapter. This obliterates the need to consider the nutritional value of the various foodsources for determining the "best" foodsource and, subsequently, the optimal trail(s).

[14] Although maze is less demanding than free navigation, the utilization of biologically inspired heuristics and soft computing techniques has been put forward for efficiently handling the task. For instance, a repellent-like pheromone (footnote 4) has been used for blocking dead-ends (Yan & Yuan 2003), while a pulse propagating artificial neural network (Caulfield & Kinser 1999) has been put forward for determining the shortest trail between a start- and an end-point; however, translating the artificial neural network into an ant colony requires at least as many ants as there are possible trails, with each ant instructed to follow a distinct trail.

Elementary motion of an ant during the creation of a given trail consists of a transition from one traversable cell of the grid to an adjacent traversable and not already visited cell; selection is made from between up to eight cells for interior cells and five/three cells for edges/corners of the grid. Each ant performs a single transition at each time-step. Ant motion is synchronous, whereby no limit is placed on the number of ants that can simultaneously occupy the same location of the environment[15]. This implies that each ant transition is performed independently of the transitions of the other ants during the same time-step; still, each transition uniformly influences the transitions of the all the ants in the colony during the next time-step.

A directional trail comprises distinct pair-wise adjacent cells[16] that connect the nest and the foodsource. The ants of the colony perform 500 directional trails, namely 250 nest-to-foodsource and 250 foodsource-to-nest trails corresponding to odd- and even-numbered directional trails, respectively. POOCA operation terminates only after the last ant has completed its $500^{th}$ directional trail; in the meantime, all ants continue navigating in order to prevent dissipation of the created trail(s).

Although uniform in terms of ant behaviour, synchronous motion entails that all kinds of elementary motion (horizontal, vertical and diagonal) are identical, an assumption that can only be accounted for either by variable speed ($\sqrt{2}$ for the ratio of diagonal over horizontal or vertical ant-transition speed) or by pauses in the motion of ants performing horizontal or vertical transitions. Hence, the assumption of uniform elementary motion does not guarantee accurate trail length evaluation or the identification of changes in direction of motion. An example is given in Figure 1, where all trails (a-d) comprise seven cells (POOCA length of 7), but only trail (a) has an actual (Euclidean) length of 6[17], with trails (b-d) having Euclidean lengths of $4+2\sqrt{2}$, $6\sqrt{2}$ and $6\sqrt{2}$, respectively; furthermore, while trails (c-d) have identical lengths and Euclidean lengths, trail (d) has only one change in direction and is thus smoother than trail (c) which has four changes in direction.

For the concurrent evaluation of POOCA trail length and smoothness, two kinds of changes in direction are discerned:

- Global changes, corresponding to distinct trail-merging patterns during operation that lead to different final trails (e.g. Figure 1(a), 1(c) and 1(d)). Although directly resolvable when these changes elongate the created trail, supplementary constraints are needed when no elongation is observed; these constraints may be related to the construction of the agent and the needs of the navigation task, e.g. avoidance of sharp turns versus minimization of changes in direction irrespective of magnitude (Figure 2).
- Local changes, concerning elementary unnecessary deviations in otherwise straight parts of a trail (e.g. Figure 1(b)). Recurring local changes generate a rugged-trail effect that is clearly suboptimal as well as hard to navigate. Furthermore, it is possible for a local - and originally confined - change to gradually propagate along

[15] This is unlike Panait & Luke (2004b), where ant transitions are sequentially performed at each time-step and a limit is placed on the number of ants that can occupy the same cell at the same time-step; excessive ant congestion in an area means that some ants may have to remain stationary until the area becomes less congested, whereby the blocked ants can move again.

[16] With each visited cell appearing only once in the trail.

[17] Euclidean length is measured from the centre of each cell of the grid.

the trail during operation and to cause more local and/or global changes in direction as well as trail elongation.

Pheromone lies in the interval [0,1]. All cells are initialized to a pheromone concentration value of 0.5, except from the nest that is assigned a constant value of 1. The location of the foodsource remains unknown until it is first reached by an ant, whereby it is also assigned a constant value of 1. The same is true of the location of the obstacles that are initially unknown and become incorporated in the environment as soon as an ant of the colony tries to access them, at which time a constant pheromone value of 0 is assigned to the uncovered obstacle cell. No reconstruction of free space or of the shapes, sizes and total number of the obstacles is attempted, whereby it is possible for free-space and obstacle cells to remain unidentified at the completion of POOCA operation (Undeger & Polat 2007).

During POOCA operation, it is possible for the pheromone concentration of a group of cells to increase/decrease disproportionately to that of the other cells. To this end, pheromone normalization (like Blum & Dorigo 2004) over the entire grid is performed at each time-step as soon as the first directional trail of the ant colony is completed. Normalization is not applied before that in order to prevent premature locking on the parts of the (practically random) trails created early on; the minor increments in pheromone up to that point ensure that the first completed directional trail and the other partial trails are only faintly demarcated on the grid, thus precluding pheromone saturation of any part of the environment.

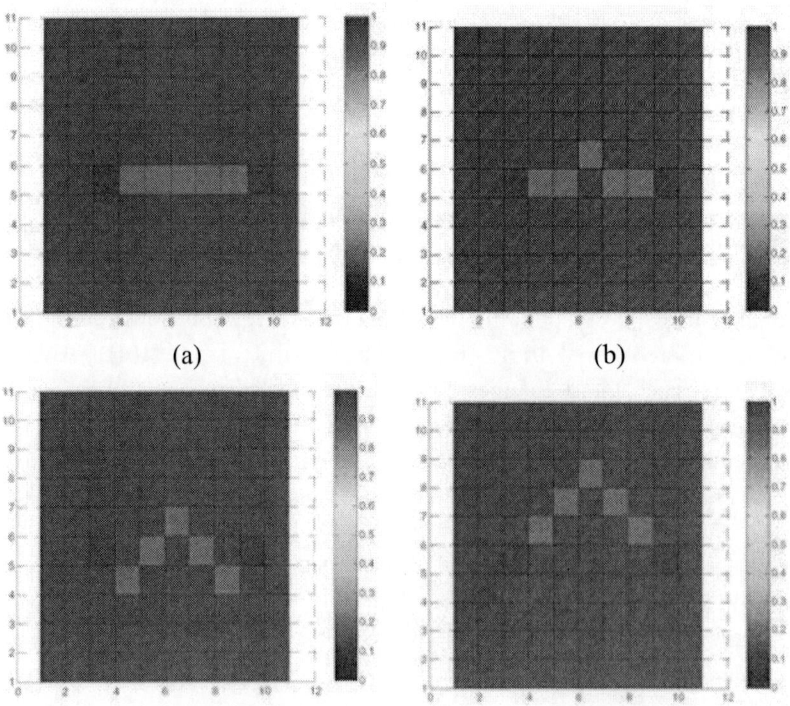

(a) (b) (c) (d)

Figure 1. POOCA and Euclidean-based trail length estimation for trails composed of seven cells

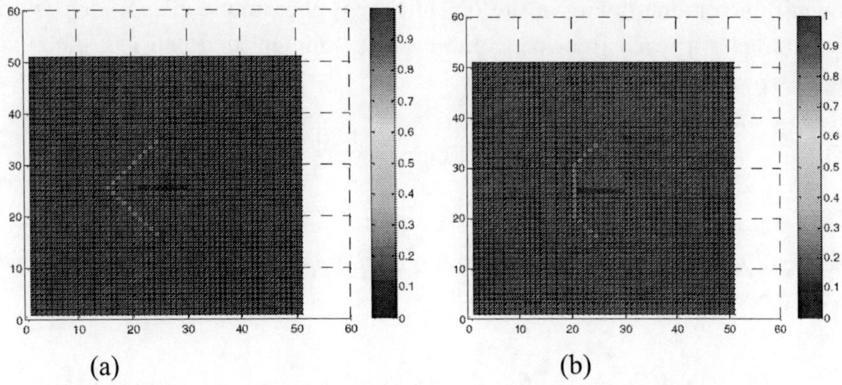

Figure 2. Although the two trails are of equal POOCA length 21, trail (a) corresponds to a single large global change, while trail (b) contains two smaller global changes

## 4.3. POOCA Operation

Whenever a free-space cell $i$ is visited by an ant of the colony, its pheromone concentration is incremented. The total update in pheromone concentration is implemented according to

$$phero\_update_{ti} = phero_{ti} + \sum_{j} increment_{tij} \tag{1}$$

where $phero_{ti}$ and $phero\_update_{ti}$ denote the pheromone concentration of cell $i$ at the beginning and end (after all ants have realized their transitions) of the $t$th time-step, respectively. Parameter $increment_{tij}$ denotes the amount of pheromone that is deposited on cell $i$ by each ant $j$ of the colony during the $t$th time-step and is given by

$$increment_{tij} = \begin{cases} 0 & ant\ j\ does\ not\ visit\ cell\ i \\ \dfrac{1}{\max\{X,Y\}} \cdot \dfrac{1}{(500 - c_j)} & ant\ j\ visits\ cell\ i \\ & during\ its\ c_j th\ trail \end{cases} \tag{2}$$

indicating that no pheromone is deposited by ants that do not visit the cell during the $t$th time-step, while each ant that visits the cell at the $t$th time-step increases the pheromone concentration of the cell by an amount that is inversely proportional to the largest dimension of the grid and proportional to the $c_j$th directional trail currently constructed by the ant ($1 \le c_j \le 500$). As already explained in section 4.1., Equation 2 imitates the varying amount of pheromone laid by real ants depending on their feeding status and is useful in communicating the $j$th ant's current knowledge of the environment: small increments are employed during the first random trails at the beginning of POOCA operation, while progressively larger increments are applied as trail creation becomes more informed.

Following pheromone laying at the $t$th time-step, pheromone evaporation is applied via the *decay* parameter to each free-space and each yet-unidentified cell $i$ of the environment, producing $phero\_evaporate_{ti}$

$$phero\_evaporate_{ti} = \begin{cases} (1 - decay)phero\_update_{ti} & \text{for free-space or yet unidentified cells} \\ phero\_update_{ti} & \text{otherwise} \end{cases} \quad (3)$$

Subsequently, the pheromone concentrations $phero_{(t+1)i}$ of all cells $i$ of the grid become available for the next ($t$+1th) time-step via

$$phero_{(t+1)i} = phero\_evaporate_{ti} \quad (4)$$

As mentioned at the end of section 4.2., pheromone normalization is applied at each time-step following the creation of the very first directional trail; implemented between Equations (3) and (4), normalization scales the pheromone concentrations of all free-space and yet unidentified cells $i$ of the grid in the interval [0.15 0.85].

Unlike pheromone laying, evaporation and normalization, the remaining two processes of ant transition and pheromone diffusion require long-term memory. Each ant transition is implemented as a pure roulette-wheel selection process, thus closely imitating real ant operation (Goss et al. 1989; Deneubourg et al. 1990). Initially, the transition probability $prob_{ii*}$ from cell $i$ to each adjacent cell $i*$ (excluding known obstacle cells) that has not been visited during the current trail of the ant[18] is calculated according to

$$prob_{ii*} = \frac{in_{ii*}(k + phero_{ti*})^2}{\sum_I in_{iI}(k + phero_{tI})^2} \quad (5)$$

where $phero_{ti}^{*}$ and $phero_{tI}$ denote the pheromone concentration of cell $i*$ and $I$ (with $I$ ranging over all cells $i*$ that are candidates for transition) during the $t$th time-step, respectively. Parameters $in_{ii*}$ and $in_{iI}$ denote the inertia values corresponding to ant transitions from cell $i$ to each cell $i*$ and $I$, respectively[19]. Finally, parameter $k$ simulates the non-linear positive reinforcement and random exploration behaviour of the Iridomyrmex humilis ant colony (Deneubourg at al. 1990): both the square of the current pheromone levels of the cells that are candidate for transition and the non-zero probability of performing a transition to any adjacent cell are conveyed. If no cell can be found for transition, i.e. all adjacent cells constitute either obstacle-cells or part of the current directional trail, the ant returns to its origin (nest or foodsource) and re-initiates foraging at the next time-step.

Diffusion takes place whenever a directional trail is completed by an ant of the colony. It is applied between pheromone laying (Equation 1) and evaporation (Equation 3) and is implemented via a recursive procedure applied exactly once to each free-space and unidentified cell of the grid that does not belong to the completed trail[18] as follows

---

[18] Hence the need for memory.

[19] These values are based on the directional agreement between each possible transition and the previous transition of the ant; memory is again necessary for remembering the direction of the previous transition of each ant.

$$diff_{tijc_j} = \frac{\sum_I phero\_update_{tI}}{I} \frac{1}{(r+1)} \frac{500 - c_j}{500} \quad (6)$$

where $diff_{tijcj}$ denotes the increase in the pheromone concentration of cell $i$ that is located $r$ recursions away from the just completed $c_j$th directional trail[18] of ant $j$ during the $t$th time-step. The first quotient of Equation 6 denotes the local average of the pheromone concentrations $phero\_update_{tI}$ calculated over the direct neighbours $I$ of cell $i$, while the other two quotients impose a reduction in the diffusion of pheromone away from the trail and for every successive directional trail completed by ant $j$. At each recursion $r$, the calculated amount of diffusion is added to the pheromone concentration synchronously for the cells of the grid that belong to this recursion and before the $r$+1th recursion takes place according to

$$phero\_update_{ti} = phero\_update_{ti} + diff_{tijc} \quad (7)$$

where $phero\_update_{ti}$ on the right hand side of Equation 7 is given by Equation 1.

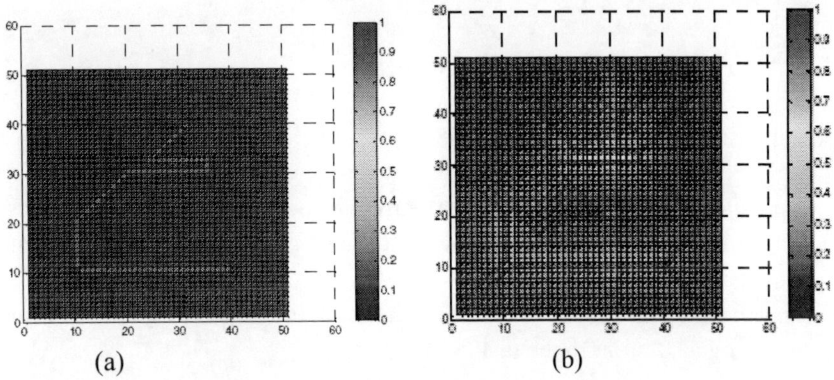

Figure 3. A just-completed directional trail extracted from its environment before (a) and after diffusion and normalization (b)

Diffusion propagates as follows: all the free-space and unidentified cells neighbouring at least one cell of the trail (i.e. being one cell away from one or more cells of the trail) are subjected to an increase in their pheromone concentration at the first recursion ($r$=1 in Equation 6). At the second recursion ($r$=2), all the free-space or unknown cells neighbouring at least one of the previously updated cells (i.e. being two cells away from the trail) have their pheromone values incremented in the same fashion but by a smaller amount. Diffusion propagates over the grid, while - at the same time - progressively diminishing away from the trail at each successive recursion. In case more than one ant complete their directional trails at the same time-step, the recursions of identical values of $r$ are implemented synchronously for all completed trails. An illustration of diffusion is given in Figure 3 for a trail extracted from its environment; higher pheromone values appear near the trail, at narrow areas between parts of the trail, and at concave bends of the trail (i.e. for cells that are near more cells of the created trail). These differences in pheromone concentrations facilitate the eventual annihilation of winding parts of trails and the eventual creation of shorter and straighter trails.

A change in the environment is implemented once all ants have completed 500 directional trails. Operation is re-initialized at the next time-step in the modified environment with the application of

(I) diffusion of the existing trail(s),
(II) normalization of the pheromone values of all cells other than those constituting part of the trail(s) in the interval [0.15,0.85], and
(III) assignment of 0.5 to the pheromone concentrations of all the cells that constitute part of the trail(s),

and proceeds until a further 500 directional trails are performed by all ants in the modified environment. Steps (I-III) create extended areas of intermediate pheromone concentration over as well as around the existing trail(s), thus simulating pheromone laying of real ant colonies in altered areas between – as well as beyond - already created pheromone trails. Consequently, the ant colony can escape from parts of the old trail(s) that constitute clearly sub-optimal trails for the modified environment, while – at the same time - retaining parts of the trail(s) that do not significantly affect trail optimality.

## 4.4. POOCA Trail Optimization via Evolution

Genetic algorithms (GA's, Goldberg 1989) constitute a main branch of EC that employ:

1. a population of chromosomes; each chromosome represents a candidate solution to the task under optimization and is composed of genes, where each gene stands for a salient characteristic of the task;
2. a fitness function which expresses the suitability of a given chromosome in constituting a solution to the task.

GA operation can be summarised as follows. Two genetic operators, reproduction and selection, are applied repeatedly (for a sufficient number of generations) to the population. At the beginning of each generation, a subset of chromosomes from the population is initially isolated for reproduction. Reproduction employs (i) crossover, which swaps homologous genes of pairs (or groups) of the isolated chromosomes, and (ii) mutation, which slightly alters - with a small probability - each gene of every new chromosome. Subsequently, selection picks the fittest - new and mutated - chromosomes that are to be included in the population of the next generation. The repeated application of reproduction and selection promotes the inclusion of chromosomes of gradually increasing fitness from the entire solution-space[20] in the evolving population. The proper choice of the various GA parameter values ensures that at least one chromosome of the population will eventually constitute a (near-)optimal solution to the task at hand.

---

[20] Crossover and mutation are complementary: while the chromosomes resulting from crossover resemble their parent chromosomes whereby search focuses upon promising areas of the solution space, the mutated chromosomes may have distinct characteristics from the chromosomes from which they are derived whereby search is extended randomly away from good points of the solution space.

A GA is employed for coordinating pheromone laying, evaporation and diffusion, thus ensuring the consistent creation of (near-)optimal trails. To this end, the combination of appropriate values for

(i1) *decay* (Equation 3),
(i2) $in_0$, $in_{45}$, $in_{90}$, $in_{135}$, and $in_{180}$ (Equation 5) implementing the biases for straight ahead motion and for motion deviating by ±45°, ±90°, ±135° and 180° from straight ahead motion, respectively,
(i3) *k* (Equation 5), and
(i4) *ant_no*, expressing the number of ants in the colony,

is determined. While parameters (i1)-(i3) influence trail optimality, parameter (i4) affects trail creation efficiency. Each chromosome of the GA population comprises eight genes representing parameters (i1)-(i4), with the possible gene values ranging within the intervals shown in the middle column of Table 1.

Three criteria of POOCA accuracy and efficiency are employed, namely

(ii1) $opt\_length / length$, where *opt_length* denotes the length of the optimal trail(s) for the particular environment and *length* stands for the length of the created trail,
(ii2) $1 - (local\_no / length)$, where *local_no* denotes the number of local changes in direction found in the created trail, and
(ii3) $(500.opt\_length) / (step\_no.ant\_no)$, where *step_no* expresses the total number of time-steps performed until termination of POOCA operation.

The maxima of criteria (ii1) and (ii2) equal 1, for shortest trails and no local changes in direction, respectively. However, criterion (ii3) practically never reaches unity but decreases steeply for total numbers of time-steps exceeding the number of time-steps needed to traverse the optimal trail 500 times and for more than one ant in the colony. The GA fitness function combines (i.e. evaluates the weighted sum of) parameters (i1)-(i4) for determining values that consistently allow the efficient creation of (near-) optimal trails. A small set of validation problems is used to this purpose, where all the problems involve optimal trails of fixed length 20 on a 50x50 square grid and concern:

- static obstacle-free environments configured such that horizontal and diagonal[21] optimal trails are created,
- static obstacle-free environments, where operation begins from established sub-optimal L-shaped trails; following the application of steps (I-III) of section 4.3., the suboptimal trails must be transformed into optimal diagonal trails (also used in Panait & Luke (2004a) and Panait & Luke (2004b)), and

[21] Such trails allow the accurate estimation of local and global changes in direction.

- static environments with a single obstacle that may be either horizontal of width one or diagonal of width two[22].

**Table 1. Parameters to be optimized via GA**

| Parameters | initial range | optimal value |
|---|---|---|
| *decay* | [0.0005:0.0005:0.15] | 0.001 |
| $in_0$ straight ahead motion | [0.5:0.5:5] | 2 |
| $in_{45}$ ±45° | [0.1:0.1:*in*] | 1.5 |
| $in_{90}$ ±90° | [0.1:0.1:$in_{45}$] | 1.5 |
| $in_{135}$ ±135° | [0.1:0.1:$in_{90}$] | 1 |
| $in_{180}$ 180° | [0.1:0.1:$in_{135}$] | 1 |
| *k* | [0.1:0.1:1] | 0.2[23] |
| *ant_no* | [5:5:100] | 10 |

Initial default normalized weights of [0.333 0.333 0.333] are used for criteria (ii1)-(ii3). The fitness value of a given chromosome is computed as the average of the weighted sums of parameters (i1)-(i4), with fifty tests repeated for each validation problem.

The GA procedure implemented in this chapter differs slightly from the general GA description given at the beginning of this section. The initial GA population comprises 25 chromosomes; instead of purely random, the creation of the initial chromosomes is such that the entire range of each parameter (middle column of Table 1) is uniformly covered. After the fitness value of each chromosome is evaluated, crossover is applied 25 times via roulette-wheel selection, resulting in 50 new chromosomes. All 75 (old and new) chromosomes are subjected to mutation, with each gene modified with a probability of 0.05 by an amount equal to the step shown in the middle column of Table 1. Subsequently, the new population is created by selecting - via roulette-wheel - 25 of the 75 mutated chromosomes. The GA optimization process is terminated after 100 generations or as soon as the maximum fitness value reaches a plateau, i.e. does not change by more than ±0.05 for 10 successive generations.

The values of parameters (i1)-(i4) resulting from the GA optimization process on the validation problems are shown in the rightmost column of Table 1. A further local search around the default normalized weights [0.333 0.333 0.333] on the same validation problems resulted in new weights of [0.4 0.2 0.4] that maximize both the average and the maximum fitness value of the GA population on these problems; criteria (ii1)-(ii3) now reach average values of 0.95, 0.97 and 0.047, respectively, and the fitness function reaches a value of 0.59.

Before presenting more results of POOCA performance when using the optimal values of parameters (i1)-(i4), it is worth describing the operation observed for the validation navigation problems. At the beginning of operation, each ant follows its own trail, to a large extent randomly and independently of the other ants in the colony. Ant transitions are marked by small increments in pheromone concentration, with normalization and diffusion applied as soon as the first nest-to-foodsource trail is completed. Both the completed trail and the partly

[22] The obstacle widths are such that the ants are obliged to circumvent the obstacles rather than go through them.

[23] The significantly smaller value of *k* employed in this chapter (*k*=2 in Deneubourg et al. (1990)) accommodates for the normalized pheromone concentrations as well as for the importance of straight-ahead motion.

formed trails are weak, whereby the global application of diffusion creates a rolling pheromone landscape around all them; consequently, locking to a specific non-optimal trail created early on in the navigation process is delayed. By preferring to navigate in areas of higher rather than lower pheromone concentration, the ants invariably become influenced by the diffused pheromone landscape in their subsequent navigation and trail creation patterns. Each completed trail and the ensuing diffusion further contributes to the pheromone landscape, which begins to resemble a network of wide and fuzzy areas of high pheromone concentration connecting the nest and the foodsource. When near each other, the trails form islands of high pheromone concentration, which – aided by inertia, by the gradually strengthening pheromone laying and by the progressive weakening of pheromone diffusion – are transformed into progressively straighter and narrower trails. The creation of valid, circle-free, short and smooth trails is further encouraged by the fact that a cell cannot be visited more than once during a directional trail (whereby circles are drastically reduced), and the assignment of maximum, non-decaying pheromone values of 1 of the nest and foodsource (whereby these cells are assigned an increased probability of being preferred for transition over neighbouring free-space cells). The ant colony eventually converges upon a single one-cell wide, short and smooth (near-) optimal trail; it is mentioned that, for the parameter values selected by GA, a cell belong to a final trail only if its pheromone concentration is no less than 0.83. On average, two local changes in direction are detected in every three trails, with occurrence being independent of the environment or the existence of obstacles.

When lower inertia values than those shown in the rightmost column of Table 1 are assigned to changes in direction of ant motion, twisting trails are created with more frequent local changes in direction; conversely, when higher inertia values are assigned to changes in direction of ant motion, stretches of straight trails and unnecessary global changes in direction are observed which result in significantly longer trails. Finally, values of *decay* lower than 0.001 do not guarantee the creation of a single trail at the end of POOCA operation, while significantly higher values cause dissipation of the created trail.

# 5. Navigation Problems

Equipped with the optimal parameter values and fitness function weights determined in section 4.4., POOCA operation is investigated for a variety of problems involving a single nest and a single foodsource in static as well as dynamic environments. The average trail length and the average number of time-steps required until POOCA termination as well as their normalized expressions[24] are used in the following as measures of trail optimality and computational complexity, respectively.

## 5.1. Static Problems

Static problems involve a constant nest, a constant foodsource and an environment that is either obstacle-free or contains constant obstacles.

[24] Corresponding to the inverse of criteria (ii1) and (ii3), in the latter case without the *ant_no* parameter which is now set to 10.

### *5.1.1. Obstacle-free navigation*

Three kinds of problems are investigated:

(i) finding an optimal trail between the nest and the foodsource,

(ii) reconstructing an optimal trail subsequent to its partial destruction, and

(iii) converging upon an optimal trail starting off from a sub-optimal trail.

Navigation problems (i) are studied for open space as well as for narrow (of width 9 and 16) straight and cornered corridors on various nest-foodsource configurations and grid sizes. 50x50 grids are employed for corridor navigation; optimal trail lengths between 5 and 25, between 25 and 45, and larger than 45, with steps of 5, involve straight (horizontal or vertical) corridors only, both straight and cornered corridors, and cornered corridors only, respectively. In order to examine the same optimal trail lengths in open-space navigation, the horizontal, vertical and diagonal optimal trails are constructed on 50x50 grids for optimal trail lengths up to 45 and on 50x$S$ for optimal trail lengths longer than 45, where

$$S = 5(ceil(L/5) + 1), \qquad L > 45 \tag{8}$$

Table 2 and Figure 4 exemplify POOCA operation accuracy and efficiency for these problems. The mean and standard deviation of the trail length as well as the average number of time-steps required until POOCA termination are shown in Table 2, averaged over all the navigation problems of the same nature tested for a given optimal trail length. Additionally, Figure 4 depicts the ratio of average over optimal trail length, the standard deviation of the trail length and the average number of time-steps until POOCA termination for increasing optimal trail lengths. Performance is satisfactory overall, with (cornered) corridor navigation being superior to open-space navigation. In more detail, trail optimality is practically independent of the optimal trail length (Table 2 and Figure 4(a)), with the variation in trail length constituting a function of optimal trail length (Table 2 and Figure 4(b)). It can also be seen that computational efficiency depends upon both the optimal trail length and the total navigable space (Table 2 and Figure 4(c)); efficiency is lower for optimal trails traversing a small part of the environment and higher for optimal trails traversing a significant part of the environment, the latter being due to the restriction in direction selection effectuated by the edges of the grid. Owing to the progressive expansion of the environment in accordance with the increase in trail length for open space navigation, the slope of the corresponding curve in Figure 4(c) is constant; conversely, and owing to the fixed size of the navigating environment for corridor navigation, the slope of the corresponding curve is constant for trail lengths up to 30, gradually drops for lengths between 35 and 70, and eventually floors for even longer trails. Finally, when compared to optimal trail lengths, the mean trail lengths demonstrate that local changes in direction do not significantly affect trail length for either environment.

An example of POOCA corridor navigation and trail evolution is shown in Figure 5. Figure 5(a-b) illustrates the 120$^{th}$ trail of an ant of the colony (extracted from the navigating environment for ease of viewing) before and after diffusion, respectively, while Figure 5(c-d) demonstrates progressive convergence into a shorter and smoother trail, after 400 and 500 directional trails have been completed by all ants in the colony, respectively. It is interesting that, when navigating in the narrower corridors of width 9, the final trail has a roughly equal distance from the two sides. Generated by the combination of inertia and diffusion, the observed isotropic pheromone concentration is superior to the oscillatory or erroneous motion observed in a number of mobile RN approaches, where the walls of narrow corridors are perceived as obstacles coercing the robots either to halt on the spot or to initiate a circling behaviour; the reader is referred to Chang (2005) for more details.

Figure 6 highlights the importance of diffusion for the gradual creation of smooth and short trails; again, for ease of understanding, only one or two trails are shown at the same time extracted from the rest of the navigating environment. Figure 6(a-b) shows the 150$^{th}$ directional trail of an ant before and after diffusion, respectively; Figure 6(c-d) shows the same for the 132$^{nd}$ directional trail completed by another ant at the next-time step; Figure 6(e) combines the two trails prior to diffusion of the second trail, while Figure 6(f) demonstrates how the pheromone concentrations of areas near local changes in direction (especially at their concave sides) and at locations where the two trails converge or cross each other increase after diffusion of the second trail; in fact, 10 ants are adequate for creating - and moving within - a band of high pheromone concentration that joins the nest and the foodsource. Combined with inertia to change in direction of motion and the diminishing diffusion of POOCA as operation progresses, the band gradually shrinks to a one-cell wide smooth and straight trail.

**Table 2. POOCA performance for navigation problems (i)**

| Optimal trail length | Open space | | | (Cornered) corridor | | |
|---|---|---|---|---|---|---|
| | Mean | Std | Time-steps | Mean | Std | Time-steps |
| 5 | 5.0434 | 0.1979 | 4 928 | 5.0101 | 0.0033 | 3 527 |
| 10 | 10.1218 | 0.4352 | 9 773 | 10.0864 | 0.2405 | 7 110 |
| 15 | 15.1568 | 0.5448 | 14 482 | 15.0694 | 0.3136 | 10 712 |
| 20 | 20.2073 | 0.6061 | 18 042 | 20.1053 | 0.3642 | 13 353 |
| 25 | 25.2096 | 0.5714 | 22 970 | 25.1282 | 0.3884 | 16 984 |
| 30 | 30.2470 | 0.6247 | 26 740 | 30.1208 | 0.3854 | 21 751 |
| 35 | 35.2564 | 0.6328 | 30 612 | 35.1483 | 0.4046 | 22 583 |
| 40 | 40.2869 | 0.7010 | 37 941 | 40.1675 | 0.4677 | 28 928 |
| 45 | 45.3118 | 0.7939 | 45 200 | 45.2385 | 0.6247 | 31 363 |
| 50 | 50.3458 | 0.8715 | 51 499 | 50.2886 | 0.7296 | 33 327 |
| 55 | 55.3404 | 0.8974 | 53 242 | 55.2688 | 0.6943 | 36 627 |
| 60 | 60.3799 | 0.9666 | 59 552 | 60.3022 | 0.7890 | 37 547 |
| 65 | 65.5064 | 1.1824 | 62 165 | 65.3175 | 0.8192 | 41 266 |
| 70 | 70.6036 | 1.2936 | 70 639 | 70.3772 | 0.9875 | 46 208 |
| 75 | 75.6641 | 1.3342 | 71 963 | 75.4495 | 1.0134 | 46 629 |
| 80 | 80.7647 | 1.5194 | 78 768 | 80.5279 | 1.1471 | 47 016 |
| 85 | 85.9463 | 1.7827 | 85 332 | 85.6364 | 1.3076 | 47 765 |
| 90 | 90.9363 | 1.8774 | 92 078 | 90.7071 | 1.4178 | 48 369 |
| 95 | 96.1007 | 1.9821 | 97 843 | 95.8189 | 1.4941 | 49 369 |

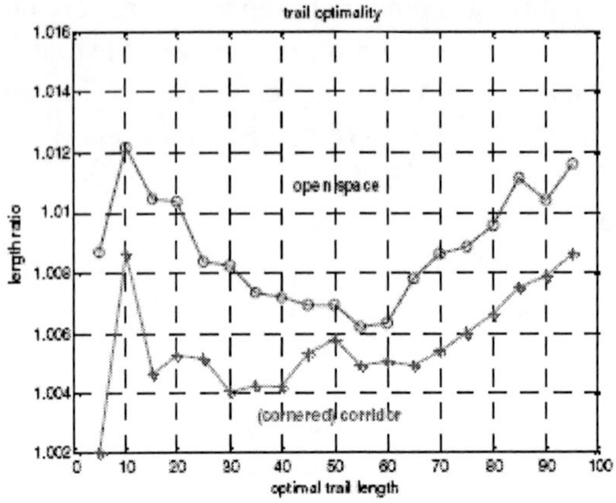


(a)

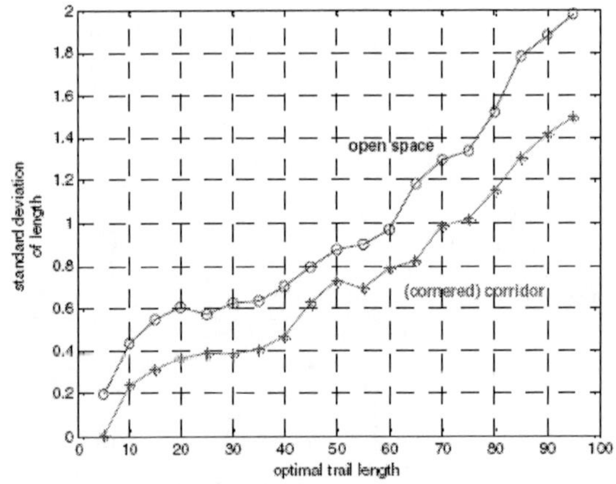


(b)

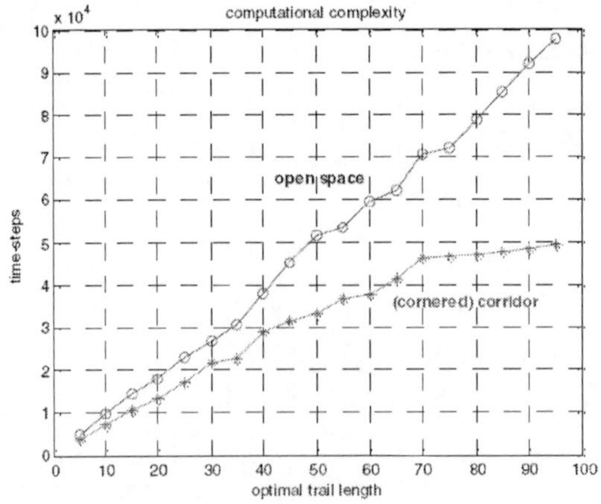


(c)

Figure 4. Graphical evaluation of POOCA operation as a function of optimal trail length for navigation in problems (i); normalized trail optimality (a); standard deviation of trail length (b); computational complexity (c).

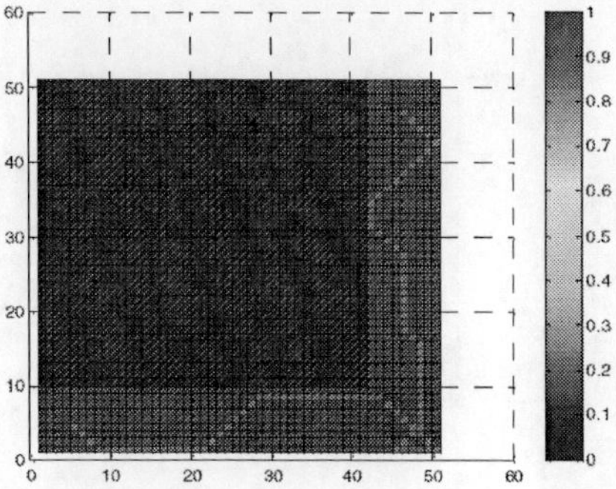


(a)

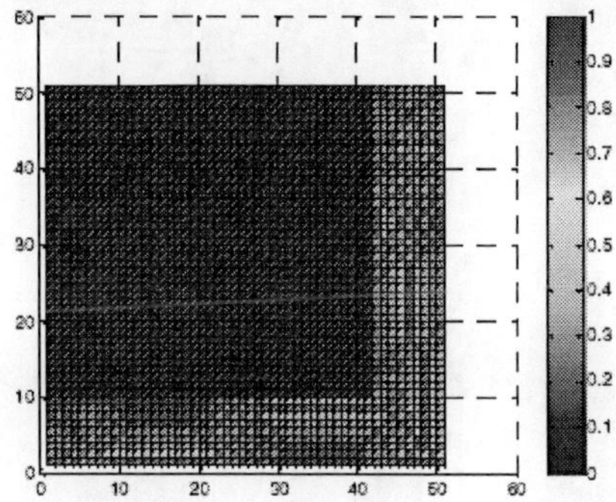


(b)

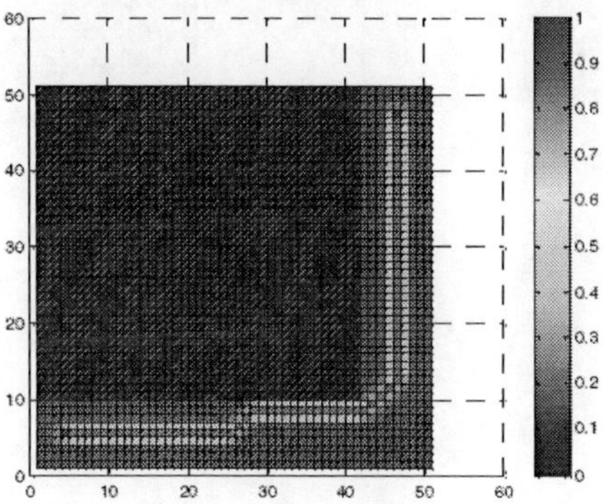


(c)

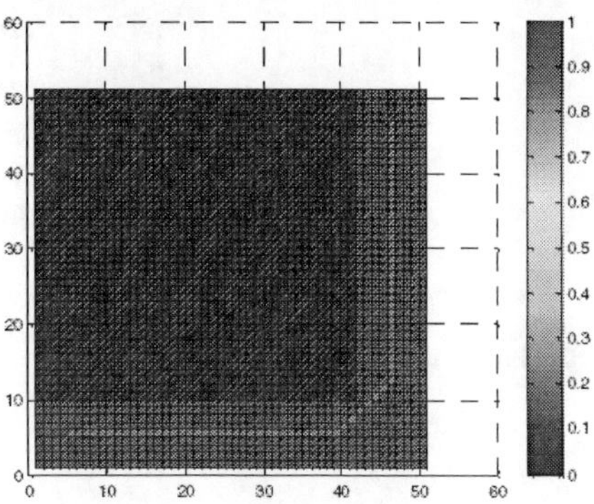


(d)

Figure 5 POOCA operation for obstacle-free navigation on a 9x50 cornered corridor

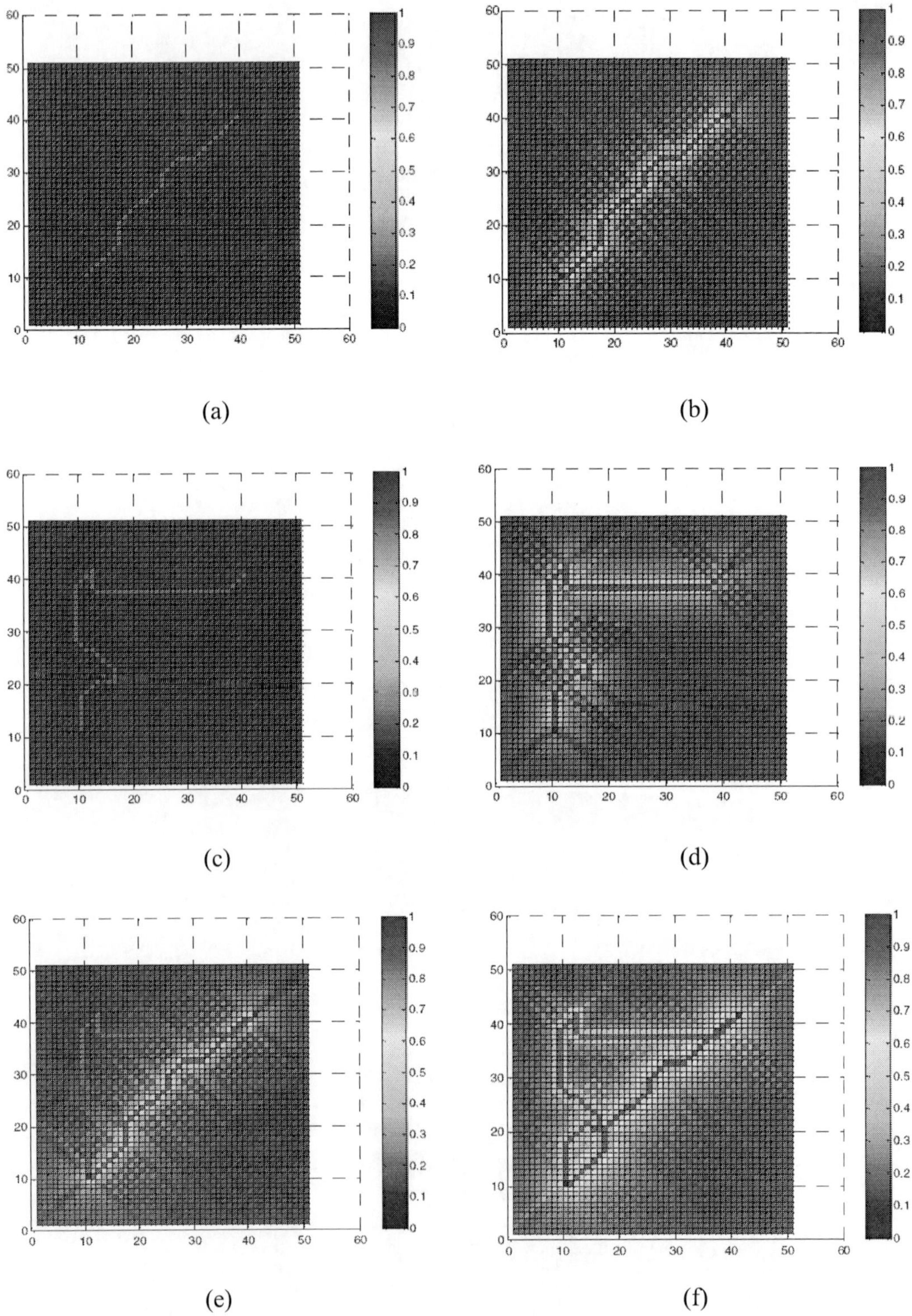


Figure 6. The effect of diffusion for the creation of (near-)optimal trails

The same environments are used for navigation problems (ii). Optimal trails between the nest and the foodsource are partially deleted such that that the two parts of the remaining trails are at least two cells long[25] and the lengths of the missing parts of the trails range between 5 and 45 with steps of 5; POOCA operation is initialized with the application of steps (I-III) of section 4.3.

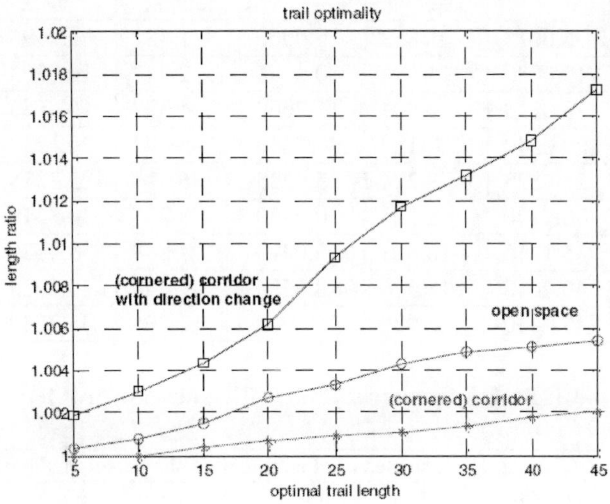


(a)

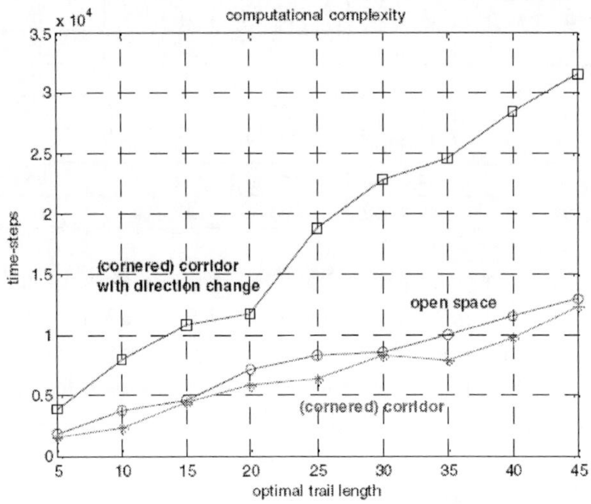


(b)

Figure 7. Graphical evaluation of POOCA operation for trail reconstruction after the partial destruction of an optimal trail, as a function of missing trail length; normalized trail optimality (a); computational complexity (b)

---

[25] The remaining parts provide an indication of the direction of the original trail for open space and corridors. For cornered corridors, and especially when it is the bending part of the trail that is missing, the indications of direction of the original trail are conflicting.

**Table 3. POOCA accuracy and efficiency for navigation problems (ii)**

| Missing trail length | Open space | | (Cornered) corridor | | Cornered corridor with direction change | |
|---|---|---|---|---|---|---|
| | Mean | Time-steps | Mean | Time-steps | Mean | Time-steps |
| 5 | 5.0015 | 1 838 | 5.0000 | 1 482 | 5.0096 | 3 808 |
| 10 | 10.0080 | 3 688 | 10.0000 | 2 347 | 10.0303 | 7 926 |
| 15 | 15.0225 | 4 603 | 15.0060 | 4 392 | 15.0655 | 10 829 |
| 20 | 20.0540 | 7 127 | 20.0140 | 5 792 | 20.1238 | 11 692 |
| 25 | 25.0825 | 8 224 | 25.0225 | 6 328 | 25.2325 | 18 786 |
| 30 | 30.1290 | 8 525 | 30.0330 | 8 206 | 30.3510 | 22 883 |
| 35 | 35.1715 | 10 003 | 35.0490 | 7 848 | 35.4620 | 24 594 |
| 40 | 40.2040 | 11 526 | 40.0720 | 9 668 | 40.5920 | 28 483 |
| 45 | 45.2430 | 12 929 | 45.0945 | 12 306 | 45.7740 | 31 563 |

**Table 4. POOCA accuracy and efficiency for problems (iii)**

| Optimal trail length | L-shaped original trail | | U-shaped original trail | |
|---|---|---|---|---|
| | Mean | Time-steps | Mean | Time-steps |
| 5 | 5.6437 | 6 413 | 5.5574 | 6 535 |
| 10 | 11.6320 | 12 634 | 11.1347 | 14 860 |
| 15 | 16.4795 | 23 540 | 16.6322 | 26 838 |
| 20 | 22.5240 | 31 785 | 22.2982 | 35 894 |
| 25 | 27.7205 | 45 198 | 27.3376 | 48 430 |
| 30 | 33.8747 | 61 930 | 33.2614 | 68 020 |
| 35 | 38.7302 | 70 897 | 38.4850 | 77 869 |
| 40 | 44.6136 | 87 871 | 44.3436 | 96 513 |
| 45 | 49.4440 | 104 683 | 49.8147 | 114 978 |

As shown in Table 3 and Figure 7, POOCA operation is similar to, but slightly better than, that observed for problems (i), in other words filling in missing parts of the trails is in general more accurate than when constructing the trails from scratch. The superiority of corridor over open space trail reconstruction which was observed for problems (i) remains for problems (ii) but is not as evident; this is due to the bias towards straight ahead motion that is provided by the remaining parts of the trails and facilitates open space navigation in particular. Conversely, trail reconstruction is slightly less accurate and prolonged for corridor navigation when a change in direction occurs in the missing part of the trail. This degradation appears to be a function of the length of the missing trail and becomes more accentuated when trail reconstruction extends to the remaining parts of the trail. The average number of time-steps required until POOCA termination is independent of the length of the original trail, but dependent on the length and - especially – the straightness of the missing trail. A comparison between Tables 3 and 2 as well as between Figures 7 and 4 further demonstrates these points.

For problems (iii), initial sub-optimal L- and U- trails (Panait & Luke 2004a) appear constructed on 50x50 grids such that the corresponding optimal trails that connect the nest and the foodsource are diagonal or horizontal/vertical, respectively, and range in length between 5 and 45 with steps of 5. As for problems (ii), POOCA operation begins with the application of steps (I-III) of section 4.3. and proceeds with gradual trail shortening and smoothing towards areas of higher pheromone concentration, namely towards concave parts of the bending trail(s). As can be observed in Table 4, the creation of (straight) optimal trails is not always achieved, a phenomenon that is mostly due to the unsynchronized smoothing over and straightening of the trails. When local changes in direction are generated near each other, it is not unlikely for them to propagate to other parts of the evolving trail and elongate the final trail. As shown in Table 4, the (L- or U-) shape of the original trail does not significantly affect accuracy, although it influences efficiency with convergence accomplished more rapidly for L-shaped original trails. An illustration of optimal trail convergence, starting off from a U-shaped trail, is given in Figure 8. The result of the application of steps (I-II) and (III) of section 4.3. is shown in Figure 8(a-b), respectively, while the gradual trail evolution towards a progressively straighter trail after 250 and 350 directional trails have been completed by the 10 ants, respectively, is illustrated in Figure 8(c-d); convergence into the final optimal trail is shown in Figure 8(e). A point worth stressing here is the importance of step (III) of section 4.3. for re-initializing operation following a change in the environment. As depicted in Figure 8(a), the pheromone landscape resulting from the application of steps (I-II) still holds the memory of the trail created prior to the change in the environment, thereby rendering it extremely difficult to escape from the original trail. Conversely, the application of step (III) shown in Figure 8(b) decreases the pheromone concentration of the original trail and transforms the surrounding landscape into a fuzzy area of relatively high pheromone concentration; POOCA can now either swiftly reconstruct the previous trail or escape from it and create a novel trail, depending on the navigating conditions set by the modified environment.

**Table 4. POOCA accuracy and efficiency for problems (iii)**

| Optimal trail length | L-shaped original trail | | U-shaped original trail | |
|---|---|---|---|---|
| | Mean | Time-steps | Mean | Time-steps |
| 5 | 5.6437 | 6 413 | 5.5574 | 6 535 |
| 10 | 11.6320 | 12 634 | 11.1347 | 14 860 |
| 15 | 16.4795 | 23 540 | 16.6322 | 26 838 |
| 20 | 22.5240 | 31 785 | 22.2982 | 35 894 |
| 25 | 27.7205 | 45 198 | 27.3376 | 48 430 |
| 30 | 33.8747 | 61 930 | 33.2614 | 68 020 |
| 35 | 38.7302 | 70 897 | 38.4850 | 77 869 |
| 40 | 44.6136 | 87 871 | 44.3436 | 96 513 |
| 45 | 49.4440 | 104 683 | 49.8147 | 114 978 |

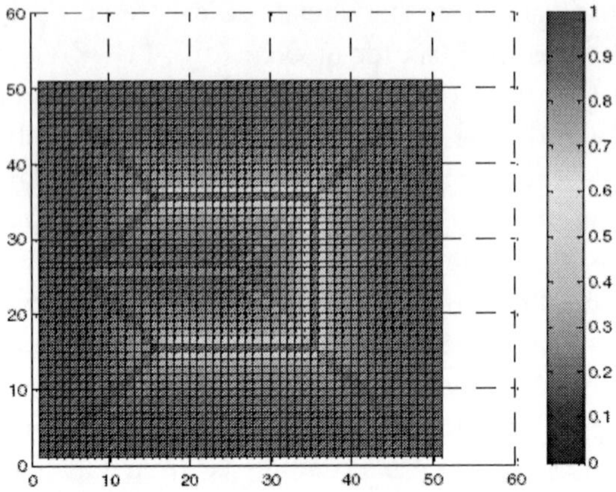


(a)

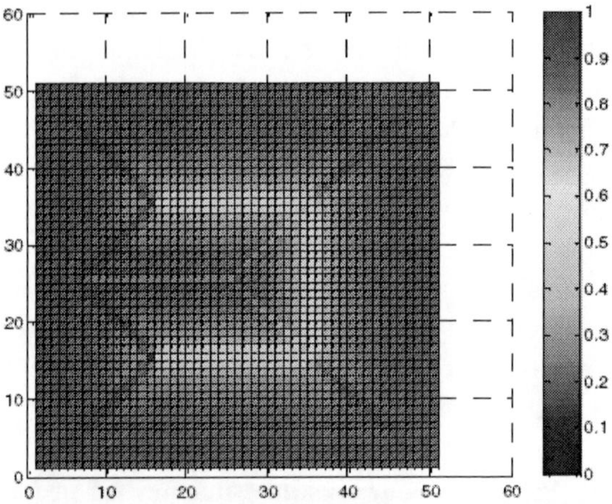


(b)

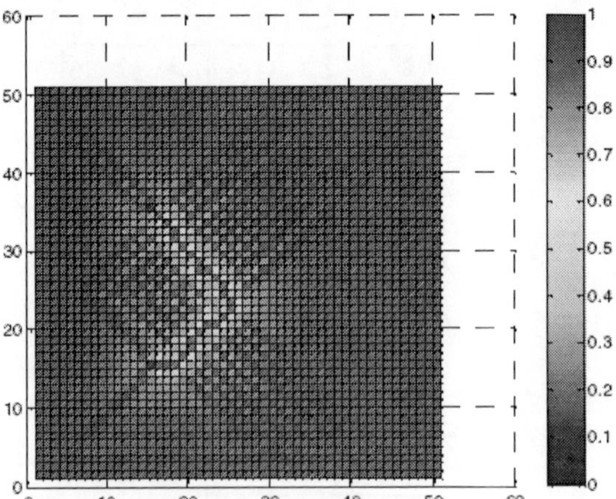


(c)

Figure 8. Continued

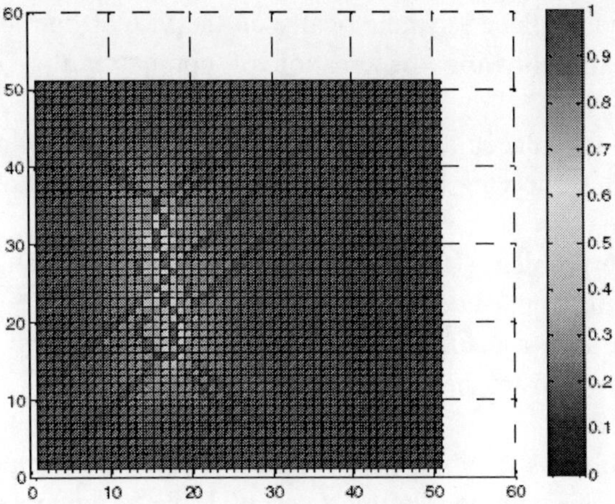


(d)

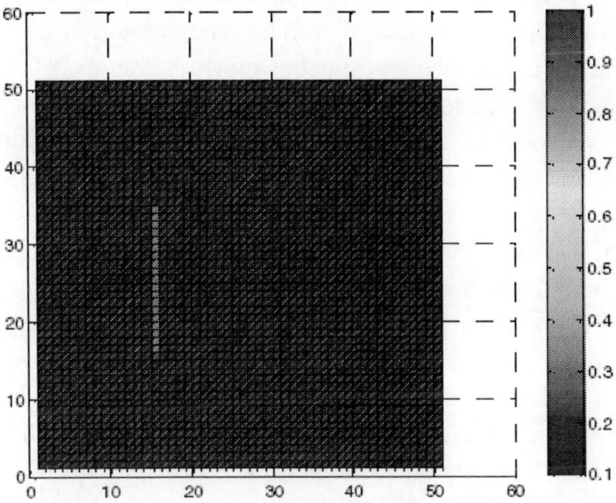


(e)

Figure 8. Successful transformation of a suboptimal U-shaped trail into a straight optimal trail

### *5.1.2. Navigation in environments cluttered with obstacles*

Navigation in static environments cluttered with obstacles is investigated for both single obstacles and a multitude of obstacles. The 50x50 grid and the same nest-foodsource configurations as for obstacle-free navigation (section 5.1.1) are employed, with obstacles of different shapes and sizes[26] allowing the creation of optimal trail lengths between 5 and 75 with steps of 5.

Navigation in environments cluttered with single obstacles is focused upon:

(i) a convex obstacle whose location does not affect trail creation (dummy obstacle),

[26] Obstacles occupy between 0.04 to 36% of the grid and are composed of combinations of horizontal and vertical bars of width 1 and diagonal bars of width 2.

(ii) a convex obstacle placed symmetrically on the virtual line joining the nest and the foodsource, thus allowing the creation of optimal trail(s) on either side of the obstacle,

(iii) a convex obstacle placed asymmetrically on the virtual line joining the nest and the foodsource, thus allowing the creation of optimal trail(s) on one (the "shorter") side of the obstacle only,

(iv) the dead-cycle problem (Undeger & Polat 2007; Zhu & Yang 2007), where a non-convex obstacle is placed symmetrically on the virtual line joining the nest and the foodsource in such a configuration that the ants are coerced to navigate inside the obstacle and away from the foodsource.

For navigation problems (i), POOCA operation is equally accurate to and slightly more efficient than open-space navigation (leftmost part of Table 5 compared to the leftmost part of Table 2). When obstacles are small and located clearly away from the optimal trail, convergence dovetails that of open-space navigation. Efficiency increases for larger obstacles, with POOCA operation approaching that of corridor navigation for very large obstacles[27].

Problems (ii) and (iii) implement unconstrained versions of the "double bridge" experiments for branches of equal and different lengths, respectively. No systematic preference of side is detected for a symmetrically placed object (e.g. Figure 2), although the choice of side is determined quite early on, when about 50 to 75 trails have been completed by the 10 ants. As shown in the middle columns of Table 5, POOCA operation appears dependent on obstacle size with slower convergence observed for larger obstacles; this phenomenon is due both to the mounting trail length and to the growing distance between the two candidate trails. The slightly higher average trail length than that observed for problems (i) is due to local changes in direction propagating along the trail and occasionally elongating it. The rightmost part of Table 5 demonstrates that POOCA operation is even slower and less accurate for an asymmetrically placed obstacle (problem (iii)). The fall in accuracy is caused mainly by the non-consistent convergence upon the "shorter" side when the shortest trail(s) that can be created on each side of the obstacle differ by no more than 10%. Additionally, for problems involving a less than 5% difference between the shortest trail(s) on each side of the obstacle, it is quite common for both trails to remain at the end of POOCA operation, i.e. for convergence upon a single trail not to be consistently accomplished. It appears that the small colony of 10 ants is not adept at distinguishing between such small differences in the lengths of trails evolving independently of each other[28]. Overall, trail smoothness (in terms of global directional changes) appears to be more important that absolute trail length minimization for navigation in environments cluttered with obstacles.

Problem (iv) examines POOCA operation under adverse navigating circumstances. A dead-cycle involves a hollow obstacle that is placed in such a configuration that the ants/agents originating from the nest get trapped inside the obstacle and – once outside it – are coerced to move away from the foodsource and back towards the nest. Owing to the limited

[27] The free-space part of the environment is not narrow enough to produce an effect similar to the isotropic pheromone concentration observed for 9-cell wide corridors (section 5.1.1. and Figure 5).

[28] Tests on asymmetrically placed obstacles using larger numbers of ants in the colony have shown that this problem can be practically eradicated with a ten-fold increase in the colony size. Such an implementation, however, significantly increases the computational complexity (time of execution, memory requirements etc.) of POOCA and has not been followed, at the expense of the occasional creation of sub-optimal or multiple trails.

range of robot sensors, the dead-cycle problem constitutes and especially challenging RN problem, regardless of the use or not of memory (Undeger & Polat 2007): the created trails are significantly longer than necessary when memory is used, while a cyclic behaviour and an inability to reach the foodsource are observed when no memory is used.

**Table 5. POOCA accuracy and efficiency in environments cluttered with single convex objects**

| Trail length | Dummy obstacle | | Symmetrically placed obstacle | | Asymmetrically placed obstacle | |
|---|---|---|---|---|---|---|
| | Mean | Time-steps | Mean | Time-steps | Mean | Time-steps |
| 5 | 5.0254 | 4 073 | 5.2516 | 6 582 | 5.3072 | 7 004 |
| 10 | 10.1045 | 8 116 | 10.4194 | 11 105 | 10.4795 | 12 547 |
| 15 | 15.1139 | 13 220 | 15.5335 | 16 267 | 15.8351 | 17 984 |
| 20 | 20.1467 | 16 938 | 20.7618 | 19 928 | 21.0806 | 20 682 |
| 25 | 25.1741 | 20 411 | 25.9159 | 24 974 | 26.4697 | 24 573 |
| 30 | 30.2043 | 23 690 | 31.3004 | 25 654 | 31.8876 | 26 427 |
| 35 | 35.2105 | 28 303 | 36.5975 | 31 393 | 37.2415 | 33 093 |
| 40 | 40.2331 | 34 951 | 41.9429 | 36 438 | 42.8449 | 38 723 |
| 45 | 45.2725 | 41 281 | 47.2083 | 42 742 | 48.3696 | 44 357 |
| 50 | - | - | 52.5069 | 51 194 | 53.7428 | 50 526 |
| 55 | - | - | 57.8452 | 55 482 | 59.2746 | 54 414 |
| 60 | - | - | 62.9961 | 59 729 | 64.7951 | 58 212 |
| 65 | - | - | 68.7629 | 63 933 | 70.3278 | 61 919 |
| 70 | - | - | 73.5982 | 68 096 | 75.9428 | 65 537 |
| 75 | - | - | 79.2337 | 72 216 | 81.5372 | 69 064 |

**Table 6. POOCA accuracy and efficiency for the dead-cycle problem**

| Optimal trail Length | Free space (%) (not occupied by the obstacle) | Mean obstacle size | Mean | Time-steps |
|---|---|---|---|---|
| 37 | 95 | 12x12 | 38.2852 | 42 853 |
| 51 | 75 | 25x25 | 55.7839 | 73 131 |
| 67 | 55 | 34x34 | 73.8841 | 415 269 |

For the following tests, hollow square obstacles with an opening on one side are employed. The locations of the nest and the foodsource as well as the centre of mass of the obstacle remain constant and are placed on the line of symmetry formed by nest and the foodsource; the size of the obstacle varies so as to occupy between 5 and 45% of the environment and the opening of the obstacle always faces towards the nest. It can be observed from Table 6 that the difficulty of the navigation task increases as the amount of free space is reduced:

- For smaller obstacles (up to 15% of the grid), the ants either escape the obstacle altogether or quickly explore its concavity and begin navigating towards the foodsource; as a consequence, accuracy and efficiency are only slightly affected. This can be verified by comparing the first row of Table 6 with the leftmost columns of the 7-8th rows of Table 2.
- For larger obstacles, both the probability that the ants will visit the obstacle and the amount of time spent exploring it increase. The resulting longer trails are subject to more accentuated evaporation, whereby the difference in pheromone concentration within and without the obstacle is reduced; consequently, trail creation and convergence are significantly delayed. A comparison of the last two rows of Table 6 and the corresponding rows of the leftmost part of Table 2 illustrates a rise in mean trail length and a marked decline in computational efficiency for large instances of the dead-cycle problem.

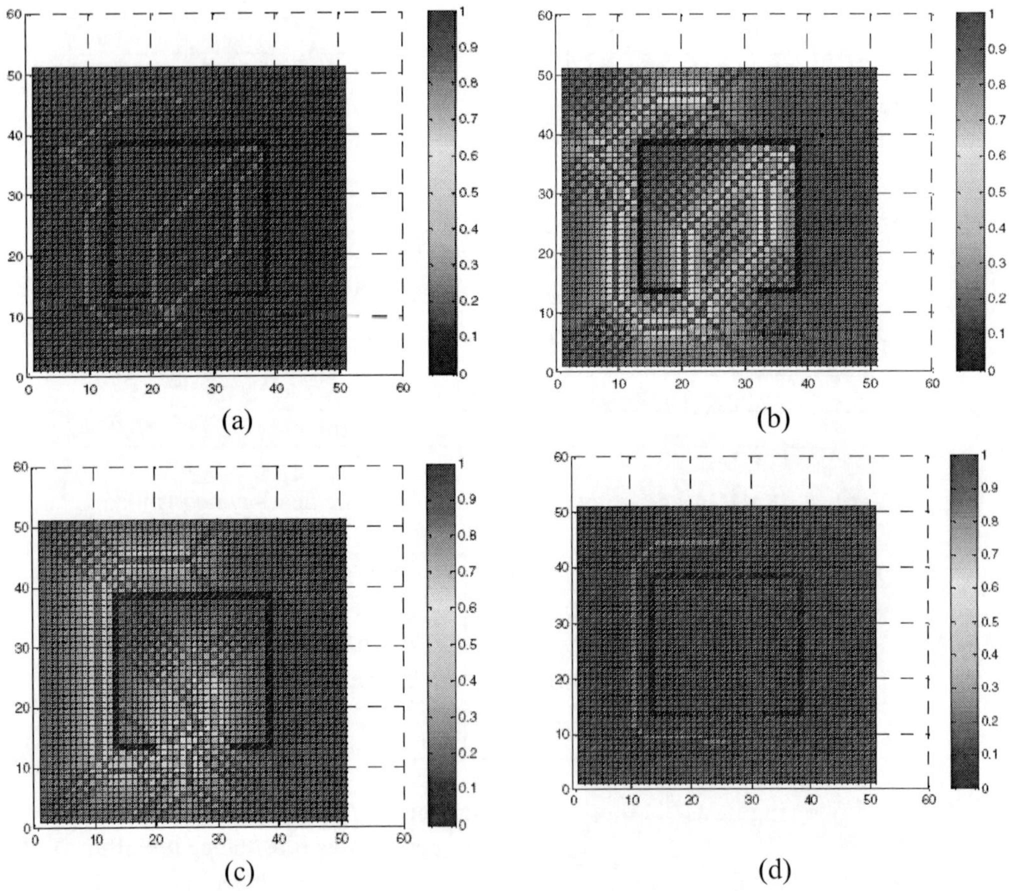

Figure 9. POOCA operation for the dead-cycle problem, with the concave obstacle occupying 25% of the grid.

The evolution of POOCA operation is illustrated in Figure 9 for a 25x25 obstacle; Figure 9(a-b) depicts a characteristic far-from-optimal trail (extracted from its environment) of an ant exploring the obstacle during its 150$^{th}$ trail, before and after diffusion, respectively. It is still quite likely for an ant of the colony to visit the obstacle, although the amount of time spent exploring it is reduced compared to that of the initial trails. Figure 9(c) demonstrates gradual smoothing of the trail after 300 directional trails have been created by all the ants of the colony, whereby the obstacle-related part of the trail progressively shrinks, while Figure 9(d) depicts the final trail constructed at the end of POOCA operation. It is important that - even for this small ant colony - near-optimal trails are constructed[29].

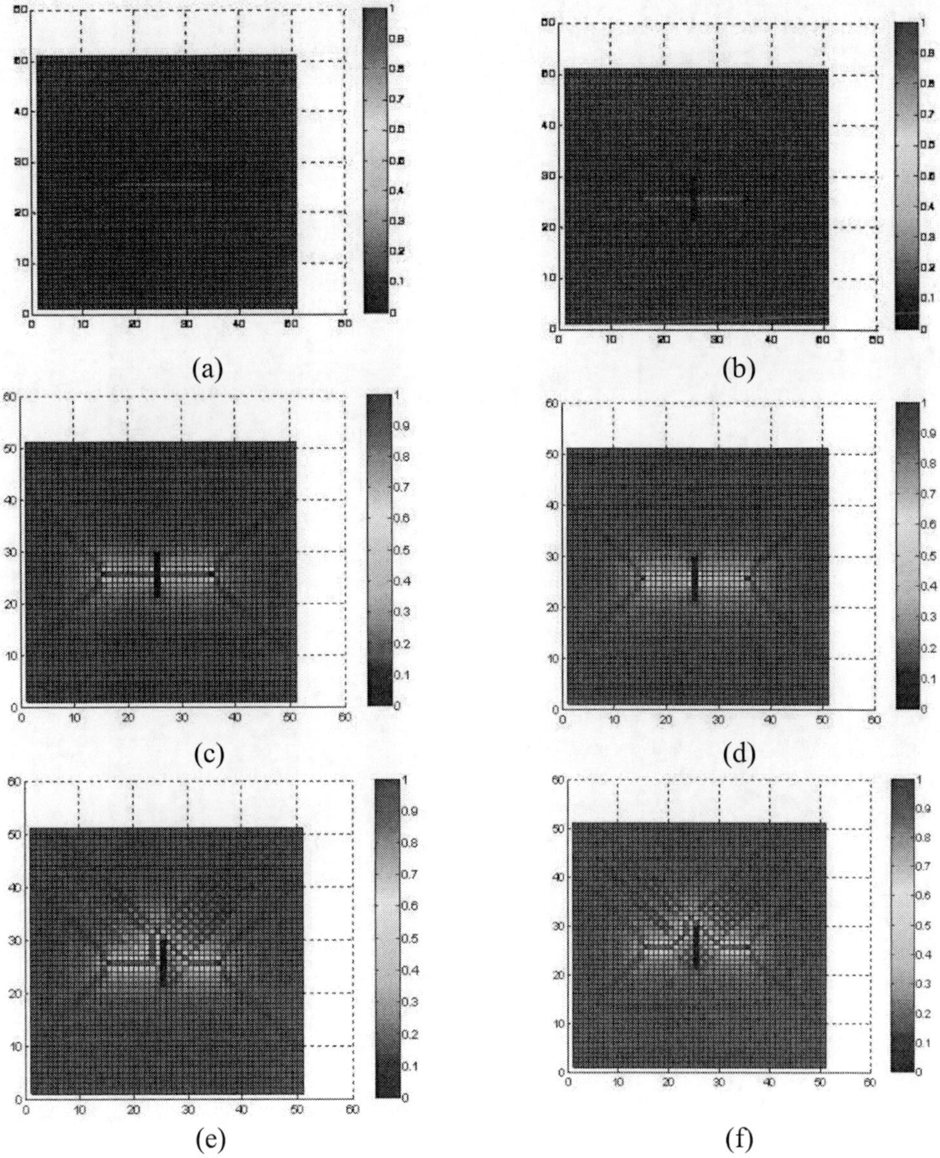


Figure 10. Continued

[29] Similar to the "double bridge" experiments, faster convergence is accomplished by a 25 and 80-fold increase in the colony size for 75 and 55% of free space, respectively, at the expense – however - of a disproportionate increase in the time of execution and memory requirements.

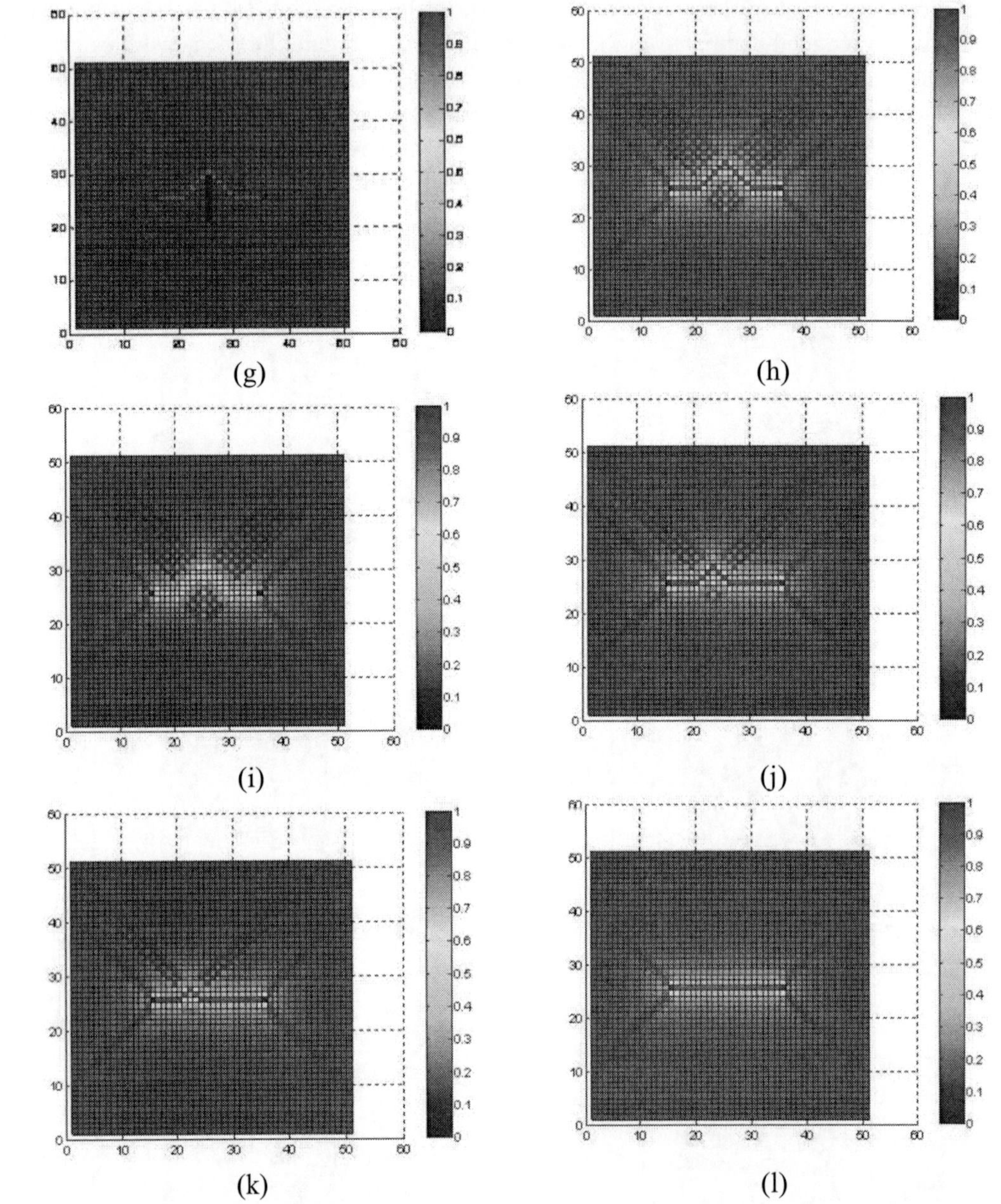


Figure 10. A dynamic environment involving an obstacle that is placed symmetrically on the virtual line joining the nest and the foodsource and is, subsequently, removed.

Ultimately, some navigation problems involving more than one convex obstacle are examined on 50x50 grids. Some obstacles are placed and sized such that they do not affect trail creation, others are placed symmetrically and others yet asymmetrically on the virtual line joining the nest and the foodsource. Additionally, relaxed versions of the "multiple bridge" problems (Mazer et al. 1998; Borisov & Vasilyev 2002; Undeger & Polat 2007; Zhu & Yang 2007) are tested; the implemented environments involve multiple wide areas (reminiscent of the corridors used in the "multiple bridge" problems) connecting the nest and the foodsource and, hence, promote the construction of an assortment of (near-)optimal trails. As for single obstacles, the optimal trail length constitutes a function of the proportion of free space on the grid.

Analogous results to those concerning single obstacles are observed. The final trail upon which POOCA converges is determined to a large extent by the trails constructed at the beginning of POOCA operation, with trail smoothness being more important than exact trail length. Owing to the significantly larger number of candidate (near-)optimal trails, the similarity of POOCA convergence to the trail creation process of real ants (footnote 6) becomes obvious: parts of the trails constructed during the first 80-120 directional trails of the ants are used for constructing the final trail, with diffusion smoothing over the locations where parts of different trails are combined. Similar to problems (ii) with single obstacles, differences in trail length not exceeding 15% of the optimal trail(s) are not consistently distinguished and a choice of trails within this margin is converged upon.

## 5.2. Dynamic Environments

Dynamic problems (Ishda & Korf 1995; Panait & Luke 2004a) involve changes in the navigating environment and are represented here as combinations of the static problems investigated in section 5.1.; it is reminded that each change in the environment takes place after the 10 ants have completed 500 directional trails, is followed by steps (I-III) of section 4.3. and terminates as soon as another 500 directional trails have been completed by the ant colony. The dynamic problems include:

(i) nest and/or foodsource relocation in both obstacle-free environments and in environments cluttered with obstacles,
(ii) obstacle appearance, with the obstacle placed either symmetrically or asymmetrically on the virtual line joining the nest and the foodsource,
(iii) obstacle relocation such that either or both the old and new location of the obstacle interfere with the optimal trail or not,
(iv) obstacle disappearance, with the obstacle originally placed either symmetrically or asymmetrically on the virtual line joining the nest and the foodsource.

It has been found that POOCA accuracy does not differ significantly from that observed when the ant colony navigates each component static problem. The total number of time-steps required until final convergence lies within the margin [-5.63%, 7.81%] of the sum of the total number of steps required for each static problem. The sign and degree of deviation depend on the amount of trail reconstruction that becomes necessary from the change in the environment, e.g. if few parts of the originally created trail must be rebuilt or if global trail creation is required.

Some examples of POOCA operation are shown in Figures 10-11. Figure 10 demonstrates a combination of problems (ii) and (iv), where an obstacle appears symmetrically on the virtual line joining the nest and the foodsource in an originally obstacle-free environment; following trail reconstruction, the obstacle is removed. The optimal trail converged upon in the original obstacle-free environment is shown in Figure 10(a). Obstacle

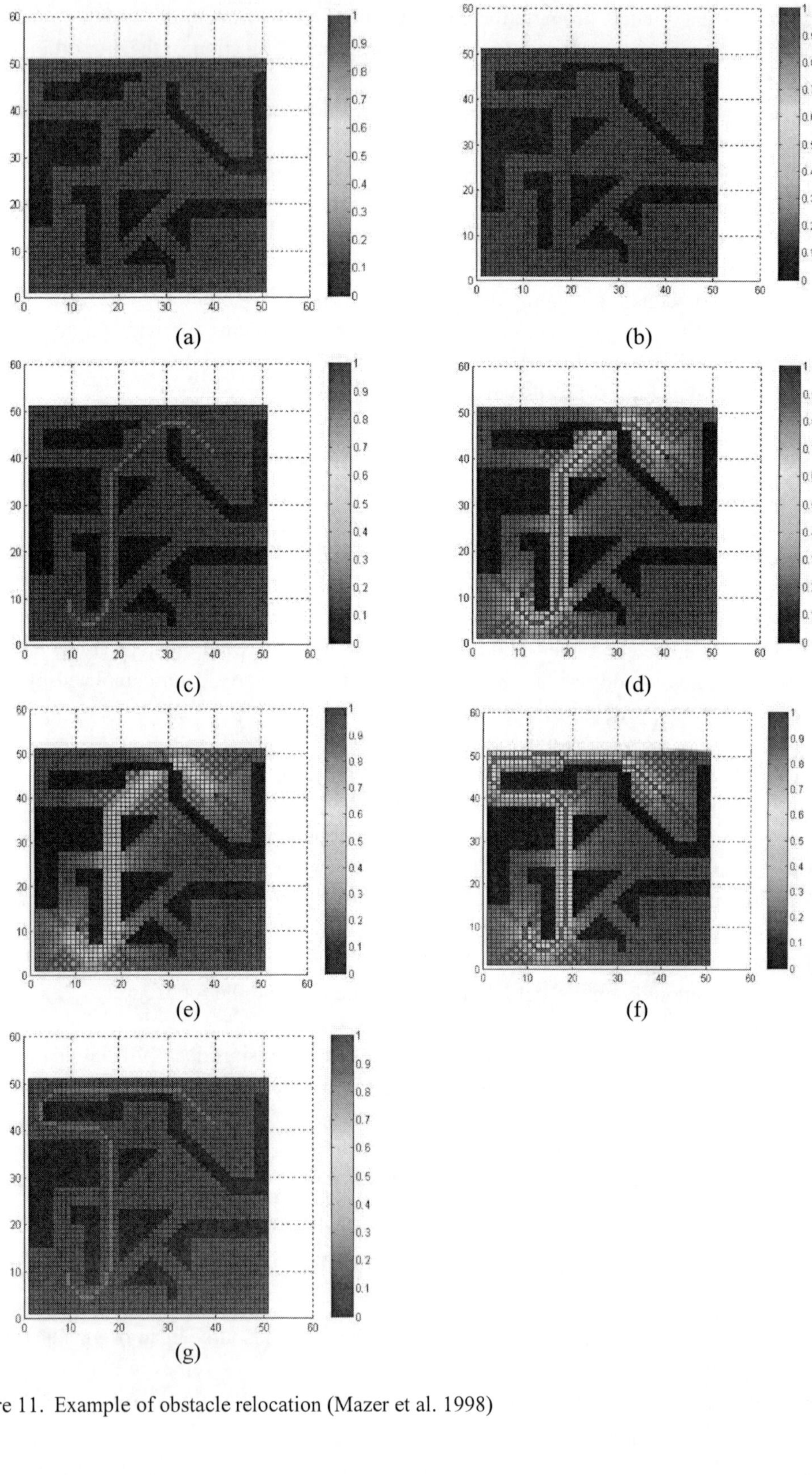


Figure 11. Example of obstacle relocation (Mazer et al. 1998)

appearance (Figure 10(b)) results in the application of steps (I-II) and (III) of section 4.3. (Figure 10(c-d), respectively) and in the gradual convergence upon a novel optimal trail (Figure 10(e-g), respectively) after 300, 400 and 475 trails, respectively, have been completed by the 10 ants. A new change in the environment (obstacle disappearance) reinitializes POOCA operation via steps (I-II) and (III) of section 4.3. (shown in Figure 10(h-i), respectively,) and causes the gradual restoration of the original optimal trail, as seen after 300, 400 and 475 trails (Figure 10(j-l), respectively) have been completed by all the ants in the colony.

Finally, Figure 11 gives an example of POOCA operation for an instance of obstacle relocation (problem (iii)) in an environment cluttered with obstacles; the problem is taken from Mazer et al. (1998) and Figure 11(a-b) illustrates the environment before and after obstacle relocation, respectively. The near-optimal trail converged upon in the original environment is shown in Figure 11(c). Obstacle relocation reinitializes POOCA operation via the application of steps (I-II) and (III) (Figure 11(d-e), respectively) and progresses with the partial reconstruction of the trail around the blocked location, as shown after 350 and 500 directional trails have been completed by all ants in the colony (Figure 11(f-g), respectively).

## 6. Future Research

POOCA operation needs to be studied for larger environments and more foodsources; it is likely that the optimal parameter values coordinating the main POOCA mechanisms will have to be re-evaluated. The dependence of those parameters on grid size and number of foodsources will also need to be established.

It would also be worthwhile investigating additional aspects of navigation in order to improve POOCA performance. For instance, incorporation of the global changes in direction in the estimation of trail optimality would be desirable. In parallel to that, grids composed of hexagonal grids (Rajashekhara et al., 2006) could be used, as horizontal, vertical and diagonal transitions are all of the same length. It would also be useful to consider the addition of the third dimension (Grah et al. 2005), whereby efficient navigation in both level areas and slopes could be handled concurrently.

It has been observed that, especially for narrow corridor navigation, the evolving trails tend not to neighbour obstacle cells or edges of the grid. An extension worth implementing concerns establishing safety margins – which need not necessarily be of a uniform width for both sides - between obstacles and navigable free-space; an approach similar to that of Willms & Yang (2008) could be adopted.

Finally, it would be interesting to extend POOCA operation to more than one ant colony foraging the environment at the same time. Different social frameworks could be developed with the aim at maximally exploiting the foodsource(s), where the colonies co-operate with each other, compete against each other, or select a time-varying gain-maximization strategy for when to co-operate with and when to compete against each other.

## 7. Conclusion

Progressive Organization of co-Operating Colonies/Collections of Ants/Agents (POOCA) has been introduced as a novel robot navigation and obstacle avoidance approach that is capable of efficiently as well as accurately operating in stationary and dynamic unknown environments. POOCA extends the pheromone-inspired co-operative multi-agent system learning paradigm while also advancing swarm robotics, ant colony optimization and co-operative multi-agent learning.

POOCA follows the streak of existing pheromone-based co-operative foraging multi-agent systems in its biological inspiration, namely the utilization of (i) stigmetry and minimum individual memory for collective foraging, (ii) constant pheromone evaporation, and (iii) evolutionary computation for parameter optimization. However, it differs from those approaches in that it simulates minimal and uniformly applied notions of ant colony foraging such as (i) a single type of additive and progressively intensifying pheromone that reflects each ant's increasing knowledge of the environment, (ii) inertia to constant direction of motion that discourages abrupt directional changes, and (iii) diminishing pheromone diffusion that implements the stereo-like pheromone sensing of real ants, whereby winding trails and unnecessary changes in direction of motion are gradually smoothed over. Each modification of the environment triggers diffusion and lowering of the pheromone concentration of the existing trail(s); inspired by real ants and aimed at the swift creation of a novel (near-)optimal trail, this process strikes a balance between retaining still useful parts and breaking away from sub-optimal parts of the original trail(s).

Using only 10 ants, POOCA has established its ability to uniformly, accurately as well as efficiently create (near-)optimal trails in a variety of static and dynamic environments represented by square-cell grids of size up to 50x100 and involving a single nest, a single foodsource and no, a single or multiple obstacles.

## Acknowledgments

The author wishes to thank Professor Nigel C. Steele for his succinct as well as discreet counsel during the preparation of this chapter.

## Dedication

This chapter is dedicated to my mother, Helen-Kalliopi, who always shared my fascination with real ants, pictures/drawings of ants, as well as POOCA ants.

## References

Akesson, S. & Wehner, R. (2002). Visual navigation in desert ants Cataglyphis fortis: are snapshots coupled to a celestial system of reference?, *Journal of Experimental Biology*,

*205*, 1971-1978.

Alupoaei, S. & Katkoori, S. (2004). Ant colony system application to macrocell overlap removal, IEEE Transactions on *VLSI Systems*, *12*, 1118-1122.

Asada, M. (1990). Map building for a mobile robot from sensory data, *IEEE Transactions on Systems, Man, and Cybernetics*, *20*, 1326-1336.

Barraquand, J. & Latombe, J. C. (1993). Nonholonomic multibody mobile robots: controllability and motion planning in the presence of obstacles, *Algorithmica, 10*, 121-155.

Beckers, R., Deneubourg, J. L. & Goss, S. (1992a). Trail laying behaviour during food recruitment in the ant Lasius niger (L), *Insectes Sociaux*, *39*, 59-72.

Beckers, R., Deneubourg, J. L. & Goss, S. (1993). Modulation of trail laying in the ant Lasius niger (Hymeoptera: Formicidae) and its role in the collective selection of a food source, *Journal of Insect Behavior*, *6*, 751-759.

Bell, J. E. & McMullen, P. R. (2004). Ant colony optimization techniques for the vehicle routing problem, *Advanced Engineering Informatics*, *18*, 41-48.

Blum, C. & Dorigo, M. (2004). The hyper-cube framework for ant colony optimization, *IEEE Transactions on Systems, Man, and Cybernetics – Part B*, *34*, 1161-1172.

Blum, C. (2005a). Ant colony optimization: introduction and recent trends, *Physics of Life Reviews*, *2*, 353-373.

Blum, C. (2005b). Bean-ACO – hybridizing and colony optimization with beam search: an application to open shop scheduling, *Computers and Operations Research*, *32*, 1565-1591.

Bonabeau, E., Dorigo, M. & Theraulaz, G. (1999). *Swarm Intelligence: From Natural to Artificial Systems*, Oxford University Press, Oxford, U. K.

Borenstein, J. & Koren, Y. (1989). Real-time obstacle avoidance for fast mobile robots, *IEEE Transactions on Systems, Man and Cybernetics*, *19,* 1179-1187.

Borenstein, J. & Koren, Y. (1991). The vector field histogram-fast obstacle avoidance for mobile robots, *IEEE Transactions on Robotic Automation*, *7*, 278-288.

Borisov, A. & Vasilyev, A. (2002). Learning classifier systems in autonomous agent control tasks, *Proceedings of the 5th International Conference on Application of Fuzzy Systems and Soft Computing* ("ICAFS-2002"), September, 17-18 2002, Milan, Italy, 36-42.

Brauer, W. & Weiss, G. (1998). *Multi-machine scheduling – a multi-agent learning approach,* Proceedings of the Third International Conference on Multi-Agent Systems, July 4-7 1998, Paris, France, 42-48.

Breed, M. D., Fewell, J. H., Moore, A. J. & Williams, K. R. (1987). Graded recruitment in a ponerine ant, *Behavioral Ecology and Sociobiology*, *20*, 407-411.

Bruckstein, A. M. (1993). Why the ant trails look so straight and nice, *The Mathematical Intelligencer*, *15*, 59-62.

Bui, T. N. & Rizzo, J. R. (2004). Finding maximum cliques with distributed ants, *Proceedings of GECCO 2004* (Deb K. et al. eds) *Springer*, 24-35.

Bullnheimer, B., Hartl, R. F. & Strauss, C. (1999). Applying the ant system to the vehicle routing problem, Proceedings of Meta-Heuristics International Conference, July 21-24 1997, Sophia-Antipolis, France, *Advances and Trends in Local Search Paradigms for Optimization* (Voss S. Martello S. Osman I. H. Roucairol C. eds.) 285-296.

Bäck, T. (1996). *Evolutionary Algorithms in Theory and Practice*, Oxford University. Press, Oxford, U. K.

Canny, J. (1988). *The Complexity of Robot Motion Planning*, MIT Press, Cambridge MA, U. S. A.

Caulfield, H. J. & Kinser, J. M. (1999). Finding the shortest path in the shortest time using PNN's, *IEEE Transactions on Neural Networks 10* 604-606.

Chalupsky, H., Gil, Y., Knoblock, C. A., Lerman, K., Oh, J., Pynadath, D., Russ, T. & Tambe, M. (2002). Electric elves: agent technology for supporting human organizations, *AI Magazine*, *32*, AAAI Press (10 pages).

Chang, C. (2005). Using sensor habituation in mobile robots to reduce oscillatory movements in narrow corridors, *IEEE Transactions on Neural Networks*, *16*, 1582-1589.

Choset, H. & Nagatani, K. (2001). Topological simultaneous localization and mapping (SLAM). toward exact localization without explicit localization, IEEE *Transactions on Robotics & Automation*, *17*, 125-137.

Collett, T. S. & Waxman, D. (2005). Ant navigation: reading geometrical signposts, *Current Biology Dispatch*, *15*, R171.

Collins, R. & Jefferson, D. (1991). An Artificial neural network representation for artificial organisms, *Parallel Problem Solving from Nature* In: H. P., Schwefel, R. Manner, eds. Springer-Verlag, Berlin, Germany) 259-263.

Collins, R. & Jefferson, D. (1992). AntFarm: towards simulated evolution, *Artificial Life II* In: C., Langton, C., Taylor, J. D., Farmer, S. Rassmussen, eds. Addison-Welsey, Upper Saddle River, NJ, U. S. A. 579-601.

Colorni, A., Dorigo, M., Maniezzo, V. & Trubian, M. (1994). Ant system for job-shop scheduling, Belgian Journal of Operations Research, *Statistics and Computer Science*, *34*, 39-53.

Coombs, D. & Roberts, K. (1993). Centering behaviour using peripheral vision, Proceedings of the *IEEE Conference on Computer Vision and Pattern Recognition,* IEEE Society Press, Los Alamitos, CA, 440-451.

Costa, D. & Hertz, A. (1997). Ants can color graphs, *Journal of the Operational Research Society*, *48*, 295-305.

d' Ettore, P. & Heinze, J. (2001). Sociobiology of slave-making ants, *Acta Ethologica*, *3*, 67-82.

de Biseau, J. C., Deneubourg, J. L. & Pasteels, J. C. (1991). Collective flexibility during mass recruitment in the ant Myrmica sabuleti (Hymenoptera: Formicidae), *Psyche*, 98, 323-336.

Deneubourg, J. L., Aron, S., Goss, S. & Pasteels, J. M. (1990). The self organizing exploratory pattern of the Argentine ant, *Journal of Insect Behavior, 3*, 159-168.

Denny, J. A., Wright, J. H. & Grief, B. (2001). Foraging efficiency in the wood ant, Formica rufa: is time of the essence in trail following? *Animal Behaviour*, *61*, 139-146.

di Caro, G. & Dorigo, M. (1998). AntNet: distributed stigmetric control for communications networks, *Journal of Artificial Intelligence Research, 9*, 317-365.

Dorigo, M. & Blum, C. (2005). Ant colony optimization theory: a survey, *Theoretical Computer Science*, *344*, 243-278.

Dorigo, M. & Gambardella, L. M. (1997). Ant colony system: a cooperative learning approach to the travelling salesman problem, IEEE *Transactions on Evolutionary Computation*, *1*, 53-66.

Dorigo, M. & Stutzle, T. (2004). *Ant Colony Optimization*, MIT Press, Cambridge, MA, U. S. A.

Dorigo, M., Birattari, M. & Stutzle, T. (2006). Ant colony optimization: artificial ants as a computational intelligence technique, *IEEE Computational Intelligence Magazine*, 28-38.

Dorigo, M., di Caro, G. & Gambardella, L. M. (1999). Ant algorithms for discrete optimization, *Artificial Life*, *5*, 137-172.

Dorigo, M., Maniezzo, V. & Colorni, A. (1996). Ant system: optimisation by a colony of cooperating agents, *IEEE Transactions on Systems, Man, and Cybernetics*, *26*, 29-41.

Dresner, K. & Stone, P. (2004). Multiagent traffic management: a reservation-based intersection control mechanism, Proceedings of the Third International Joint Conference on Autonomous Agents and Multi agent Systems (AAMAS-2004), July 19-23 2004, New York, U. S. A., 530-537

Fewell, J. H. (1990). Directional fidelity as a foraging constraint in the western harvester ant, Pogonomyrmex occidentalis, *Oceologia*, *82*, 45-51.

Fourcassie, V. & Deneubourg, J. L. (1994). The dynamics of collective exploration and trail-formation in Monomorium pharaonis: experiments and model, *Physiological Entomology*, *19*, 291-300.

Fournier, J. R. L. & Pierre, S. (2005). Assigning cells to switches in mobile networks using an ant colony optimization heuristic, *Computer Communications*, *28*, 65-73.

Franz, M. O. & Mallot, H. A. (2000). Biomimetic robot navigation, *Robotics and Autonomous Systems, 30*, 133-153.

Franz, M. O., Scholkopf, B., Mallot, H. A. & Bulthoff, H. H. (1998a). Learning view graphs from robot navigation, *Autonomous Robots*, *5*, 111-125.

Franz, M. O., Scholkopf, B., Mallot, H. A. & Bulthoff, H. H. (1998b). Where did I take that snapshot? Scene based homing by image matching, *Biological Cybernetics*, *79*, 191-202.

Fukushi, T. (2001). Homing in wood ants Formica japonica: use of the skyline panorama, *Journal of Experimental Biology, 204*, 2063-3072.

Gajpal, Y. & Rajendran, C. (2006). An ant-colony optimization algorithm for minimizing the completion-time variance of jobs in flowshops, *International Journal of Production Economics*, *101*, 259-272.

Galindo, C., Fernandez-Madrigal, J. A., Gonzalez, J., Saffioti, A. & Buschka, P. (2007). Life-long optimization of the symbolic model of indoor environments for a mobile robot, *IEEE Transactions on Systems, Man, and Cybernetics – Part B: Cybernetics*, 37, 1290-1304.

Gallistel, C. R. (1993). *The Organization of Learning*, MIT Press, Cambridge MA, U. S. A.

Gambardella, L. M. & Dorigo, M. (2000). Ant colony system hybridized with a new local search for the sequential ordering problem, INFORMS *Journal on Computing*, *3*, 237-255.

Gambardella, L. M., Taillard, E. D. & Dorigo, M. (1999). Ants colonies for the QAP, *Journal of the Operations Research Society*, *50*, 167-176.

Ge, S. S. & Cui, Y. J. (2002). Dynamic motion planning for mobile robots using potential field methods, *Autonomous Robots*, *13*, 207-222.

Goldberg, D. E. (1989). *Genetic Algorithms in Search, Optimization and Machine Learning,* Addison-Wesley Publishing Company Inc., New York, NY, U. S. A.

Gonzalez, J., Ollero, A. & Reina, A. (1994). Map building for a mobile robot equipped with a laser rangefinder, in Proceedings of the *IEEE International Conference on Robotics & Automation*, San Diego, CA, U. S. A., May 8-13 1994, 1904-1909.

Goss, S., Aron, S., Deneubourg, J. L. & Pasteels, J. M. (1989). Self-organized shortcuts in the

Argentine ant, *Naturwissenschaften*, *76*, 579-581.

Grah, G., Wehner, R. & Ronacher, B. (2005). Path integration in a three-dimensional maze: ground distance estimation keeps desert ants Cataglyphis fortis on course, *The Journal of Experimental Biology*, *208*, 4005-4011.

Grasse, P. P. (1959). La reconstruction du nid et les coordinations interindividuelles chez Bellicositermes Natalensis et Cubitermes sp. La theorie de la stigmetrie: essai d' interpretation du comportement des termites constructeurs, *Insectes Sociaux*, *6*, 41-81.

Gutjahr, W. J. & Rauner, M. S. (2007). An ACO algorithm for a dynamic regional nurse-scheduling problem in Austria, *Computers & Operations Research*, *34*, 642-666.

Hangartner, W. (1969). Structure and variability of the individual odor trail in Solenopsis geminate Fabr. (Hymenoptera, Formicidae), *Zettsschrift fur vergleichende Psychologie*, *62*, 111-120.

Heusse, M., Guerin, S., Snyers, D. & Kuntz, P. (1998). Adaptive agent-driven routing and load balancing in communication networks, *Advances in Complex Systems*, *1*, 237-254.

Holland, J. H. (1975). *Adaptation in Natural and Artificial Systems*, The University of Michigan Press, MI, U. S. A.

Holldobler, B. & Lumsden, D. J. (1980). Territorial strategies in ants, *Science*, *210*, 732-739.

Holldobler, B. & Wilson, E. O. (1990). *The Ants*, Harvard University Press, Cambridge, MA, U. S. A.

Horn, D. J. (1976). *Biology of Insects*, W. B. Saunders, Philadelphia, PA, U. S. A.

Huhns, M. & Singh, M. (1998). *Agents and multiagent systems: themes, approaches and challenges, Reading in Agents* (Huhms M. Singh M. eds.), Morgan Kauffman Publishers Inc. , San Francisco, CA, U. S. A. 1-23.

Hwang, Y., Xavier, P., Chen, P. & Watterberg, P. (1998). Motion planning with SANDROS and the configuration space toolkit, in *Practical Motion Planning in Robotics* (Gupta K. K. del Pobil A. P eds), Wiley, Hoboken, NJ, U. S. A.

Iba, H. (1998). Evolutionary learning of communicating agents, *Information Sciences*, *108*, 181-205.

Ishda, T. & Korf, R. E. (1995). Moving target search: a real-time search for changing goals, *IEEE Transactions on Pattern Analysis and Machine Intelligence*, *18*, 617-628.

Jackson, D. E., Holcombe, M. & Ratnieks, F. L. W. (2004). Trail geometry gives polarity to ant foraging networks, *Nature*, *432*, 907-909.

Jacobson, M. (1972). *Insect Sex Pheromones*, Academic Press, New York, U. S. A.

Jennings, N., Sycara, K. & Wooldridge, M. (1998). A roadmap of agents research and development, *Autonomous Agents and Multi-Agent Systems*, 1, 7-39.

Jim, K. C. & Giles, C. L. (2000). Taking helps: evolving communicating agents for the predator-prey pursuit problem, *Artificial Life*, *6*, 237-254.

Kaebling, L., Littman, M. & Moore, A. (1996). Reinforcement learning: a survey, *Journal of Artificial Intelligence Research, 4*, 237-285.

Khatib, O. (1986). Real-time obstacle avoidance for manipulators and mobile robots, *International Journal of Robotic Research, 5*, 90-98.

Kitano, H., Asada, M., Kuniyoshi, Y., Noda, I. & Osawa, E. (1997). RoboCup: the robot world cup initiative, *Proceedings of the First International Conference on Autonomous Agents (Agents'97),* (Johnson W. L. Hayes-Roth B. eds.) ACM Press, New York, NY, U. S. A. 340-347.

Kohone,n, T. *Self-Organising Maps – Third Extended Edition* (2001). Springer-Verlag,

Berlin, Germany.

Kuipers, B. J. & Byun, Y. T. (1987). A qualitative approach to robot exploration and map-learning, in Proceedings of the Workshop on *Spatial Reasoning and Multi-Sensor Fusion*, October, 5-7, St Charles, IL, U. S. A. 390-404.

Kuipers, B. J. & Byun, Y. T. (1991). A robot exploration and mapping strategy based on a semantic hierarchy of spatial representations, *Robotics and Autonomous Systems, 9*, 47-63.

Lai, X. C., Ge, S. S. & Al Mamun, A. (2007). Hierarchical incremental path planning and situation-dependent optimized dynamic motion planning considering acceleration, *IEEE Transactions on Systems, Man and Cybernetics: B Cybernetics, 37*, 1541-1554.

Lamiraux, F., Bonnafous, D. & Lefebvre, O. (2004). Reactive path deformation for nonholonomic mobile robots, *IEEE Transactions on Robotic Automation*, 20, 967-977.

Lee, Z. J., Lee, C. Y. (2005). A hybrid search algorithm with heuristics for resource allocation problem, *Information Sciences*, *173*, 155-167.

Leerink, L. R., Schultz, S. R. & Jabri, M. A. (1995). A reinforcement learning exploration strategy based on ant foraging mechanisms, *Proceedings of the Sixth Australian Conference on Neural Networks,* Sydney, Australia.

Leonard, J. & Durrant-Whyte, H. F. (1991). Simultaneous map building and localization for an autonomous mobile robot, Proceedings of the IEEE International Workshop on *Intelligent Robots and Systems*, November 3-5 1991, Osaka, Japan, 1442-1447.

Levitt, T. S. & Lawton, D. T. (1990). Qualitative navigation for mobile robots, *Artificial Intelligence, 44*, 305-360.

Lim, A., Lin, J., Rodrigues, B. & Xiao, F. (2006). Ant colony optimization with hill climbing to solve the bandwidth minimization problem, *Applied Soft Computing*, *6*, 180-188.

Lopez-Ibanez, M., Paquete, L. & Stultze, T. (2004). On the design of ACO for the biobjective quadratic assignment problem, Proceedings of ANTS 2004 (Lecture Notes in *Computer Science 3172*, In: M. Dorigo, M., Birattari, C., Blum, L. M., Gambardella, F., Mondada, T., Stultze, eds. 214-225.

Maniezzo, V. & Colorni, A. (1999). The ant system applied to the quadratic assignment problem, *IEEE Transactions on Knowledge and Data Engineering, 11*, 769-778.

Mataric, M. (1994). Reward functions for accelerated learning, *Eleventh International Conference on Machine Learning*, July 10-13,1994, New Brunswick, N. J., U. S. A., 181-189.

Mazer, B., Ahuactzin, J. M. & Bessiere, P. (1998). The Ariadne's clew algorithm, *Journal of Artificial Intelligence Research, 9*, 295-316.

McKerrow, P. J. (1991). *Introduction to Robotics*, Addison-Welsey, New York, U. S. A.

Merkle, D., Middendorf, M. & Schmeck, H. (2002). Ant colony optimization for resource-constrained project scheduling, IEEE *Transactions on Evolutionary Computation*, *6*, 333-346.

Minguez, J. & Montano, L. (2004). Nearness diagram (ND) navigation: collision avoidance in troublesome scenarios, *IEEE Transactions on Robotic Automation, 20*, 45-59.

Monekosso, N. D. & Remagnino, P. (2001). Phe-Q: a pheromone based Q-learning, *Proceedings of the Australian Joint Conference on Artificial Intelligence*, 345-355.

Nakamura, M. & Kurumatani, K. (1996). Formation mechanism of pheromone pattern and control of foraging behaviour in an ant colony model, In: C. G. Langton, & K. Shimohara, eds. *Artificial Life V: Proceedings of the Fifth International Workshop on the*

*Synthesis and Simulation of Living Systems*, May 16-18, Nara, Japan, MIT Press, Cambridge, MA, U. S. A. 67-76.

Nelson, R. C. (1991). Visual homing using an associative memory, *Biological Cybernetics*, *65*, 281-291.

Nilsson, N. J. (1980). *Principles of Artificial Intelligence,*, Tioga Publishing Co., Wellsboro, PA, U. S. A.

Nunes, L. & Oliveira, E. (2004). Learning from multiple sources, Proceedings of the *Third International Joint Conference on Autonomous Agents and Multi agent Systems* (AAMAS-2004), July 19-23 2004, New York, U. S. A., 1106-1113.

Oriolo, G., Ulivi, G. & Vendittelli, M. (1998). Real time map building and navigation for autonomous robots in unknown environments, *IEEE Transactions on Systems, Man and Cybernetics: B Cybernetics, 28*, 318-333

Ostergaard, E., Sukhatme, G. & Mataric, M. (2001). Emergent bucket brigading – a simple mechanism for improving performance in multi-robot constrained space foraging tasks, *Proceedings of the Fifth International Conference on Autonomous Agents*, May 28–June 1 2001, Montreal, Quebec, Canada.

Panait, L. & Luke, S. (2005). Cooperative multi-agent learning: the state of the art, *Autonomous Agents and Multi-Agent Systems*, *11*, 387- 434.

Panait, L. A. & Luke, S. (2004a). A pheromone-based utility model for collaborative foraging, *Proceedings of the Third International Joint Conference on Autonomous Agents and Multiagent Systems* (AAMAS'04), July 19-23 2004, New York U. S. A. 36-43.

Panait, L. A. & Luke, S. (2004b). Ant foraging revisited, (Pollack J. B. Bedau M. Husbands P. Ikegami T. Watson R. A. eds.) Proceedings of the Ninth International Conference on the Simulation and Synthesis of Living Systems (ALIFE9), September 12-15 2004, Boston MA, U. S. A.

Panait, L. A. & Luke, S. (2004c). Learning ant foraging behaviors, Proceedings of the Ninth International Conference on the Simulation and Synthesis of Living Systems (ALIFE9), September 12-15 2004, Boston, MA, U. S. A. (Pollack J. B. Bedau M. Husbands P. Ikegami T. Watson R. A. eds.).

Parpinelli, R. S., Lopes, H. S. & Freitas, A. A. (2002). Data mining with an ant colony optimization algorithm, *IEEE Transactions on Evolutionary Computation*, *6*, 321-332.

Poncela, A., Perez, E. J., Bandera, A., Urdiales, C. & Sandoval, F. (2002). Efficient integration of metric and topological maps for directed exploration of unknown environments, *Robotic autonomous Systems*, *41*, 21-39.

Potter, M., Meeden, L. & Schultz, A. (2001). Heterogeneity in the coevolved behaviors of mobile robots: the emergence of specialists, Proceedings of the Seventeenth International Conference on Artificial Intelligence (IJCAI-2001), August 4-10 2001, Seattle, WA, U. S. A. 1337-1343.

Rajashekhara Prabhudesai, A. B. & Chaudhuri, S. (2006). Qualitative visual environment retrieval, *IEEE Transactions on Systems, Man, and Cybernetics – Part B: Cybernetics*, *36*, 1373-1380.

Resnick, M. (1994). *Turtles, Termites, and Traffic Jams - Explorations in Massively Parallel Microworlds*, MIT Press, Cambridge, MA, U. S. A.

Riley, P. & Veloso, M. (2000). On behaviour classification in adversarial environments, *Distributed Autonomous Robotic Systems* (Parker L. Bekey G. Barhen J. eds.) Springer-Verlag, Berlin,Germany, *4*, 371-380.

Robinson, E. J. H., Jackson, D. E., Holcombe, M. & Ratnieks, F. L. W. (2005). Insect communication: "no entry" signal in ant foraging, *Nature*, *438*, 442.

Rozin, V. & Margaliot, M. (2006). The fuzzy ant, 2006 IEEE International Conference on Fuzzy Systems, July 16-2 2006, *Vancouver BC, Canada*, 1679-1686.

Rupe, J., Akolly, E. & Sheaffer, C. (2003). A neural network model of the search behaviorof Cataglyphis bicolour, *MICS 2003 - 36$^{th}$ Annual Midwest Instruction and Computing Symposium*, April, 11-12, 203, Duluth MN, U. S. A.

Salustowicz, R., Wiering, M. & Schmidhuber, J. (1998). Learning team strategies: soccer case studies, *Machine Learning*, *33*, 2/3 263-282.

Santos-Victor, J., Sandini, G., Curotto, F. & Garibaldi, S. (1995). Divergent stereo for robot navigation,: a step forward to a robotic bee, *International Journal of Computer Vision*, *14*, 159-177.

Sauter, J., Matthews, R. S., Van Parunak, H. & Brueckner, S. (2002). Evolving adaptive pheromone path planning mechanisms, Proceedings of the First International Joint Conference on Autonomous Agents and Multi-Agent Systems (AAMAS-02) 434-440.

Sauter, J., Van Parunak, H., Brueckner, S. & Matthews, R. S. (2001). Tuning synthetic pheromones with evolutionary computing, *Proceedings of the Evolutionary Computation and Multi-Agent Systems (ECOMAS)* (Smith R. E. Bonacina C. Hoile C. Marrow P. (eds), San Francisco, CA, USA 321-324.

Schneider, J., Wong, W. K., Moore, A. & Riedmiller, M. (1999). Distributed value functions, *Proceedings of the Sixteenth International Conference on Machine Learning,* June 27-30, 1999, Bled, Slovenia, 371-378.

Schoonderwoerd, R., Holland, O., Bruten, J. & Rothkrantz, L. (1996). Ant-based load balancing in telecommunication networks, *Adaptive Behavior, 5*, 169-207.

Schultz, A. & Grenfenstette, Adams, W. (1996). Pobo-shepherd: learning complex robotic behaviors, Robotics and Manufacturing: *Recent Trends in Research and Applications*, *6*, 763-768.

Schultz, T. R. (2000). In search of ant ancestors, *Proceedings of the National Academy of Science*, USA 97, 14028-14029.

Sen, S. & Sekaran, M. (1996). Multiagent coordination with learning classifier systems, Proceedings of the IJCAI Workshop on Adaptation and Learning in Multi-Agent Systems (Weiss G. Sen S. eds.), Springer-*Verlag, Berlin, Germany*, *1042*, 218-233.

Sharpe, T. & Webb, B. (1998). Simulated and situated models of chemical trail following in ants, *From Animals to Animats*, *5*, Proceedings of the SAB'98 (Pfeifer R. Blumberg B. Meyer J. -A. Wilson S. W eds.), MIT Press, Cambridge, MA, 195-204.

Shygelska, A. & Hoos, H. H. (2005). An ant colony optimisation algorithm for the 2D and 3D hydrophobic polar protein folding problem, *BMC Bioinformatics*, *6*, 1-22.

Shyu, S. J., Lin, B. M. T. & Hsiao, T. S. (2006). Ant colony optimization for the cell assignment problem in PCS networks, *Computers & Operations Research*, *33*, 1713-1740.

Silva, C. A., Sousa, J. M. C., Runkler, T. & Palm, R. (2005). Soft computing optimization methods applied to logistic processes, *International Journal of Approximate Reasoning*, *40*, 280-301.

Smith, R. C. & Cheeseman, P. (1986). On the representation and estimation of spatial uncertaintly, *The International Journal of Robotics Research*, 5, 56-68.

Sommer, S. & Wehner, E. (2004). The ant's estimation of distance travelled: experiments with desert ants Cataglyphis fortis, *Journal of Computational Physiology*, A 190, 1-6.

Steeb, R., Cammarata, S., Hayes-Roth, F., Thorndyke, P. & Wesson, R. (1998). Distributed intelligence for air fleet control, Readings in Distributed Artificial Intelligence (Bond A. Gasser L. eds.), Morgan Kauffman Publishers Inc. , San Francisco, CA, U. S. A., 90-101.

Stentz, A. (1995). The focussed D* algorithm for real-time replanning, Proceedings of the International Joint Conference of Artificial Intelligence,, August 19-21, 1995, Montreal, Canada, 1652-1659.

Stone, P. & Veloso, M. M. (2000). Multiagent systems: a survey from a machine learning perspective, *Autonomous Robots*, *8*, 345-383.

Stutzle, T. & Dorigo, M. (1999). ACO algorithms for the quadratic assignment problem, *New Ideas in Optimisation* (Corne D. Dorigo M. Glover F. eds.), Mc-Graw-Hill, London, U. K.

Sumpter, D. J. T. & Beekman, M. (2003). From nonlinearity to optimality: pheromone trail foraging by ants, *Animal Behaviour*, *66*, 273-280.

Sutton, R. (1988). Learning to predict by the methods of temporal differences, *Machine Learning*, *3*, 9-44.

Tangamchit, P., Dolan, J. & Khosla, P. (2002). The necessity of average rewards in cooperative multirobot learning, Proceedings of the *IEEE Conference on Robotics and Automation*, May 11-15 2002 Washington D. C. , U. S. A. 2 1296- 1301.

Thrun, S. & Bucken, A. (1996). Integrating grid-based and topological maps for mobile robot navigation, in Proceedings of the AAAI 13th National Conference on *Artificial Intelligence,*, August, 4-8, 1996, *Portland, Oregon*, U. S. A. 946-951.

Thrun, S., Fox, D. & Burgard, W. (1998). Probabilistic mapping of an environment by a mobile robot, in *Proceedings of the IEEE International Conference on Robotics & Automation*, May 16-20 1998, Leuven, Belgium, 1546-1551.

Tomatis, N., Nourbakhsh, I. & Siegwart, R. (2003). Hybrid simultaneous localization and map building: a natural integration of topological and metric, *Robotic Autonomous Systems*, *44*, 3-14.

Trullier, O., Wiener, S. I., Berthoz, A. & Meyer, J. A. (1997). Biologically based artificial navigation systems: review and prospects, *Progress in Neurobiology*, *51*, 483-544.

Tseng, L. Y. & Chen, S. C. (2006). A hybrid metaheuristic for the resource-constrained project scheduling problem, *European Journal of Operational Research*, *175*, 707-721.

Undeger, C. & Polat F. (2007). Real-time edge follow: a real-time path search algorithm, *IEEE Transactions on Systems, Man, and Cybernetics – Part B: Cybernetics, 37*, 860-872.

Waldner, J. P. (2007). *Nanocomputers and Swarm Intelligence*, Wiley-ISTE, London, U. K.

Van Dyke Parunak, H. (1996). *Applications of distributed artificial intelligence in industry*, Foundations of Distributed Artificial Intelligence (O'Hare G. M. P. , Jennings N. R. eds.), John Wiley & Sons, Hoboken, NJ, U. S. A. 139-164.

van Dyke Parunak, H., Brueckner, S. A., Matthews, R. & Sauter, J. (2005). Pheromone learning for self-organising agents, *IEEE Transactions on Systems, Man, and Cybernetics – Part A: Systems and Humans*, *35*, 316-326.

Varga, L. Z., Jennings, N. R. & Cockburn, D. (1994). Integrating intelligent systems into a cooperating community for electricity distribution management, *International Journal of Expert Systems with Applications*, *7*, 563-579.

Vaughan, R. T., Stoy, K., Sukhatme, G. S. & Mataric, M. J. (2000). Whistling in the dark:

cooperative trail following in uncertain localization space, In: C., Sierra, M. Gini, & J. S. Rosenschein, eds. *Proceedings of the Fourth International Conference on Autonomous Agents*, Barcelona, Spain, June 3-7 2000, ACM Press, New York, NY U. S. A. 187-194.

Vaughan, R. T., Stoy, K., Sukhatme, G. S. & Mataric, M. J. (2002). LOST: localization-space trails for robot teams, *IEEE Transactions on Robotics and Automation*, *8*, 796-812.

Webb, B. (1995). Using robots to model animals: a cricket test, *Robotics and Autonomous Systems, 16*, 117-134.

Weber, K., Venkatesh, S. & Srinivisan, M. V. (1997). Insect inspired behaviours for the autonomous control of mobile robots, *From Living Eyes to Seeing Machines* (Srinivisan M. V. Venkatesh S. eds), Oxford University Press, Oxford, U. K. , 226-248.

Wehner, R. & Menzel, R. (1969). Homing in the ant Cataglyphis bicolour, *Science*, *164*, 192-194.

Wehner, R. & Srinivasan, M. (1981). Searching behavior of desert ants, genus cataglyphis, *Journal of Comparative Physiology, 142*, 315-358.

Weiss, G. (1997). Distributed Artificial intelligence Meets Machine learning: Learning in Multi-Agent Environments, *Lecture Notes in Artificial Intelligence Number 1221*, Springer-Verlag, Berlin, Germany.

Weiss, G. (1999). *Multi-Systems: A Modern Approach to Distributed Artificial Intelligence*, MIT Press, Cambridge, MA, U. S. A.

Verbeek, K. & Nowe, A. (2002). Colonies of learning automata, IEEE Transactions on Systems, *Man, and Cybernetics-Part B*, *32*, 772-780.

Werner, G. M. & Dyer, M. G. (1993). Evolution of herding behavior in artificial animals, *From Animals to Animats: Proceedings of the Second International Conference on Simulation of Adaptive Behavior (SAB92)*, December 7-11 1992, Honolulu, Hawai, 393-399.

White, T., Pagurek, B. & Oppacher, F. (1998). ASGA: improving the ant system by integration with genetic algorithms, *Proceedings of the Third Annual Conference on Genetic Programming* In: R. S., Koza, W. Banzhaf, K., Chellapilla, K., Deb, M., Dorigo, D. B., Fogel, M. H., Garzon, D. E., Goldberg, H. Iba, R. Riolo, eds. Morgan Kauffman Publishers Inc., San Francisco, CA, U. S. A), July 22-25, 1998, Madison, WI, U. S. A. 610-617.

Willms, A. R. & Yang, X. (2008). Real-time robot path planning via a distance-propagating dynamic system with obstacle clearance, *IEEE Transactions on Systems, Man, and Cybernetics–Part B: Cybernetics*, *38*, 884-892.

Wilson, E. O. (1963). Pheromones, *Scientific American*, *208*, 100-114.

Wodrich, M. & Bilchev, G. (1997). Cooperative distributed search: the ants' way, *Journal of Control and Cybernetics*, *26*, 413-446.

Wooldridge, M., Bussmann, S. & Klosterberg, M. (1996). Production sequencing as negotiation, *Proceedigns of the First International Conference on the Practical Application of Intelligent Agents and Multi-Agent Technology* (PAAM-96), April 1996, London, U. K., 709-726.

Yan, Z. & Yuan, C. W. (2003). Ant colony optimization for navigating complex labyrinths, In: G., Wang, Q., Liu, Y. Yao, & A. Skowron, eds. Proceedings of the 9th International Conference on *Rough Sets, Fuzzy Sets, Data Mining, and Granular Computing (RSFDGrC 2003)*, May 26-29 2003, Chongqing, China 445-448.

Zhao, J. & Schmidhuber, J. (1996). Incremental self-improvement for life-tile multi-agent reinforcement learning, Proceedings of the Fourth International Conference on *Simulation of Adaptive Behavior: From Animals to Animats 4*, September 9-13 1996, Cape Cod, MA, U. S. A., MIT Press, Cambridge, MA, U. S. A. (Maes P. Mataric M. Meyer J. A. Pollack J. Wilson S. W. eds.) 516-525

Zhu, A. & Yang, S. X. (2007). Neurofuzzy-based approach to mobile robot navigation in unknown environments, *IEEE Transactions on Systems, Man, and Cybernetics-Part C: Applications and Reviews*, *37*, 610-621.

Ziegler, P. E. & Wehner, R. (1997). Time-sources of memory decay in vector-based and landmark-based systems of navigation in desert ants Cataglyphis fortis, *Journal of Computational Physiology*, *181*, 13-20.

In: Ant Colonies
Editor: Emily C. Sun

ISBN: 978-1-61122-023-0


*Chapter 2*

# ANT COLONY SOLUTION TO THE OPTIMAL TRANSFORMER SIZING AND EFFICIENCY PROBLEM IN POWER SYSTEMS

***Marina A. Tsili*[1] *and Eleftherios I. Amoiralis*[2,*]**
[1]Faculty of Electrical & Computer Engineering,
National Technical University of Athens,
University Campus, Athens, Greece
[2]Department of Production Engineering and Management,
Technical University of Crete,
University Campus, Chania, Greece

## ABSTRACT

This chapter proposes a stochastic optimization method, based on ant colony optimization, for the optimal choice of transformer sizes to be installed in a distribution network. This method is properly introduced to the solution of the optimal transformer sizing problem, taking into account the constraints imposed by the load the transformer serves throughout its life time and the possible transformer thermal overloading. The possibility to upgrade the transformer size one or more times throughout the study period results to different sizing paths, and ant colony optimization is applied in order to determine the least cost path, taking into account the transformer capital cost as well as the energy loss cost during the study period. The method is expanded for the optimal choice of transformer efficiency to serve the loads of the considered network. For a given transformer capacity, the possibility to install transformers of different efficiency throughout the study period is investigated with the objective to minimize the total installation and loss cost. The results of the proposed method demonstrate the benefits of its application in distribution network planning.

---

* Corresponding author: mtsili@central.ntua.gr, eamir@tee.gr

# 1. INTRODUCTION

The objective of the optimal transformer sizing problem in a multi-year planning period is to select the transformer sizes (i.e., rated capacities) and the years of transformer installation so as to serve a distribution substation load at the minimum total cost (i.e., sum of transformer purchasing cost plus transformer energy loss cost). Oversizing a transformer can result in higher no-load losses, while undersizing a transformer can result in higher load losses. The proper size of a transformer depends on various economic factors as well as its losses. Due to the large amount of installed distribution transformers in power systems, the impact of their proper sizing, also referred as kVA sizing, is particularly crucial to their design and can result to significant economic benefits to electric utilities and other transformer users. There are several factors involved in the process of sizing a transformer, e.g. expected future growth of the load to be served, installation altitude, ambient temperature, insulation, number of phases, efficiency, losses, capital cost throughout the transformer commission time, cost of the energy, and interest rate. During the solution of the transformer sizing problem, careful consideration must be given to the fact that the possible transformer capacities are discrete instead of continuous and that the option to upgrade the transformer size one or more times throughout the study period can result to different sizing strategies that have to be considered as well.

It is therefore clear that the optimal choice of the transformer size cannot be straightforward, by installing a transformer of sufficient capacity to meet the load demand in the final year of the study period, a strategy usually adopted by electric utilities. On the other hand, it must be treated as a constrained minimization problem, taking into account all possible sizing strategies. Deterministic optimization methods may be used for the solution of this problem, such as dynamic programming [1] or integer programming [2]. However, the wide spectrum of transformer sizes and various load types involved in the electric utility distribution system make the transformer sizing a difficult combinatorial optimization problem, since the space of solutions is huge. That is why stochastic optimization methods may prove to provide more robust solutions. The use of such methods in transformer sizing is not encountered in the technical literature or is partially included in the analysis, e.g. as a tool to forecast the loads to be served [3].

In this chapter, the Optimal Transformer Sizing (OTS) problem is solved by means of the heuristic Ant System method using the Elitist strategy, called Elitist Ant System (EAS). EAS belongs to the family of Ant Colony Optimization (ACO) algorithms. Dorigo has proposed the first EAS in his Ph.D. thesis [4] and later on in [5][6]. The EAS is a biologically inspired meta-heuristics method in which a colony of artificial ants cooperates in finding good solutions to difficult discrete optimization problems. Cooperation is the key design component of ACO algorithms, i.e. allocation of the computational resources to a set of relatively simple agents (artificial ants) that communicate indirectly by stigmergy [7], i.e. by indirect communication mediated by the environment. In other words, a set of artificial ants cooperates in dealing with a problem by exchanging information via pheromones deposited on a graph.

In the bibliography, ACO algorithms have been applied to solve a variety of well-known combinatorial optimization problems, such as routing problem [8], travelling salesman problem [9], assignment problem [10], scheduling problem [11], fault section estimation problem [12], ship berthing problem [13], and subset [14] problems.

In power systems, ACO algorithms have been applied to solve the optimum generation scheduling problem [15][16], combined heat and power economic dispatch problem [17], and the optimum switch relocation and network reconfiguration problems for distribution systems [18][19][20]. More details on ACO implementation in the solution of other problems are described in [21].

EAS was introduced in the solution of the OTS problem in case of one (three-phase, oil-immersed, self-cooled (ONAN)) distribution transformer with constant economic factors in [22], and was extended in [27][28] to take into account all details of the economic analysis, such as the inflation rate that influences the energy loss cost and the transformer investment as well as the installation and depreciation cost in a real distribution network, constituting an efficient methodology for transformer planning. The present chapter presents the application of EAS ACO algorithm to both optimal transformer sizing/efficiency problem. First, the OTS problem is solved as a constrained optimization problem, following the procedure described in Section 2. The most important constraint is the load to be served by the transformer throughout its life cycle, as well as the respective transformer thermal loading, evaluated through detailed calculation of the winding temperature variation, as described in Section 3. The objective function to be minimized includes the transformer capital cost as well as the energy loss cost (Section 4). The EAS method (Section 5) is adapted to the considered problem and the results of its implementation (Section 6) demonstrate its suitability for the solution of OTS and the benefits from its application in comparison to simplified transformer sizing approaches. Section 7 expands the application of EAS method to the determination of the optimal efficiency of transformers of the capacities selected by ACO in Section 6. Since thermal limitations are not imposed in this case, the number of possible installation strategies is significantly increased and the problem becomes more complex. Moreover, Section 8 presents the implementation of ACO algorithm in Matlab code, revealing in detail the various steps of the method during the solution of optimal transformer sizing/efficiency problem.

## 2. Overview of the Proposed Method

### 2.1. Optimal Transformer Sizing

The OTS problem consists in finding the proper capacities and technical characteristics of transformers to be installed in a distribution network so that the overall installation and energy loss cost over the study period is minimized and the peak loading condition is met [1]. The proposed solution to the OTS problem is graphically shown in Figure 1.

The process of the optimal transformer sizing is realized through the following steps, described in the diagram of Figure 1:

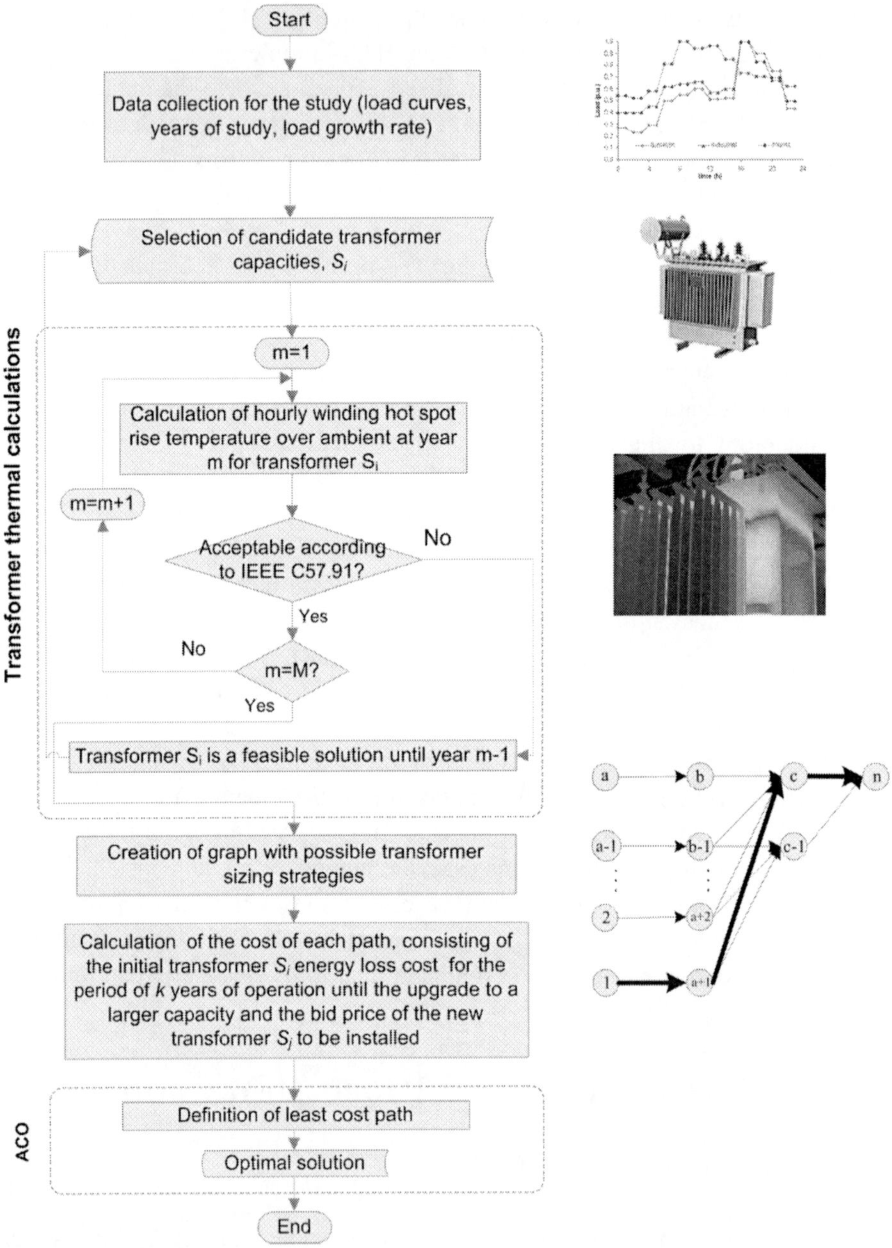


Figure 1. Flowchart illustrating the main steps of the proposed method for the solution of the optimal transformer sizing problem

- Collection of data concerning the special characteristics of the load at each substation of the considered network. These data consist of the typical daily load curve and the expected load growth rate over the study period.
- Selection of possible candidate transformer sizes according to tables of standard transformer sizes, although non-standard sizes can be also considered.
- Determination of the feasible number of years that each potential transformer can serve the load of each substation, based on thermal calculations (Section 3). This step

involves calculation of hourly winding hot spot rise temperature over ambient at each year $m$ of the study for each potential transformer $S_i$.

- Determination of the possible transformer sizing strategies (per substation) throughout the study period, consisting of combinations of the potential transformer capacities and the years that they may operate in order to serve the considered load.
- Calculation of the energy loss cost for each transformer (through the method presented in Section 4) of the network for the periods defined by the strategies of the previous step.
- Creation of the graph with all possible combinations of transformer sizes and years of replacement, for the solution of the OTS problem with the use of EAS, according to the procedure described in Section 5, for each substation of the studied distribution network. The cost of each path consists of the energy loss cost of the installed transformer $S_i$ for the period of years of operation until the upgrade to a larger capacity and the bid price of the new transformer $S_j$ to be installed minus the remaining value of transformer $S_i$.
- Selection of the least cost transformer sizing path per substation, with the use of EAS. This path corresponds to the optimal transformer sizing strategy.

## 2.2. Optimal Transformer Efficiency Selection

The Optimal Transformer Efficiency Selection problem consists in finding the most efficient design of transformers of a given size (capacity) to be installed in a distribution network so that the overall installation and energy loss cost over the study period is minimized. The capacity of each substation is chosen based on the capacity $S_M$ that is able to serve the considered load up to the final year of the study, as determined by the thermal calculations of Section 3. Many different transformer designs can be developed to meet the requirements of this capacity. The efficiency of these designs is determined by their total losses (i.e. the sum of no load and load losses). The lower the losses, the higher the manufacturing cost of a design, so a compromise between the initial investment cost and the cost of losses throughout the study period has to be determined. The ACO algorithm is used to derive the optimal installation strategy according to the following steps (Figure 2):

- Collection of data concerning the special characteristics of the load at each substation of the considered network. These data consist of the typical daily load curve and the expected load growth rate over the study period.
- Selection of possible candidate transformer sizes according to tables of standard transformer sizes, although non-standard sizes can be also considered.
- Determination of the transformer capacity $S_M$ that can serve the load of each substation up to year $M$ (final year) of the study, based on thermal calculations (Section 3). This step involves calculation of hourly winding hot spot rise temperature over ambient at each year $m$ of the study for each potential transformer $S_i$. The calculation is repeated until the capacity $S_M$ that can serve the load for the $M$ years of the study is determined.

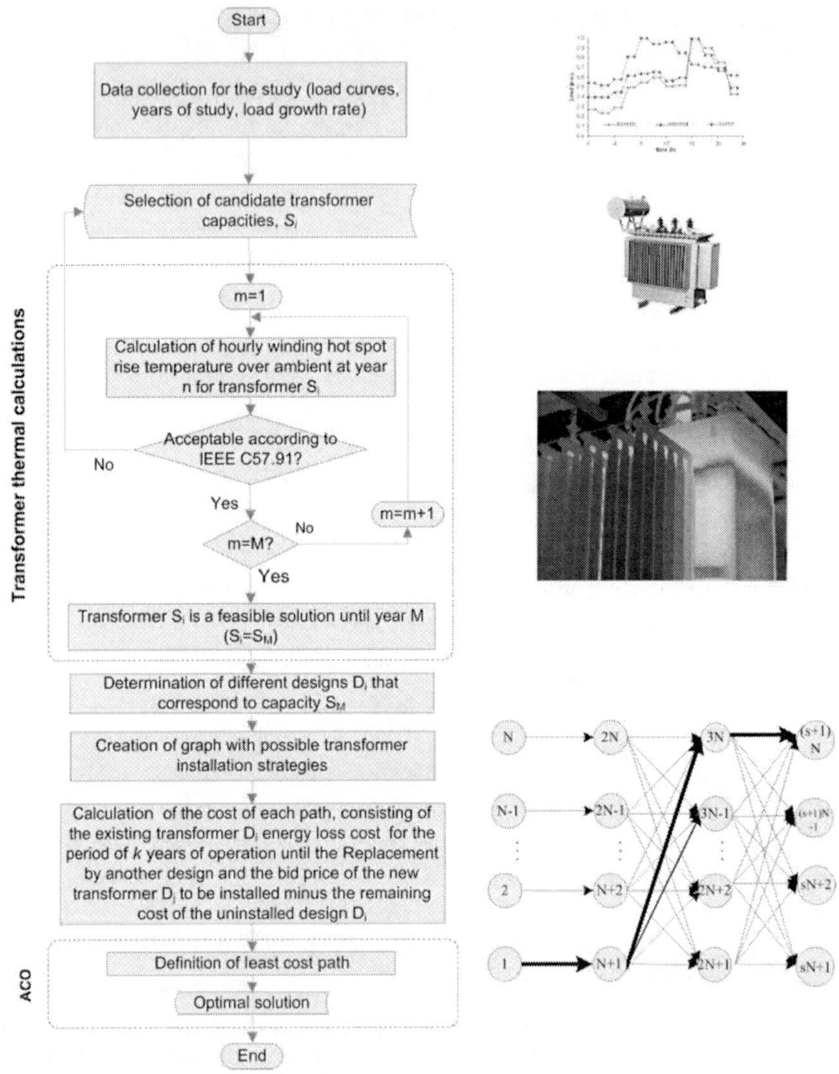


Figure 2. Flowchart illustrating the main steps of the proposed method for the solution of the optimal transformer efficiency selection problem

- Determination of the possible transformer designs that correspond to the above capacity.
- Determination of the possible transformer installation strategies (per substation) throughout the study period, consisting of combinations of different transformer designs and the years that they may operate in order to serve the considered load. It must be noted that, since thermal limitations are not imposed in this case, the number of possible installation strategies is significantly increased and the problem becomes more complex than the one of Section 2.1.
- Calculation of the energy loss cost for each transformer (through the method presented in Section 4) of the network for the periods defined by the strategies of the previous step.

- Creation of the graph with all possible combinations of transformer designs and years of replacement, for the solution of the Optimal Transformer Efficiency problem with the use of EAS, according to the procedure described in Section 7, for each substation of the studied distribution network. The cost of each path consists of the energy loss cost of the installed transformer design $D_i$ for the period of years of operation until the replacement by another design and the bid price of the new design $D_j$ to be installed minus the remaining value of transformer $D_i$.
- Selection of the least cost transformer sizing path per substation, with the use of EAS. This path corresponds to the optimal transformer installation strategy.

## 3. Calculation of Transformer Thermal Loading

The transformer thermal calculation is implemented according to the guidelines imposed by the IEEE Standard C57.91-1995 (R2002), [23]. The main equations used in these calculations are described in the followings (all temperatures are expressed in °C).

### 3.1. Top-Oil Temperature Calculation

The top-oil temperature rise $\Delta\Theta_{TO}$ at a time after a step load change is given by the following equation:

$$\Delta\Theta_{TO} = \Delta\Theta_{TO,U} - \Delta\Theta_{TO,i} \cdot \left(1 - e^{-1/\tau_{TO}}\right) + \Delta\Theta_{TO,i} \qquad (1)$$

where $\Delta\Theta_{TO,i}$ and $\Delta\Theta_{TO,U}$ are the initial and ultimate top-oil rise over ambient temperature during the considered time period, while $\tau_{TO}$ is the oil time constant (in hours) for the considered load, deriving from the value of the time constant at the rated load $\tau_{TO,R}$, calculated through equation (2) [23],

$$\tau_{TO} = \tau_{TO,R} \frac{\left(\frac{\Delta\Theta_{TO,U}}{\Delta\Theta_{TO,R}}\right) - \left(\frac{\Delta\Theta_{TO,i}}{\Delta\Theta_{TO,R}}\right)}{\left(\frac{\Delta\Theta_{TO,U}}{\Delta\Theta_{TO,R}}\right)^{\frac{1}{n}} - \left(\frac{\Delta\Theta_{TO,i}}{\Delta\Theta_{TO,R}}\right)^{\frac{1}{n}}} \qquad (2)$$

where $n$ is an empirical exponent equal to 0.8 for self-cooled transformers.

The constant $\tau_{TO,R}$ is a function of the weight of the core and coil assembly $WCC$ (in kilograms), the weight of tank and fittings $WT$ (in kilograms), the volume of oil $VO$ (in liters), the top-oil rise over ambient temperature at rated load $\Delta\Theta_{TO,R}$ (equal to 60°C for the considered distribution transformers) and the total loss at rated load $P_{T,R}$ (in watts) according to the following equation (applicable to self-cooled transformers):

$$\tau_{TO,R} = (0.0272 \cdot WCC + 0.01814 \cdot WT + 5.034 \cdot VO)\frac{\Delta\Theta_{TO,R}}{P_{T,R}} \quad (3)$$

A typical value of $\tau_{TO,R}$ equal to 2.5 hours can be considered for distribution transformers larger than 200kVA, while for smaller capacities, a value of 3.5 hours may be adopted [24].

The initial top-oil rise over ambient temperature $\Delta\Theta_{TO,i}$ is equal to the value $\Delta\Theta_{TO}$ calculated at the previous interval of the considered load cycle. The ultimate top-oil rise over ambient temperature is calculated with the use of the top-oil rise over ambient temperature at rated load $\Delta\Theta_{TO,R}$ (equal to 60°C for the considered distribution transformers), the ratio $K$ of the load at the considered interval to the rated load and the ratio R of the load loss at rated load to no-load loss:

$$\Delta\Theta_{TO,U} = \Delta\Theta_{TO,R} \cdot \left(\frac{K^2 \cdot R + 1}{R + 1}\right)^n \quad (4)$$

For the first interval of the studied load cycle, an initial value of $\Delta\Theta_{TO,i}$ equal to zero may be arbitrarily chosen. After completing the above calculations for all the intervals of the load cycle, the final $\Delta\Theta_{TO,U}$ of the cycle can be used as the new value of $\Delta\Theta_{TO,i}$ of the first interval and the process may be repeated to obtain stable temperature profiles.

### 3.2. Winding Hottest Spot Temperature Calculation

The winding hottest spot temperature rise over top-oil temperature $\Delta\Theta_H$ at a time after a step load change is given by the following equation:

$$\Delta\Theta_H = (\Delta\Theta_{H,U} - \Delta\Theta_{H,i}) \cdot \left(1 - e^{\frac{-1}{\tau_w}}\right) + \Delta\Theta_{H,i} \quad (5)$$

where $\Delta\Theta_{H,i}$ and $\Delta\Theta_{H,U}$ represent the initial and ultimate winding hottest spot temperature rise over top-oil temperature during the considered time period and $\tau_w$ stands for the winding time constant at hot spot location (in hours). The typical value of $\tau_w$ is less than 0.1 hours [25], thus (3) may be simplified to the following equation:

$$\Delta\Theta_H = \Delta\Theta_{H,U} \quad (6)$$

The ultimate winding hottest spot temperature rise over top-oil temperature is:

$$\Delta\Theta_{H,U} = \Delta\Theta_{H,R} \cdot K^{2m_f} \quad (7)$$

where $\Delta\Theta_{H,R}$ is the winding hottest spot temperature rise over top-oil temperature at the rated load (a value of 15°C is suggested by the standard, when the actual test values are not available) and $m_f$ is an empirical factor, equal to 0.8 for self-cooled transformers.

Finally, the winding hottest spot temperature at the considered interval is the sum of $\Delta\Theta_{TO}$, $\Delta\Theta_H$ and the average ambient temperature $\Theta_A$ during the cycle:

$$\Theta_H = \Theta_A + \Delta\Theta_{TO} + \Delta\Theta_H \qquad (8)$$

## 3.3. Insulation Aging

Although the IEEE standard specifies that operation at hottest spot temperature above 140°C results to potential risks for the transformer integrity, this value must not be considered as the maximum one during the calculations carried out for the determination of the transformer loading limits. This is due to the fact that thermal aging is a cumulative process, therefore operation above the rating should be examined in conjunction with its consequences upon the normal life expectancy of the transformer. For the study of the present chapter, a maximum hot-spot temperature of 120°C has been chosen, based on the relative aging rate of the insulation in the transformer [24].

## 3.4. Overloading Capability

In order to determine the transformer loading limits, the calculation of the hottest spot temperature is repeated for each year of the study period, at an hourly basis, according to the daily load curve. In order to remain on the safe side, the peak load curve of the considered year is used in the calculations. The yearly load growth rate $s$ is taken into account for the derivation of the per unit load $K_t^k$ of hour $t$ at year $k$ of the study according to the per unit load $K_t^0$ of hour $t$ at year 0:

$$K_t^k = K_t^0 \cdot (1+s)^k \qquad (9)$$

Figure 3 shows the winding hottest spot temperature variation for eight distribution transformers of rated capacity 160, 190, 220, 250, 300, 400, 500 and 630 kVA and ratio $R$ of the load loss at rated load to no-load loss equal to 5.61, 6.63, 6.9, 5.23, 5.68, 4.73, 5.44 and 7.11, respectively, serving an industrial load of initial peak value equal to 150 kVA, at the 25th year of the study period, for a load growth rate of 2.7%. The scale of the left axis in Figure 3 corresponds to the values of the load curve $K_t^k$ (expressed in kVA, since the per unit values are different on the basis of the rated capacity of each transformer), illustrated as bar diagram. The scale of the right axis in Figure 3 indicates the winding hottest spot variation, in °C (corresponding to the eight transformer ratings of Figure 3). The thermal calculation is based on a typical load curve of an industrial consumer, with the use of an ambient temperature equal to 40°C. As can be observed from Figure 3, the 160, 190 and 220 kVA transformers overcome the limit of 120°C so they are not suitable to serve the load at the 25th year of the study period.

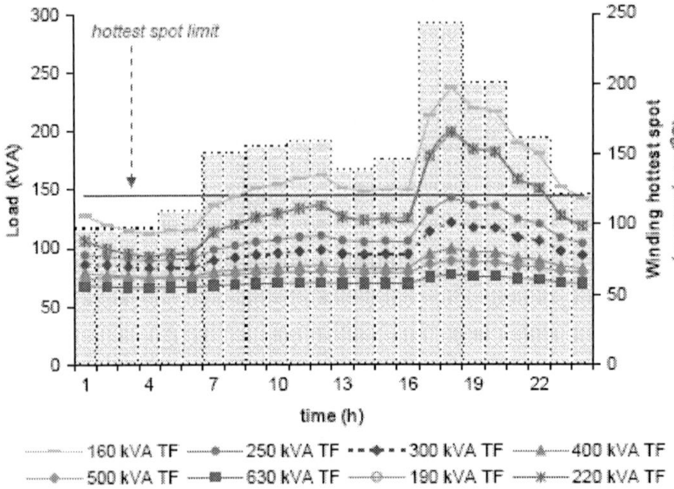


Figure 3. Winding hottest spot temperature variation of eight transformer (TF) ratings

## 4. Calculation of Transformer Energy Loss Cost

The calculation of annual transformer energy loss cost of the potential sizing paths is realized with the use of the energy corresponding to the transformer no load loss (*NLL*) $E_{NLL}$ (in kWh) for each year of operation and the energy corresponding to the load loss (*LL*), $E_{LL}^k$ (in kWh) for each *k*-th year of operation. These energies are calculated according to (10) and (11), respectively:

$$E_{NLL} = NLL \cdot HPY \tag{10}$$

$$E_{LL}^k = LL \cdot \left[ l_f \cdot \frac{S_{\max,0}^l}{S_{nom}^l} (1+s)^k \right]^2 \cdot HPY \tag{11}$$

where $S_{\max,0}^l$ is the initial peak load of the substation load type *l* (in kVA), $S_{nom}^l$ is the nominal power of the transformer that serves load type *l* (in kVA), *HPY* is the number of hours per year, equal to 8760, and $l_f$ is the load factor, i.e. the mean transformer loading over its lifetime (derived from the load curve of each consumer type served by the considered substation). The cost of total energy corresponding to the transformer *NLL* for each *k*-th year $C_{NLL}^k$ (in €) and the cost of energy corresponding to the transformer *LL* for each *k*-th year $C_{LL}^k$ (in €) are calculated as follows:

$$C_{NLL}^k = E_{NLL} \cdot CYEC^k \tag{12}$$

$$C_{LL}^{k} = E_{LL}^{k} \cdot CYEC^{k} \tag{13}$$

where $CYEC^k$ denotes the present value of the energy cost (in €/kWh) at the $k$-th year. Finally, the total cost of the transformer energy loss $C_L^k$ for the $k$-th year is given by:

$$C_{L}^{k} = C_{NLL}^{k} + C_{LL}^{k} \tag{14}$$

# 5. Elitist Ant System Method

## 5.1. Mechanism of EAS Algorithm

The EAS is an evolutionary computation optimization method based on ants' collective problem solving ability. This global stochastic search method is inspired by the ability of a colony of ants to identify the shortest route between the nest and a food source, without using visual cues.

The operation mode of EAS algorithm is as follows: the artificial ants of the colony move, concurrently and asynchronously, through adjacent states of a problem, which can be represented in the form of a weighted graph. This movement is made according to a transition rule, called *random proportional* rule, through a stochastic mechanism. When ant $k$ is in node $i$ and has so far constructed the partial solution $s^p$, the probability of going to node $j$ is given by:

$$p_{ij}^{k} = \begin{cases} \dfrac{\tau_{ij}^{\alpha} + n_{ij}^{\beta}}{\sum\limits_{c_{il} \in N(s^p)} \tau_{il}^{\alpha} + n_{il}^{\beta}}, & \text{if } c_{ij} \in N(s^p) \\ 0 & \text{, otherwise} \end{cases} \tag{15}$$

where $N(s^P)$ is the set of feasible nodes when being in node $i$, i.e. edges $(i,l)$ where $l$ is the node not yet visited by the ant $k$. The parameters $\alpha$ and $\beta$ control the relative importance of the pheromone versus the heuristic information value $\eta_{ij}$, given by:

$$n_{ij} = \frac{1}{d_{ij}} \tag{16}$$

where $d_{ij}$ is the weight of each edge. Regarding parameters $\alpha$ and $\beta$, their role is as follows: if $\alpha$ = 0, those nodes with better heuristic preference have a higher probability of being selected. However, if $\beta$ = 0, only the pheromone trails are considered to guide the constructive process, which can cause a quick stagnation, i.e. a situation where the pheromone trails associated with some transitions are significantly higher than the remainder, thus making the ants build the same solutions. Hence, there is a need to establish a proper balance between the importance of heuristic and pheromone trail information.

Individual ants contribute their own knowledge to other ants in the colony by depositing pheromones, which act as chemical "markers" along the paths they traverse. Through indirect communication with other ants via foraging behavior, a colony of ants can establish the shortest path between the nest and the food source over time with a positive feedback loop known as stigmergy. As individual ants traverse a path, pheromones are deposited along the trail, altering the overall pheromone density. More trips can be made along shorter paths and the resulting increase in pheromone density attracts other ants to these paths. The main characteristic of the EAS technique is that (at each iteration) the pheromone values are updated by all the *k* ants that have built a solution in the iteration itself. The pheromone $\tau_{ij}$, associated with the edge joining nodes *i* and *j*, is updated as follows [5][26]:

$$\tau_{ij} = (1-\rho)\cdot\tau_{ij} + \sum_{m=1}^{k}\Delta\tau_{ij}^{k} + \varepsilon\cdot\tau_{ij}^{elite} \quad (17)$$

where $\rho \in (0,1]$ is the evaporation rate, *k* is the number of ants, $\varepsilon$ is the number of elitist ants, and $\Delta\tau_{ij}^{k}$ is the quantity of pheromone laid on edge (i, j) by ant k, calculated as follows:

$$\Delta\tau_{ij}^{k} = \begin{cases} \dfrac{Q}{L_k}, & \text{if ant } k \text{ used edge}(i,j) \text{ in its tour} \\ 0, & \text{otherwise} \end{cases} \quad (18)$$

where $Q$ is a constant for pheromone update, and $L_k$ is the length (or the weight of the edge) of the tour constructed by ant *k*. Furthermore, shorter paths will tend to have higher pheromone densities than longer paths since pheromone density decreases over time due to evaporation [5][6]. This shortest path represents the global optimal solution and all the possible paths represent the feasible region of the problem.

## 5.2. OTS Implementation Using the EAS Algorithm

In this work our interest lies in finding the optimum choice of distribution transformers capacity sizing, so as to meet the load demand for all the years of the study period. To achieve so, a graph shown in Figure 4 is constructed, representing the sizing paths.

The graph has *s* stages and each stage indicates a time period (in years) the limits of which are defined by the need to replace one of the considered transformer sizes due to violation of its thermal loading limits. Therefore, stage *s* has one node less in comparison with stage (*s-1*), stage (*s-2*) has one node less in comparison with stage (*s-1*), etc. The first stage indicates the beginning of the study, comprising number of nodes equal to the number of potential transformer capacities $N_T$, while *s* represents the end of the study period (consisting of the largest necessary rated capacity able to serve the load at the final year of the study). Symbols *X*, *Y*, *Z*, *W* refer to the different rated powers ($X < Y < Z < W$). It is important to point out that it is meaningless to connect for example node 1 to node (c-1) due to the fact that it corresponds to installation of a transformer with lower rated power than the one already in operation (only upgrade of the sizes can be considered). Furthermore, the arcs between the nodes are directed from the previous stage to the next one (backward movement is not allowed) since each stage represents a forward step in the time of the study. Nodes 1 to $a_n$ (Figure 4) are designated as the source nodes corresponding to each potential transformer size and node $n$ is designated as the destination node (Figure 4). The use of multiple source nodes enables the examination of more potential solutions of the problem. The numbering of $n$ nodes of the graph of Figure 4 is realized upwards for each stage, i.e. the bottom node of the 1$^{st}$ stage is node 1, while the last node of the 1$^{st}$ stage is $a_n$ (where $a_n$ corresponds to the number of nodes of the 1$^{st}$ stage). Accordingly, the 2$^{nd}$ stage begins with node $a_n$+1 while its last node is numbered $b_n$ (where $b_n$ is the number of nodes of the 3$^{rd}$ stage), 3$^{rd}$ stage begins with node $b_n$+1 and ends at node $c_n$ (where $c_n$ is the number of nodes of the 3$^{rd}$ stage), etc., concluding to the $s$-th stage, which comprises only node $n$. The objective of the colony agents is to find the least-cost path between nodes that belong to first stage and node $n$ that belongs to $s$-th stage. Three quantities are associated with each arc: the arc weight, the pheromone strength, and the agent learning parameter. Based on these characteristics, the weight of each arc is calculated.

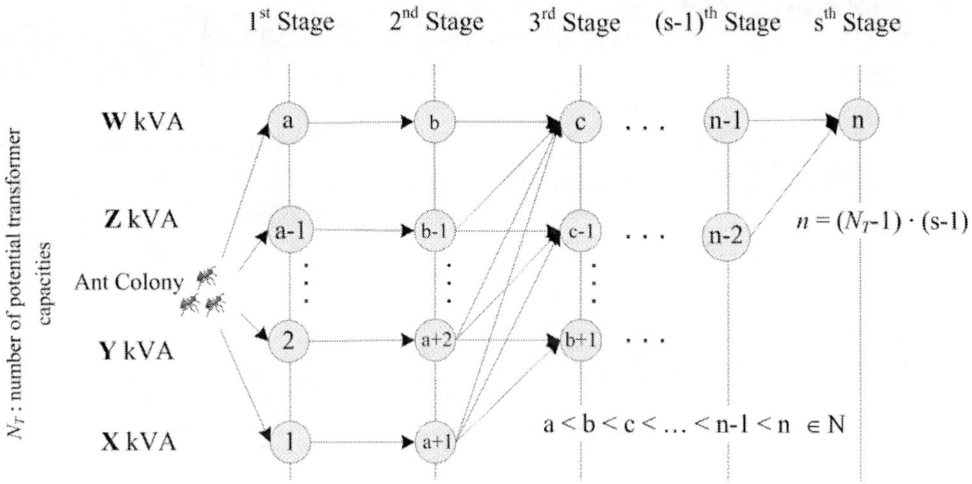


Figure 4. The directed graph used for the OTS problem [27] [28]

## 6. Application of ACO Algorithm to Optimal Transformer Sizing Problem

The proposed method is applied for the optimal choice of the transformer sizes of a practical distribution network. Figure 5 illustrates the single line diagram of the examined distribution network, corresponding to a typical Medium Voltage (MV) network encountered in rural areas of Greece. A High Voltage/Medium Voltage (HV/MV) power transformer supplies a distribution feeder. Sixteen of the twenty nodes in the network of Figure 5, correspond to distribution substations, comprising Medium Voltage/Low Voltage (MV/LV) distribution transformers, while the remaining nodes correspond to intersection points. Eight different types of substations are indicated on the diagram of Figure 5, namely Types 1 to 8, described in the followings:

1. *Type 1*: domestic load of initial peak value equal to 150 kVA (at the year 1 of the study) with a growth rate equal to 4% for 29 years, resulting to final peak value of 467.80 kVA (at the 30$^{th}$ year of the study).
2. *Type 2*: tourist load of initial peak value equal to 150 kVA with a growth rate equal to 4.5% for 29 years, resulting to final peak value of 537.61 kVA (at the 30$^{th}$ year of the study),
3. *Type 3*: tourist load of initial peak value equal to 125 kVA with a growth rate equal to 4.5% for 29 years, resulting to final peak value of 448.00 kVA (at the 30$^{th}$ year of the study),
4. *Type 4*: domestic load of initial peak value equal to 175 kVA with a growth rate equal to 4% for 29 years, resulting to final peak value of 545.76 kVA (at the 30$^{th}$ year of the study),
5. *Type 5*: industrial load of initial peak value equal to 200 kVA with a growth rate equal to 4% for 29 years, resulting to final peak value of 623.73 kVA (at the 30$^{th}$ year of the study),
6. *Type 6*: domestic load of initial peak value equal to 230 kVA with a growth rate equal to 4% for 29 years, resulting to final peak value of 717.29 kVA (at the 30$^{th}$ year of the study).
7. *Type 7*: industrial load of initial peak value equal to 50 kVA with a growth rate equal to 2.7% for 29 years, resulting to final peak value of 108.27 kVA (at the 30$^{th}$ year of the study).
8. *Type 8*: industrial load of initial peak value equal to 75 kVA with a growth rate equal to 2.7% for 29 years, resulting to final peak value of 162.41 kVA (at the 30$^{th}$ year of the study).

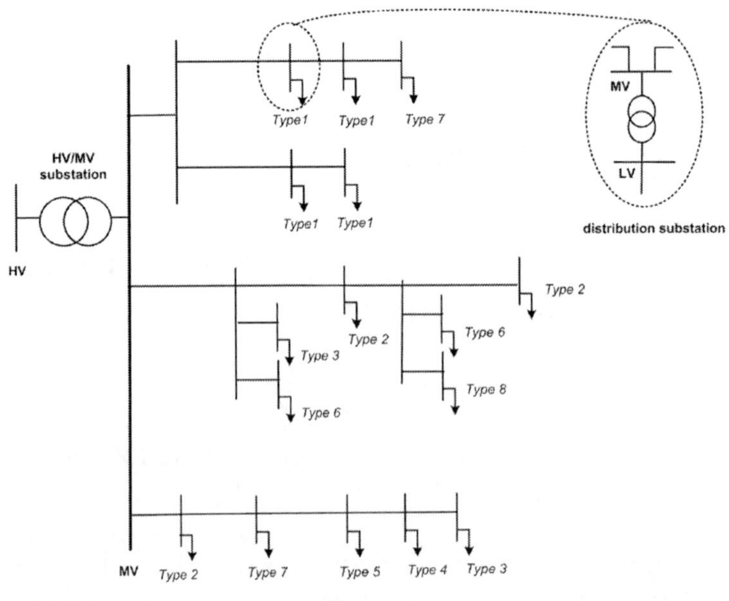


Figure 5. Single line diagram of the examined distribution network

Three consumer types are encountered in the nodes of Figure 5, namely domestic, tourist, and industrial, with daily loading profiles that correspond to load factor $l_f$ equal to 0.55, 0.75, and 0.61, respectively. The load of each node is served by a distribution substation, comprising a 20/0.4 kV distribution transformer, as illustrated in the diagram.

In the case of the Type 1-6 substations, six transformer ratings are considered, namely 160, 250, 300, 400, 500, and 630 kVA. In the case of the Type 7-8 substations, due to the smaller initial peak value and growth rate of the considered load, intermediate capacities (between 160 and 250 kVA) were included in the study, resulting to a range of five ratings consisting of 160, 190, 220, 250, and 300 kVA. The ratings of 400, 500 and 630 kVA were not included in the range for this type of substation, since their capacities are significantly larger than the served load. Table 1 lists the main technical characteristics and bid price of the considered transformers. Initially, thermal calculation study was carried out in order to find the exact periods where each transformer can meet the load expectations of the above six types of substations. The calculations described in Section 3 and illustrated in Figure 3 were repeated for the six transformers and each year of the study, resulting to the time periods of Table 1 (indicated as years of thermal durability, i.e. years that the transformer is able to withstand the respective thermal loading). According to Table 1, transformers up to 500 kVA are suitable to serve the loads of Type 1-4 substations, since their thermal durability covers the study period (therefore, the thermal durability of 630 kVA transformers is not examined in these cases). In the case of Type 5 and 6 substations, transformers of 160 kVA cannot be used since the initial peak load results to excessive thermal overloading, and only the ratings 250 to 630 kVA can be considered. In the case of Type 7-8 substations, all considered ratings are suitable to serve the load up to the final year of the study. The periods derived in Table 1 were used to define the stages of the graph of Figure 4. In order to define the weight of each arc in the graph of Figure 4, the energy loss cost calculation of each transformer for the studied period was based on the annual energy loss cost calculation described in Section 4. The energy loss cost $C_L^{i \to j}$ corresponding to the transition from node $i$ ($p$-th year of the study period) to $j$ ($q$-th year of the study period), is computed by:

$$C_L^{i \to j} = \sum_{k=p+1}^{q} C_L^k \qquad (19)$$

**Table 1. Technical parameters and thermal withstand of the transformers used in the solution of the OTS problem**

| Transformer technical parameters | | | | Transformer thermal withstand (yr) per type of substation load | | | | | | | |
|---|---|---|---|---|---|---|---|---|---|---|---|
| Size (kVA) | Bid price (€) | NLL (kW) | LL (kW) | Type 1 | Type 2 | Type 3 | Type 4 | Type 5 | Type 6 | Type 7 | Type 8 |
| 160 | 5275 | 0.454 | 2.544 | 5 | 4 | 8 | 3 | 0 | 0 | 30 | 30 |
| 190 | 5801 | 0.537 | 2.920 | - | - | - | - | - | - | 30 | 30 |
| 220 | 6327 | 0.619 | 3.296 | - | - | - | - | - | - | 30 | 30 |
| 250 | 6853 | 0.702 | 3.672 | 16 | 14 | 18 | 14 | 10 | 7 | 30 | 30 |
| 300 | 6932 | 0.738 | 4.186 | 21 | 18 | 23 | 19 | 15 | 12 | 30 | 30 |
| 400 | 9203 | 0.991 | 4.684 | 28 | 25 | 28 | 26 | 22 | 19 | - | - |
| 500 | 10296 | 1.061 | 5.771 | 30 | 30 | 30 | 30 | 28 | 24 | - | - |
| 630 | 12197 | 1.094 | 7.774 | - | - | - | - | 30 | 30 | - | - |

When the transition from node $i$ to $j$ corresponds to transformer size upgrade from $S_i$ to $S_j$, the installation cost $I_{i\to j}$ derives from:

$$I_{i\to j} = BP^p_{S_j} - R^p_{S_i}, \tag{20}$$

$$R^p_{S_i} = BP_{S_i} \cdot \left[ \frac{(1+r)^M - (1+r)^m}{(1+r)^M - 1} \right], \tag{21}$$

where $BP^p_{S_j}$ is the present value of the bid price of the transformer to be installed at the $p$-th year of the study period, $R^p_{S_i}$ is the remaining value of the uninstalled transformer, $BP_{S_i}$ is the transformer $S_i$ bid price, $r$ is the inflation rate, $M$ are the years of the transformer lifetime and $m$ are the years that the transformer was under service.

Table 2 lists the cost of four arcs of Figure 6, calculated according to Sections 4 and 6. The cost of the arc between nodes 11 and 17 (15th to 22th year of the study) of Figure 6 is analytically calculated as follows:

$$C_L^{11\to17} = \sum_{k=16}^{22} C_L^k = \sum_{k=16}^{22} C_{NLL}^k + C_{LL}^k$$

$$\Rightarrow C_L^{11\to17} = E_{NLL} \cdot \sum_{k=16}^{22} CYEC^k + E_{LL} \cdot \sum_{k=16}^{22} CYEC^k$$

$$\Rightarrow C_L^{11\to17} = AF \cdot HPY \cdot \sum_{k=16}^{22} CYEC^k + LL \cdot HPY \cdot l_f^2 \cdot \sum_{k=16}^{22} CYEC^k$$

$$\Rightarrow C_L^{11\to17} = 1.094 \cdot 8760 \cdot 1 \cdot 0.729 + 7.774 \cdot 8760 \cdot 0.61^2 \cdot 0.729$$

$$\Rightarrow C_L^{11\to17} = 6986.3 + 18472.9 = 25459€$$

$BP^{15}_{630\,kVA} = 21035$ €, from (21) $R^{15}_{300kVA} = 4388$ €

$$I_{11\to17} = BP^{15}_{630\,kVA} - R^{15}_{300\,kVA} = 16647€$$

$$\textbf{arc cost}_{11\text{-}17} = C_L^{11\to17} + I_{11\to17} = 32663\ €$$

Figures 6, 7 and 8 illustrate the graph used by the proposed ACO method for the solution of the OTS problem for Type 5, Type 7 and Type 8 substation load of Figure 5, respectively, using the transformers of Table 1. The graphs of Figure 7 and 8 comprise more nodes than the one of Figure 6, since all candidate transformer sizes can serve the load up to the final year of the study, therefore resulting to the presence of five nodes (i.e. five capacities) at each stage, an overall of thirty nodes. This configuration is consistent to the general graph of Figure 4,

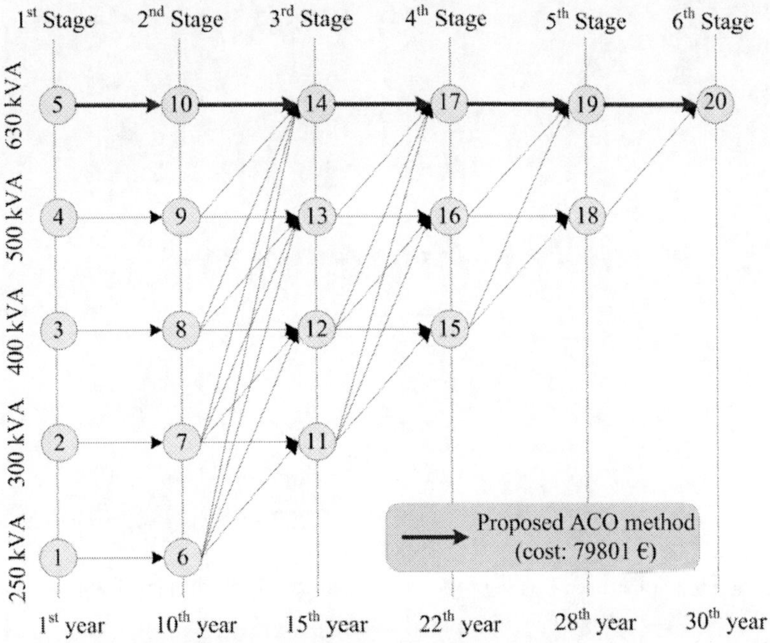


Figure 6. The directed graph used by the proposed ACO method for the Type 5 substation load

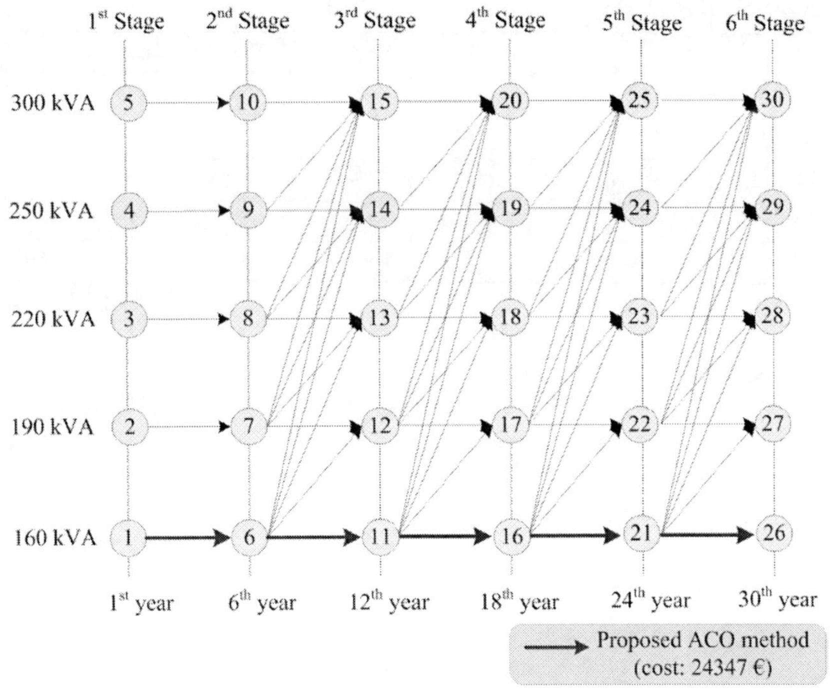


Figure 7. The directed graph used by the proposed ACO method for the Type 7 substation load

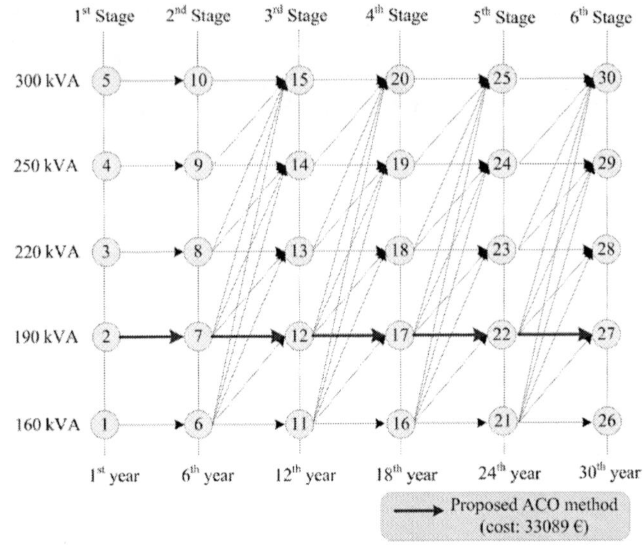


Figure 8. The directed graph used by the proposed ACO method for the Type 8 substation load

**Table 2. Cost of indicative arcs in the graph of Figure 6 (substation Type 5)**

| Arc | Cost of the arc | Value (€) | Arc | Cost of the arc | Value (€) |
|---|---|---|---|---|---|
| $2 \to 7$ | $C_L^{2\to 7} + BP_{300}^{1st-year}$ | 17972 | $17 \to 19$ | $C_L^{17\to 19}$ | 23601 |
| $11 \to 17$ | $C_L^{11\to 17} + I_{11\to 17}$ | 32663 | $19 \to 20$ | $C_L^{19\to 20}$ | 11185 |
| $1 \to 6$ | $C_L^{1\to 6} + BP_{250}^{1st-year}$ | 19389 | $12 \to 15$ | $C_L^{12\to 15}$ | 19673 |
| $6 \to 11$ | $C_L^{6\to 11} + I_{6\to 11}$ | 14816 | $15 \to 19$ | $C_L^{15\to 19} + I_{15\to 19}$ | 47230 |
| $11 \to 15$ | $C_L^{11\to 15} + I_{11\to 15}$ | 31156 | $5 \to 10$ | $C_L^{5\to 10} + BP_{630}^{1st-year}$ | 21738 |
| $15 \to 18$ | $C_L^{15\to 18} + I_{15\to 18}$ | 45575 | $10 \to 14$ | $C_L^{10\to 14}$ | 72618 |
| $18 \to 20$ | $C_L^{18\to 20} + I_{18\to 20}$ | 43831 | $14 \to 17$ | $C_L^{14\to 17}$ | 16016 |

where, for the purpose of generality, the lack of several nodes in the ultimate stages is indicated. Moreover, since, according to Table 1, the years to serve the load are equal for all transformer capacities (i.e. 30 years), the thermal durability could not be used as a criterion for the derivation of the stages of Figure 7 and 8. For this purpose, the whole period of the study was divided to five equal periods of 6 years, in order to derive the same number of stages as the ones in the graphs corresponding to the other types of substations. We tested several values for each parameter, i.e. $\alpha \in \{0,0.5,1,2,5\}$, $\beta \in \{0,0.5,1,2,5\}$, $\rho \in \{0.1,0.3,0.5,0.7,1\}$. Table 3 includes the data of the optimal sizing strategies for each type of substation of Figure 5 and Table 1. The optimal solutions of Table 3 were obtained using $k$=20, $\alpha$=2, $\beta$=0.5, $\rho$=0.5, $Q$=2.7, max iterations=2000. According to Figure 6, the optimal sizing path yielded by the proposed method corresponds to installation of the largest rated capacity that can serve the expected load at the end of the study period. The same optimal path is selected for Types 1-4 and 6 of the substation loads of the considered network, corresponding to the costs listed in Table 3. This is due to the fact that transformers with rated power significantly larger than the served load operate under low load current, thus consuming less annual energy losses (and consequently having less annual energy loss cost), in comparison with transformers of rated power close to the served load. In the case of Figure 7, the optimal sizing path corresponds to the installation of the rated capacity larger than the maximum peak load at the end of the study (equal to 108.27 kVA for this type of substation), i.e. 160kVA, instead of the maximum available capacity that can serve the expected load at the end of the study period (i.e. 300kVA). The same conclusion applies for Type 8 substation, where the installation of the 190kVA capacity from the first year of the study is selected, i.e. the capacity that is larger than the maximum peak load at the end of the study (equal to 162.41 kVA for this type of substation).

**Table 3. Results of the proposed method for the OTS problem of Figure 5**

| Transformer cost | Substation load types | | | | | | | |
|---|---|---|---|---|---|---|---|---|
| | Type 1 | Type 2 | Type 3 | Type 4 | Type 5 | Type 6 | Type 7 | Type 8 |
| Installation cost (€) | 10677 | 10296 | 10677 | 10677 | 12648 | 12648 | 5470 | 6015 |
| Energy loss cost (€) | 48529 | 61195 | 66372 | 56025 | 67153 | 70047 | 18877 | 26863 |
| Total cost (€) | 59206 | 71491 | 77049 | 66702 | 79801 | 82695 | 24347 | 32878 |
| Number of substations | 4 | 3 | 2 | 1 | 1 | 2 | 2 | 1 |
| Total installation cost (€) | 42708 | 30888 | 21354 | 10677 | 12648 | 25296 | 10940 | 6015 |
| Total energy loss cost (€) | 194116 | 183585 | 132744 | 56025 | 67153 | 140094 | 37754 | 26863 |
| Overall cost (€) | 236824 | 214473 | 154098 | 66702 | 79801 | 165390 | 48694 | 32878 |

According to the results of Table 3, the energy loss cost is the main component that influences the total cost difference between the proposed and the conventional sizing method, compared to the installation cost. The importance of transformer energy losses can be observed through the curves of Figure 9, indicating the variation of the energy loss cost of the considered transformer capacities for the Type 1 substation load throughout the study period (corresponding to load factor equal to 0.55, for domestic load). Figure 10 illustrates the variation of the energy loss cost of the considered transformer capacities for the Type 7 substation load throughout the study period (corresponding to load factor equal to 0.61, for industrial load), where the difference in the energy loss cost between 160 kVA (the optimal transformer) and 300 kVA (the largest available capacity) is verifying the selection of the optimal sizing path. Finally, Figure 11 shows the variation of the energy loss cost of the considered transformer capacities for the Type 8 substation load through-out the study period (corresponding to load factor equal to 0.61, for industrial load), which has different behaviour in comparison to Figure 9 and 10. In this case, it is clear that for the first 15 years of the study, the 160 kVA transformer is the one with the best (less) annual energy cost, while for the next 15 years of the study it becomes the worst transformer, in terms of annual energy cost. Under these circumstances, neither the larger nor the smaller transformer capacity through the study period can serve successfully the considered load (75 kVA). As a result of the above and based on the optimization algorithm, i.e. the proposed ACO method, the transformer rating of 190 kVA is selected as the optimum one.

Based on the aforementioned case studies and taking into consideration Figures 6-8, we conclude that the key to deal with the optimal transformer sizing problem is to select an ideal transformer size at the first year of the study period (30 years), which will remain constant throughout this period. In particular, it is not worth upgrading the transformer size during the study because the present value of the bid price (of the new transformer to be installed) increases dramatically the cost of the upgrade arc value (i.e. the arc that represents transformer size upgrading, namely arcs that direct from smaller to higher transformer sizes),

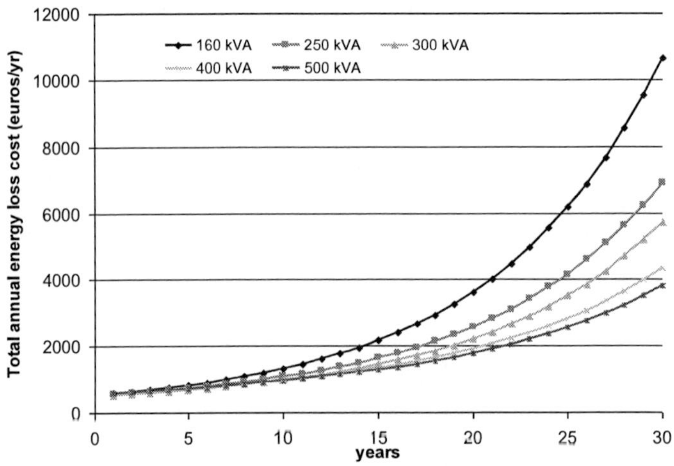


Figure 9. Total annual energy loss cost curves corresponding to the five transformer ratings serving load of Type 1 substation

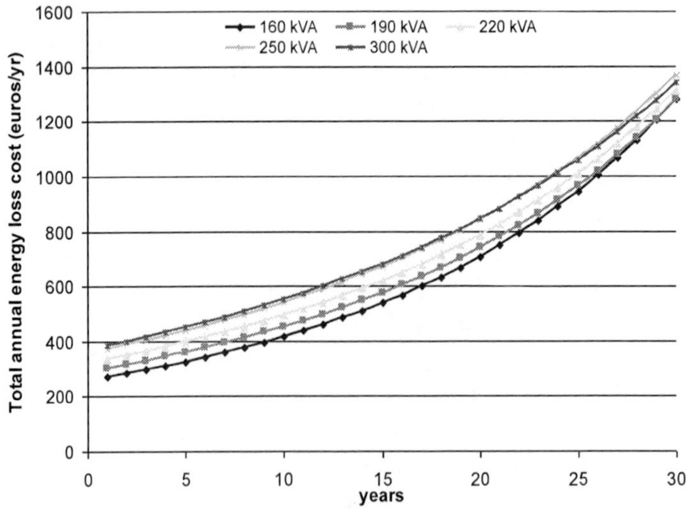


Figure 10. Total annual energy loss cost curves corresponding to the five transformer ratings serving load of Type 7 substation

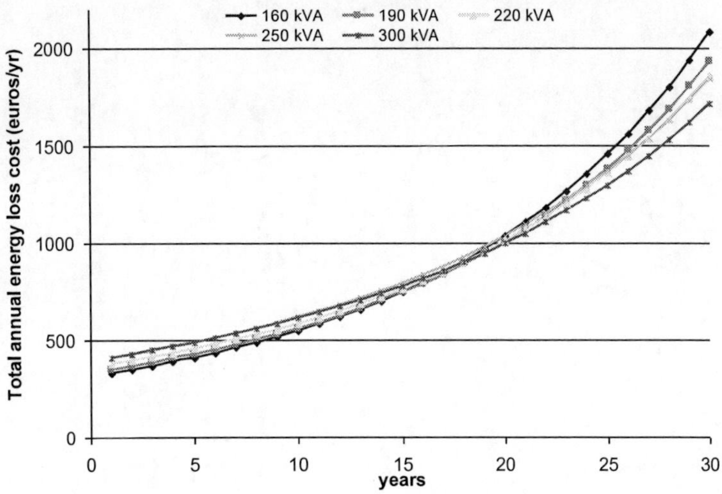


Figure 11. Total annual energy loss cost curves corresponding to the five transformer ratings serving load of Type 8 substation

while at the same time the value of the energy cost remains relatively smaller. The present remaining value of the uninstalled transformer is usually not high enough to compensate this cost difference. This observation can be also confirmed from Figures 8-10. To be more precise, it is clear that there are transformer sizes able to serve the considered load with less annual energy losses and consequently less annual energy loss cost in comparison with the remaining transformer designs during the period of the 30 years (e.g. in the case of Figure 10, the 160 kVA rating corresponds to less energy loss than the selected 190 kVA rating, thus in terms of less energy consumption, the selection to upgrade from 160 kVA to 190 kVA would be the optimal one), however the economic surplus due to the additional transformer purchase overcomes the need to upgrade the transformer during the study. In a nutshell, the initial transformer choice is a key issue in the optimal transformer sizing problem, based on the load properties and the economic forecast.

## 7. Application of ACO Algorithm to Optimal Transformer Efficiency Selection Problem

Next to the optimal transformer sizing, i.e. the selection of transformer capacities to serve the loads of the network of Figure 5, ACO is applied for the optimal efficiency selection of the transformer to be installed at each substation.

In this case the objective of ACO is to determine the optimum choice of distribution transformers design of a given capacity, so as to minimize the installation and loss cost for all the years of the study period. The application of the method presents several variations in relation to the graph of Figure 4, as depicted in the graph of Figure 12, representing the possible efficiency paths.

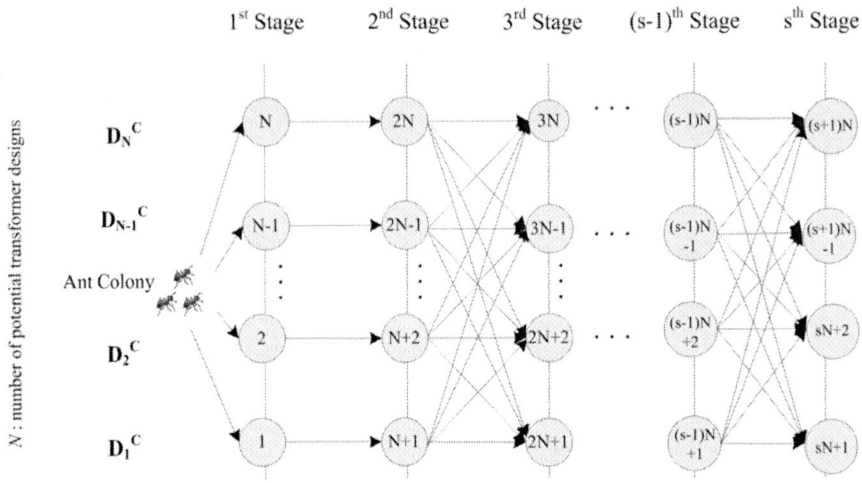


Figure 12. The directed graph used for the Optimal Transformer Efficiency selection problem

As in the case of Figure 4, the graph has $s$ stages and each stage indicates a time period (in years). Since all considered transformers are able to serve the load and their thermal withstand is equal to the study period, the limits of the stages of Figure 12 are now defined by division of the study period to five equal intervals of six years. All stages have equal number of nodes, since it is possible to use anyone of the examined designs at each year of the study. The first stage indicates the beginning of the study, comprising number of nodes equal to the number of potential transformer capacities $N$, while $s$ represents the end of the study period. Symbols $D_1^C, D_2^C, D_{N-1}^C, D_N^C$ refer to the different designs of the examined rated capacity $C$. In the case of the graph of Figure 12 it is possible to connect nodes of upper levels to nodes of lower levels (e.g. node $2N$-$1$ to $2N+2$) since this connection corresponds to installation of a transformer with equal rated power to the one already in operation (that can serve the considered load without any thermal withstand problem). However, the arcs between the nodes are directed from the previous stage to the next one (backward movement is not allowed) since each stage represents a forward step in the time of the study. Nodes 1 to $N$ (Figure 12) are designated as the source nodes corresponding to each potential transformer design and nodes $sN+1$ to $(s+1)N$ are designated as the destination nodes (Figure 12). The use of multiple source nodes enables the examination of more potential solutions of the problem. The numbering of n nodes of the graph of Figure 12 is realized upwards for each stage, i.e. the bottom node of the 1$^{st}$ stage is node 1, while the last node of the 1$^{st}$ stage is $N$ (where $N$ corresponds to the number of designs). Accordingly, the 2nd stage begins with node $N+1$ while its last node is numbered $2N+1$ (the number of nodes of all stages is equal to $N$), 3rd stage begins with node $2N+1$ and ends at node $3N$, etc., concluding to the s-th stage, which comprises nodes $sN+1$ to $(s+1)N$. The objective of the colony agents is to find the least-cost path between nodes that belong to first stage and nodes that belong to s-th stage.

Many different transformer designs can be developed to meet the requirements of a particular transformer specification. These designs will have varying amounts of core steel and copper or aluminum conductors with differing no-load and load losses. The lowest cost design that meets all the applicable performance standards and requirements is generally referred to as the low efficiency design [29]. For the purposes of the analysis, seven different transformer designs (three-phase, oil-immersed, 50 Hz distribution transformers) per kVA rating were considered, with different losses and efficiency levels. The thermal calculations of Section 3 (depicted in the flowchart of Figure 2) are not repeated in this case, since the capacities that are able to serve the loads of the substations of Figure 5 up to the final year of the study are already determined in the previous Section.

In the case of Substation Types 1-4, ACO method resulted to the installation of a 500 kVA transformer from the first year of the study. In this Section, the possibility to select among seven different designs with nominal power equal to 500 kVA is considered. The specifications of these designs are listed in Table 4. This table indicates the difference in the manufacturing cost (reflected in the bid price) as a function of the transformer efficiency. In this case, $D_7^{500kVA}$ is the low efficiency design, since it corresponds to the lowest manufacturing cost and higher losses, while $D_1^{500kVA}$ is the high efficiency design with the highest bid price. $D_4^{500kVA}$ can be considered a standard efficiency design, having intermediate bid price and efficiency values. As can be seen from Table 4, the three designs with higher total losses (namely $D_5^{500kVA}$, $D_6^{500kVA}$ and $D_7^{500kVA}$) are less expensive than $D_4^{500kVA}$. On the other hand, designs $D_1^{500kVA}$, $D_2^{500kVA}$ and $D_3^{500kVA}$, with lower total losses than $D_4^{500kVA}$ transformer are more expensive. In the case of Substation Types 5 and 6, ACO method resulted to the installation of a 630 kVA transformer from the first year of the study. The specifications of the seven different designs with nominal power equal to 630 kVA that are considered in this Section are listed in Table 5. In this case, $D_1^{630kVA}$ is the low efficiency design, since it corresponds to the lowest manufacturing cost and higher losses, while $D_7^{630kVA}$ is the high efficiency design with the highest bid price. In the case of Substation Type 7, ACO method resulted to the installation of a 160 kVA transformer from the first year of the study. The specifications of the seven different designs with nominal power equal to 160 kVA that are considered in this Section are listed in Table 6. In this case, $D_7^{160kVA}$ is the low efficiency design, since it corresponds to the lowest manufacturing cost and higher losses, while $D_1^{160kVA}$ is the high efficiency design with the highest bid price. Finally, in the case of Substation Type 8, ACO method resulted to the installation of a 190 kVA transformer from the first year of the study. The specifications of the seven different designs with nominal power equal to 190 kVA that are considered in this Section are listed in Table 7. In this case, $D_1^{190kVA}$ is the low efficiency design, since it corresponds to the lowest manufacturing cost and higher losses, while $D_7^{190kVA}$ is the high efficiency design with the highest bid price. It must be noted that all the designs of Tables 4-7 are different than the ones of Table 1 (for the 160, 190, 500 and 630kVA ratings), thus the cost of the conventional installation strategies in this Section differ from the ones yielded in Section 6.

The optimal solution for Type 4 substation corresponds to the directed graph of Figure 13, while the optimal paths corresponding to Type 1-4 Substations are listed in detail in Table 8. The conventional selection strategy corresponds to the installation of the transformer with

**Table 4. Technical parameters of 500 kVA transformers used in the optimal efficiency selection of Type 1-4 Substations**

| 500 kVA transformer technical parameters | | | |
|---|---|---|---|
| | Bid price (€) | NLL (kW) | LL (kW) |
| $D_1^{500kVA}$ | 10308 | 1.692 | 4.408 |
| $D_2^{500kVA}$ | 9339.0 | 0.586 | 4.891 |
| $D_3^{500kVA}$ | 8197.0 | 0.697 | 4.106 |
| $D_4^{500kVA}$ | 7555.0 | 0.662 | 5.044 |
| $D_5^{500kVA}$ | 7080.0 | 0.586 | 5.85 |
| $D_6^{500kVA}$ | 6003.0 | 0.828 | 5.024 |
| $D_7^{500kVA}$ | 4085.0 | 0.668 | 7.973 |

**Table 5. Technical parameters of 630 kVA transformers used in the optimal efficiency selection of transformer to serve Type 5 and 6 substation loads**

| 630 kVA **transformer** technical parameters | | | |
|---|---|---|---|
| | Bid price (€) | NLL (kW) | LL (kW) |
| $D_1^{630kVA}$ | 4870.0 | 1.098 | 9.358 |
| $D_2^{630kVA}$ | 6758.0 | 0.774 | 6.974 |
| $D_3^{630kVA}$ | 8190.0 | 0.782 | 6.049 |
| $D_4^{630kVA}$ | 8739.0 | 0.762 | 5.849 |
| $D_5^{630kVA}$ | 9137.0 | 0.782 | 5.204 |
| $D_6^{630kVA}$ | 9374.0 | 0.645 | 6.123 |
| $D_7^{630kVA}$ | 10965 | 0.654 | 5.113 |

the lowest bid price among the designs of Table 8 (i.e. $D_7^{500kVA}$) for all the years of the study period. The proposed ACO method suggests an optimal path consisting of the installation of a transformer of low no-load and load losses and higher bid price (i.e. $D_3^{500kVA}$) for the first 5 stages of the study period (resulting to an overall of 24 years) and its replacement by $D_7^{500kVA}$ for the 6 last years of the study. Despite the higher purchasing price, the selection of $D_3^{500kVA}$ results to significantly decreased loss costs through the first 4 stages of the study, thus resulting to an overall cost equal to 67376€ which is 8.6% cheaper than the overall cost yielded by the conventional installation strategy (i.e. 73185€). Figure 14 depicts the difference in the loss costs of the examined designs $D_1^{500kVA}$ - $D_7^{500kVA}$ influencing the overall cost of Table 8.

**Table 6. Technical parameters of 160 kVA transformers used in the optimal efficiency selection of transformer to serve Type 7 substation load**

| 160 kVA transformer technical parameters | | | |
|---|---|---|---|
| | Bid price (€) | NLL (kW) | LL (kW) |
| $D_1^{160kVA}$ | 1762 | 0.475 | 3.19 |
| $D_2^{160kVA}$ | 2397 | 0.299 | 2.498 |
| $D_3^{160kVA}$ | 2464 | 0.345 | 2.152 |
| $D_4^{160kVA}$ | 2674 | 0.299 | 2.168 |
| $D_5^{160kVA}$ | 3244 | 0.297 | 2.053 |
| $D_6^{160kVA}$ | 3435 | 0.242 | 2.19 |
| $D_7^{160kVA}$ | 4219 | 0.244 | 1.934 |

**Table 7. Technical parameters of 190 kVA transformers used in the optimal efficiency selection of transformer to serve Type 8 substation load**

| 190 kVA transformer technical parameters | | | |
|---|---|---|---|
| | Bid price (€) | NLL (kW) | LL (kW) |
| $D_1^{190kVA}$ | 2294 | 0.528 | 3.254 |
| $D_2^{190kVA}$ | 2598 | 0.523 | 2.304 |
| $D_3^{190kVA}$ | 3330 | 0.35 | 2.317 |
| $D_4^{190kVA}$ | 3565 | 0.299 | 2.44 |
| $D_5^{190kVA}$ | 5125 | 0.327 | 2.51 |
| $D_6^{190kVA}$ | 5244 | 0.338 | 2.047 |
| $D_7^{190kVA}$ | 5571 | 0.323 | 2.416 |

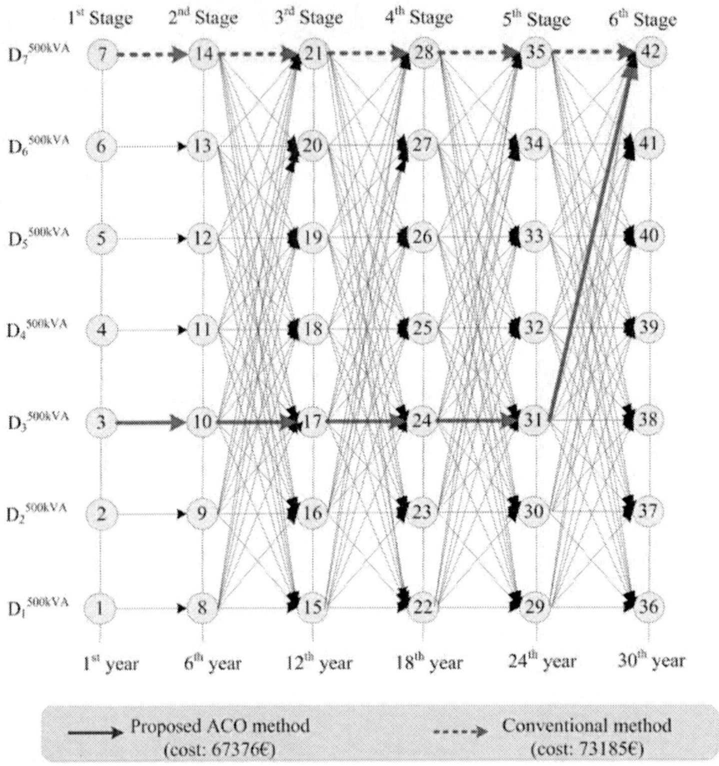


Figure 13. The directed graph used by the proposed ACO method for the selection of the optimal transformer efficiency to serve Type 4 substation load

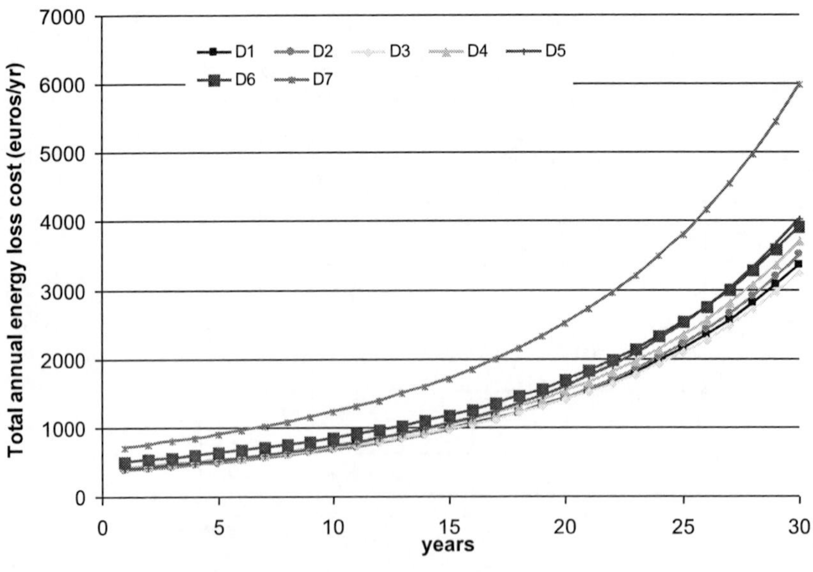


Figure 14. Total annual energy loss cost curves corresponding to the seven transformer designs serving load of Type 4 substation

**Table 8. Optimal and conventional transformer installation strategies for the substations of Figure 5**

| Type | | Stage 1 | Stage 2 | Stage 3 | Stage 4 | Stage 5 | Stage 6 | Cost(€) |
|---|---|---|---|---|---|---|---|---|
| 1 | Conventional | $D_7^{500kVA}$ | $D_7^{500kVA}$ | $D_7^{500kVA}$ | $D_7^{500kVA}$ | $D_7^{500kVA}$ | $D_7^{500kVA}$ | 62834 |
| | ACO | $D_3^{500kVA}$ | $D_3^{500kVA}$ | $D_3^{500kVA}$ | $D_3^{500kVA}$ | $D_3^{500kVA}$ | $D_7^{500kVA}$ | 59460 |
| 2 | Conventional | $D_7^{500kVA}$ | $D_7^{500kVA}$ | $D_7^{500kVA}$ | $D_7^{500kVA}$ | $D_7^{500kVA}$ | $D_7^{500kVA}$ | 100633 |
| | ACO | $D_3^{500kVA}$ | $D_3^{500kVA}$ | $D_3^{500kVA}$ | $D_3^{500kVA}$ | $D_3^{500kVA}$ | $D_7^{500kVA}$ | 89148 |
| 3 | Conventional | $D_7^{500kVA}$ | $D_7^{500kVA}$ | $D_7^{500kVA}$ | $D_7^{500kVA}$ | $D_7^{500kVA}$ | $D_7^{500kVA}$ | 80321 |
| | ACO | $D_3^{500kVA}$ | $D_3^{500kVA}$ | $D_3^{500kVA}$ | $D_3^{500kVA}$ | $D_3^{500kVA}$ | $D_7^{500kVA}$ | 73380 |
| 4 | Conventional | $D_7^{500kVA}$ | $D_7^{500kVA}$ | $D_7^{500kVA}$ | $D_7^{500kVA}$ | $D_7^{500kVA}$ | $D_7^{500kVA}$ | 73185 |
| | ACO | $D_3^{500kVA}$ | $D_3^{500kVA}$ | $D_3^{500kVA}$ | $D_3^{500kVA}$ | $D_3^{500kVA}$ | $D_7^{500kVA}$ | 67376 |
| 5 | Conventional | $D_1^{630kVA}$ | $D_1^{630kVA}$ | $D_1^{630kVA}$ | $D_1^{630kVA}$ | $D_1^{630kVA}$ | $D_1^{630kVA}$ | 80155 |
| | ACO | $D_7^{630kVA}$ | $D_3^{500kVA}$ | $D_3^{500kVA}$ | $D_3^{500kVA}$ | $D_3^{500kVA}$ | $D_7^{500kVA}$ | 53823 |
| 6 | Conventional | $D_1^{630kVA}$ | $D_1^{630kVA}$ | $D_1^{630kVA}$ | $D_1^{630kVA}$ | $D_1^{630kVA}$ | $D_1^{630kVA}$ | 83641 |
| | ACO | $D_7^{630kVA}$ | $D_3^{500kVA}$ | $D_3^{500kVA}$ | $D_3^{500kVA}$ | $D_3^{500kVA}$ | $D_7^{500kVA}$ | 55725 |
| 7 | Conventional | $D_1^{160kVA}$ | $D_1^{160kVA}$ | $D_1^{160kVA}$ | $D_1^{160kVA}$ | $D_1^{160kVA}$ | $D_1^{160kVA}$ | 23209 |
| | ACO | $D_7^{160kVA}$ | $D_7^{160kVA}$ | $D_7^{160kVA}$ | $D_7^{160kVA}$ | $D_7^{160kVA}$ | $D_7^{160kVA}$ | 16078 |
| 8 | Conventional | $D_1^{190kVA}$ | $D_1^{190kVA}$ | $D_1^{190kVA}$ | $D_1^{190kVA}$ | $D_1^{190kVA}$ | $D_1^{190kVA}$ | 24829 |
| | ACO | $D_7^{190kVA}$ | $D_7^{190kVA}$ | $D_7^{190kVA}$ | $D_7^{190kVA}$ | $D_7^{190kVA}$ | $D_7^{190kVA}$ | 30472 |

**Table 9. Results of the proposed method for the Optimal Transformer Efficiency selection problem of Figure 4**

| Transformer cost | Substation load types | | | | | | | |
|---|---|---|---|---|---|---|---|---|
| | Type 1 | Type 2 | Type 3 | Type 4 | Type 5 | Type 6 | Type 7 | Type 8 |
| Conventional cost (€) | 62834 | 100633 | 80321 | 73185 | 80155 | 83641 | 23209 | 30472 |
| Optimum cost (€) | 59460 | 89148 | 73380 | 67376 | 53823 | 55725 | 16078 | 24829 |
| Number of substations | 4 | 3 | 2 | 1 | 1 | 2 | 2 | 1 |
| Total conventional cost (€) | 251336 | 301899 | 160642 | 73185 | 80155 | 167282 | 46418 | 30472 |
| Total optimum cost (€) | 237840 | 267444 | 146760 | 67376 | 53823 | 111450 | 32156 | 24829 |
| Difference (%) | 5,7% | 12,9% | 9,5% | 8,6% | 48,9% | 50,1% | 44,4% | 22,7% |

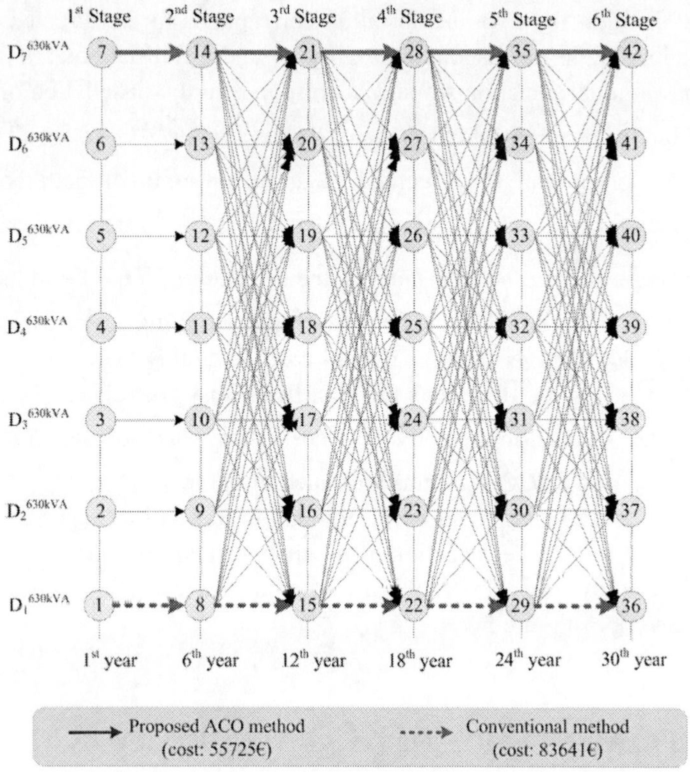


Figure 15. The directed graph used by the proposed ACO method for the selection of the optimal transformer efficiency to serve Type 6 substation load

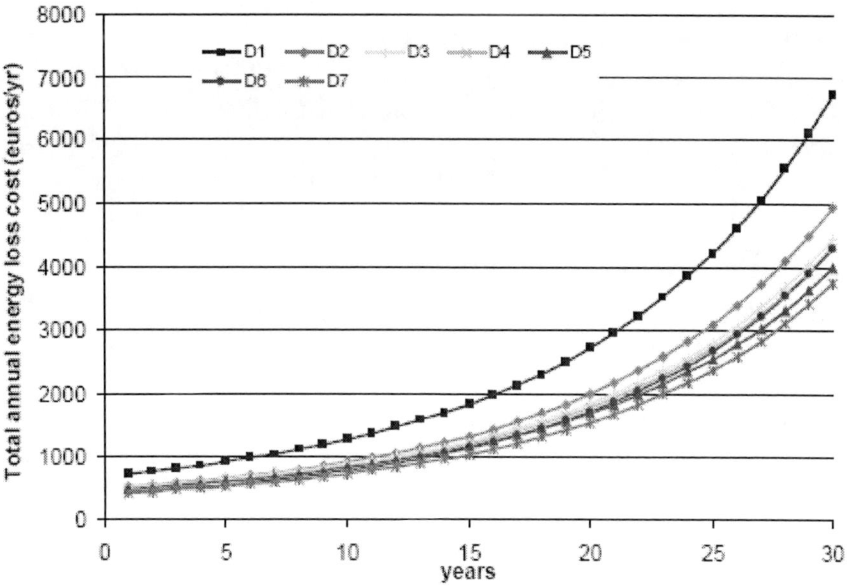


Figure 16. Total annual energy loss cost curves corresponding to the seven transformer designs serving load of Type 6 substation

The optimal solution for Type 6 substation corresponds to the directed graph of Figure 15, while the optimal paths corresponding to Type 5 and 6 Substations are listed in detail in Table 8. The conventional selection strategy corresponds to the installation of the transformer with the lowest bid price among the designs of Table 8 (i.e. $D_1^{630kVA}$) for all the years of the study period. The proposed ACO method suggests an optimal path consisting of the installation of a transformer of the highest bid price (i.e. $D_7^{630kVA}$) for all the years of the study period. As in the case of Type 1-4 Substations, the selection of $D_7^{630kVA}$ results to significantly decreased loss costs throughout the study period, thus resulting to an overall cost equal to 55725€ which is 50.1% cheaper than the overall cost yielded by the conventional installation strategy (i.e. 83641€). Figure 16 depicts the significant loss cost difference of the examined designs $D_1^{630kVA}$ - $D_7^{630kVA}$ resulting to overall cost difference up to 50% between the conventional and proposed ACO solutions presented in Table 8.

The optimal installation strategies corresponding to Substation Types 7 and 8 are similar to the one of Types 5 and 6 (i.e. selection of the transformer with the highest bid price from the first year of the study) and their details are listed in Table 8. Table 9 lists the overall cost results for the network of Figure 5.

## 8. Implementation of ACO Algorithm in Matlab

The present Section presents the implementation of ACO algorithm to the selection of the optimal transformer efficiency selection problem presented in the previous section.

**%ACO**

```
%Ant colony optimization for solving the optimal transformer
% sizing/efficiency
                                    %Date: 01/07/2010

clc
clear
% This code creates a 36x36 matrix that can be used as input to ACO.

% stage2 = 6 expresses that stage 1 is located at the 6th year.
stage1 = 1;
stage2 = 6;
stage3 = 12;
stage4 = 18;
stage5 = 24;
stage6 = 30;

% D1 - D2 - D3 - D4 - D5 - D6 - D7: Different Transformer Designs -
% Nominal Power in kVA
D1 = 190;
```

```
D2 = 190;
D3 = 190;
D4 = 190;
D5 = 190;
D6 = 190;
D7 = 190;

% BP1 - BP2 - BP3 - BP4 - BP5 - BP6 - BP7: Bid Price of each
%Transformer Design
BP1 = 2294;
BP2 = 2598;
BP3 = 3330;
BP4 = 3565;
BP5 = 5125;
BP6 = 5244;
BP7 = 5571;

% NLL1 - NLL2 - NLL3 - NLL4 - NLL5 - NLL6 - NLL7: No Load
%losses of each Transformer Design in kW
NLL1 = 0.528;
NLL2 = 0.523;
NLL3 = 0.35;
NLL4 = 0.299;
NLL5 = 0.327;
NLL6 = 0.338;
NLL7 = 0.323;

% LL1 - LL2 - LL3 - LL4 - LL5 - LL6 - LL7: Load losses of each
% Transformer Design in kW
LL1 = 3.254;
LL2 = 2.304;
LL3 = 2.317;
LL4 = 2.44;
LL5 = 2.51;
LL6 = 2.047;
LL7 = 2.416;

%Availability factor
AF = 1;

%Load factor
l_f = 0.61;

%Hours per year
HPY = 8760;

%Electricity cost in euro/kWh
CYEC = 0.054;
```

```
%load growth factor
s =           0.027;

%peak load
Smax_0 = 75;

%inflation rate
i_r = 0.037;

%Transformer life time in years
transformer_life = 30;

%Electricity cost growth in euro/kWh
CYEC_growth = zeros(30,1);

CYEC_growth(1,1) = CYEC * (1 + i_r);
for i = 2:30
 CYEC_growth(i,1) = CYEC_growth(i-1,1) * (1 + i_r);
end

%Bid price growth in euro
BP_growth = zeros(30,7);

BP_growth(1,1) = BP1 * (1 + i_r);
BP_growth(1,2) = BP2 * (1 + i_r);
BP_growth(1,3) = BP3 * (1+ i_r);
BP_growth(1,4) = BP4 * (1 + i_r);
BP_growth(1,5) = BP5 * (1 + i_r);
BP_growth(1,6) = BP6 * (1 + i_r);
BP_growth(1,7) = BP7 * (1 + i_r);
for i = 2:30
 BP_growth(i,1) = BP_growth(i-1,1) * (1 + i_r);
 BP_growth(i,2) = BP_growth(i-1,2) * (1 + i_r);
 BP_growth(i,3) = BP_growth(i-1,3) * (1 + i_r);
 BP_growth(i,4) = BP_growth(i-1,4) * (1 + i_r);
 BP_growth(i,5) = BP_growth(i-1,5) * (1 + i_r);
 BP_growth(i,6) = BP_growth(i-1,6) * (1 + i_r);
 BP_growth(i,7) = BP_growth(i-1,7) * (1 + i_r);
end

%Tt_energy_Dx is a 30x5 matrix where x is the transformer design
%index
%1st column --> Energy of the no load losses in kWh/yr
%2nd column --> Energy of the load losses in kWh/yr
%3rd column --> Cost of the no load losses in euro
%4th column --> Cost of the load losses in euro
%5th column --> Total energy cost of Dx transformer in euro
%D1 data
```

```
Tt_energy_D1 = zeros(30,5);
for i=1:30
 Tt_energy_D1(i,1) = NLL1 * HPY * AF;
 Tt_energy_D1(i,2) = LL1 * HPY * ((1 + s)^i * l_f*(Smax_0/D1))^2;
 Tt_energy_D1(i,3) = Tt_energy_D1(i,1) * CYEC_growth(i,1);
 Tt_energy_D1(i,4) = Tt_energy_D1(i,2) * CYEC_growth(i,1);
 Tt_energy_D1(i,5) = Tt_energy_D1(i,3) + Tt_energy_D1(i,4);
end

%D2 data
Tt_energy_D2 = zeros(30,5);
for i=1:30
 Tt_energy_D2(i,1) = NLL2 * HPY * AF;
 Tt_energy_D2(i,2) = LL2 * HPY * ((1 + s)^i * l_f*(Smax_0/D2))^2;
 Tt_energy_D2(i,3) = Tt_energy_D2(i,1) * CYEC_growth(i,1);
 Tt_energy_D2(i,4) = Tt_energy_D2(i,2) * CYEC_growth(i,1);
 Tt_energy_D2(i,5) = Tt_energy_D2(i,3) + Tt_energy_D2(i,4);
end

%D3 data
Tt_energy_D3 = zeros(30,5);
for i=1:30
 Tt_energy_D3(i,1) = NLL3 * HPY * AF;
 Tt_energy_D3(i,2) = LL3 * HPY * ((1 + s)^i * l_f*(Smax_0/D3))^2;
 Tt_energy_D3(i,3) = Tt_energy_D3(i,1) * CYEC_growth(i,1);
 Tt_energy_D3(i,4) = Tt_energy_D3(i,2) * CYEC_growth(i,1);
 Tt_energy_D3(i,5) = Tt_energy_D3(i,3) + Tt_energy_D3(i,4);
end

%D4 data
Tt_energy_D4 = zeros(30,5);
for i=1:30
 Tt_energy_D4(i,1) = NLL4 * HPY * AF;
 Tt_energy_D4(i,2) = LL4 * HPY * ((1 + s)^i * l_f*(Smax_0/D4))^2;
 Tt_energy_D4(i,3) = Tt_energy_D4(i,1) * CYEC_growth(i,1);
 Tt_energy_D4(i,4) = Tt_energy_D4(i,2) * CYEC_growth(i,1);
 Tt_energy_D4(i,5) = Tt_energy_D4(i,3) + Tt_energy_D4(i,4);
end
%D5 data
Tt_energy_D5 = zeros(30,5);
for i=1:30
 Tt_energy_D5(i,1) = NLL5 * HPY * AF;
 Tt_energy_D5(i,2) = LL5 * HPY * ((1 + s)^i * l_f*(Smax_0/D5))^2;
 Tt_energy_D5(i,3) = Tt_energy_D5(i,1) * CYEC_growth(i,1);
 Tt_energy_D5(i,4) = Tt_energy_D5(i,2) * CYEC_growth(i,1);
 Tt_energy_D5(i,5) = Tt_energy_D5(i,3) + Tt_energy_D5(i,4);
end
```

```
%D6 data
Tt_energy_D6 = zeros(30,5);
for i=1:30
 Tt_energy_D6(i,1) = NLL6 * HPY * AF;
 Tt_energy_D6(i,2) = LL6 * HPY * ((1 + s)^i * l_f*(Smax_0/D6))^2;
 Tt_energy_D6(i,3) = Tt_energy_D6(i,1) * CYEC_growth(i,1);
 Tt_energy_D6(i,4) = Tt_energy_D6(i,2) * CYEC_growth(i,1);
 Tt_energy_D6(i,5) = Tt_energy_D6(i,3) + Tt_energy_D6(i,4);
end

%D7 data
Tt_energy_D7 = zeros(30,5);
for i=1:30
 Tt_energy_D7(i,1) = NLL7 * HPY * AF;
 Tt_energy_D7(i,2) = LL7 * HPY * ((1 + s)^i * l_f*(Smax_0/D7))^2;
 Tt_energy_D7(i,3) = Tt_energy_D7(i,1) * CYEC_growth(i,1);
 Tt_energy_D7(i,4) = Tt_energy_D7(i,2) * CYEC_growth(i,1);
 Tt_energy_D7(i,5) = Tt_energy_D7(i,3) + Tt_energy_D7(i,4);
end

%Total Energy cost of each transformer design
%D1 - D2 - D3 - D4 - D5 - D6 - D7
tec = zeros(30,7);
for i=1:30
 tec(i,1) = Tt_energy_D1(i,5);
 tec(i,2) = Tt_energy_D2(i,5);
 tec(i,3) = Tt_energy_D3(i,5);
 tec(i,4) = Tt_energy_D4(i,5);
 tec(i,5) = Tt_energy_D5(i,5);
 tec(i,6) = Tt_energy_D6(i,5);
 tec(i,7) = Tt_energy_D7(i,5);
end

%Bid Price & remaining value of each transformer design in euro
%D1 - D2 - D3 - D4 - D5 - D6 - D7
BP = zeros(30,7);
for i=1:30
 BP(i,1) = BP_growth(i,1);
 BP(i,2) = BP_growth(i,2);
 BP(i,3) = BP_growth(i,3);
 BP(i,4) = BP_growth(i,4);
 BP(i,5) = BP_growth(i,5);
 BP(i,6) = BP_growth(i,6);
 BP(i,7) = BP_growth(i,7);
end

remaining_value = zeros(30,7);
for i=1:30
```

```
remaining_value(i,1) = BP1 * ((((1 + i_r)^transformer_life)- ...
 (1 + i_r)^i)/((1+i_r)^transformer_life-1));
remaining_value(i,2) = BP2 * ((((1 + i_r)^transformer_life)- ...
 (1 + i_r)^i)/((1+i_r)^transformer_life-1));
remaining_value(i,3) = BP3 * ((((1 + i_r)^transformer_life)-...
 (1 + i_r)^i)/((1+i_r)^transformer_life-1));
remaining_value(i,4) = BP4 * ((((1 + i_r)^transformer_life)-...
 (1 + i_r)^i)/((1+i_r)^transformer_life-1));
remaining_value(i,5) = BP5 * ((((1 + i_r)^transformer_life)-...
 (1 + i_r)^i)/((1+i_r)^transformer_life-1));
remaining_value(i,6) = BP6 * ((((1 + i_r)^transformer_life)-...
 (1 + i_r)^i)/((1+i_r)^transformer_life-1));
remaining_value(i,7) = BP7 * ((((1 + i_r)^transformer_life)-...
 (1 + i_r)^i)/((1+i_r)^transformer_life-1));
end

%Energy demand to move from the 1st stage to the 2nd stage
energy_1_2_power_a = 0;
energy_1_2_power_b = 0;
energy_1_2_power_c = 0;
energy_1_2_power_d = 0;
energy_1_2_power_e = 0;
energy_1_2_power_f = 0;
energy_1_2_power_g = 0;

for i = 1:stage2
 energy_1_2_power_a = tec(i,1)+ energy_1_2_power_a;
 energy_1_2_power_b = tec(i,2)+ energy_1_2_power_b;
 energy_1_2_power_c = tec(i,3)+ energy_1_2_power_c;
 energy_1_2_power_d = tec(i,4)+ energy_1_2_power_d;
 energy_1_2_power_e = tec(i,5)+ energy_1_2_power_e;
 energy_1_2_power_f = tec(i,6)+ energy_1_2_power_f;
 energy_1_2_power_g = tec(i,7)+ energy_1_2_power_g;
end

%Energy demand to move from the 2nd stage to the 3rd stage
energy_2_3_power_a = 0;
energy_2_3_power_b = 0;
energy_2_3_power_c = 0;
energy_2_3_power_d = 0;
energy_2_3_power_e = 0;
energy_2_3_power_f = 0;
energy_2_3_power_g = 0;

for i = (stage2+1):stage3
 energy_2_3_power_a = tec(i,1)+ energy_2_3_power_a;
 energy_2_3_power_b = tec(i,2)+ energy_2_3_power_b;
 energy_2_3_power_c = tec(i,3)+ energy_2_3_power_c;
```

```
 energy_2_3_power_d = tec(i,4)+ energy_2_3_power_d;
 energy_2_3_power_e = tec(i,5)+ energy_2_3_power_e;
 energy_2_3_power_f = tec(i,6)+ energy_2_3_power_f;
 energy_2_3_power_g = tec(i,7)+ energy_2_3_power_g;
end

%Energy demand to move from the 3rd stage to the 4th stage
energy_3_4_power_a = 0;
energy_3_4_power_b = 0;
energy_3_4_power_c = 0;
energy_3_4_power_d = 0;
energy_3_4_power_e = 0;
energy_3_4_power_f = 0;
energy_3_4_power_g = 0;

for i = (stage3+1):stage4
 energy_3_4_power_a = tec(i,1)+ energy_3_4_power_a;
 energy_3_4_power_b = tec(i,2)+ energy_3_4_power_b;
 energy_3_4_power_c = tec(i,3)+ energy_3_4_power_c;
 energy_3_4_power_d = tec(i,4)+ energy_3_4_power_d;
 energy_3_4_power_e = tec(i,5)+ energy_3_4_power_e;
 energy_3_4_power_f = tec(i,6)+ energy_3_4_power_f;
 energy_3_4_power_g = tec(i,7)+ energy_3_4_power_g;
end

%Energy demand to move from the 4th stage to the 5th stage
energy_4_5_power_a = 0;
energy_4_5_power_b = 0;
energy_4_5_power_c = 0;
energy_4_5_power_d = 0;
energy_4_5_power_e = 0;
energy_4_5_power_f = 0;
energy_4_5_power_g = 0;

for i = (stage4+1):stage5
 energy_4_5_power_a = tec(i,1)+ energy_4_5_power_a;
 energy_4_5_power_b = tec(i,2)+ energy_4_5_power_b;
 energy_4_5_power_c = tec(i,3)+ energy_4_5_power_c;
 energy_4_5_power_d = tec(i,4)+ energy_4_5_power_d;
 energy_4_5_power_e = tec(i,5)+ energy_4_5_power_e;
 energy_4_5_power_f = tec(i,6)+ energy_4_5_power_f;
 energy_4_5_power_g = tec(i,7)+ energy_4_5_power_g;
end

%Energy demand to move from the 5th stage to the 6th stage
energy_5_6_power_a = 0;
energy_5_6_power_b = 0;
energy_5_6_power_c = 0;
```

```
energy_5_6_power_d = 0;
energy_5_6_power_e = 0;
energy_5_6_power_f = 0;
energy_5_6_power_g = 0;

for i = (stage5+1):stage6
 energy_5_6_power_a = tec(i,1)+ energy_5_6_power_a;
 energy_5_6_power_b = tec(i,2)+ energy_5_6_power_b;
 energy_5_6_power_c = tec(i,3)+ energy_5_6_power_c;
 energy_5_6_power_d = tec(i,4)+ energy_5_6_power_d;
 energy_5_6_power_e = tec(i,5)+ energy_5_6_power_e;
 energy_5_6_power_f = tec(i,6)+ energy_5_6_power_f;
 energy_5_6_power_g = tec(i,7)+ energy_5_6_power_g;
end

ant = zeros(36, 36);
%1st Stage
ant(1,2) = energy_1_2_power_a + BP(stage1,1);
ant(1,3) = energy_1_2_power_b + BP(stage1,2);
ant(1,4) = energy_1_2_power_c + BP(stage1,3);
ant(1,5) = energy_1_2_power_d + BP(stage1,4);
ant(1,6) = energy_1_2_power_e + BP(stage1,5);
ant(1,7) = energy_1_2_power_f + BP(stage1,6);
ant(1,8) = energy_1_2_power_g + BP(stage1,7);
%2nd Stage
ant(2,9) = energy_2_3_power_a;
ant(2,10) = energy_2_3_power_b + BP(stage2,2) - ...
remaining_value(stage2,1);
ant(2,11) = energy_2_3_power_c + BP(stage2,3) - ...
remaining_value(stage2,1);
ant(2,12) = energy_2_3_power_d + BP(stage2,4) - ...
 remaining_value(stage2,1);
ant(2,13) = energy_2_3_power_e + BP(stage2,5) - ...
 remaining_value(stage2,1);
ant(2,14) = energy_2_3_power_f + BP(stage2,6) - ...
 remaining_value(stage2,1);
ant(2,15) = energy_2_3_power_g + BP(stage2,7) - ...
 remaining_value(stage2,1);

ant(3,9) = energy_2_3_power_b + BP(stage2,1) - ...
 remaining_value(stage2,2);
ant(3,10) = energy_2_3_power_b;
ant(3,11) = energy_2_3_power_c + BP(stage2,3) - ...
 remaining_value(stage2,2);
ant(3,12) = energy_2_3_power_d + BP(stage2,4) - ...
 remaining_value(stage2,2);
ant(3,13) = energy_2_3_power_e + BP(stage2,5) - ...
 remaining_value(stage2,2);
```

```
ant(3,14) = energy_2_3_power_f + BP(stage2,6) - ...
 remaining_value(stage2,2);
ant(3,15) = energy_2_3_power_g + BP(stage2,7) - ...
 remaining_value(stage2,2);

ant(4,9) = energy_2_3_power_c + BP(stage2,1) - ...
 remaining_value(stage2,3);
ant(4,10) = energy_2_3_power_c + BP(stage2,2) - ...
 remaining_value(stage2,3);
ant(4,11) = energy_2_3_power_c;
ant(4,12) = energy_2_3_power_d + BP(stage2,4) - ...
 remaining_value(stage2,3);
ant(4,13) = energy_2_3_power_e + BP(stage2,5) - ...
 remaining_value(stage2,3);
ant(4,14) = energy_2_3_power_f + BP(stage2,6) - ...
 remaining_value(stage2,3);
ant(4,15) = energy_2_3_power_g + BP(stage2,7) - ...
 remaining_value(stage2,3);

ant(5,9) = energy_2_3_power_d + BP(stage2,1) - ...
 remaining_value(stage2,4);
ant(5,10) = energy_2_3_power_d + BP(stage2,2) - ...
 remaining_value(stage2,4);
ant(5,11) = energy_2_3_power_d + BP(stage2,3) - ...
 remaining_value(stage2,4);
ant(5,12) = energy_2_3_power_d;
ant(5,13) = energy_2_3_power_e + BP(stage2,5) - ...
 remaining_value(stage2,4);
ant(5,14) = energy_2_3_power_f + BP(stage2,6) - ...
 remaining_value(stage2,4);
ant(5,15) = energy_2_3_power_g + BP(stage2,7) - ...
 remaining_value(stage2,4);

ant(6,9) = energy_2_3_power_a + BP(stage2,1) - ...
 remaining_value(stage2,5);
ant(6,10) = energy_2_3_power_b + BP(stage2,2) - ...
 remaining_value(stage2,5);
ant(6,11) = energy_2_3_power_c + BP(stage2,3) - ...
 remaining_value(stage2,5);
ant(6,12) = energy_2_3_power_d + BP(stage2,4) - ...
 remaining_value(stage2,5);
ant(6,13) = energy_2_3_power_e;
ant(6,14) = energy_2_3_power_f + BP(stage2,6) - ...
 remaining_value(stage2,5);
ant(6,15) = energy_2_3_power_g + BP(stage2,7) - ...
 remaining_value(stage2,5);

ant(7,9) = energy_2_3_power_a + BP(stage2,1) - ...
```

```
 remaining_value(stage2,6);
ant(7,10) = energy_2_3_power_b + BP(stage2,2) - ...
 remaining_value(stage2,6);
ant(7,11) = energy_2_3_power_c + BP(stage2,3) - ...
 remaining_value(stage2,6);
ant(7,12) = energy_2_3_power_d + BP(stage2,4) - ...
 remaining_value(stage2,6);
ant(7,13) = energy_2_3_power_e + BP(stage2,5) - ...
 remaining_value(stage2,6);
ant(7,14) = energy_2_3_power_f;
ant(7,15) = energy_2_3_power_g + BP(stage2,7) - ...
 remaining_value(stage2,6);

ant(8,9) = energy_2_3_power_a + BP(stage2,1) - ...
 remaining_value(stage2,7);
ant(8,10) = energy_2_3_power_b + BP(stage2,2) - ...
 remaining_value(stage2,7);
ant(8,11) = energy_2_3_power_c + BP(stage2,3) - ...
 remaining_value(stage2,7);
ant(8,12) = energy_2_3_power_d + BP(stage2,4) - ...
 remaining_value(stage2,7);
ant(8,13) = energy_2_3_power_e + BP(stage2,5) - ...
 remaining_value(stage2,7);
ant(8,14) = energy_2_3_power_f + BP(stage2,6) - ...
 remaining_value(stage2,7);
ant(8,15) = energy_2_3_power_g ;

%3rd Stage
ant(9,16) = energy_3_4_power_a;
ant(9,17) = energy_3_4_power_b + BP(stage3,2) - ...
 remaining_value(stage3,1);
ant(9,18) = energy_3_4_power_c + BP(stage3,3) - ...
 remaining_value(stage3,1);
ant(9,19) = energy_3_4_power_d + BP(stage3,4) - ...
 remaining_value(stage3,1);
ant(9,20) = energy_3_4_power_e + BP(stage3,5) - ...
 remaining_value(stage3,1);
ant(9,21) = energy_3_4_power_f + BP(stage3,6) - ...
 remaining_value(stage3,1);
ant(9,22) = energy_3_4_power_g + BP(stage3,7) - ...
 remaining_value(stage3,1);

ant(10,16) = energy_3_4_power_b + BP(stage3,1) - ...
 remaining_value(stage3,2);
ant(10,17) = energy_3_4_power_b;
ant(10,18) = energy_3_4_power_c + BP(stage3,3) - ...
 remaining_value(stage3,2);
ant(10,19) = energy_3_4_power_d + BP(stage3,4) - ...
```

```
remaining_value(stage3,2);
ant(10,20) = energy_3_4_power_e + BP(stage3,5) - ...
remaining_value(stage3,2);
ant(10,21) = energy_3_4_power_f + BP(stage3,6) - ...
remaining_value(stage3,2);
ant(10,22) = energy_3_4_power_g + BP(stage3,7) - ...
remaining_value(stage3,2);

ant(11,16) = energy_3_4_power_c + BP(stage3,1) - ...
remaining_value(stage3,3);
ant(11,17) = energy_3_4_power_c + BP(stage3,2) - ...
remaining_value(stage3,3);
ant(11,18) = energy_3_4_power_c;
ant(11,19) = energy_3_4_power_d + BP(stage3,4) - ...
remaining_value(stage3,3);
ant(11,20) = energy_3_4_power_e + BP(stage3,5) - ...
remaining_value(stage3,3);
ant(11,21) = energy_3_4_power_f + BP(stage3,6) - ...
remaining_value(stage3,3);
ant(11,22) = energy_3_4_power_g + BP(stage3,7) - ...
remaining_value(stage3,3);

ant(12,16) = energy_3_4_power_d + BP(stage3,1) - ...
remaining_value(stage3,4);
ant(12,17) = energy_3_4_power_d + BP(stage3,2) - ...
remaining_value(stage3,4);
ant(12,18) = energy_3_4_power_d + BP(stage3,3) - ...
remaining_value(stage3,4);
ant(12,19) = energy_3_4_power_d;
ant(12,20) = energy_3_4_power_e + BP(stage3,5) - ...
remaining_value(stage3,4);
ant(12,21) = energy_3_4_power_f + BP(stage3,6) - ...
remaining_value(stage3,4);
ant(12,22) = energy_3_4_power_g + BP(stage3,7) - ...
remaining_value(stage3,4);

ant(13,16) = energy_3_4_power_a + BP(stage3,1) - ...
remaining_value(stage3,5);
ant(13,17) = energy_3_4_power_b + BP(stage3,2) - ...
remaining_value(stage3,5);
ant(13,18) = energy_3_4_power_c + BP(stage3,3) - ...
remaining_value(stage3,5);
ant(13,19) = energy_3_4_power_d + BP(stage3,4) - ...
remaining_value(stage3,5);
ant(13,20) = energy_3_4_power_e;
ant(13,21) = energy_3_4_power_f + BP(stage3,6) - ...
remaining_value(stage3,5);
ant(13,22) = energy_3_4_power_g + BP(stage3,7) - ...
```

```
remaining_value(stage3,5);

ant(14,16) = energy_3_4_power_a + BP(stage3,1) - ...
 remaining_value(stage3,6);
ant(14,17) = energy_3_4_power_b + BP(stage3,2) - ...
 remaining_value(stage3,6);
ant(14,18) = energy_3_4_power_c + BP(stage3,3) - ...
 remaining_value(stage3,6);
ant(14,19) = energy_3_4_power_d + BP(stage3,4) - ...
 remaining_value(stage3,6);
ant(14,20) = energy_3_4_power_e + BP(stage3,5) - ...
 remaining_value(stage3,6);
ant(14,21) = energy_3_4_power_f;
ant(14,22) = energy_3_4_power_g + BP(stage3,7) - ...
 remaining_value(stage3,6);

ant(15,16) = energy_3_4_power_a + BP(stage3,1) - ...
 remaining_value(stage3,7);
ant(15,17) = energy_3_4_power_b + BP(stage3,2) - ...
 remaining_value(stage3,7);
ant(15,18) = energy_3_4_power_c + BP(stage3,3) - ...
 remaining_value(stage3,7);
ant(15,19) = energy_3_4_power_d + BP(stage3,4) - ...
 remaining_value(stage3,7);
ant(15,20) = energy_3_4_power_e + BP(stage3,5) - ...
 remaining_value(stage3,7);
ant(15,21) = energy_3_4_power_f + BP(stage3,6) - ...
 remaining_value(stage3,7);
ant(15,22) = energy_3_4_power_g ;

%Stage 4
ant(16,23) = energy_4_5_power_a;
ant(16,24) = energy_4_5_power_b + BP(stage4,2) - ...
 remaining_value(stage4,1);
ant(16,25) = energy_4_5_power_c + BP(stage4,3) - ...
 remaining_value(stage4,1);
ant(16,26) = energy_4_5_power_d + BP(stage4,4) - ...
 remaining_value(stage4,1);
ant(16,27) = energy_4_5_power_e + BP(stage4,5) - ...
 remaining_value(stage4,1);
ant(16,28) = energy_4_5_power_f + BP(stage4,6) - ...
 remaining_value(stage4,1);
ant(16,29) = energy_4_5_power_g + BP(stage4,7) - ...
 remaining_value(stage4,1);

ant(17,23) = energy_4_5_power_b + BP(stage4,1) - ...
 remaining_value(stage4,2);
ant(17,24) = energy_4_5_power_b;
```

```
ant(17,25) = energy_4_5_power_c + BP(stage4,3) - ...
 remaining_value(stage4,2);
ant(17,26) = energy_4_5_power_d + BP(stage4,4) - ...
 remaining_value(stage4,2);
ant(17,27) = energy_4_5_power_e + BP(stage4,5) - ...
 remaining_value(stage4,2);
ant(17,28) = energy_4_5_power_f + BP(stage4,6) - ...
 remaining_value(stage4,2);
ant(17,29) = energy_4_5_power_g + BP(stage4,7) - ...
 remaining_value(stage4,2);

ant(18,23) = energy_4_5_power_c + BP(stage4,1) - ...
 remaining_value(stage4,3);
ant(18,24) = energy_4_5_power_c + BP(stage4,2) - ...
 remaining_value(stage4,3);
ant(18,25) = energy_4_5_power_c;
ant(18,26) = energy_4_5_power_d + BP(stage4,4) - ...
 remaining_value(stage4,3);
ant(18,27) = energy_4_5_power_e + BP(stage4,5) - ...
 remaining_value(stage4,3);
ant(18,28) = energy_4_5_power_f + BP(stage4,6) - ...
 remaining_value(stage4,3);
ant(18,29) = energy_4_5_power_g + BP(stage4,7) - ...
 remaining_value(stage4,3);

ant(19,23) = energy_4_5_power_d + BP(stage4,1) - ...
 remaining_value(stage4,4);
ant(19,24) = energy_4_5_power_d + BP(stage4,2) - ...
 remaining_value(stage4,4);
ant(19,25) = energy_4_5_power_d + BP(stage4,3) - ...
 remaining_value(stage4,4);
ant(19,26) = energy_4_5_power_d;
ant(19,27) = energy_4_5_power_e + BP(stage4,5) - ...
 remaining_value(stage4,4);
ant(19,28) = energy_4_5_power_f + BP(stage4,6) - ...
 remaining_value(stage4,4);
ant(19,29) = energy_4_5_power_g + BP(stage4,7) - ...
 remaining_value(stage4,4);

ant(20,23) = energy_4_5_power_a + BP(stage4,1) - ...
 remaining_value(stage4,5);
ant(20,24) = energy_4_5_power_b + BP(stage4,2) - ...
 remaining_value(stage4,5);
ant(20,25) = energy_4_5_power_c + BP(stage4,3) - ...
 remaining_value(stage4,5);
ant(20,26) = energy_4_5_power_d + BP(stage4,4) - ...
 remaining_value(stage4,5);
ant(20,27) = energy_4_5_power_e;
```

```
ant(20,28) = energy_4_5_power_f + BP(stage4,6) - ...
 remaining_value(stage4,5);
ant(20,29) = energy_4_5_power_g + BP(stage4,7) - ...
 remaining_value(stage4,5);

ant(21,23) = energy_4_5_power_a + BP(stage4,1) - ...
 remaining_value(stage4,6);
ant(21,24) = energy_4_5_power_b + BP(stage4,2) - ...
 remaining_value(stage4,6);
ant(21,25) = energy_4_5_power_c + BP(stage4,3) - ...
 remaining_value(stage4,6);
ant(21,26) = energy_4_5_power_d + BP(stage4,4) - ...
 remaining_value(stage4,6);
ant(21,27) = energy_4_5_power_e + BP(stage4,5) - ...
 remaining_value(stage4,6);
ant(21,28) = energy_4_5_power_f;
ant(21,29) = energy_4_5_power_g + BP(stage4,7) - ...
 remaining_value(stage4,6);

ant(22,23) = energy_4_5_power_a + BP(stage4,1) - ...
 remaining_value(stage4,7);
ant(22,24) = energy_4_5_power_b + BP(stage4,2) - ...
 remaining_value(stage4,7);
ant(22,25) = energy_4_5_power_c + BP(stage4,3) - ...
 remaining_value(stage4,7);
ant(22,26) = energy_4_5_power_d + BP(stage4,4) - ...
 remaining_value(stage4,7);
ant(22,27) = energy_4_5_power_e + BP(stage4,5) - ...
 remaining_value(stage4,7);
ant(22,28) = energy_4_5_power_f + BP(stage4,6) -  ...
remaining_value(stage4,7);
ant(22,29) = energy_4_5_power_g ;

%Stage 5
ant(23,30) = energy_5_6_power_a;
ant(23,31) = energy_5_6_power_b + BP(stage5,2) - ...
 remaining_value(stage5,1);
ant(23,32) = energy_5_6_power_c + BP(stage5,3) - ...
 remaining_value(stage5,1);
ant(23,33) = energy_5_6_power_d + BP(stage5,4) - ...
 remaining_value(stage5,1);
ant(23,34) = energy_5_6_power_e + BP(stage5,5) - ...
 remaining_value(stage5,1);
ant(23,35) = energy_5_6_power_f + BP(stage5,6) - ...
 remaining_value(stage5,1);
ant(23,36) = energy_5_6_power_g + BP(stage5,7) - ...
 remaining_value(stage5,1);
```

```
ant(24,30) = energy_5_6_power_b + BP(stage5,1) - ...
 remaining_value(stage5,2);
ant(24,31) = energy_5_6_power_b;
ant(24,32) = energy_5_6_power_c + BP(stage5,3) - ...
 remaining_value(stage5,2);
ant(24,33) = energy_5_6_power_d + BP(stage5,4) - ...
remaining_value(stage5,2);
ant(24,34) = energy_5_6_power_e + BP(stage5,5) - ...
 remaining_value(stage5,2);
ant(24,35) = energy_5_6_power_f + BP(stage5,6) - ...
 remaining_value(stage5,2);
ant(24,36) = energy_5_6_power_g + BP(stage5,7) - ...
 remaining_value(stage5,2);

ant(25,30) = energy_5_6_power_c + BP(stage5,1) - ...
 remaining_value(stage5,3);
ant(25,31) = energy_5_6_power_c + BP(stage5,2) - ...
 remaining_value(stage5,3);
ant(25,32) = energy_5_6_power_c;
ant(25,33) = energy_5_6_power_d + BP(stage5,4) - ...
 remaining_value(stage5,3);
ant(25,34) = energy_5_6_power_e + BP(stage5,5) - ...
 remaining_value(stage5,3);
ant(25,35) = energy_5_6_power_f + BP(stage5,6) - ...
 remaining_value(stage5,3);
ant(25,36) = energy_5_6_power_g + BP(stage5,7) - ...
 remaining_value(stage5,3);

ant(26,30) = energy_5_6_power_d + BP(stage5,1) - ...
 remaining_value(stage5,4);
ant(26,31) = energy_5_6_power_d + BP(stage5,2) - ...
 remaining_value(stage5,4);
ant(26,32) = energy_5_6_power_d + BP(stage5,3) - ...
 remaining_value(stage5,4);
ant(26,33) = energy_5_6_power_d;
ant(26,34) = energy_5_6_power_e + BP(stage5,5) - ...
 remaining_value(stage5,4);
ant(26,35) = energy_5_6_power_f + BP(stage5,6) - ...
 remaining_value(stage5,4);
ant(26,36) = energy_5_6_power_g + BP(stage5,7) - ...
 remaining_value(stage5,4);

ant(27,30) = energy_5_6_power_a + BP(stage5,1) - ...
 remaining_value(stage5,5);
ant(27,31) = energy_5_6_power_b + BP(stage5,2) - ...
 remaining_value(stage5,5);
ant(27,32) = energy_5_6_power_c + BP(stage5,3) - ...
 remaining_value(stage5,5);
```

```
ant(27,33) = energy_5_6_power_d + BP(stage5,4) - ...
 remaining_value(stage5,5);
ant(27,34) = energy_5_6_power_e;
ant(27,35) = energy_5_6_power_f + BP(stage5,6) - ...
 remaining_value(stage5,5);
ant(27,36) = energy_5_6_power_g + BP(stage5,7) - ...
 remaining_value(stage5,5);

ant(28,30) = energy_5_6_power_a + BP(stage5,1) - ...
 remaining_value(stage5,6);
ant(28,31) = energy_5_6_power_b + BP(stage5,2) - ...
 remaining_value(stage5,6);
ant(28,32) = energy_5_6_power_c + BP(stage5,3) - ...
 remaining_value(stage5,6);
ant(28,33) = energy_5_6_power_d + BP(stage5,4) - ...
 remaining_value(stage5,6);
ant(28,34) = energy_5_6_power_e + BP(stage5,5) - ...
 remaining_value(stage5,6);
ant(28,35) = energy_5_6_power_f;
ant(28,36) = energy_5_6_power_g + BP(stage5,7) - ...
 remaining_value(stage5,6);

ant(29,30) = energy_5_6_power_a + BP(stage5,1) - ...
 remaining_value(stage5,7);
ant(29,31) = energy_5_6_power_b + BP(stage5,2) - ...
 remaining_value(stage5,7);
ant(29,32) = energy_5_6_power_c + BP(stage5,3) - ...
 remaining_value(stage5,7);
ant(29,33) = energy_5_6_power_d + BP(stage5,4) - ...
 remaining_value(stage5,7);
ant(29,34) = energy_5_6_power_e + BP(stage5,5) - ...
 remaining_value(stage5,7);
ant(29,35) = energy_5_6_power_f + BP(stage5,6) - ...
 remaining_value(stage5,7);
ant(29,36) = energy_5_6_power_g ;

%copy the half matrix
ant(2,1) = ant(1,2);
ant(3,1) = ant(1,3);
ant(4,1) = ant(1,4);
ant(5,1) = ant(1,5);
ant(6,1) = ant(1,6);
ant(7,1) = ant(1,7);
ant(8,1) = ant(1,8);
%2nd Stage
ant(9,2) = ant(2,9);
ant(10,2) = ant(2,10);
ant(11,2) = ant(2,11);
```

```
ant(12,2) = ant(2,12);
ant(13,2) = ant(2,13);
ant(14,2) = ant(2,14);
ant(15,2) = ant(2,15);

ant(9,3) = ant(3,9);
ant(10,3) = ant(3,10);
ant(11,3) = ant(3,11);
ant(12,3) = ant(3,12);
ant(13,3) = ant(3,13);
ant(14,3) = ant(3,14);
ant(15,3) = ant(3,15);

ant(9,4) = ant(4,9);
ant(10,4) = ant(4,10);
ant(11,4) = ant(4,11);
ant(12,4) = ant(4,12);
ant(13,4) = ant(4,13);
ant(14,4) = ant(4,14);
ant(15,4) = ant(4,15);

ant(9,5) = ant(5,9);
ant(10,5) = ant(5,10);
ant(11,5) = ant(5,11);
ant(12,5) = ant(5,12);
ant(13,5) = ant(5,13);
ant(14,5) = ant(5,14);
ant(15,5) = ant(5,15);

ant(9,6) = ant(6,9);
ant(10,6) = ant(6,10);
ant(11,6) = ant(6,11);
ant(12,6) = ant(6,12);
ant(13,6) = ant(6,13);
ant(14,6) = ant(6,14);
ant(15,6) = ant(6,15);

ant(9,7) = ant(7,9);
ant(10,7) = ant(7,10);
ant(11,7) = ant(7,11);
ant(12,7) = ant(7,12);
ant(13,7) = ant(7,13);
ant(14,7) = ant(7,14);
ant(15,7) = ant(7,15);

ant(9,8) = ant(8,9);
ant(10,8) = ant(8,10);
ant(11,8) = ant(8,11);
```

```
ant(12,8) = ant(8,12);
ant(13,8) = ant(8,13);
ant(14,8) = ant(8,14);
ant(15,8) = ant(8,15);

%3rd Stage
ant(16,9) = ant(9,16);
ant(17,9) = ant(9,17);
ant(18,9) = ant(9,18);
ant(19,9) = ant(9,19);
ant(20,9) = ant(9,20);
ant(21,9) = ant(9,21);
ant(22,9) = ant(9,22);

ant(16,10) = ant(10,16);
ant(17,10) = ant(10,17);
ant(18,10) = ant(10,18);
ant(19,10) = ant(10,19);
ant(20,10) = ant(10,20);
ant(21,10) = ant(10,21);
ant(22,10) = ant(10,22);

ant(16,11) = ant(11,16);
ant(17,11) = ant(11,17);
ant(18,11) = ant(11,18);
ant(19,11) = ant(11,19);
ant(20,11) = ant(11,20);
ant(21,11) = ant(11,21);
ant(22,11) = ant(11,22);

ant(16,12) = ant(12,16);
ant(17,12) = ant(12,17);
ant(18,12) = ant(12,18);
ant(19,12) = ant(12,19);
ant(20,12) = ant(12,20);
ant(21,12) = ant(12,21);
ant(22,12) = ant(12,22);

ant(16,13) = ant(13,16);
ant(17,13) = ant(13,17);
ant(18,13) = ant(13,18);
ant(19,13) = ant(13,19);
ant(20,13) = ant(13,20);
ant(21,13) = ant(13,21);
ant(22,13) = ant(13,22);
ant(16,14) = ant(14,16);
ant(17,14) = ant(14,17);
ant(18,14) = ant(14,18);
```

```
ant(19,14) = ant(14,19);
ant(20,14) = ant(14,20);
ant(21,14) = ant(14,21);
ant(22,14) = ant(14,22);

ant(16,15) = ant(15,16);
ant(17,15) = ant(15,17);
ant(18,15) = ant(15,18);
ant(19,15) = ant(15,19);
ant(20,15) = ant(15,20);
ant(21,15) = ant(15,21);
ant(22,15) = ant(15,22);

%Stage 4
ant(23,16) = ant(16,23);
ant(24,16) = ant(16,24);
ant(25,16) = ant(16,25);
ant(26,16) = ant(16,26);
ant(27,16) = ant(16,27);
ant(28,16) = ant(16,28);
ant(29,16) = ant(16,29);
ant(23,17) = ant(17,23);
ant(24,17) = ant(17,24);
ant(25,17) = ant(17,25);
ant(26,17) = ant(17,26);
ant(27,17) = ant(17,27);
ant(28,17) = ant(17,28);
ant(29,17) = ant(17,29);

ant(23,18) = ant(18,23);
ant(24,18) = ant(18,24);
ant(25,18) = ant(18,25);
ant(26,18) = ant(18,26);
ant(27,18) = ant(18,27);
ant(28,18) = ant(18,28);
ant(29,18) = ant(18,29);

ant(23,19) = ant(19,23);
ant(24,19) = ant(19,24);
ant(25,19) = ant(19,25);
ant(26,19) = ant(19,26);
ant(27,19) = ant(19,27);
ant(28,19) = ant(19,28);
ant(29,19) = ant(19,29);
ant(23,20) = ant(20,23);
ant(24,20) = ant(20,24);
ant(25,20) = ant(20,25);
ant(26,20) = ant(20,26);
```

```
ant(27,20) = ant(20,27);
ant(28,20) = ant(20,28);
ant(29,20) = ant(20,29);

ant(23,21) = ant(21,23);
ant(24,21) = ant(21,24);
ant(25,21) = ant(21,25);
ant(26,21) = ant(21,26);
ant(27,21) = ant(21,27);
ant(28,21) = ant(21,28);
ant(29,21) = ant(21,29);
ant(23,22) = ant(22,23);
ant(24,22) = ant(22,24);
ant(25,22) = ant(22,25);
ant(26,22) = ant(22,26);
ant(27,22) = ant(22,27);
ant(28,22) = ant(22,28);
ant(29,22) = ant(22,29);

%Stage 5
ant(30,23) = ant(23,30);
ant(31,23) = ant(23,31);
ant(32,23) = ant(23,32);
ant(33,23) = ant(23,33);
ant(34,23) = ant(23,34);
ant(35,23) = ant(23,35);
ant(36,23) = ant(23,36);

ant(30,24) = ant(24,30);
ant(31,24) = ant(24,31);
ant(32,24) = ant(24,32);
ant(33,24) = ant(24,33);
ant(34,24) = ant(24,34);
ant(35,24) = ant(24,35);
ant(36,24) = ant(24,36);

ant(30,25) = ant(25,30);
ant(31,25) = ant(25,31);
ant(32,25) = ant(25,32);
ant(33,25) = ant(25,33);
ant(34,25) = ant(25,34);
ant(35,25) = ant(25,35);
ant(36,25) = ant(25,36);
ant(30,26) = ant(26,30);
ant(31,26) = ant(26,31);
ant(32,26) = ant(26,32);
ant(33,26) = ant(26,33);
ant(34,26) = ant(26,34);
```

```
ant(35,26) = ant(26,35);
ant(36,26) = ant(26,36);

ant(30,27) = ant(27,30);
ant(31,27) = ant(27,31);
ant(32,27) = ant(27,32);
ant(33,27) = ant(27,33);
ant(34,27) = ant(27,34);
ant(35,27) = ant(27,35);
ant(36,27) = ant(27,36);

ant(30,28) = ant(28,30);
ant(31,28) = ant(28,31);
ant(32,28) = ant(28,32);
ant(33,28) = ant(28,33);
ant(34,28) = ant(28,34);
ant(35,28) = ant(28,35);
ant(36,28) = ant(28,36);

ant(30,29) = ant(29,30);
ant(31,29) = ant(29,31);
ant(32,29) = ant(29,32);
ant(33,29) = ant(29,33);
ant(34,29) = ant(29,34);
ant(35,29) = ant(29,35);
ant(36,29) = ant(29,36);

%ACO: ant colony optimization for solving the optimal
%transformer sizing
                                        %Date: 1/07/2010
%inspired by the ACO code for the solution of the traveling salesman
% problem presented in [9]

%COMMENTS
%Changes that must be done based on stages
%1. In each stage you should define the id of the nodes
%2. For each stage you should add tha correct number of ifs' !!!
%3. Be very careful! --> You should create ifs' taking into account that
%e.g. node 4 must be connected with node 7 & 8 and not 6! and so
%on...

rand('state', sum(100*clock));
Nnode = 36; % number of nodes
Nstage = 6; % number of stages
Nants = 200; % number of ants

% node locations
xnode = [1 2 2 2 2   2 2 2 3 3 3 3 3 3 4 4 4 4 4 4 5 5 5 5 5 5 ...
```

```
 6 6 6 6 6 6 6];
ynode = [1 1 2 3 4 5 6 7 1 2 3 4 5 6 7 1 2 3 4 5 6 7 1 2 3 4 5 6 7 ...
 1 2 3 4 5 6 7];

vis = 1./ant; % visibility equals inverse of distance
phmone = .1 * ones(Nnode,Nnode); % initialized pheromones between
%nodes
maxit = 3000; % max number of iterations

a = 2; b = 0.5;

% rr - trail decay
rr = 0.5;

% Q - close to the lenght of the optimal tour
% CONSTANT FOR PHEROMONE UPDATING
Q = sum(1./(1:8));
dbest = 10^6;
e = Nstage;

% initialize tours
tour = zeros(Nants,Nstage);
tour(:,Nstage) = Nnode;
tour(:,1) = 1;

average_iteration = zeros(maxit,1);

% Ant colony optimization process
for it = 1:maxit
 for ia = 1:Nants
  for iq = 2:Nstage-1
   [iq tour(ia,:)];

   if iq == 2 %iq is the current number of stage, i.e. stage 2
    %the current node
    st = tour(ia,iq-1);
    % nxt contains the nodes to be visited at the current stage
    nxt = [2 3 4 5 6 7 8];
    prob =((phmone(st,nxt).^a).*(vis(st,nxt).^b))...
    /sum((phmone(st,nxt).^a).*(vis(st,nxt).^b));
    rnode = rand;
    for iz = 1:length(prob)
     if rnode < sum(prob(1:iz))
      newnode = iz; % next node to be visited
      break
     end % if
    end % iz
    tour(ia,iq) = nxt(1,newnode);
```

```
elseif iq == 3
st = tour(ia,iq-1);
nxt = [9 10 11 12 13 14 15];
prob =((phmone(st,nxt).^a).*(vis(st,nxt).^b))...
/sum((phmone(st,nxt).^a).*(vis(st,nxt).^b));
rnode = rand;
for iz = 1:length(prob)
 if rnode < sum(prob(1:iz))
  newnode = iz;
  break
 end % if
end % iz
tour(ia,iq) = nxt(1,newnode);

elseif iq == 4
st = tour(ia,iq-1);
nxt = [16 17 18 19 20 21 22];
prob =((phmone(st,nxt).^a).*(vis(st,nxt).^b))...
/sum((phmone(st,nxt).^a).*(vis(st,nxt).^b));
rnode = rand;
for iz = 1:length(prob)
 if rnode < sum(prob(1:iz))
  newnode = iz;
  break
 end % if
end % iz
tour(ia,iq) = nxt(1,newnode);

elseif iq == 5
st = tour(ia,iq-1);

nxt = [23 24 25 26 27 28 29];
prob =((phmone(st,nxt).^a).*(vis(st,nxt).^b))...
/sum((phmone(st,nxt).^a).*(vis(st,nxt).^b));
rnode = rand;
for iz = 1:length(prob)
 if rnode < sum(prob(1:iz))
  newnode = iz;
  break
 end % if
end % iz
tour(ia,iq) = nxt(1,newnode);

elseif iq == 6
st = tour(ia,iq-1);
nxt = [30 31 32 33 34 35 36];
prob =((phmone(st,nxt).^a).*(vis(st,nxt).^b))...
/sum((phmone(st,nxt).^a).*(vis(st,nxt).^b));
```

```
      rnode = rand;
      for iz = 1:length(prob)
       if rnode < sum(prob(1:iz))
        newnode = iz;
        break
       end % if
      end % iz
      tour(ia,iq) = nxt(1,newnode);
%     end
    end

   end % iq
  end % ia

  % calculate the length of each tour and pheromone distribution
  phtemp = zeros(Nnode,Nnode);

  dist = zeros(Nants,1);

  for ic = 1:Nants
   dist(ic,1) = 0;

   for id = 1:Nstage-1
    dist(ic,1) = dist(ic) + ant( tour(ic,id) , tour(ic,id+1) );
    phtemp( tour(ic,id) , tour(ic,id+1) ) = Q / dist(ic,1);
   end % id
  end % ic
  [dist,tour];
  [dmin,ind] = min(dist);

  if dmin < dbest
   dbest = dmin;
  end % if

  % pheromone for elite path
  ph1 = zeros(Nnode,Nnode);

  for id = 1:Nstage-1
   ph1( tour(ind,id),tour(ind,id+1) ) = Q / dbest;
  end % id

  % update pheromone trails
  phmone = (1 - rr) * phmone + phtemp + e * ph1;
  dd = zeros(it,2);
  dd(it,:) = [dbest dmin];
  [it dmin dbest];
   %keep the average solution of each iteration
  average_iteration(it,1)= sum(dist)/Nants;
```

```
end %it

colordef none
whitebg('white');
[tour,dist];
figure(1)
plot(xnode(tour(ind,:)),ynode(tour(ind,:)),xnode,ynode,'o')

figure(2)

%creates the figure which shows the convergence history of
%the total transformer cost

line('xdata',1:maxit,'ydata',average_iteration(1:it,1),'markersize',6, ...
 'erasemode','none','Color',[.2 .4 .8]);
axis auto
colordef none
whitebg('white');
title('Convergence history')
xlabel('Iterations')
ylabel('Average best solution')
drawnow

%Conventional_cost is the cost of the strategy that is followed by the
%electric utility
Conventional_cost = ant(1,2) + ant(2,9) + ant(9,16) + ...
 ant(16,23) + ant(23,30) %it has to be changed according to the path
%that corresponds to installation of the transformer with the lowest bid
%price from the first year of the study

%best_cost is the cost of the strategy that is produced by the
%proposed methodology
best_cost = min(dist)
```

The execution of the above algorithm yields the optimum path for Type 8 substation and the convergence history, depicted in the following figures. It must be noted, that due to the stochastic nature of ACO, different executions of the algorithm may result to different optimal paths. It is therefore recommended to run the algorithm more than once and observe the difference in the optimal costs that derive. The increase of the number of ants as well as the variation of parameters $a$, $\beta$ and $\rho$ are also recommended as a strategy to obtain the global optimum to the optimal transformer efficiency selection problem.

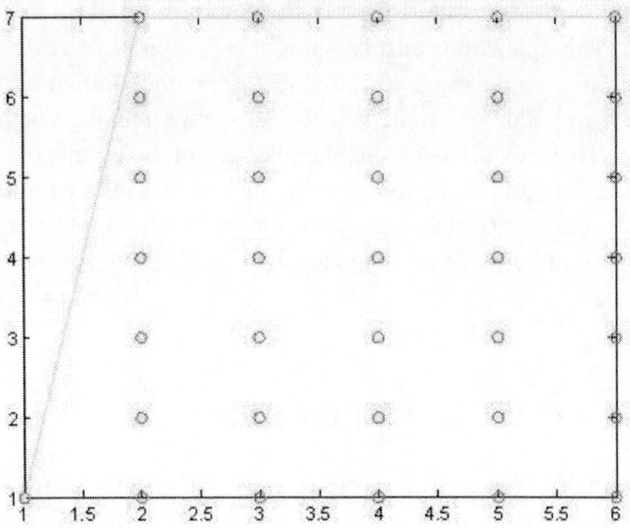


Figure 17. The least cost path derived by the execution of the matlab code

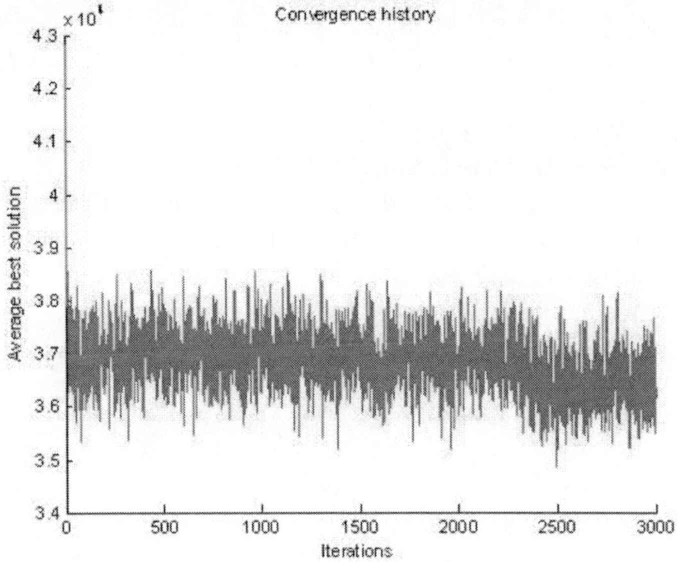


Figure 18. The convergence history graph derived by the execution of the matlab code

# 9. CONCLUSIONS

In this chapter, an EAS algorithm is proposed for the solution of the OTS planning problem by minimizing the overall transformer cost (i.e., the sum of the transformer purchasing cost plus the transformer energy loss cost) over the planning period, while satisfying all the problem constraints (i.e., the load to be served and the transformer thermal loading limit). The method is applied for the selection of the optimal size of the distribution transformers in a real network, comprising 16 distribution substations to serve a load over a period of 30 years. The application results show that the proposed EAS algorithm is very efficient because it always converges to the global optimum solution of the OTS problem. Moreover, the EAS algorithm is applied to the substations of the above network for the optimal transformer efficiency selection, i.e. the selection of the efficiency of the transformers to be installed in the network, so as to optimize the total installation and energy loss cost. Significant cost benefits up to 50% can be achieved by the application of the proposed method, indicating its importance and applicability to distribution network planning and optimization problems.

## REFERENCES

[1] Chen, C. S. & Wu, T. H. (1998). Optimal distribution transformer sizing by dynamic programming. *Electrical Power & Energy Systems*, *20*, 161-167.

[2] Jovanovic, D. (2003). Planning of optimal location and sizes of distribution transformers using integer programming. *Electrical Power & Energy Systems*, *25*, 717-723.

[3] Robinson, M., Wallace, S., Woodward, D. & Engstrom, G. (2006). US Navy power transformer sizing requirements using probabilistic analysis. *Journal of Ship Production*, *22*, 212-218.

[4] Dorigo, M. (1992). Optimization, learning and natural algorithms. Ph.D. Thesis (in Italian), *Politechnico de Milano*, Milan, Italy.

[5] Dorigo, M. & Stützle, T. (2004). *Ant colony optimization*. MIT Press.

[6] Dorigo, M., Maniezzo, V. & Colorni, A. (1996). Ant system: optimization by a colony of cooperating agents. *IEEE Transactions on Systems, Man, and Cybernetics-Part B*, *26*, 29-41.

[7] Goss, S., Aron, S., Deneubourg, J. L. & Pasteels, J. M. (1989). Self-organized shortcuts in the argentine Ant. *Naturwissenschaften*, *76*.

[8] Stützle, T., Hoos, H. H. (2000). MAX-MIN Ant system. *Future Generation Computer Systems*, *16*, 889-914.

[9] Haupt, R. L. & Haupt, S. E. (2004). Practical Genetic *Algorithms. Wiley-Interscience*.

[10] Maniezzo, V. (1999). Exact and approximate nondeterministic tree-search procedures for the quadratic assignment problem. INFORMS *Journal on Computing*, *11*, 358-369.

[11] Merkle, D., Middendorf, M. & Schmeck, H. (2002). Ant colony optimization for resource-constrained project scheduling. *IEEE Transactions on Evolutionary Computation*, *6*, 333-346.

[12] Chang, C. S., Tian, L. & Wen, F. S. (1999). A new approach to fault section estimation in power systems using Ant system. *Electric Power Systems Research*, *49*, 63–70.

[13] Tong, C. J., Lau, H. C. & Lim, A. (1999). *Ant colony optimization for the ship berthing problem*. P.S. Thiagarajan, R. Yap (Eds.): ASIAN'99, LNCS 1742, Springer-Verlag Berlin Heidelberg, 359-370.

[14] Leguizamon, G. & Michalewicz, Z. (1999). A new version of ant system for subset problems. In Proc. of the 1999 *Congress on Evolutionary Computation*, *2*, 1459-1464.

[15] Yu, I. K., Chou, C. S. & Song, Y. H. (1998). Application of the ant colony search

algorithm to short-term generation scheduling problem of thermal units. *In Proc. Int. Conf. Power Syst. Tech.*, *1*, 552-556.

[16] Huang, S. J. (2001). Enhancement of hydroelectric generation scheduling using ant colony system based optimization approaches. *IEEE Trans. Energy Conver.*, *16*, 296–301.

[17] Song, Y. H., Chou, C. S. & Stonham, T. J. (1999). Combined heat and power economic dispatch by improved ant colony search algorithm. *Electric Power Systems Research*, *52*, 115-121.

[18] Teng, J. H., Liu, Y. H. (2003). A novel ACS-based optimum switch relocation method. *IEEE Trans. Power Syst.*, *18*, 113-120.

[19] Jeon, Y. J., Kim, J. C., Yun, S. Y. & Lee, K. Y. (2003). Application of ant colony algorithm for network reconfiguration in distribution systems. *In Proc. Symp. Power Plants Power Syst. Control*, 266-271.

[20] Vlachogiannis, J. G., Hatziargyriou, N. D. & Lee, K. Y. (2005). Ant colony system-based algorithm for constrained load flow problem. *IEEE Trans. on Power Systems, 20*, 1241-1249.

[21] Blum, C. (2005). Ant colony optimization: introduction and recent trends. *Physics of Life Reviews*, *2*, 353-373.

[22] Amoiralis, E. I., Tsili, M. A., Georgilakis, P. S. & Kladas, A. G. (2007). Ant colony colution to optimal transformer sizing problem. *CD Proc. of Electrical Power Quality and Utilisation.*

[23] IEEE Guide for Loading Mineral-Oil-Immersed Transformers, *IEEE Std* C57.91, 2002.

[24] Heunis, S. W., Herman, R. (2004). A thermal loading guide for residential distribution transformers based on time-variant current load models. *IEEE Trans. Power Syst.*, *19*, 1294-1298

[25] Schneider, K. & Hoad, R. (1992). Initial transformer sizing for single-phase residential Load. *IEEE Trans. Power Delivery*, *7*, 2074-2081.

[26] Bonabeau, E., Dorigo , M. & Theraulaz, G. (1999). *Swarm intelligence from natural to artificial systems,* Oxford University Press, New York.

[27] Amoiralis, E. I., Georgilakis, P. S., Tsili, M. A. & Kladas, A. G. (2010). Ant Colony Optimisation solution to distribution transformer planning problem. *Int. J. Advanced Intelligence Paradigms.*

[28] Amoiralis, E. I., Georgilakis, P. S., Tsili, M. A. & Kladas, A. G. (2008). Ant Colony System-Based Algorithm for Optimal Multi-Stage Planning of Distribution Transformer Sizing, Lecture Notes in Computer Science, Springer-Verlag, *Part II, LNAI*, *5178*, 9-17.

[29] Haggerty, N., Malone, T., Crouse, J. (1998). Applying high efficiency transformers. *IEEE Industry Applications Magazine*, *4*, 50-56.

In: Ant Colonies
Editor: Emily C. Sun
ISBN: 978-1-61122-023-0


*Chapter 3*

# DISTRIBUTED DECISIONS: NEW INSIGHTS FROM RADIO-TAGGED ANTS

***Elva J. H. Robinson[1] and Wlodek Mandecki[2]***
[1] York Centre for Complex Systems Analysis and Department of Biology, University of York, UK
[2] PharmaSeq, Inc., New Jersey, USA

## ABSTRACT

Ant colonies have been used as model systems for the study of self-organisation. Viewing ants as identical agents following simple rules has led to many insights into the emergence of complex behaviours. However, real biological ants are far from identical in behaviour. New advances in radio-frequency identification (RFID) technology now allow the exploration of ant behaviour at the individual level, providing unprecedented insights into distributed decision-making. Two areas of decision-making have been addressed with this new technology: 1) Individual task decisions in a changing environment; 2) Collective decision-making during colony emigration. The first of these areas investigates how tasks are robustly distributed between members of a colony in the face of changing environmental conditions. The use of RFID tags on worker ants allows simultaneous monitoring of a range of factors which could affect decision-making, including age, experience, spatial location, social interactions and fat reserves. These multifactor studies have demonstrated that individual ants base some task decisions on their own physiological state, but also utilise social cues. For non-specialist tasks, self-organisation also contributes because movement patterns can cause emergent task allocation. The combination of these simple mechanisms provides the colony as a whole with a responsive work-force, appropriately allocated across tasks but flexible in response to changing environmental conditions. The second area of distributed decision-making which has benefitted from the use of RFID is the study of unanimous collective decision-making during colony emigration. RFID microtransponder tags are used to identify the ants involved in collecting information about the environment and to determine how their actions lead to the final colony-level decision. The studies using RFID technology demonstrate that ants use a very simple threshold rule to make their individual decisions; from these individual decisions emerges a sophisticated choice mechanism at the colony level. Inter-individual variation in thresholds is critical for this to be an effective decision mechanism in an unpredictable environment, so the collection of individual-level data is essential. This provides interesting insights for anyone trying to combine inputs from distributed sensors to determine a single computer action. In general, the decentralised robustness exemplified by both decision-making processes provides a benchmark for studying behaviour of other animal populations, as well having implications in designing decision-making algorithms.

## INTRODUCTION

### Distributed Decisions: Ants as a Model System

Among social animals, an individual's behaviour is determined both by its own priorities and information and also by its interactions with other members of the group. Collective behaviour occurs when groups of individuals act in a coordinated manner. In some cases a single dominant individual can determine group decisions through centralised control, for example the matriarch of a group of elephants initiating a group departure [1]. In most animal groups however, decisions about where the group will go and what it will do are distributed among many individuals or even spread across the entire group [2]. When distributed decisions are made, the contributing individuals may have differing information and differing priorities, posing challenges to collective decision-making.

Ant colonies, and other social insects, make a good model system for studying distributed decision-making because in general the differences in priorities between the individuals are small [3]. The reproductive unit is the colony, so the colony members usually share the aim of maximising colony fitness. The collective behaviour of the group is based on the simple decisions made by individuals. In case study 1 we explore how individual decisions can lead to a robust colony-wide system of division of labour. In case study 2 we show how individual decisions can interact and combine to produce a single collective action. Although the colony members share the same overall priorities, information may be very unevenly distributed across a colony, so conflicts over decision-making can still arise. In addition, while viewing ants as identical agents following simple rules has led to many insights into the emergence of complex behaviours [4], real biological ants vary in behaviour. To understand distributed decisions, we must identify the rules followed by individual members and must take into account the variation between members of a group, both in terms of information available to them and in how they act on that information. In order to do this, some means of reliably identifying the individuals is required. Radio-frequency identification technology provides an ideal solution to this problem.

### The Role of RFID Technology

Radio-frequency identification (RFID) technology allows the unique identification of large numbers of individuals. Previous methods of uniquely identifying social insects such as ants have been primarily visual, using coloured/numbered labels [5, 6], finely knotted wires [7, 8], or combinations of paint dots [9-12]. These visual methods have been used successfully in many studies, however to access the individual identity information requires a labour-intensive process (whether done by a computer or manually) to decode the visual data. For large colonies and long-term studies these methods become impractical. RFID technology directly supplies the ID of the individual studied, avoiding a time-consuming and error-prone decoding process.

RFID technology provides data on the identity of an individual in a particular place at a certain time. The position of the individual can be inferred either by its proximity to a RFID reader or by using several readers to pinpoint a 3D location, and the time of detection can be recorded automatically along with the identity. "Active" RFID tags include their own power source and can be read hundreds of metres away [13]. The weight of the batteries means that these tags are most suited to large animals. They have been used in many ecological studies of animal migration, territory use and foraging patterns [14-16]. "Passive" RFID tags do not carry their own power source, but get the power they need from the reader. They can therefore be smaller and lighter. One commonly used system is the PIT (passive integrated transponder) tag, which gets the power it needs from the radio signal it receives and uses this energy to transmit a "backscatter" signal carrying the unique ID code. Passive RFID systems have been widely used for tagging commercial fish stocks [17] and have also been used successfully in behavioural studies, for example in small mammals [18, 19] and large social insects such as bumble-bees and paper wasps [20, 21].

The new advances in radio-frequency identification (RFID) technology we describe below have provided tiny passive radio tags small enough to use on ants. This technology allows detailed exploration of ant behaviour at the individual level. By supplying the ID codes of the ants direct to the computer the system avoids the labour-intensive decoding process required for visual methods of ant marking. The individual-level data collected has provided unprecedented insights into distributed decision-making.

## METHODOLOGY

### RFID Technology

PharmaSeq has developed a unique, low cost RFID system based on light-powered microtransponders. The system also includes a reader for determining the IDs of the microtransponders together with software and a computer. In addition to its use for studying the social habits of ants, the system has been used in several applications where the small size and weight of the chip, plus low cost are key: in DNA and protein diagnostic assays [22, 23], cell assays [24], and for tagging laboratory mice [25, 26].

***Design and properties of microtransponder.*** The current PharmaSeq microtransponder (commercially called a "p-Chip") is a monolithic 500 × 500 x 100 μm integrated circuit chip that can transmit its pre-programmed identification code via radio frequency (RF). It is composed of photocells, a clock recovery circuit, a memory sequencer, logic circuits, an antenna with current driver, and memory (ROM) that stores its serial number (Figure 1a). The photocells, when illuminated, provide power to the circuitry on the chip. A loop antenna transmits the ID data via a variable magnetic field by modulating the current in the antenna.

The modulation state, and thus the current in the antenna, are dependent on the logical state of the individual bits being transmitted. The transmission bit rate is controlled by the pulse rate (on-off modulation) of the illuminating laser, which is typically operated at 1 MHz. The signal is intercepted by a nearby coil/receiver set and decoded to determine the ID. Microtransponders contain only an ID number; all other information related to the tagged specimen is contained in a database on the computer. The current design utilizes 10 bits to encode the ID, allowing 1,024 possible numbers. However, a new chip design is anticipated that will provide coding in the ROM for 30 bits, so that microtransponders will be manufactured to have as many as $2^{30}$ (approx. $10^9$) unique ID values.

Microtransponders are made with standard digital CMOS processes used in manufacturing of memory chips and computer processors. Post-processing of wafers involves backgrinding (thinning) and dicing of the wafers into individual chips. The chip surface is made of silicon dioxide, which is deposited during the electronic manufacturing process as a final passivation layer.

The stability of the RF transmitting functions of microtransponders has been tested by exposing them to a wide variety of aqueous solutions and solvents. The results showed that the microtransponders are very stable in most aqueous solutions (half-life > 4 days), moderately stable in basic solutions (half-life of about 1 day) and very stable in all of the organic solvents tested. In addition, the chips have excellent temperature stability. One hundred percent of chips incubated at up to 520°C for 8 h retained full RF activity (sample size: 100 chips). The chips have a lifetime of many years at room temperature or lower (-20°C and -80°C were tested).

***ID reader.*** The ID reader ('wand') is a hand-held device capable of reading the ID of individual microtransponders. The diagram showing the internal components is provided in Figure 2a, the specifications are presented in Figure 2b and a photograph of the ID reader is shown in Figure 2c. The wand is USB-powered and contains a USB 2.0 microcontroller, an FPGA, power regulators, a laser diode and a programmable laser current driver, an optical focusing module and an air coil pickup with an RF receiver/data slicer. The wand contains a Class 3R laser, emitting an average of 60mW of optical power at 658 nm. The ID is read when the microtransponder is placed within suitable proximity of the laser beam. The light is pulsed at 1 MHz (50% duty cycle); this pulse rate provides the data clock used by the microtransponder for synchronization of the transmitted ID data bits. The resulting ID readout from the chip is rapid (less than 0.01 sec). The timing of the pulse groups are set so that the duty cycles and average power levels fall within requirements for registration as a Class 3R laser device, meaning that protective eyewear is not necessary.

Software processes the ID readings received from the wand using an error-checking decode algorithm, with errors undetectable in $10^6$ ID reads, and stores them, along with a log of activities, in an MS SQL database or other type of file specified by the user. The available software includes DLL and LabView application programming interfaces. Exporting data directly to MS Excel is also an option.

***Advantages of providing power to microtransponders by light versus RF.*** Conventional passive RFID tags harvest power from the driving RF signal using antenna coils measuring many centimetres in diameter typically. These result in up to approximately 1% efficiency of power transfer to the tag. In the case of those RFID methods that do not use such a large external antenna, the antenna efficiency drops by orders of magnitude, severely curtailing range and efficacy. Light energy harvested by photodiodes in the PharmaSeq microtransponder returns approximately 10% efficiency in transfer. The optical power level is not bound by the same RF radiated power emissions limits set by the regulatory agencies as are the RF emitters associated with traditional RFID. Furthermore, the PharmaSeq microtransponder actually actively radiates a signal much like a small radio transmitter, as opposed to the passive backscatter method employed by passive RFID. Thus, because light-powered transponders use energy more efficiently, they can achieve greater transmission ranges with a smaller antenna and thus a smaller overall system. The wand will reliably read microtransponders under a wide variety of challenging conditions such as through clear 2 mm thick glass, 1 mm thick blue-coloured glass, a sheet of white paper or a banknote, within a cavity in a steel surgical instrument and many others. In contrast with traditional RF tags, an additional benefit of using a collimated beam of light to activate the chips is the selectivity, i.e. the ability to direct illumination onto one chip only and to achieve specificity of physical addressing.

(a)

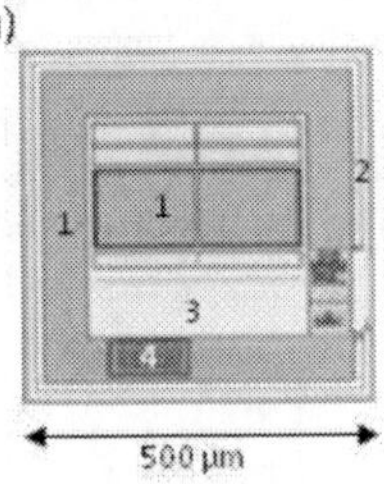


(b)

| | |
|---|---|
| Nominal dimensions of chip | 500x500x100 microns |
| Chip dimensions after dicing | 600x600x100 microns |
| Weight | 85 µg |
| Material | Silicon |
| Manufacturing process | CMOS |
| Number of ID codes | 1,024 (current)<br>$10^9$ (planned) |
| Analog RF signal | 1 MHz |
| Wavelength of laser light | 658 nm |
| Nominal cycle time[1] | 512 µs |
| Maximum read distance | 4 mm |

Figure 1. Microtransponder design. (a): Picture of a microtransponder. Key elements are 1: photocells; 2: antenna; 3: logic; 4: memory. (b): Specifications for the microtransponder. [1]Time required for one complete transmission of microtransponder memory contents

(a)

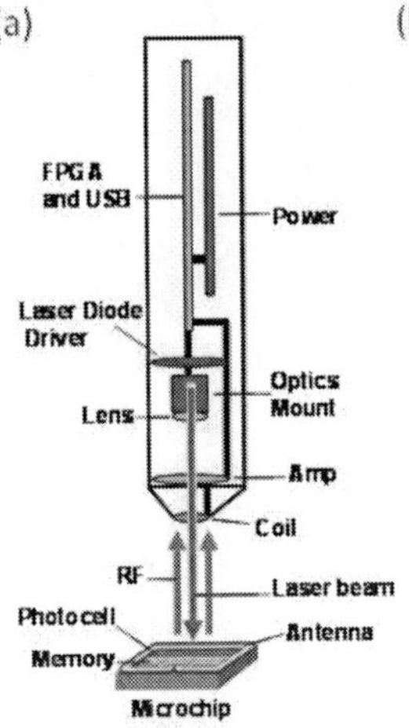


(b)

| | |
|---|---|
| Length | 175 mm |
| Diameter | 28 mm |
| Weight | 130 g |
| Laser power, average | 60 mW |
| Laser power, standby mode | 5 mW |
| Laser device class | 3R |
| Maximum read distance | 4 mm |
| Read time | <5 msec |
| Laser modulation frequency | 1 MHz |
| ID read error rate | Undetectable<br>(<<1 per $10^6$ ID reads) |
| Computer requirement | PC with Windows XP, Vista or 7 |
| Computer connection | USB |

(c)

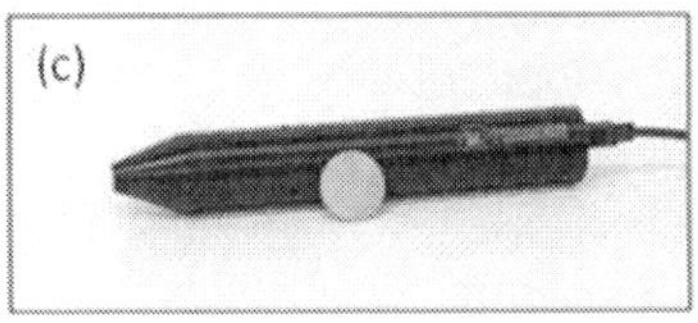

Figure 2. ID reader and workstation for reading IDs. (a) Design of the ID reader. (b) Specifications for a wand. (c) ID reader compared to the size of a U.S. quarter. Parts a and c reproduced from [25] with permission from AALAS

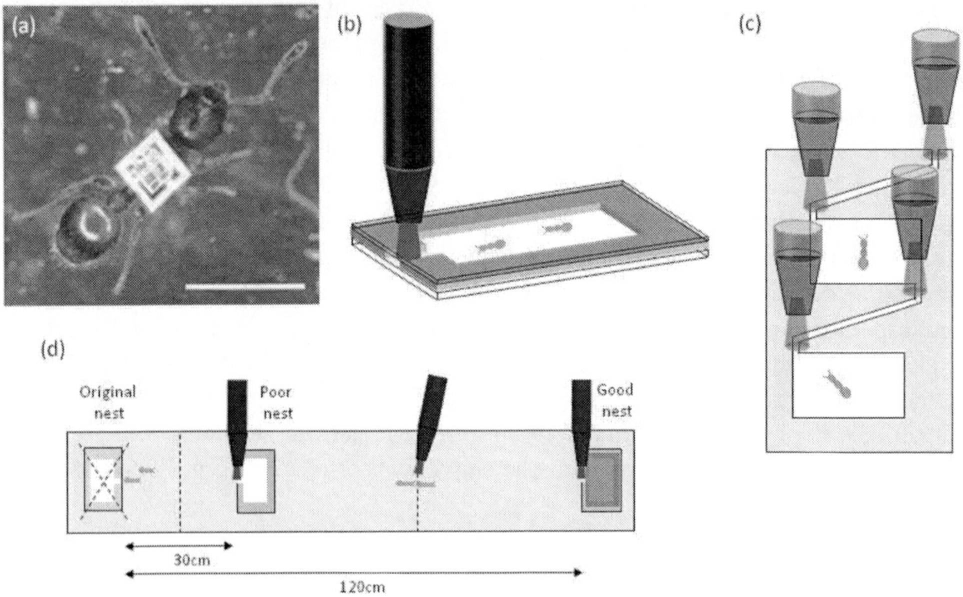


Figure 3. RFID applied to ants. (a). Radio-tagged *T. albipennis* worker. Scale bar 1mm. Photograph by N. R. Franks. (b). RFID reader over entrance to artificial ant nest (not to scale). (c) Two chamber nest used in case study 1 with two readers over each corridor. (d) Arena used for emigration experiments in case study 2. Original nest has been destroyed. Readers are located over the new nest entrances, and are also used to identify tandem running ants. Parts a and d modified with permission from [32].

## Application to Ants

The PharmaSeq RFID system has been successfully applied to the rock ant *Temnothorax albipennis* (Figure 3). This species lives in crevices in rocks and naturally forms colonies of around 100-200 individuals [27], making it possible to tag every worker in a colony and thus collect a complete behavioural dataset. For the experiments described in the two case studies, complete colonies were collected from the Dorset coast, UK, and housed in the laboratory in artificial 'crevice' nests formed of two microscope slides separated by a cardboard ring, with a single entrance corridor cut in the cardboard. Colonies were provided with water, honey solution and dead *Drosphila*.

RFID tags (microtransponders) can be glued (using Araldite Rapid™ epoxy adhesive) onto the ant's thorax under a microscope, after briefly anaesthetising the ant with carbon dioxide to immobilise it. After the RFID tag is attached, the ant must be isolated for around 3 hours. This allows the ant's natural cuticular hydrocarbons to start to cover the glue and RFID tag, reducing the amount of attention nestmates pay to the presence of the tag, and prevents nestmates from removing the tag before the glue has hardened fully. The thorax is chosen for affixing the tag because this locates the tag above the ant's centre of gravity and because, unlike the gaster, the thorax does not expand and contract as the ant feeds or uses up reserves. To tag an entire colony, the nest is opened and the workers are removed, tagged and isolated one by one. The brood is not left unattended, because the first ants to be tagged are ready to be released before the last are removed. Once all ants have been tagged, a new nest is provided and the tagged ants then relocate the brood into their new home.

*T. albipennis* workers have a mean fresh weight of 0.30mg, so an RFID microtransponder weighs around 30% of their body weight (Figure 1b). Although this initially seems a high proportion, these ants readily transport each other, and ants can carry many times their own body weight [28, 29]. The presence of the microtransponder does not have any detectable effects on the ants' speed of movement or directness of path [30], and does not appear to affect mortality. In fact, two *T. albipennis* workers tagged in January 2007 are still alive and active over 3 years later (EJHR, pers. obs. June 2010).

This species naturally has relatively two-dimensional nest geometry, making it an ideal subject for the RFID system. Readers can be fixed over certain points, e.g. the nest entrance or corridors between chambers in the nest, and the ants can be identified as they pass from one location to another [30]. *T. albipennis* workers are 2-3mm long with a head width of 0.5mm, so the microtransponder has a similar width to the ant (Figure 3a). This is ideal for maximising microtransponder detection because the RFID reader wand can be positioned over a corridor just wide enough for one ant and the microtransponder must then pass directly under the reader (Figure 3b).This detection method can be used to identify the ants entering and leaving nests or certain chambers within a sub-divided nest (Figure 3c). Using two readers above a corridor provides directional information (Figure 3c). In addition, the readers can also be moved over the surface of the nest to scan the ants present in certain areas [31] or can be hand-held to scan directly the identities of ants engaged in a specific behaviour (Figure 1d) [32]. The ants do not seem to react to the proximity of the reader, probably because the laser light is 658nm and therefore falls outside the visual range of ants (typically around 350-550nm) [33].

## DISTRIBUTED DECISIONS

### Case Study 1: Task-Allocation

Social insect colonies show impressive levels of division of labour in which certain individuals specialise on certain tasks. The benefits of division of labour identified by Adam Smith in 1776 [34], include specialisation (improvements through practice) and spatial efficiency (time is not wasted moving from one job to the next). These benefits apply to ant colonies as much as to human societies [35]. In human societies, division of labour may be organised in a 'top-down' fashion, for example with a foreman directing his workforce to different tasks. In ants there is no centralised control and yet the workers must be allocated appropriately across the different tasks, e.g. foraging, brood care and nest maintenance. Furthermore, this task allocation process must be flexible and robust in the face of changes in demand for particular tasks. The decisions regarding task allocation are distributed across the colony and the implementation of these decisions is also distributed through the individual ants' responses to perceived changes. This individually flexible behaviour provides the colony as a whole with an effective and robust system of workforce allocation.

The organisation of work in social insects is usually modelled as a threshold-based system, where individuals perform a task if the stimulus for performing that task exceeds their threshold for that task [36, 37]. Division of labour arises when individuals differ in their threshold or in the stimulus they experience. Intrinsic differences between individuals in their threshold can arise from differences in genotype [38], size [39], physiology [40], age [36] or experience [6]. Some of these differences can be flexible (e.g. physiology) while others are fixed (e.g. adult size). Differing levels of stimulus can be experienced because of an individual's spatial location [41] or their social interactions [42]. The effects of many of these factors have been studied in isolation, but using the RFID system allows simultaneous monitoring of a range of factors which could affect decision-making. Size is unlikely to be an important predictor in *T. albipennis*, because the workers are monomorphic [43]. Also, colonies are relatively genetically uniform as they are usually monogynous and monoandrous [27, 44]. The most important factors are therefore likely to be: age, physiology, experience, spatial factors and social interaction.

Foraging in an essential task for every colony, and it is interesting because it represents a division between individuals which stay in the safety of the nest and those which take the risky decision to go outside. There is clear specialisation in foraging in *T. albipennis* (Figure 4), with some workers making no trips outside the nest and others making many.

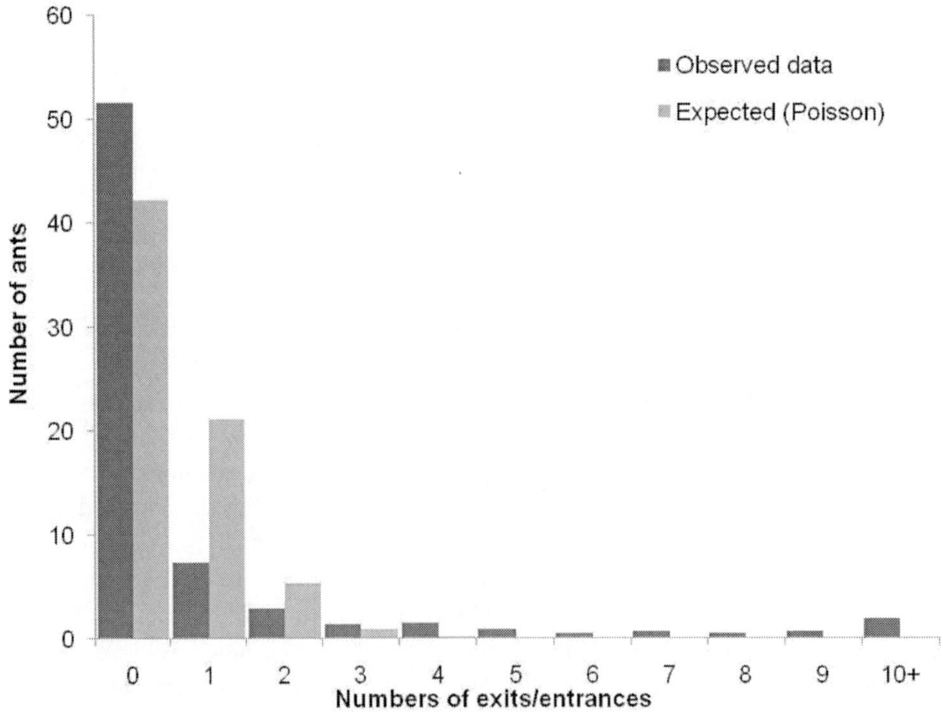


Figure 4. Foraging activity distribution. Distribution of trips outside the nest, observed data mean across 5 colonies. Observed data are significantly more skewed towards some ants making a very high number of exits than the distribution that would be generated if decisions to exit were made at random (Poisson distribution) [30]

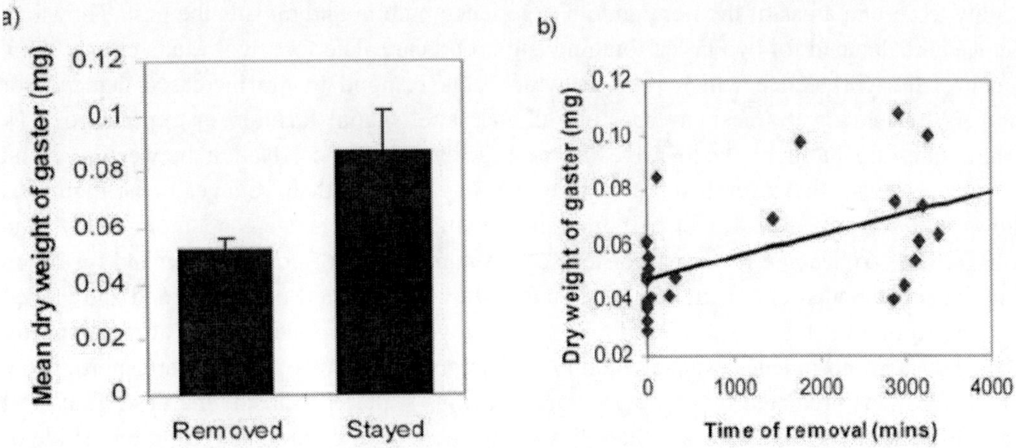


Figure 5. Corpulence and foraging propensity. a) Corpulence of ants which left the nest and were removed versus those that stayed in the nest, mean across five colonies +SD. b) Change in corpulence of ants leaving the nest against removal time, data from one sample colony. Corpulence is significantly higher among ants that stayed in the nest, and increases significantly during the removal period [30]

Robinson et al. [30] collected data on experience, physiology and social interactions, and tested how well these predicted an ant's decision to leave the nest to forage. For each ant, experience was based on that ant's number of previous trips outside the nest, physiology on the ant's corpulence (fat stores) and social interactions on the number of nest-mates returning to the nest prior to the focal ant's departure. The best predictors were social interactions and corpulence, with ants being more likely to leave the nest if they were lean and if many nest-mates had just returned. This fits well with the threshold-stimulus model, suggesting that the ants could use a corpulence threshold to determine how likely they are to leave the nest, and this could interact with stimulus from returning nestmates which activate other ants to leave. This leads to foraging occurring in bouts [30]. Robinson et al. [30] then tested what would happen in the absence of any returning ants. Since no ants return to the nest, no food is coming in, so we would expect a steady increase in demand for food, e.g. brood hunger signalling. The threshold model predicts that as the stimulus increases over time, higher threshold ants should be stimulated to leave the nest, leading to an increase in the corpulence of ants that leave the nest over time, and a significant difference between the corpulence of those that leave and those that stay. This is exactly what is seen (Figure 5). Corpulence was the significant factor in predicting when an ant left the nest, and experience did not seem to play a role [30].

The role of a corpulence-related threshold in determining allocation to the task of foraging seems clear. However, corpulence may correlate with an ant's location in the nest. In several species the more peripheral ants are leaner than more centrally located ones [43, 45-47], leading to the hypothesis that less corpulent ants are more likely to leave the nest simply because they are more likely to encounter the nest entrance or be contacted by returning nestmates. In addition, corpulence may correlate with age, with older individuals being leaner [31, 48]. Foragers are generally observed to be older individuals [49-51], so this suggests the hypothesis that less corpulent ants are leaving the nest because they are older, not because of their associated physiology. Robinson et al. [31] tested these hypotheses by RFID-tagging colonies of ants and matching up for each individual its age cohort, corpulence, spatial fidelity to certain areas of the nest, and its experience both in and outside the nest. They then changed the demand for two tasks: foraging and brood care. The foraging results clearly show that it is the corpulence which predicts which ants respond to the increased demand for foragers by leaving the nest, irrespective of their age, spatial location or experience [31]. Leaner ants are more likely to leave the nest. Although the correlation between age and corpulence meant that overall more mature ants left the nest than younger ones, Figure 6a shows that for any given level of corpulence, mature workers were no more likely than younger ones to become foragers. For the second manipulation (increased demand for brood care), ants responded one of in two ways: either they moved onto the new brood and tended it, or transported it back to the brood pile. Ants moved onto the new brood at random with respect to age, corpulence, spatial fidelity and experience; however, ants transporting the brood were best predicted by corpulence and previous experience inside the nest. That is, it was the leaner ants and those who had previously spent a lot of time patrolling the inside of the nest which transported the brood (Figure 6b & 6c). This suggests that corpulence could be related to a general threshold for work, not just foraging. However, the role of previous experience patrolling the nest indicates that certain ants may simply be more likely to stumble across the newly added brood and respond by transporting it to the main brood pile. This suggests a task encounter model, where any ant can do the job, but some are more likely to encounter it than others.

Why use different systems for these two tasks? Foraging is a complex task involving navigating the unpredictable outside world. If, as seems to be the case, lean foragers pass on the food they collect to other workers and remain lean, then over time leaner ants will become the most experienced. In addition, leaner foragers will have a greater capacity for feeding in the field, may be less likely to attract predators and are less of a loss to the colony if they do not return. In addition corpulence will also give a good indication of the hunger state of the colony – if the colony's food reserves are low, more individuals will be lean enough to respond to the hunger stimulus and go out to forage. In contrast, brood care in ants seems to be a less specialised task, to which any ant can contribute [52]. Using a task encounter model provides a simple self-organised mechanism for the colony to ensure that ants are appropriately allocated. Overall, out of all the factors considered (age, physiology, experience, spatial factors and social interaction) it is physiology, social interaction and spatially-specific experience that seem to be the most important in determining individual task-decisions. The combination of these simple mechanisms provides the colony as a whole with a responsive work-force, appropriately allocated across tasks but flexible in response to changing environmental conditions.

## Case Study 2: Nest Choice and Emigration

Many processes within an ant colony can occur in parallel, for example foraging and brood care in case study 1 in which individuals constantly make and implement individual decisions about which tasks to perform. However, in certain situations a whole colony must come to a unanimous decision about a collective action which must be implemented in a coordinated manner. One such collective decision occurs when a colony decides to relocate.

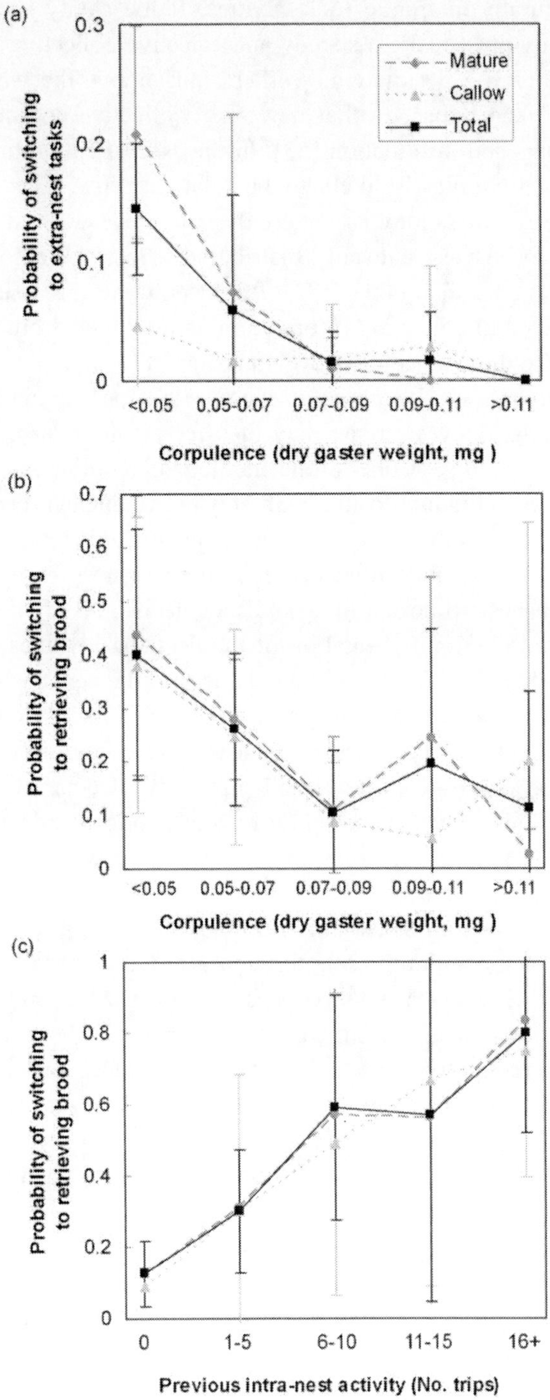


Figure 6. Task-switching in ants. The probabilities of switching to a) external (foraging) tasks and b) transporting brood decrease significantly with increasing corpulence [31]. c) The probability of switching to transporting brood increases significantly with previous intra-nest activity [31]. Differences between age cohorts (mature and callow) are not statistically significant [31]. Probabilities, mean of 6 colonies ±SD; Diamond, mature; triangle, callow; square, total. Figure reproduced with permission from [31]

*T. albipennis* live naturally in fragile rock cavities. If the cavity in which these ants nest breaks open, the colony must make a speedy and effective collective decision to move to a new home. Having chosen a destination, workers must move the whole colony, including immobile eggs, larvae and pupae, to that new site. Collective decisions are influenced by conflict, time-constraints and information [53]. In the case of emigrating ants, all individuals share the same aim, so conflict is likely to be relatively low. The time-constraints are a significant factor because the colony is potentially vulnerable while it makes its choice, and information is likely to be very unevenly distributed across the colony, with some scouts encountering more nest-sites than others [32]. Robinson et al. [32] used the RFID system to identify the ants involved in collecting information about the environment, and to determine how their actions lead to the final colony-level decision.

The emigration process in *T. albipennis* starts with scouts going out to search for new nest-sites. Scouts finding a new nest-site may then recruit nestmates. *T. albipennis* workers recruit using 'tandem-running', a one-to-one method of recruitment whereby an informed individual leads another individual to the goal, staying in antennal contact most of the way [54]. The following ant learns the route and is subsequently able to lead more ants to the new site [55]. Scouts assess the number of nestmates in the new nest by their encounter rate [56]. When this measure reaches a 'quorum threshold', the decision is made to accept that site and implementation begins [57]. Implementation of the decision involves informed ants rapidly transporting adult nestmates, brood items and the queen to the new nest-site [57, 58].

When more than one possible nest-site is available, as is likely to be the case in the wild, ant colonies are able to choose between nests based on a range of attributes including light level, cavity dimensions, size of entrance and proximity of conspecifics [55, 59-62]. Two mechanisms have previously been proposed for how this collective decision is made. The first is 'recruitment latency' whereby the time that ants wait between discovering a nest-site and first recruiting to that nest is dependent on the quality of that nest [55]. If two equidistant sites of differing quality are offered, this should mean that recruitment to the better nest will start earlier, leading to an accumulation of ants through positive feedback, and this nest reaching the quorum threshold before the poorer nest does. The second previously proposed mechanism is direct comparison, and suggests that ants visiting both nests can compare their qualities and choose to recruit to the better one [55]. These mechanisms have been used as the basis for several models of collective decision-making [57, 63-65]. However, Franks et al. [66] showed that *T. albipennis* colonies are able to choose a good nest even when it is 9 times further away than a poor one. In these experiments the good nest was over 2.5m away – a considerable distance to cover for 2mm-long ants. In theory the extra travel time required to return from this distant good nest should cancel out any benefits of recruitment latency. It seems questionable whether direct comparison of nests would be a sufficient mechanism with the nests so far apart. To investigate this, Robinson et al. [32] ran a similar set of experiments with a nearby low quality nest and a distant high quality nest but with all the workers RFID-tagged. By fixing RFID readers above the entrances to the new nests, it was possible to identify all the ants which entered the two nests during the searching and assessment phase. A hand-held RFID reader was also used to identify ants involved in tandem running. The results showed no evidence of the recruitment latency mechanism [32]. Intriguingly, even when the travel time differences were removed from the recruitment latency data, there were still no quality-dependent differences in recruitment latency, conflicting with earlier studies. The results also showed no evidence that direct comparison played a significant role in decision-making. An average of only around 1 ant per colony had the opportunity to visit both nests before recruiting, and these ants were no more likely to recruit to the good nest than to the poor nest [32]. Informed ants that had visited both nests did not even return more quickly to the better nest than uninformed ants finding it for the first time. There was also no evidence that ants performed recruitment at a higher rate to the better nest, or for longer [32]. How then did the colonies manage to make their collective choice?

The data collected clearly showed that ants discovering the near, poor quality, nest might either continue re-visiting that poor nest, or might discover the father away, good quality nest. In contrast, ants that discovered the more distant good nest first were highly likely to continue to re-visit that nest, and unlikely to discover the other nest (Figure 7). In both cases these ants are uninformed about the quality of the other nest available, so clearly their decision about whether to search for alternatives or not is based on the quality of the first nest they find. This suggests the ants are using an internal threshold of acceptability: if the nest exceeds this threshold they accept it, making repeat visits and going on to start recruitment. If the nest does not reach this threshold, they reject it and continue searching.

How does this simple threshold mechanism fit with previously proposed mechanisms of quality-dependent recruitment latency and direct comparison of alternatives? Interestingly, all empirical demonstrations of quality-dependent differences in recruitment latency came from studies in which a colony was given either a single poor nest or a single good nest [55, 64, 67, 68]. If ants use a threshold rule and a colony is offered only a poor nest, then ants finding that nest are likely to reject it and continue searching. However, as it is the only nest available they will keep finding it and rejecting it until eventually, due to assessment errors or within-colony threshold variation, some ants will accept the nest and recruit nestmates, leading to an apparent 'long recruitment latency'. In contrast if a colony is offered only a good nest, it is likely to exceed the acceptance threshold of the first ants to find the nest, so they will accept it and start to recruit, leading to an apparent 'short recruitment latency'. Recruitment latency differences can thus be explained as side-effects of the threshold rule [32]. If a colony is offered two nests of differing qualities, ants finding the good nest first are likely to accept it and start recruiting, whereas ants finding the poor nest first are likely to reject it and keep searching. By chance they will then find the good nest, accept it and start recruitment. This leads to the 'apparent comparison' phenomenon, but without the ants actually having to remember and compare the qualities of the different nests. Analytical and simulation modelling confirm that the simple threshold model is sufficient to explain the behavioural data previously thought to support other mechanisms [69].

Insect brains can be considered limited because they do not contain the parallel neural pathways which would allow sensory inputs to be processed in different ways to extract information that can be used to compute extra variables from this sensory information [70]. Social insects can share information collected by different workers and can thus circumvent these limits to make collective decisions based on variables not directly sensed by the individuals. In house-hunting ants, a very simple individual mechanism leads to sophisticated collective decision-making. The best option can be chosen, even if it is further away and therefore harder to sample. At a collective level, the different options are effectively compared but without any individuals having to make a direct comparison (see Box 1). This mechanism works well under time-constraints because the colonies are rapidly able to choose a nearby site if it is good enough. The mechanism can also cope with uneven distribution of information because informed individuals recruit others and no individual needs to have visited more than one nest. A distribution of acceptance thresholds within the colony (or high error in individual assessments) will help the ant colony to function effectively in a range of environments. On the one hand, the very low threshold ants are beneficial because they mean that even a low quality nest will be accepted eventually, if it is all that is available, preventing the colony being trapped in a no-choice situation. On the other hand, very high threshold ants are beneficial because they will constantly search for alternatives, ensuring the colony does not settle for second best. This provides interesting insights for anyone trying to combine inputs from distributed sensors to determine a single computer action. This suggests that using a range of sensors with differing levels of sensitivity will provide a network with a more effective collective decision-making mechanism. It also suggests that the computational power required by the hub of the network is low, as it does not need to directly compare sensor input values.

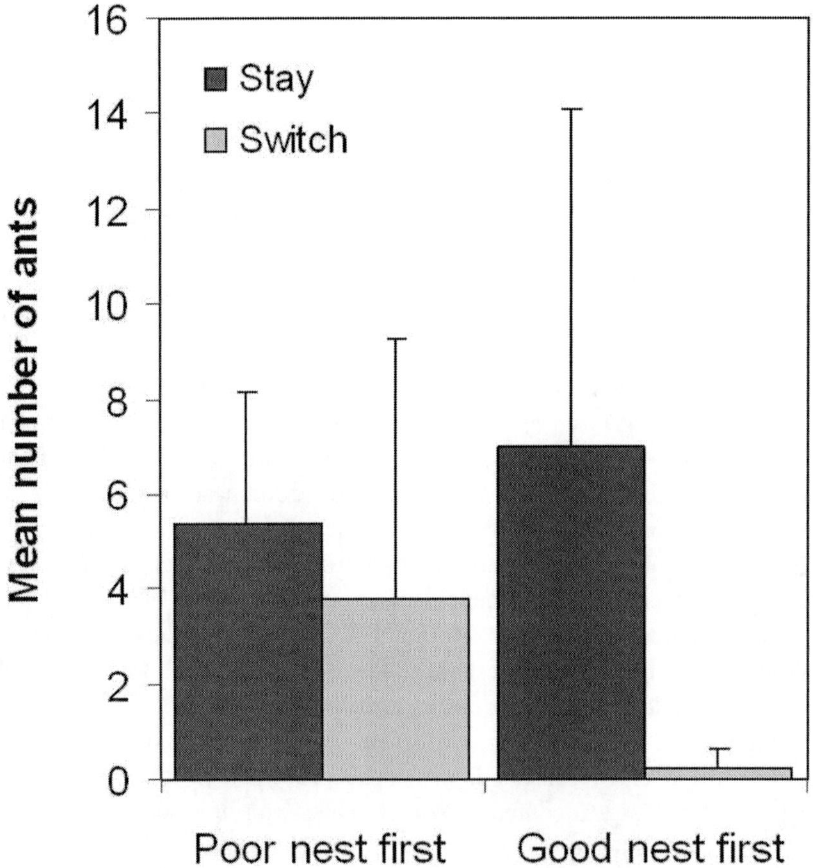


Figure 7. Searching behaviour of house-hunting ants. Ants which make an independent visit to one nest (i.e. not by being recruited), and then either continue to visit that nest only (stay) or visit the other nest (switch). Means from 9 colonies, +SD. Figure modified with permission from [32]

### Box 1. Levels of Decision-Making

Two distinct decision-making mechanisms are:

1) Direct comparison of alternatives
2) Sequential search using a threshold

When direct comparisons are used, the chooser must sample the available options for some period and then use memory of previous options to make a comparison and find the best one. Sequential search methods, in contrast, require no memory or sampling period. Here the chooser samples the available options sequentially and accepts the first to exceed their internal threshold. They need hold no memory of previously encountered options and their decision is based solely on the current option under assessment, not on the general environment.

Intriguingly, ants use contrasting methods of decision-making to those made by ant colonies. As discussed in the main text, ants use a threshold-based sequential search process and will 'satisfice', i.e. accept the first nest that satisfies their individual acceptance threshold and then cease searching. However, this is not what is seen when we take a step back and observe colony-level behaviour. Here a colony which has accepted a nest of good quality will nevertheless later 'upgrade' if an even higher quality nest becomes available [70]. This means the colony does not 'satisfice' but rather effectively makes a comparison between its own nest and the new one available. This colony-level comparison process is mediated by the simple individual-level sequential search process: in a colony with a wide distribution of acceptance thresholds there will be some very 'choosy' high threshold ants that continue to search, even though the colony is housed in a good nest and the majority are satisfied. If these high threshold ants find a new very high quality nest which does exceed their threshold, then they will recruit nestmates.

This very high quality nest is likely to exceed the threshold of these new recruits too, so a quorum will be reached at the new nest and the colony will move. Thus an effective group-level comparison can emerge from simple sequentially searching subunits.

## Conclusion

### Future Directions

One major advantage of the RFID system is that it provides the potential for automatic manipulation of individual behaviour. Automatic doors operated in conjunction with the RFID system would allow the exclusion of specific identified individuals from certain locations. This would make it possible to control both the information available to certain individuals and their opportunity to contribute to shared decisions. This kind of manipulation experiment will quantify the influence of key individuals and will determine just how distributed colony-decisions really are. The system also provides scope for collecting longitudinal data on the same colony to test whether the contributions of individuals change over time. Combined with manipulation experiments, this would allow the test of whether changes are intrinsic with age or whether it is the ants' experience which most affects its later decision-making behaviour. The system could also be used with other ant species to provide cross-species comparison data and could also be applied to a range of other areas of interest, including foraging organisation, colony budding, inter-colony competition, task-partitioning and reproductive conflict.

### Distributed Decisions

The two case studies described here clearly show the benefit of detailed individual-level data for understanding collective processes. Using the RFID system to locate and identify individual ants as they carry out the essential colony tasks of foraging and brood care has shown how very simple individual rules can lead to an effective division of labour for the colony and that by means of these rules, the colony is able to respond rapidly to changes in demand for certain tasks. We also demonstrated that individuals use very simple rules to decide on suitable new nest sites during colony emigration. By identifying the ants involved in recruiting nest-mates, we were able to explore how these individual rules lead to a collective decision – the relocation of the colony.

These investigations into the mechanisms of distributed decision-making give us further insights into the success of social insects. Ants continually face dynamic organisational problems and have been evolving to manage these problems for 80 million years [71]. The decentralised robustness of distributed decision-making, as demonstrated by ants, should be an inspiration to engineers designing human systems. The importance of avoiding detailed centralised control is increasingly recognised [72]. We will benefit from studying the highly evolved distributed organisation of ant colonies and applying these insights to the dynamic problems in our modern society.

## Acknowledgments

We thank Richard G. Morris for helpful advice and assistance, and Efrain Rodriguez for reading the manuscript. The case studies described were carried out in collaboration with Nigel R. Franks and Ofer Feinerman; we thank them for all their contributions. This work was supported in part by grants from Engineering and Physics Research Council UK [EP/D076226/1, supporting EJHR] and National Institutes of Health, USA [GM087834 to WM]. EJHR gratefully acknowledges current support from the Royal Society, UK.

## References

[1] Poole, J. H. K., Payne, L.W. R. & Moss, C. J. (1988). The social contexts of some very low frequency calls of African elephants. *Behavioral Ecology and Sociobiology*, *22(6)*, 385-392.

[2] Conradt, L. & Roper, T. J. (2003). Group decision-making in animals. *Nature*, *421*,

155-158.

[3] Bourke, A. F. G. & Franks, N. R. (1995). Social Evolution in Ants. *Monographs in Behaviour and Ecology*, ed. J.R. Krebs and T. Clutton-Brock., Princeton, New Jersey: Princeton University Press., *529*.

[4] Camazine, S., Deneubourg, J. L., Franks, N. R. & Sneyd, J. et al., (2001). *Self-Organization in Biological Systems*. Princeton Studies in Complexity., Princeton and Oxford: Princeton, University Press. 217-156.

[5] Fénéron, R., Durand, J. L. & Jaisson, P. (1996). Relation between behaviour and physiological maturation in a ponerine ant. Behaviour, *133*, 791-806.

[6] Ravary, F., Lecoutey, E., Kaminski, G. & Châline, N. et al., (2007). Individual experience alone can generate lasting division of labor in ants. *Current Biology*, *17(15)*, 1308-1312.

[7] Mirenda, J. T. & Vinson, S. B. (1979). A marking technique for adults of the red imported fire ant. *The Florida Entomologist*, *62(3)*, 279-281.

[8] Abraham, M. & Pasteels, J. M. (1980). Social behavior during nest-moving in the ant *Myrmica rubra* (L.) Hymenoptera, Formicidae). *Insectes Sociaux*, *27*, 127-147.

[9] Möglich, M. & Hölldobler, B. (1974). Social carrying behavior and division of labor during nest moving in ants. *Psyche*, *81(2)*, 219-236.

[10] Traniello, J. F. A. (1987). Individual and social strategies of foraging in the ant *Formica schaufussi*, in *Chemistry and Biology of Social Insects*, J. Eder and H. Rembold, Editors., Verlag J. Peperny: Munich., 511-512.

[11] Beckers, R., Deneubourg, J. L. & Goss, S. (1992). Trails and U-turns in the selection of a path by the ant *Lasius niger*. *Journal of Theoretical Biology*, *159(4)*, 397-415.

[12] Langridge, E. A., Sendova-Franks, A. B. & Franks, N. R. (2008). The behaviour of ant transporters at the old and new nests during successive colony emigrations *Behavioral Ecology and Sociobiology, 62*, 1851-1861.

[13] Reynolds, D. R. & Riley, J. R. (2002). Remote-sensing, telemetric and computer-based technologies for investigating insect movement: a survey of existing and potential techniques. *Computers and Electronics in Agriculture*, *35*, 271-307.

[14] White, A. M., Swaisgood, R. R. & Czekala, N. (2007). Ranging patterns in white rhinoceros, *Ceratotherium simum simum*: implications for mating strategies. *Animal Behaviour*, *74*, 349-356.

[15] Ainley, D. G., Ribic, C. A., Ballard, G. & Heath, S. et al., (2004). Geographic structure of Adelie Penguin populations: Overlap in colony-specific foraging areas. *Ecological Monographs*, *74(1)*, 159-178.

[16] Balme, G., Hunter, L. & Slotow, R. (2007). Feeding habitat selection by hunting leopards *Panthera pardus* in a woodland savanna: prey catchability versus abundance. *Animal Behaviour*, *74*, 589-598.

[17] Fuller, S. A., Henne, J. P., Seals, J. & Mudrak, V. A. (2008). Performance of commercially available passive integrated transponder (PIT) tag systems used for fish identification and interjurisdictional fisheries management. *North American Journal of Fisheries Management*, *28(2)*, 386-393.

[18] Kerth, G., Ebert, C. & Schmidtke, C. (2006). Group decision making in fission-fusion societies: evidence from two-field experiments in Bechstein's bats. *Proceedings of the Royal Society of London Series B*, *273*, 2785-2790.

[19] Patriquin, K. J., Leonard, M. L., Broders, H. G. & Garroway, C. J. (2010). Do social

networks of female northern long-eared bats vary with reproductive period and age? *Behavioral Ecology and Sociobiology*, *64*, 899-913.

[20] Sumner, S., Lucas, E., Barker, J. & Isaac, N. (2007). Radio-tagging technology reveals extreme nest-drifting behavior in a eusocial insect. *Current Biology*, *17(2)*, 140-145.

[21] Streit, S., Bock, F., Pirk, C. W. W. & Tautz, J. (2003). Automatic life-long monitoring of individual insect behaviour now possible. *Zoology*, *106*, 169-171.

[22] Lin, X., Flint, J., Azaro, M. & Coradetti, T. et al. (2007). Microtransponder-based multiplex assay for genotyping cystic fibrosis. *Clinical Chemistry*, *53*, 1372-1376.

[23] Li, J., Wang, Z., Gryczynski, I. & Mandecki, W. Silver nanoparticle-enhanced fluorescence in microtransponder-based immuno- and DNA hybridization assays. submitted.

[24] Mandecki, W., Ardelt, B., Coradetti, T. & Davidowitz, H. et al., (2006). Microtransponders, the miniature RFID electronic chips, as platforms for cell growth in cytotoxicity assays. *Cytometry Part A*, *69A*, 1097-1105.

[25] Gruda, M. C., Pinto, A., Craelius, A. & Davidowitz, H. et al., A system for tagging laboratory mice with light-activated microtransponders. *Journal of the American Association for Laboratory Animal Science*, in press.

[26] Pharma Seq, (2010). Inc. www.pharmaseq.com/pages/rfid.html.

[27] Partridge, L.W., Partridge, K. A. & Franks, N. R. (1997). Field survey of a monogynous leptothoracine ant (Hymenoptera, Formicidae): Evidence of seasonal polydomy? *Insectes Sociaux*, *44(2)*, 75-83.

[28] Nielsen, M. G. (2001). Energetic cost of foraging in the ant *Rhytidoponera aurata* in tropical Australia. *Physiological Entomology, 26(3)*, 248-253.

[29] Nielsen, M. G., Jensen, T. F. & Holm-Jensen, I. (1982). Effect of load carriage on the respiratory metabolism of running worker ants of *Camponotus herculeanus* (Formicidae). *Oikos*, *39*, 137-142.

[30] Robinson, E. J. H., Richardson, T. O., Sendova-Franks, A. B. & Feinerman, O. et al., (2009). Radio-tagging reveals the roles of corpulence, experience and social information in ant decision making. *Behavioral Ecology and Sociobiology*, *63(5)*, 627-636.

[31] Robinson, E. J. H., Feinerman, O. & Franks, N. R. (2009). Flexible task allocation and the organisation of work in ants. *Proceedings of the Royal Society of London Series B*, *276*, 4373-4380.

[32] Robinson, E. J. H., Smith, F. D., Sullivan, K. M. E. & Franks, N. R. (2009). Do ants make direct comparisons? *Proceedings of the Royal Society of London Series B*, *276*, 2635-2641.

[33] Briscoe, A. D. & Chittka, L. (2001). The evolution of color vision in insects. *Annual Review of Entomology*, *46*, 471-510.

[34] Smith, A. (1776). *An Inquiry into the Nature and Causes of the Wealth of Nations*, ed. K. Sutherland., Oxford: Oxford World Classics. 618.

[35] Oster, G. F. & Wilson, E. O. (1978). *Caste and Ecology in the Social Insects.*, Princeton, New Jersey: Princeton University Press. 352.

[36] Robinson, G. E. (1987). Regulation of honey-bee age polyethism by juvenile hormone. *Behavioral Ecology and Sociobiology*, *20(5)*, 329-338.

[37] Bonabeau, E. & Théraulaz, G. (1999). Role and variability of response thresholds in the regulation of division of labor in insect societies, in *Information Processing in Social*

*Insects*, C. Detrain, J.L. Deneubourg, and J.M. Pasteels, Editors., Birkhäuser: Basel, Switzerland., 141-163.

[38] Robinson, G. E. & Page, R. E. (1988). Genetic determination of guarding and undertaking in honey-bee colonies. *Nature, 333*, 356-358.

[39] Wilson, E. O. (1953). The origin and evolution of polymorphism in ants. *Quarterly Review of Biology*, *28(2)*, 136-156.

[40] Robinson, E. J. H. (2009). Physiology as a caste-defining feature. *Insectes Sociaux*, *56(1)*, 1-6.

[41] Tofts, C. (1993). Algorithms for task allocation in ants (a study of temporal polyethism theory). *Bulletin of Mathematical Biology*, *55*, 891-918.

[42] Greene, M. J. & Gordon, D. (2007). Interaction rate informs harvester ant task decisions. *Behavioral Ecology*, *18*, 451-455.

[43] Blanchard, G. B., Orledge, G. M., Reynolds, S. E. & Franks, N. R. (2000). Division of labour and seasonality in the ant *Leptothorax albipennis*: worker corpulence and its influence on behaviour. *Animal Behaviour*, *59*, 723-738.

[44] Pearson, B., Raybould, A. F. & Clarke, R. T. (1995). Breeding-behavior, relatedness and sex-investment ratios in *Leptothorax tuberum* Fabricius. *Entomologia Experimentalis et Applicata*, *75(2)*, 165-174.

[45] Gentry, J. B. (1974). Response to predation by colonies of Florida harvester ant, *Pogonomyrmex badius*. *Ecology, 55(6)*, 1328-1338.

[46] Tschinkel, W. R. (1987). Seasonal life history and nest architecture of a winter-active ant, *Prenolepis imparis*. *Insectes Sociaux*, *34(3)*, 143-164.

[47] Tschinkel, W. R. (1998). Sociometry and sociogenesis of colonies of the harvester ant, *Pogonomyrmex badius*: worker characteristics in relation to colony size and season. *Insectes Sociaux*, *45(4)*, 385-410.

[48] Toth, A. L. & Robinson, G. E. (2005). Worker nutrition and division of labour in honeybees. *Animal Behaviour*, *69*, 427-435.

[49] Gordon, D. M., „J. Chu, A., Lillie, M. & Tissot, et al., (2005). Variation in the transition from inside to outside work in the red harvester ant *Pogonomyrmex barbatus*. *Insectes Sociaux*, *52(3)*, 212-217.

[50] Seeley, T. D. (1982). Adaptive significance of the age polyethism schedule in honeybee colonies. *Behavioral Ecology and Sociobiology*, *11(4)*, 287-293.

[51] Schmid-Hempel, P. & Schmid-Hempel, R. (1984). Life duration and turnover of foragers in the ant *Cataglyphis bicolor* (Hymenoptera, Formicidae). *Insectes Sociaux*, *31*, 345-360.

[52] Muscedere, M. L., Willey, T. A. & Traniello, J. F. A. (2009). Age and task efficiency in the ant *Pheidole dentata*: young minor workers are not specialist nurses. *Animal Behaviour*, 2009, *77*, 911-918.

[53] Conradt, L. & Roper, T. J. (2009). Conflicts of interest and the evolution of decision sharing. *Philosophical Transactions of the Royal Society B-Biological Sciences*, *364,* 807-819.

[54] Möglich, M. (1978). Social organization of nest emigration in Leptothorax (Hym. Form.). *Insectes Sociaux*, *25*, 205-225.

[55] Mallon, E. B., Pratt, S. C. & Franks, N. R. (2001). Individual and collective decision-making during nest site selection by the ant *Leptothorax albipennis*. *Behavioral Ecology and Sociobiology*, *50(4)*, 352-359.

[56] Pratt, S. C. (2005). Quorum sensing by encounter rates in the ant *Temnothorax albipennis*. *Behavioral Ecology*, *16*, 488-496.

[57] Pratt, S. C., Mallon E. B., Sumpter, D. J. T. & Franks, N. R. (2002). Quorum sensing, recruitment, and collective decision-making during colony emigration by the ant *Leptothorax albipennis*. *Behavioral Ecology and Sociobiology*, *52(2)*, 117-127.

[58] Franks, N. R. & Sendova-Franks, A. B. (2000). Queen transport during ant colony emigration: a group-level adaptive behaviour. *Behavioral Ecology*, *11*, 315-318.

[59] Franks, N. R., Mallon, E. B., Bray, H. E. & Hamilton, M. J. et al. (2003). Strategies for choosing between alternatives with different attributes: exemplified by house-hunting ants. *Animal Behaviour*, *65*, 215-223.

[60] Franks, N. R., Dornhaus, A., Metherell, B. & Nelson, T. et al. (2006). Not everything that counts can be counted: ants use multiple metrics for a single nest trait. *Proceedings of the Royal Society of London Series B*, *273*, 165-169.

[61] Mallon, E. B. & Franks, N. R. (2000). Ants estimate area using Buffon's needle. *Proceedings of the Royal Society of London Series B*, *267(1445)*, 765-770.

[62] Franks, N. R., Dornhaus, A., Hitchcock, G. & Guillem, R. et al. (2007). Avoidance of conspecific colonies during nest choice by ants. *Animal Behaviour*, *73(3)*, 525-534.

[63] Planqué, R., Dornhaus, A., Franks, N. R. & Kovacs, T. et al. (2007). Weighted waiting in collective decision-making. *Behavioral Ecology and Sociobiology*, *61(3)*, 347-356.

[64] Pratt, S. C., Sumpter, D. J. T., Mallon, E. B. & Franks, N. R. (2005). An agent-based model of collective nest site choice by the ant *Temnothorax albipennis. Animal Behaviour*, *70*, 1023-1036.

[65] Marshall, J. A. R., Dornhaus, A., Franks, N. R. & Kovacs, T. (2005). Noise, cost and speed-accuracy trade-offs: decision-making in a decentralised system. *Journal of the Royal Society: Interface*, *3*, 243-254.

[66] Franks, N. R., Hardcastle, K. A., Collins, S. & Smith, F. D. et al., (2008). Can ant colonies choose a far-and-away better nest over an in-the-way poor one*? Animal Behaviour*, *76*, 323-334.

[67] Pratt, S. C. (2005). Behavioral mechanisms of collective nest-site choice by the ant *Temnothorax curvispinosus*. *Insectes Sociaux*, *52*, 383-392.

[68] Pratt, S. C. & Sumpter, D. J. T. (2006). A tunable algorithm for collective decision making. *Proceedings of the National Academy of Sciences of the USA*, *103(43)*, 15906-15910.

[69] Robinson, E. J. H., Franks, N. R., Ellis, S. & Okuda, S. et al., *A simple threshold rule for sophisticated collective decision-making.* submitted.

[70] Chittka, L. & Niven, J. (2010). Are bigger brains better? *Current Biology*, *19(21)*, R995-R1008.

[71] Wilson, E. O., Carpenter, F. M. & Brown, W. L. (1967). The first Mesozoic ants. *Science, 157*, 1038-1039.

[72] Prokopenko, M., Wang, P., Foreman, M. & Valencia, P. et al., (2005). On connectivity of reconfigurable impact networks in ageless aerospace vehicles. *Robotics and Autonomous Systems*, *53(1)*, 36-58.

In: Ant Colonies
Editor: Emily C. Sun
ISBN: 978-1-61122-023-0


*Chapter 4*

# IMPACTS, ECOLOGY AND DISPERSAL OF THE INVASIVE ARGENTINE ANT

***Eiriki Sunamura[1], Shun Suzuki[1], Hironori Sakamoto[2], Koji Nishisue[1], Mamoru Terayama[1] and Sadahiro Tatsuki[1]***

[1]Graduate School of Agricultural and Life Sciences, University of Tokyo, Bunkyo-ku, Tokyo, Japan

[2]Graduate School of Environmental Sciences, Hokkaido University, Kita-ku, Sapporo, Japan

## ABSTRACT

Introduction of alien organisms is a major risk that follows international trade. Ants are among the most harmful groups of invasive organisms, with five species, including the Argentine ant *Linepithema humile*, listed among the world's 100 worst invasive species by the IUCN. We review the damage, ecology, and dispersal of invasive ants, with the Argentine ant as a representative. Invasive ants attain high population densities in the introduced range, and cause damage to ecosystems, agriculture, and human well-being by the sheer number. The high density may stem partly from formation of expansive 'supercolonies' (a supercolony is a large network of cooperative nests). In the Argentine ant, the high consistency of their supercolony identities makes them important units in inferring the dispersal history of this species. We highlight two topics in the dispersal history of the species: 1) formation of an unprecedented intercontinental supercolony by the 150th year of international trade; 2) recent successive introductions to Pan-Pacific region seemingly in accordance with globalization.

## INTRODUCTION

Introduction of alien organisms is a major risk that accompanies international trade. Global biodiversity is being lost at an unprecedented rate [Pimm et al. 1995], and biological invasion is one of its main causes, along with changes in land use, climate, and biogeochemical cycles [Vitousek 1994; Vitousek et al. 1996; Wilcove et al. 1998; Sala et al. 2000]. Alien species have strong competitive ability against indigenous species, often owing to release from natural enemies [Mitchell and Power 2003; Torchin et al. 2003]. For instance, introduced Nile perch in Lake Victoria may have caused disappearance of hundreds of endemic fish species by predation and competition [Witte et al. 1992]. Introduced species are also economically destructive [Pimentel et al. 2005; Xu et al. 2006; Pejchar and Mooney 2009]. In the Great Lakes region of the U.S.A., maintenance of water intake pipes clogged by introduced zebra mussels costs millions of dollars every year [Pejchar and Mooney 2009]. Moreover, introduced species threaten human health, as represented by the cases of disease outbreak mediated by alien mosquitoes [Juliano and Lounibos 2005]. In order to stop the damage by invasive alien species, prevention of introduction and spread, as well as control of established population, should be addressed [Mack et al. 2000; Simberloff et al. 2005; Hulme 2006]. Because eradication or successful management is often very difficult and costly, and because globalization is accelerating transportation of alien species, many authors put more emphasis on preventive approaches [Ricciarddi and Rasmussen 1998; Mack et al. 2000; Leung et al. 2002; Perrings et al. 2002; Westphal et al. 2008; Hulme 2009]. Prevention requires knowledge on pathways of dispersal, and corresponding quarantine system and surveillance network.

Ants are recognized as one of the most harmful groups of alien species. In fact, 17 invertebrate species are listed among the world's 100 worst invasive species by the IUCN (International Union for Conservation of Nature), and five of them are ants [Lowe et al. 2000]. The five species comprise the Argentine ant *Linepithema humile*, the big-headed ant *Pheidole megacephala*, the little fire ant *Wasmannia auropunctata*, the red imported fire ant *Solenopsis invicta*, and the yellow crazy ant *Anoplolepis gracilipes*. All of these species attain high population densities in the introduced range, and directly or indirectly displace indigenous ants, other invertebrates, vertebrates and plants [Holway et al. 2002]. They also become agricultural pests by tending honeydew producing homopteran insects (aphids, scale insects and mealybugs). Furthermore, they are significant nuisance pests in urban areas that invade buildings with high frequency and in large numbers. In particular, the red imported fire ant and the little fire ant are pronounced sanitary pests that torment farmers, gardeners and those indoor, with their poison stings [Rhoades et al. 1989; Wetterer and Porter 2003]. The damage to livestock, wildlife, and public health caused by *Solenopsis* fire ants in the U.S.A. can be $1 billion per year [Pimentel et al. 2005]. Despite the enormous efforts to cope with introduced invasive ants, no truly effective control methodology has been established: eradication or successful management is extremely hard with existing methods [Soeprono and Rust 2004; Silverman and Brightwell 2008]. Given the hardship of control, preventive measures should be strengthened to suppress ant invasions. However, knowledge on their invasion history and pathways of dispersal is still limited. For the big-headed ant and yellow crazy ant, even their native ranges have not been clarified [Holway et al. 2002].

In this chapter we review the pest status (consequences of invasion), ecology (intrinsic characteristics that enhance invasion success), and dispersal (an ultimate cause of invasion) of invasive ants, with the Argentine ant (Fig. 1) as an exponent. This species is one of the most intensively studied invasive ants. In most sections of this review, brief comparisons are made between Argentine ants and other invasive ants.

Figure 1. The Argentine ant *Linepithema humile*. Upper: a worker carrying a larvae; lower: a fertile queen. Workers are 2.2-2.6 mm in length and from light to dark brown in color [Newell and Barber 1913]. Queens are 4.5-5 mm long. Photographs by Taku Shimada.

# THE ARGENTINE ANT *LINEPITHEMA HUMILE*: PEST STATUS

## Distribution and Habitat

The Argentine ant is native to the Paraná River drainage of northern Argentina and surrounding countries in South America [Tsutsui et al. 2001; Wild 2007]. During the last 150 years, this species has been unintentionally introduced to all continents except Antarctica and many oceanic islands with Mediterranean or mild temperate climate [Suarez et al. 2001; Roura-Pascual et al. 2004; Wetterer and Wetterer 2006; Wetterer et al. 2009]. First recorded from Madeira somewhere between 1847 and 1858, Argentine ants landed in Europe (Portugal and France), North America (Louisiana and California), and Africa (South Africa) during 1890-1910, Central America (Mexico and Bermuda) and Australia (Victoria, Western Australia, New South Wales, and Tasmania) around 1940-1950, and finally Asia (Japan) in 1993, and have spread in each area. Ecological niche characteristics of Argentine ants are similar between native and introduced ranges: in the introduced range Argentine ants typically become established along coastal areas and major river corridors [Suarez et al. 2001; Espadaler and Gómez 2003; Roura-Pascual et al. 2006, 2009a]. Dry inlands and high-elevation areas are rarely invaded. Access to permanent sources of water or soil moisture may be important abiotic conditions for establishment [Holway 1998a; Menke et al. 2007, 2009]. Argentine ants mostly invade disturbed environments such as urban districts and agricultural land, but they sometimes penetrate natural environments [Holway et al. 2002], where impacts on endemic species are of particular concern (e.g. South Africa's fynbos shrub land [Bond and Slingsby 1984] and Hawaii's subalpine shrub land [Cole et al. 1992]).

Although native range and optimal abiotic conditions (e.g. climate and nesting microhabitat) vary among invasive ant species, predominant establishment in disturbed environment [Holway et al. 2002] and occasional infestation in natural environment (e.g. Galápagos Islands for little fire ants [Lubin 1984]; tropical rain forest of Christmas Island for yellow crazy ants [O'Dowd et al. 2003]) is the common pattern among species.

## Impacts

There are many similarities among invasive ant species in their effects on local ecosystems, economy, and human well-being, with the *Solenopsis* fire ants and the little fire ant causing additional effects with their stings [Holway et al. 2002]. Here we survey case studies with Argentine ants.

### *1) Impacts on Ecosystems*

Ecological impacts of the introduced Argentine ants range over many taxa and are caused by various means [Holway et al. 2002; Lach 2003; Ness and Bronstein 2004; Krushelnycky et al. 2005; Lach & Thomas 2008]. Among the impacts, effects on invertebrates are the most notable. Argentine ants competitively displace almost all of the native ant species throughout the invaded area [North America: Erickson 1971; Ward 1987, Human and Gordon 1997, Holway 1998b; Australia: Heterick 2000, Walters 2006, Rowles and O'Dowd 2009a Asia: Miyake et al. 2002, Touyama et al. 2003; Europe: Cammell et al. 1996, Carpintero et al.

2005; Africa: Bond and Slingsby 1984] by their large number and aggressiveness [Human and Gordon 1999; Holway 1999; Rowles and O'Dowd 2007; Carpintero and Reyes-López 2008]. Argentine ants can also reduce the abundance or diversity of non-ant ground-dwelling invertebrates or change their composition [Cole et al. 1992; Human and Gordon 1997; Bolger et al. 2000; Krushelnycky and Gillespie 2008; Rowles and O'Dowd 2009a], probably by predation or competition, though in some ecosystems the impacts are little apparent [Holway 1998; Walters 2006]. The affected species are from many orders (e.g. Collembola, Diptera, Lepidoptera, Coleoptera and Araneae) and functional groups (e.g. decomposers, herbivores, predators and scavengers). Wide range of rare, floral, or arboreal invertebrates may also be affected by Argentine ant infestation [Huxel 2000; Altleld and Stiling 2006, 2009; Lach 2007, 2008; Krushelnycky and Gillespie 2008; Nygard et al. 2008].

Abundances of certain vertebrate species are reported to decline as Argentine ants invade. One well-studied example is the coastal horned lizard *Phynosoma coronatum* in southern California [Fisher et al. 2002]. This reptile feeds mainly on ants, and Argentine ants are unsuitable nutritional alternatives to native ants they displace [Suarez et al. 2000; Suarez and Case 2002]. Argentine ants also negatively affect the abundance of the grey shrew *Notiosorex crawfordi* in southern California [Laakkonen et al. 2001]. The mechanism is unknown, but the authors suggest the disruption of native arthropod community by the Argentine ants may affect the prey availability of the shrew. Such indirect effects can be widespread because Argentine ants displace many native species, as described above. Other than reptiles and mammals, invasive ants often damage birds [Holway et al. 2002]. In the case of Argentine ants, nest predations have been observed for many birds [Newell and Barber 1913], including endangered species such as the California gnatcatcher *Polioptila californica californica* [Sockman 1997] and Hawaiian goose Nene *Branta sandvicensis* [Krushelnycky et al. 2005]. However, relative importance of predation pressure by Argentine ants compared to those by other ants, mammals and birds, has been little addressed [Sockman 1997; Suarez et al. 2005].

Plants may be negatively affected by Argentine ants by several, and often indirect, means. First, plants may suffer disruption of ant-plant mutualism on seed dispersal [Rodriguez-Cabal et al. 2009]. In not a few plant species, ants disperse the seeds in lieu of an elaiosome, a lipid-rich appendage attractive to ants [Giladi 2006]. They transport seeds to their nest, consume only the elaiosome, and then dispose the intact seeds in a nest chamber or a refuse pile outside. This not only enables distant dispersal of the seeds, but also reduces location and consumption of the seeds by predators. Argentine ants do not replace native ants as seed dispersers, especially for large seeds, in many places around the world: they transport seeds for only short distances, leave the seeds above ground (leading to high rates of predation), and thus change the plant community structure [Bond and Slingsby 1984; Christian 2001; Carney et al. 2003; Gómez et al. 2003; Rowles and O'Dowd 2009b] Second, plants can suffer disruption of pollination and consequent reduction of seed-set by Argentine ants [Blancafort and Gómez 2005]. Ants are generally poor pollinators [Hölldobler and Wilson 1990], and consumption of floral nectar by Argentine ants might be costly to insect-pollinated plants [Holway et al. 2002]. In South Africa, Argentine ants can be strong competitors with the honeybee for nectar, collecting 42% of the nectar of black ironbark before honeybees start foraging in the morning [Buys 1987]. Pollination failure can also be induced by direct displacement of pollinators [Blancafort and Gómez 2005]. Argentine ants can aggressively drive flower-visiting pollinators away [Lach 2007]. They can also displace pollinators by preying on the larvae or disturbing the nests [Cole et al. 1992]. Third,

Argentine ants can damage plants by tending homopteran insects [Altfeld and Stiling 2006], as in agriculture (see below). Effect of Argentine ants on plant mortality has not been understood well. There is a case where plants experience reduced mortality owing to exclusion of herbivores by Argentine ants, despite the negative effect of Homoptera tending [Altfeld and Stiling 2009]. However, it might not be the general pattern. In Christmas Island, sooty mold induced by mutualism of yellow crazy ant and Homoptera have led to the conspicuous deaths of trees [O'Dowd et al. 2003].

### *2) Impacts on Agriculture*

Argentine ants have been widely recognized as agricultural pests, mainly for causing outbreaks of phloem-feeding homopteran insects [Newell and Barber 1913; Vega and Rust 2001]. In the introduced range, Argentine ants form mutualistic relationships with various homopteran species opportunistically [Holway et al. 2002; Lester et al. 2003]. Like many other ant species, Argentine ants protect these insects from predators or parasitoids in exchange of carbohydrate-rich honeydew. They displace natural enemies of Homoptera [Flanders 1945; Bartlett 1961; Daane et al. 2007; Mgocheki and Addison 2009] or selectively remove parasitized homopteran individuals [Frazer and Van den Bosch 1973]. Outbreak of homopteran insects is detrimental to crop growth because of excess consumption of the phloem, injury on the product appearance by galls, transmission of pathogens, and encouragement of the growth of sooty mold over the leaves. Homoptera outbreak via mutualism with Argentine ants is documented from citrus orchards, vineyards [e.g. Phillips and Sherk 1991; Addison and Samways 2000; Daane et al. 2007], and many other crops [Lester et al. 2003]. A few studies compared the intensity of Homoptera tending between Argentine and native ants. These studies suggested the moderate or strong ability of Argentine ants to displace parasitoids compared to other ants [Martinez-Ferrer et al. 2003; Mgocheki and Addison 2009]. In these laboratory experiments, colony size of studied ants was controlled. The effects of Homoptera tending by Argentine ants would be increased in the field, considering the high density of this species. According to some scientists in the U.S.A., homopteran outbreak was observed only in association with Argentine ants [Newell and Barber 1913; Phillips and Sherk 1991].

Argentine ants also directly damage crops. In Japan, we often hear complaints from owners of fields and kitchen gardens such as: Argentine ants infest figs before humans harvest; Argentine ants damage and deform root crops (e.g. carrot and white radish) [E. Sunamura, personal communication].

### *3) Impacts in Urban Area*

Argentine ants are nuisance pests that inhabit urban districts and frequently intrude structures [e.g. Gordon et al. 2001]. Examples of damages in Japan include: swarm on foods; bite humans and pets; crawl into bed and disturb sleep; these annoyances occur so often that the residents get on the verge of nervous breakdown [E. Sunamura, personal communication]. In the U.S.A., Argentine ants went on a rampage as household pests soon after the initial introduction [Newell and Barber 1913], forcing some people to move to uninfested localities and making real estate values of invaded districts fall [De Ong 1916]. The continuous effort to control Argentine ants since then to the present [Newell and Rouge 1909; Brightwell and Silverman 2009] also bears out their significance as an urban pest, as well as the hardship of control. Indeed, ants are today ranked among the greatest urban pests by the structural pest control industry in the U.S.A., and Argentine ants account for a considerable portion of the number of ant control instances by pest management professionals (e.g. 85% in San Diego) [Field et al. 2007].

## Ecology

In this section we review the ecology of Argentine ants relevant to their invasiveness. Because of the ecological and economic significance, ecology of Argentine ants has been investigated intensively in the introduced range. Though not yet plenty, knowledge on the ecology of the native South American population has been much updated in recent years.

The native habitat of the Argentine ant, the Paraná River drainage [Wild 2004, 2007], is an unstable environment with repeated flooding [LeBrun et al. 2007]. In such an environment with frequent disturbance, characteristics such as high reproductive ability (typical of r-strategists), high migration ability, and broad dietary spectrum, may be adaptive. The following characteristics of Argentine ants may have evolved in such a context, but those characteristics may also allow their establishment, abundance, and frequent human-mediated dispersal out of the native range.

### *1) Polygyny [Multi-Queen System]*

In many ant species, a nest contains a single reproductive queen [Hölldobler and Wilson 1990]. However, in Argentine ants, a nest contains multiple queens (>10 queens/1000 workers) [Keller et al. 1989]. An individual queen lays up to dozens of eggs per day [Abril et al. 2008].

### *2) Colony Budding*

In many ant species, winged queens undertake mating flight and found new nests at distant sites from their natal nests [Hölldobler and Wilson 1990]. In contrast, Argentine ant queens do not engage in mating flight, and instead they mate within natal nests [Markin 1970a; Passera et al. 1988]. New nests are founded by colony budding, in which queens leave for new nesting sites nearby the natal nests, accompanied by workers on foot [Ingram and Gordon 2003]. Because queens undertaking colony budding can rely on worker forces from the start, they reach their maximum fecundity earlier and thus have a higher intrinsic rate of natural increase, compared to queens undertaking mating flight and founding nests independently [Tsuji and Tsuji 1996]. Simulations showed that when nest mortality is dependent on the nest size [e.g. in local competition: Holway and Case 2001; Walters and MacKay 2005; Sagata and Lester 2009], colony budding is more adaptive than independent founding by mating flight, under frequent disturbances [Nakamaru et al. 2007].

### *3) Opportunistic Nesting Behavior*

Argentine ants readily relocate nests when nest conditions become unfavorable [Gordon et al. 2001; Heller and Gordon 2006]. Other than digging shallow nests in the soil, Argentine ants make use of various microhabitats for nesting sites such as under mulch, under paving stones, between cracks in stone wall and concrete blocks, within and under flowerpots, inside empty cans, in garbage bags and garbage boxes [Vega and Rust 2001; S. Tatsuki, personal communication]. These traits may increase the chance of human transportation of this species.

#### *4) Supercoloniality*

In typical ant species, colonies are composed of one or several cooperative nests, and territorial aggression among conspecifics from neighboring nests is commonly observed [Hölldobler and Wilson 1990]. In Argentine ants, however, individuals can move freely among many nests without incurring territorial aggression (nests are often interconnected with trails), and the aggregation of mutually non-aggressive nests is referred to as a 'supercolony'. Formation of a supercolony reduces the cost associated with territorial defense, and enable Argentine ants to invest in colony growth [Holway et al. 1998].

Supercoloniality may have arisen from the traits of polygyny and colony budding, but one supercolony can cover an extremely large area. For example, Argentine ants form a vast supercolony for more than 6000 km along the Mediterranean coast, though the supercolony is not perfectly continuous [Giraud et al. 2002]. Such large-scale supercolonies are common in the introduced range [>900 km across coastal California, U.S.A.: Tsutsui et al. 2000; >900 km across New Zealand: Corin et al. 2007a; >80 km across Melbourne City, Australia: Suhr et al. 2009; >400 km across Japan: Sunamura et al. 2009a].

Territorial aggression occurs among individuals from different supercolonies [Thomas et al. 2006]. When individuals from different supercolonies encounter, they usually run away or attack each other. The attack often escalates to fierce fight, where individuals incur severe injuries (lose legs and antennas) or die. In Europe, two populations different from the aforementioned supercolony exist, one expanding over >700 km along the Iberian Mediterranean coast [Giraud et al. 2002], and the other recently found from Corsica [Blight et al., in press]. Other than the large one in California, the U.S.A. harbors several, much smaller supercolonies in California [Tsutsui et al. 2003] and the southeastern part of the country [Buczkowski et al. 2004]. In Japan, three small supercolonies (<1 km in diameter) were found from Kobe Port, other than the largest one in the country [Sunamura et al. 2007]. These supercolony identities were confirmed by behavioral experiments in which individuals from distant localities were artificially put together, but the behavioral patterns in these laboratory experiments may be consistent with the actual behavioral patterns in the field [Thomas et al. 2006]. In Japan, combats among Argentine ant individuals have been observed in the contact zone of distinct supercolonies in Kobe Port (Fig. 2).

Argentine ants in the introduced range are characterized by single massive supercolonies and a few smaller supercolonies. In contrast, Argentine ants in the native range form multiple, mutually incompatible supercolonies that are typically less than hundreds of meters in diameter [Tsutsui et al. 2000; Heller 2004; Pedersen et al. 2006; Vogel et al. 2009]. For example, Vogel et al. [2009] found as many as 11 supercolonies along the 3 km study transect. The difference in supercolony size and number between the introduced and native range may have arisen from introduction of a few supercolonies from the native range to new environments [Tsutsui et al. 2000; Giraud et al. 2002; Helanterä et al. 2009]. The release from fierce competition with conspecific supercolonies may enable Argentine ants in the introduced range to attain elevated population density [Suarez et al. 1999; Tsutsui et al. 2000]. High population density may be responsible for the displacement of native ants and other species by numerical advantage, prominent outbreak of homopteran insects in agricultural environment, and terrible nuisance in urban area [Holway et al. 2002; Silverman and Brightwell 2008].

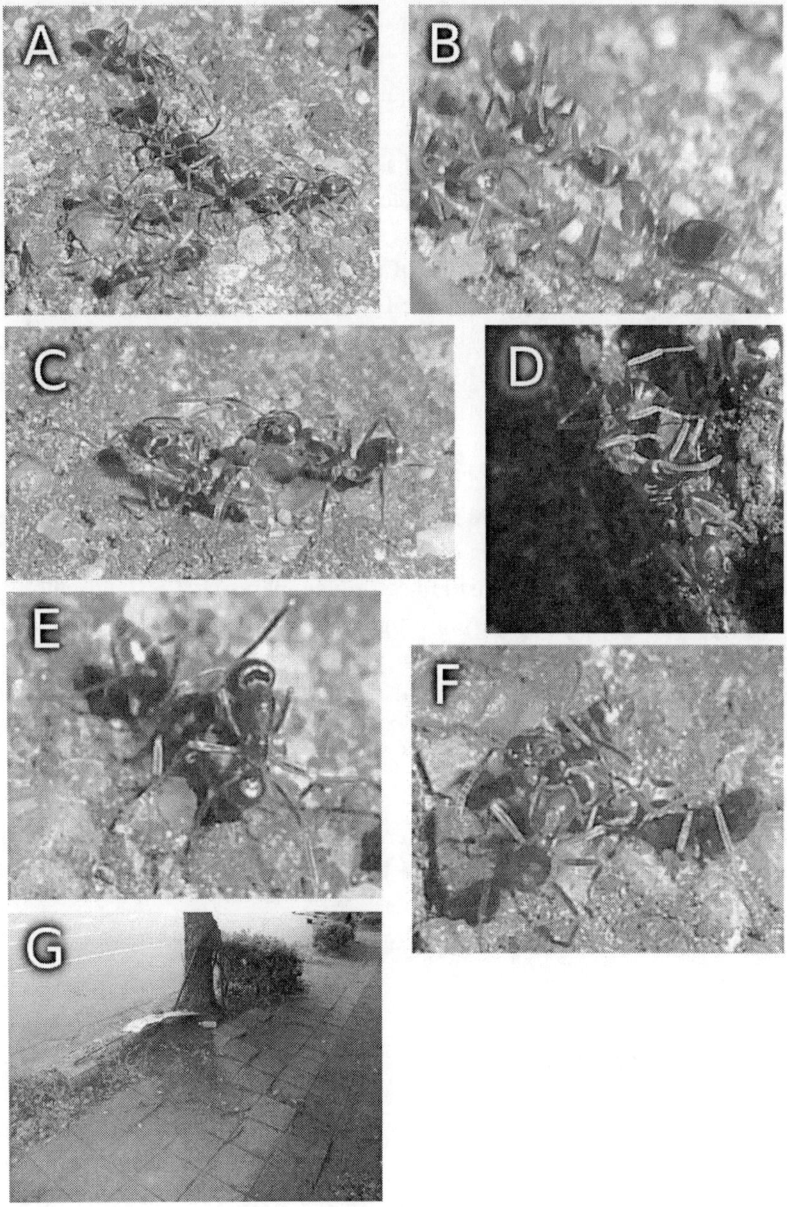


Figure 2. Aggressive interactions between Argentine ant supercolonies in the field. In Kobe Port, Japan, by-ship multiple introductions may have led to the distribution of mutually compatible supercolonies. A) Trails of different supercolonies collide and turn into chaos. Two individuals in the center flex their gasters menacingly. B) Two workers bite each other's mandibles. C) The left worker tries to run away, but the right worker bites it in the leg. D) The upper worker bites the lower individual in the petiole and emits chemical defensive compounds from the gaster. E) Two workers bite each other. The front individual uses chemical weapon. F) Fights often lead to death (right). The winner (lower left) meets another opponent (upper left), and the war continues. G) Pavement of Maya Wharf, Kobe Port, where the ant combat (A-E) was observed. This is the first record of field observation of aggressive interaction between supercolonies in Japan (April 2009). Photographs by Eiriki Sunamura.

***5) Broad Dietary Spectrum***

Argentine ants are omnivorous [LeBrun et al. 2007], and show flexible patterns of food resource use [Tillberg et al. 2007]. They prey on live arthropods, scavenge dead animals, and collect plant remains in the field [Abril et al. 2007]. They swarm on meat, vegetables and sweets in houses [E. Sunamura, personal obseravtion]. Among the broad dietary spectrum, however, Argentine ants feed mainly on liquid food such as the honeydew produced by homopteran insects [Markin 1970b; Abril et al. 2007]. Mass consumption of the carbohydrate-rich honeydew in the introduced range might fuel Argentine ant activity, as well as reduce the trophic level of Argentine ants to maintain high population density [Davidson 1998; Grover et al. 2007; Tillberg et al. 2007].

As described above, preadaptation (e.g. of the colony structure) to disturbed habitat, and numerical dominance gained by formation of expansive supercolony and perhaps dietary flexibility, may contribute to the success of Argentine ants in the introduced range (see also Suarez et al. 2008). Supercoloniality and omnivory are common among the invasive ant species (some species undergo mating flight along with colony budding) listed by the IUCN [Lowe et al. 2000] and other notorious ants (e.g. garden ant *Lasius neglectus*: Cremer et al. 2008) [Passera 1994; Holway et al. 2002]. In addition to these factors, release from natural enemies, a general cause of invader's success, may contribute to the success of these ants. For example, more than 30 natural enemies of *Solenopsis* fire ants have been discovered in their native South America (e.g. social parasitic ants, mites, parasitic flies and entomopathogenic microsporidia) [Williams et al. 2003]. As for the Argentine ants, however, natural enemies in the native range have not been detected [but see Markin and McCoy 1968; Tsutsui et al. 2003; Reuter et al. 2005; Touyama et al. 2008]. Finally, release from interspecific competition may be also important [LeBrun et al. 2007]. Fire ants and Argentine ants co-occur in a part of their native ranges, and competition with supercolonies of each other appears to be as fierce as that with supercolonies of their own species. Because an ant species, which possesses any one of the above characteristics, is not necessarily invasive, invasiveness of alien ants might arise from addition of some characteristics or their synergistic effect.

## CONTROL

Major control methods currently used for Argentine ants are chemical means such as toxic baits and barrier treatments [Soeprono and Rust 2004; Silverman and Brightwell 2008]. Argentine ants are readily susceptible to the active ingredients, but treatments often fail to achieve successful control. The difficulties in controlling Argentine ants are backed by the formation of a supercolony [Silverman and Brightwell 2008]. Partial treatments of a supercolony may achieve temporary decline or elimination of Argentine ants, but members of the supercolony soon move into the vacant space from surrounding areas by tracking trails, relocating nests, or budding. For example, in a survey of homeowners living in a neighborhood infested with Argentine ants in California, approx. 40% of homeowners who hired professional pest control services did not obtain satisfactory results, with Argentine ants continuing to come back [Klotz et al. 2008]. There are a few important cases where feasibility of eradication was shown for incipient small colonies with intense bait applications and follow-up surveys (a quarter of 26 ha residential area of Bunbury, Australia: Davis et al.

1998; 9.3 ha natural environment on Tiritiri Matangi Island, New Zealand: Harris 2002), but it is virtually impossible to eradicate large infestations, with limited resources and numerous stakeholders [Forschler 1997; Silverman and Brightwell 2008].

Control of other invasive ants faces the same problem with Argentine ants, since they also form supercolonies. However, eradication from small infestation or successful large-scale management have been achieved in concerned natural environments, with adequate evaluation of distribution range, sufficient resources, and good cooperation among stakeholders (big-headed ant *Pheidole megacephala* in northern Australia [Hoffmann and O'Connor 2004; Hoffmann, in press]; little fire ant *Wasmannia auropunctata* in Santa Fe and Marchena Islands, Galápagos [Abedrabbo 1994; Causton et al. 2005]; yellow crazy ant *Anoplolepis gracilipes* in some part of Seychelles and Christmas Island [Haines and Haines 1978; Green and O'Dowd 2009]). For fire ants, release trials of natural enemies moved from their native range have been conducted, and successful establishment of self-sustaining populations has been confirmed for two species of parasitic flies [Graham et al. 2003; Porter et al. 2004] and an entomopathogenic microsporidium [Williams et al. 1999].

# DISPERSAL

## Means of Dispersal

International dispersal of Argentine ants naturally depends on human activity [Suarez et al. 2001]. The type of commerce involved is obscure. Even for exotic ants as a whole [McGlynn 1999], there have been few systematic analyses. In the case of the U.S.A., 94% of the ants intercepted in commerce at its border between 1927 and 1985 (394 records in total) were detected on plants (only one record for Argentine ants and no record for fire ants *Solenopsis invicta* and *Solenopsis richteri*, though they are now widespread in the country: see Lewis et al. 1992) [Suarez et al. 2005]. Major means of transportation for ants intercepted at the New Zealand border between 1955-2005 were fresh produce of air cargo and air passenger, as well as container of maritime cargo (The big-headed ant *Pheidole megacephala* was the number 1 intercepted species, and the yellow crazy ant and Argentine ant were among the top 20 species) [Ward et al. 2006]. There have been few records of Argentine ant interception at Japan's border: the first record was made recently (2005) from air plants, which came from Guatemala through Los Angeles by airway [T. Kishimoto, personal communication]. The air plants were infested by a colony with approx. 150 workers and two queens. Occurrence of Argentine ants has not been recorded from Guatemala [Wetterer et al. 2009], but the country includes areas suitable for their establishment [Roura-Pascual et al. 2004; Hartley et al. 2006].

The primary mode of dispersal of introduced Argentine ants within countries or continents is also human-mediated long distance jump dispersal [Suarez et al. 2001; Ward et al. 2005; Okaue et al. 2007; Blight et al. 2009; Pitt et al. 2009; Roura-Pascual et al. 2009b], which can proceed at a rate of >100 km/year [Suarez et al. 2001]. Unaided dispersal of Argentine ants is made exclusively via colony budding on foot, generally at a rate of only <300 m/year [Suarez et al. 2001]. The dual model of dispersal, human-mediated jump dispersal and colony budding, may be a general rule in invasive ants, but some species (e.g. *Solenopsis invicta*) show more complex patterns of dispersal because they also undertake mating flight [Holway et al. 2002; Espadaler et al. 2007].

Statistics on what vehicles Argentine ants use in jump dispersal events are scarce, but potted plants or nursery stock have often been cited in the literature [Newell and Barber 1913; Smith 1965; Costa and Rust 1999]. These may be one of the major means of human-mediated dispersal for invasive ants in general [e.g. Lewis et al. 1992; Ugelvig et al. 2008]. Steamboats and railroads were also a major means of Argentine ant dispersal in the U.S.A. at the beginning of the last century [Newell and Barber 1913], but their relative contribution might have declined with the development of other means of transportation. Roura-Pascual et al. (2009b) suggested with simulations the relatively low but certain contribution of the cork industry in the Argentine ant jump dispersal in the Iberian Peninsula. For *Solenopsis invicta* and *S. richteri* intercepted at the California border during 1987-1992 (758 records in total), the sources were divided into nursery stock, agricultural shipments, non-agricultural shipments, empty trucks, rental trucks, and autos [Lewis et al. 1992]. Among them, non-agricultural shipments (e.g. pallets, roofing materials and carpets) comprised the most (approx. 300 records), followed by empty trucks and agricultural shipments (approx. 200 and 180 records, respectively). In Florida and probably in other parts of the southern U.S.A. also, road maintenance practice with soil depot may be a major source for dispersal of the polygyne form of *Solenopsis invicta* [King et al. 2009].

## Keys to Infer Dispersal History of Argentine Ants: Relevance of Supercolony Identity

In attempts to reconstruct the dispersal history of alien species, genetic analyses and historical records provide vital information. In the case of Argentine ants, their social structure is also closely related to dispersal history. Previous studies showed genetic homogeneity within supercolonies [Tsutsui et al. 2000; Giraud et al. 2002; Corin et al. 2007a; Suhr et al. 2009], but differences in presence/absence or frequencies of microsatellite loci, and even lack of gene flow between supercolonies [Jaquiéry et al. 2005; Thomas et al. 2006; Pedersen et al. 2006]. This suggests that distinct supercolonies in the introduced range represent independent sources of introduction. On the other hand, a supercolony in the introduced range may derive from a single introduction, or repeated introductions of a single source or perhaps very similar sources.

Argentine ants use hydrocarbons on their cuticle, the outer layer of the exoskeleton, to discriminate members and non-members of supercolonies [Liang and Silverman 2000; Greene and Gordon 2007; Torres et al. 2007], like many other ant species use their cuticular hydrocarbons to discriminate members and non-members of nests [Howard and Blomquist 2005]. Workers share similar cuticular hydrocarbon profiles (compounds and their relative proportions) within supercolonies, whereas workers from distinct supercolonies have different hydrocarbon profiles [Suarez et al. 2002; Sunamura et al. 2009a]. Many studies have suggested that cuticular hydrocarbon profiles are genetically based in Argentine ants [e.g. Tsutsui et al. 2000; Giraud et al. 2002; Suarez et al. 2002]. Behavioral patterns between Argentine ant colonies also remain consistent under usual rearing conditions in laboratories

[Giraud et al. 2002; Suarez et al. 2002], but under extreme rearing condition where the ants are fed with only a particular insect prey, prey-derived hydrocarbons are acquired by Argentine ants and inter-colony behavioral patterns are strongly affected [Liang and Silverman 2000]. This shows that cuticular hydrocarbon profiles are influenced by environment. However, such a phenomenon has never been observed in the field [Helanterä et al. 2009]. Environment-mediated change in hydrocarbon profiles is unlikely to happen in the field, because prey species which can induce the change may be limited [Liang et al. 2001], and Argentine ants usually consume a variety of food resources, not specific prey [Markin 1970b; Abril et al. 2007].

Supercolonies expanding for hundreds or thousands of kilometers in the introduced range [Tsutsui et al. 2000; Giraud et al. 2002] may have been formed via numerous human-mediated dispersal events of particular source populations. Evidence supporting this view has been obtained from studies on social structure in recently invaded countries, New Zealand and Japan [Corin et al. 2007a; Sunamura et al. 2009a]. In both countries, Argentine ants were noted in the early 1990s, and now show patchy distribution resulting from human-mediated dispersal [Ward et al. 2005; Okaue et al. 2007]. In New Zealand, behavioral and genetic experiments demonstrated lack of aggression among all of the sampled localities and that the local colonies may originate from a single source population from Australia [Corin et al. 2007a, b]. In Japan, genetic similarity and lack of aggression among all of the localities, except Kobe Port, were revealed [Sunamura et al. 2007, 2009a]. In addition, chemical analysis demonstrated similarity of cuticular hydrocarbon profiles among disjunctive members of the supercolony [Sunamura et al. 2009a]. These results suggest that supercolonies expand via human-mediated jump dispersal, without experiencing significant change in hydrocarbon profiles and recognition patterns by founder effect and change in environment concomitant to the dispersal.

The apparent permanence of supercolony identity in Argentine ants makes it an important unit in inferring their dispersal history, although it is necessary to confirm behavioral data with genetic data because the possibilities of a new supercolony arising from mutation in the introduced range and effect of non-genetic factors on social structure cannot be excluded [Liang and Silverman 2000; Blight et al., in press]. It must be noted that the relationship between supercolony identity and dispersal history varies among ant species. Invasive ants come from many subfamilies in which supercoloniality may have evolved independently [Helanterä et al. 2009] via different mechanisms [Keller and Ross 1998; Fournier et al. 2005].

## Dispersal History

There have been few systematic genetic studies examining international dispersal events of Argentine ants, and limited cases where introduction pathways were suggested. Tsutsui et al. [2001] suggested with microsatellite data that many of the introduced populations around the world originated from the southern part of Paraná River drainage. Wetterer and Wetterer [2006] suggested the route from South America through Madeira to Portugal with a combination of mitochondrial data, behavioral data and historical records. Tsutsui et al. [2001] suggested with microsatellite data that the population of Maui Island derived from one of the two distinct populations of Hawaii Island. Corin et al. [2007b] suggested with mitochondrial data and interception records introduction from Australia to New Zealand. Buczkowski et al. [2004] revealed that microsatellite alleles of the large supercolony of California were a subset of the total alleles of the diminutive supercolonies in southeastern U.S.A., but relationships between the large supercolony and each of the small supercolonies were not reported. There have been some other speculations based on historical records that need to be verified with future research. For example, it was speculated that Argentine ants first reached U.S.A. in New Orleans from Brazil via coffee ship [Foster 1908]. Also, Argentine ants are thought to have entered South Africa via cattle fodder from Argentina during the Anglo-Boer War [Skaife 1955]. In France, Argentine ants were apparently introduced with orchids and ferns imported from South America to green houses in the Côte d'Azur [Passera 1994]. Argentine ants are thought to have landed in Hawaii either with troops in the Second World War [Passera 1994] or with goods from California [Zimmerman 1941].

Though not reached through identification of specific introduction pathways, supercolony identities and their genetic analyses have provided information on more general patterns of dispersal. The presence of several, behaviorally and genetically distinct supercolonies in many introduced areas around the world [Giraud et al. 2002; Tsutsui et al. 2003; Buczkowski et al. 2004; Sunamura et al. 2009a] suggests that Argentine ants have come out of their native range at least several times, and that multiple introductions into a country is a common pattern. Intensive investigations of Argentine ant social structure at fine spatial scales, especially in the hubs for international trade, have so far been scarce, but such an approach may help identify focal ports of entry. For example, localization of three out of four Japanese supercolonies in Kobe Port may indicate direct, multiple introductions into the port via international trade [Sunamura et al. 2007, 2009a]. Also, Argentine ant colonies in seaport sites in Victoria, Australia, are mutually non-aggressive but exhibit relatively high antennation frequency to recognize each other, possibly due to multiple introductions from slightly different sources [Björkman-Chiswell et al. 2008].

With knowledge on the social structure of Argentine ants in various introduced countries accumulated, studies on the relationships among supercolonies around the world are now becoming a trend in Argentine ant research. Wetterer and Wetterer [2006] found that the supercolony of Madeira and the largest supercolony in southern Europe are mutually non-aggressive. Brandt et al. [2009] performed comprehensive analyses using supercolonies from various introduced areas of the world (North America, Hawaii, Europe, and Australia), and showed that the largest supercolonies in respective areas are genetically very similar and have very similar cuticular hydrocarbon profiles. These results suggested that the large supercolonies arose from a common introduction pathway, or perhaps even from the same native supercolony, and that they might be mutually non-aggressive. During the same period, Sunamura et al. [2009b] examined behavioral relationships among supercolonies from California, Europe, and Japan, and found that the largest supercolonies in these areas are indeed mutually non-aggressive. Their focal populations were selected based on their finding that the large supercolony of Japan has cuticular hydrocarbon profile apparently similar to those of the large supercolonies in California and Europe [Liang et al. 2001; de Biseau et al. 2004]. These studies suggest the presence of a transcontinental supercolony, although the behavioral assay merits more replication. This supercolony is the largest cooperative unit ever known from any social insect species that exhibits intraspecific aggression. Moreover, the extent of this ant society is paralleled by human society only. This supercolony is also a very unique existence in the point that humans created it unwittingly via international trade. Given the formation of an expansive supercolony is responsible for the invasiveness and difficulties in control of Argentine ants, the global-scale supercolony might be another 'inconvenient truth'.

How was the intercontinental supercolony created? Wetterer and Wetterer [2006] proposed an interesting hypothesis regarding the dispersal history of the largest supercolony in Europe. Argentine ants were first discovered out of their native range on Madeira between 1847 and 1858, followed by detection in some localities in Portugal in 1890s. At that time, Madeira was an important hub for commerce between Portugal and its colonies in South America. Based on behavioral, genetic, and historical evidence, it was suggested that the European large supercolony originated from the route from South America to Portugal via Madeira, and then throughout southern Europe. The finding that the European supercolony is a part of the intercontinental supercolony gives rise to an intriguing hypothesis that descendants of the most ancient introduced population have spread to many parts of the world, without forgetting their roots. Expansion of very restricted propagules in the introduced range has also been suggested for the garden ant *Lasius neglectus*, though supercolony identity may be less persistent in this species [Ugelvig et al. 2008]. The hypothesis for Argentine ants needs to be tested cautiously. For example, we do not yet fully understand the distribution pattern of supercolonies in the native range. Are native populations comprised of thousands of mutually distinct supercolonies, or are they a mosaic of a countable number of mutually incompatible supercolonies? In other words, are genetic and chemical (in terms of cuticular hydrocarbon) profiles inexhaustible or limited? Are important ports in the native range dominated by a particular supercolony?

Another recent trend in ant invasion is the successive introductions to the Pan-Pacific region. In the nearly 100 or more years of invasion histories, the red imported fire ant had been confined in the southeastern U.S.A. and Middle America, and the Argentine ant has not penetrated Asia, until 1990s [Callcott and Collins 1996; Suarez et al. 2001]. However, the red imported fire ant was noted in California in 1998 [anonymous 1999], Australia in 2001 [Lach and Thomas 2008], New Zealand on three occasions since 2001 (each time soon eradicated) [Pascoe 2002; Corin et al. 2008], Taiwan in 2003 [Chen et al. 2006], Hong Kong, Macao, and mainland China in 2005 [Zhang et al. 2007]. Australia, New Zealand, Taiwan, and China may have received multiple introductions [Henshaw et al. 2005; Corin et al. 2008; Yang et al. 2008]. Argentine ants were noted in New Zealand in 1990 [Green 1990], and in Japan in 1993 [Sugiyama 2000]. Though establishment has not been confirmed, an Argentine ant male individual was recorded from North Korea [Radchenko 2005]. Also, Thailand, Fiji and Singapore were included among the sources for Argentine ants intercepted at New Zealand border [Corin et al. 2007b]. Sunamura et al. [2009a] concluded from supercolony number that Japan might have received at least four introductions. However, the large supercolony of Japan may actually derive from more than one introduction. The Argentine ant colony in Yanai, the southernmost distribution patch of the large supercolony, possesses unique microsatellite alleles [Hirata et al. 2008], and is likely to represent a different invasion history from the other parts of the supercolony. Because this supercolony belongs to the transcontinental supercolony, separate introductions from some of its world domain are possible [Sunamura et al. 2009b].

Rigorous studies to elucidate the cause are yet to be performed. However, globalization and liberalization may be at least partly responsible. Global-scale analysis showed that the overall degree of international trade best explains the number of invasive alien species in a country [Westphal et al. 2008]. Growth in the volume and complexity of international trade, combined with the liberalization of regulatory regimes to encourage trade, increase the frequency of introductions along existing pathways and the number of new pathways [Perrings et al. 2002]. Global increase in trade volume might have promoted the recent introductions of invasive ants to previously unexplored territories in the Pan-Pacific region. At the same time, perhaps already invaded areas of the world have also received new introductions, but the new introductions might have been confounded with the local spread of the older invasions. New introductions may be especially hard to be noticed in areas where spread of the ant is close to equilibrium [e.g. Argentine ants in the Iberian Peninsula: Roura-Pascual et al. 2009b]. This explanation appears consistent with the more marked introductions of the red imported fire ant compared to the Argentine ant in recent years. The red imported fire ant has the potential to invade large portions of all continents, but had not gone out of North and Middle America until recently [Morrison et al. 2004]. In contrast, of the potential geographical range of Argentine ants, the major vulnerable areas left uninvaded until 1990 were only southeastern Asia or tropical coastal Africa [Roura-Pascual et al. 2004; Hartley et al. 2006]. Already invaded areas merit investigation of the presence/absence of recent introductions. However, increase in transportations of exotic ants might have been specifically high in the Pan-Pacific region. For instance, Asian countries have achieved great economic growth in recent decades [The Global Social Change Research Project 2007], and may have met a dramatic rise in invasive species propagule pressure, as shown for China [Ding et al. 2008]. Important hubs for the trade between Asian countries and the trading partners (perhaps other parts of the Pan-Pacific region for the type of commerce involved in ant transportation) may suffer similar risks, as was the case for Argentine ants in Madeira [Wetterer and Wetterer 2006].

## CONCLUSION

International trade has spread Argentine ants over many parts of the world during the last 150 years, and has constructed an unparalleled ant colony in history. The damage caused by the invasion has been tremendous, and there may be still various impacts yet to be uncovered by scientists. Now the ant invasion is accelerated, apparently in accordance with the rapid growth in the volume of international trade. Increase in trade volume should be accompanied by advance in preventive measures against increased chance of invasions. Studies on the behavior and genetics of invasive ants around major ports may elucidate a number of introductions to the ports and thus focal ports of entry, as well as a link between focal ports. Such biological information, as well as trends in economy, may constitute vital components to reconstruct dispersal history, as well as predict dynamics of invasive ant dispersal at the global scale.

## ACKNOWLEDGMENTS

We would like to thank all of our current and previous collaborators, co-operators, and colleagues for nourishing our view on the subject. Special thanks go to Yukio Ishikawa and

Ayako Hamada for their assistance, encouragement and advice, and to Taku Shimada for providing photographs of Argentine ants. This work was supported by the Grant-in Aid for JSPS Fellows (20-6386) to Eiriki Sunamura.

## REFERENCES

Abedrabbo, S. (1994). Control of the little fire ant *Wasmannia auropunctata*, on Santa Fe Island in the Galápagos Islands. In Williams, D. F. (Eds.), *Exotic ants: biology, impact, and control introduced species* (pp. 219-227). Westview Press, Boulder, Colorado.

Abril, S., Oliveras, J. & Gómez, C. (2007). Foraging activity and dietary spectrum of the Argentine ant (Hymenoptera: Formicidae) in invaded natural areas of the northeast Iberian Peninsula. *Environmental Entomology, 36,* 1166-1173.

Abril, S., Oliveras, J. & Gómez, C. (2008). Effect of temperature on the oviposition rate of Argentine ant queens (*Linepithema humile* Mayr) under monogynous and polygynous experimental conditions. *Journal of Insect Physiology, 54,* 266-272.

Addison, P. & Samways, M. J. (2000). A survey of ants (Hymenoptera: Formicidae) that forage in vineyards in the Western Cape Province, South Africa. *African Entomology, 8,* 251-260.

Altfeld, L. & Stiling, P. (2006). Argentine ants strongly affect some but not all common insects on *Baccharis halimifolia. Environmental Entomology, 35,* 31-36.

Altfeld, L. & Stiling, P. (2009). Effects of aphid-tending Argentine ants, nitrogen enrichment and early-season herbivory on insects hosted by a coastal shrub. *Biological Invasions, 11,* 183–191.

Anonymous. (1999). Fire ant invades southern California. *California Agriculture, 53,* 5.

Bartlett, B. R. (1961). The influence of ants upon parasites, predators, and scale insects. *Annals of the Entomological Society of America, 54,* 543-551.

Björkman-Chiswell, B. T., van Wilgenburg, E., Thomas, M. L., Swearer, S. E. & Elgar, M. A. (2008). Absence of aggression but not nestmate recognition in an Australian population of the Argentine ant *Linepithema humile*. *Insectes Sociaux, 55,* 207-212.

Blancafort, X. & Gómez, C. (2005). Consequences of the Argentine ant, *Linepithema humile* (Mayr), invasion on pollination of *Euphorbia characias* (L.) (Euphorbiaceae). *Acta Oecologica, 28,* 49–55.

Blight, O., Orgeas, J., Renucci, M., Tirard, A. & Provost, E. (2009). Where and how Argentine ant (*Linepithema humile*) spreads in Corsica? *Comptes Rendus Biologies, 332,* 747-751.

Blight, O., Renucci, M., Tirard, A., Orgeas, J. & Provest, E. (in press). A new colony structure of the invasive Argentine ant (*Linepithema humile*) in Southern Europe. *Biological Invasions*.

Bolger, D. T., Suarez, A. V., Crooks, K. R., Morrison, S. A. & Case, T. J. (2000). Arthropods in urban habitat fragments in southern California: area, age, and edge effects. *Ecological Applications, 10,* 1230–1248.

Bond, W. & Slingsby, P. (1984). Collapse of an ant-plant mutalism: the Argentine ant (*Iridomyrmex humilis*) and myrmecochorous Proteaceae. *Ecology, 65,* 1031-1037.

Brightwell, R. J. & Silverman, J. (2009). Effects of honeydew-producing hemipteran denial on local Argentine ant distribution and boric acid bait performance. *Journal of Economic Entomology, 102,* 1170-1174.

Brandt, M., van Wilgenburg, E. & Tsutsui, N. D. (2009). Global-scale analyses of chemical ecology and population genetics in the invasive Argentine ant. *Molecular Ecology, 18,* 997-1005.

Buczkowski, G., Vargo, E. L. & Silverman, J. (2004). The diminutive supercolony: the Argentine ants of the southeastern United States. *Molecular Ecology, 13,* 2235-2242.

Buys, B. (1987). Competition for nectar between Aregntine ants (*Iridomyrmex humilis*) and honeybees (*Apis mellifera*) on black ironbark (*Eucalyptus sideroxylon*). *South African Journal of Zoology, 22,* 173-174.

Callcott, A. A. & Collins, H. L. (1996). Invasion and range expansion of imported fire ants (Hymenoptera: Formicidae) in North America from 1918-1995. *Florida Entomologist, 79,* 240-251.

Cammell, M. E., Way, M. J. & Paiva, M. R. (1996). Diversity and structure of ant communities associated with oak, pine, eucalyptus and arable habitats in Portugul. *Insectes Sociaux, 43,* 37-46.

Carney, S. E., Byerley, M. B. & Holway, D. A. (2003). Invasive Argentine ants (*Linepithema humile*) do not replace native ants as seed dispersers of *Dendromecon rigida* (Papaveraceae) in California, USA. *Oecologia, 135,* 576-582.

Carpintero, S., Reyes-López, J. & Arias de Reyna, L. (2005). Impact of Argentine ants (*Linepithema humile*) on an arboreal ant community in Doñana National Park, Spain. *Biodiversity and Conservation, 14,* 151–163.

Carpintero, S. & Reyes-López, J. (2008). The role of competitive dominance in the invasive ability of the Argentine ant (Linepithema humile). *Biological Invasions, 10,* 25-35.

Causton, C. E., Sevilla, C. R. & Porter, S. D. (2005). Eradication of the little fire ant, *Wasmannia auropunctata* (Hymenoptera: Formicidae), from Marchena Island, Galápagos: on the edge of success? *Florida Entomologist, 88,* 159-168.

Chen, J. S. C., Shen, C. & Lee, H. (2006). Monogynous and polygynous red imported fire ants, *Solenopsis invicta* Buren (Hymenoptera: Formicidae), in Taiwan. *Environmental Entomology, 35,* 167-172.

Christian, C. E. (2001). Consequences of a biological invasion reveal the importance of mutualism for plant communities. *Nature, 413,* 635-639.

Cole, F. R., Medeiros, A. C., Loope, L. L. & Zuehlke, W. W. (1992). Effects of the Argentine ant on arthropod fauna of Hawaiian high-elevation shrubland. *Ecology, 73,* 1313-1322.

Corin, S. E., Abbott, K. A., Ritchie, P. A. & Lester, P. J. (2007a). Large scale unicoloniality: the population and colony structure of the invasive Argentine ant (*Linepithema humile*) in New Zealand. *Insectes Sociaux, 54,* 275-282.

Corin, S. E., Lester, P. J., Abbott, K. L. & Ritchie, P. A. (2007b) Inferring historical introduction pathways with mitochondrial DNA: the case of introduced Argentine ants (*Linepithema humile*) into New Zealand. *Diversity and Distributions, 13,* 510-518.

Corin, S. E., Ritchie, P. A. & Lester, P. J. (2008). Introduction pathway analysis into New Zealand highlights a source population 'hotspot' in the native range of the red imported fire ant (*Solenopsis invicta*). *Sociobiology, 52,* 129-143.

Costa, H. S. & Rust, M. K. (1999). Mortality and foraging rates of Argentine ant (Hymenoptera: Formicidae) colonies exposed to potted plants treated with fipronil. *Journal of Agricultural and Urban Entomology, 16,* 37-48.

Cremer, S., Ugelvig, L. V., Drijfhout, F. P., Schlick-Steiner, B., Steiner, F. M., Seifert, B., Hughes, D. P., Schulz, A., Petersen, K. S., Konrad, H., Stauffer, C., Kiran, K., Espadaler, X., d'Ettorre, P., Aktaç, N., Eilenberg, J., Jones, G. R., Nash, D. R., Pedersen, J. S. & Boomsma, J. J. (2008). The evolution of invasiveness in garden ants. *PloS ONE, 3,* e3838.

Daane, K. M., Sime, K. R., Fallon, J. & Cooper, M. L. (2007). Impacts of Argentine ants on mealybugs and their natural enemies in California's coastal vineyards. *Ecological Entomology, 32,* 583-596.

Davidson, D. W. (1998). Resource discovery versus resource domination in ants: a functional mechanism for breaking the trade-off. *Ecological Entomology, 23,* 484-490.

Davis, P. R., van Schagen, J. J., Widmer, M. A. & Craven, T. J. (1998). The trial eradication of Argentine ants in Bunbury, Western Australia. *Internal report, Social Insect Research Section, Agriculture Western Australia.*

de Biseau, J.-C., Passera, L., Daloze, D. & Aron, S. (2004). Ovarian activity correlates with extreme changes in cuticular hydrocarbon profile in the highly polygynous ant, *Linepithema humile*. *Journal of Insect Physiology, 50,* 585-593.

De Ong, E. R. (1916). Municipal control of the Argentine ant. *Journal of Economic Entomology, 9,* 468-472.

Ding, J., Mack, R. N., Lu, P., Ren, M. & Huang, H. (2008). China's booming economy is sparking and accelerating biological invasions. *BioScience, 58,* 317-324.

Erickson, J. M. (1971). The displacement of native ant species by the introduced Argentine ant *Iridomyrmex humilis* mayr. *Psyche, 78,* 257-266.

Espadaler, X. & Gómez, C. (2003) The Argentine ant, *Linepithema humile*, in the Iberian Peninsula. *Sociobiology, 42,* 187-192.

Espadaler, X., Tartally, A., Schultz, R., Seifert, B. & Nagy, Cs. (2007). Regional trends and preliminary results on the local expansion rate in the invasive garden ant, *Lasius neglectus* (Hymenoptera, Formicidae). *Insectes Sociaux, 54,* 293-301.

Field, H. C., Evans Sr., W. E., Hartley, R., Hansen, L. D. & J. H. Klotz. (2007). A survey of structural ant pests in the southwestern U.S.A. (Hymenoptera: Formicidae). *Sociobiology, 49,* 151-164.

Fisher, R. N., Suarez, A. V. & Case, T. J. (2002). Spatial patterns in the abundance of the coastal horned lizard. *Conservation Biology, 16,* 205–215.

Flanders, S. E. (1945). Coincident infestations of *Aonidiella citrina* and *Coccus hesperidum*, a result of ant activity. *Journal of Economic Entomology, 38,* 711-712.

Foster, E. (1908). The introduction of Iridomyrmex humilis (Mayr) into New Orleans. *Journal of Economic Entomology, 1,* 289-293.

Forschler, B. (1997). A prescription for ant control success. *Pest Control, 65,* 34-38.

Fournier, D., Estoup, A., Orivel, J., Foucaud, J., Jourdan, H., Le Breton, J. & Keller, L. (2005). Clonal reproduction by males and females in the little fire ant. *Nature, 435,* 1230-1234.

Frazer, B. D. & Van den Bosch, R. (1973). Biological control of the walnut aphid in California: the interrelationship of the aphid and its parasite. *Environmental Entomology, 2,* 561-568.

Giladi, I. (2006). Choosing benefits or partners: a review of the evidence for the evolution of myrmecochory. *Oikos, 112,* 481-/492.

Giraud T., Pedersen, J. S. & Keller, L. (2002). Evolution of supercolonies: the Argentine ants of southern Europe. *Proceedings of the National Academy of Sciences of the United States of America, 99,* 6075-6079.

Gómez, C., Pons, P. & Bas, J. M. (2003). Effects of the Argentine ant *Linepithema humile* on seed dispersal and seedling emergence of *Rhamnus alaternus*. *Ecography, 26,* 532-538.

Gordon, D. M., Moses, L., Falkovitz-Halpern, M. & Wong, E. H. (2001). Effect of weather on infestation of building by the invasive Argentine ant, *Linepithema humile* (Hymenoptera: Formicidae). *The American Midland Naturalist, 146,* 321-328.

Graham, L. C. F., Porter, S. D., Pereira, R. M., Dorough, H. D. & Kelley, A. T. (2003). Field releases of the decapitating fly *Pseudacteon curvatus* (Diptera: Formicidae) in Alabama, Florida, and Tennessee. *Florida Entomologist, 86,* 334-339.

Green, O. R. (1990). Entomologist sets new record at Mt Smart for *Iridomyrmex humilis* established in New Zealand. *The Weta, 13,* 14-16.

Green, P. T. & O'Dowd, D. J. (2009). Management of invasive invertebrates: lessons from the management of an invasive alien ant. In Clout, M. N. & Williams, P. A. (Eds.), *Invasive Species Management: a Hand Book of Principles and Techniques* (pp. 153-172). Oxford University Press.

Greene, M. J. & Gordon, D. M. (2007). Structural complexity of chemical recognition cues affects the perception of group membership in the ants *Linepithema humile* and *Aphaenogaster cookerelli*. *The Journal of Experimental Biology, 210,* 897-905.

Grover, C. D., Kay, A. D., Monson, J. A., Marsh, T. C. & Holway, D. A. (2007). Linking nutrition and behavioural dominance: carbohydrate scarcity limits aggression and activity in Argentine ants. *Proceedings of the Royal Society B: Biological Sciences, 274,* 2951-2957.

Haines, I. H. & Haines, J. B. (1978). Pest status of the crazy ant, *Anoplolepis longipes* (Jerdon) (Hymenoptera: Formicidae), in the Seychelles. *Bulletin of Entomological Research, 68,* 627-638.

Harris, R. J. (2002). Potential impact of the Argentine ant (*Linepithema humile*) in New Zealand and options for its control. *Science for Conservation, 196,* 1-36.

Hartley, S., Harris, R. & Lester, P. J. (2006). Quantifying uncertainty in the potential distribution of an invasive species: climate and the Argentine ant. *Ecology Letters, 9,* 1068-1079.

Helanterä, H., Strassmann, J. E., Carrillo, J. & Queller, D. C. (2009). Unicolonial ants: where do they come from, what are they and where are they going? *Trends in Ecology and Evolution, 24,* 341-349.

Heller, N. E. (2004). Colony structure in introduced and native populations of the invasive Argentine ant, *Linepithema humile*. *Insectes Sociaux, 51,* 378-386.

Heller, N. E. & Gordon, D. M. (2006). Seasonal spatial dynamics and causes of nest movement in colonies of the invasive Argentine ant (*Linepithema humile*). *Ecological Entomology, 31,* 499-510.

Henshaw, M. T., Kunzmann, N., Vanderwoude, C., Sanetra, M. & Crozier, R. H. (2005). Population genetics and history of the introduced fire ant, *Solenopsis invicta* Buren (Hymenoptera: Formicidae), in Australia. *Australian Journal of Entomology, 44,* 37-44.

Heterick, B. E. (2000). Influence of Argentine and coastal brown ant (Hymenoptera: Formicidae) invasions on ant communities in Perth gardens, Western Australia. *Urban Ecosystems, 4,* 277-292.

Hirata, M., Hasegawa, O., Toita, T. & Higashi, S. (2008). Genetic relationships among populations of the Argentine ant *Linepithema humile* introduced into Japan. *Ecological Research, 23,* 883-888.

Hoffmann, B. D. (in press). Ecological restoration following the local eradication of an invasive ant in northern Australia. *Biological Invasions*.

Hoffmann, B. D. & O'Connor, S. (2004). Eradication of two exotic ants from Kakadu National Park. *Ecological Management and Restoration, 5,* 98-105.

Hölldobler, B. & Wilson, E. O. (1990). *The Ants.* Cambridge, Mass: The Belknap Press of Harvard University Press.

Holway, D. A. (1998a). Factors governing rate of invasion: a natural experiment using Argentine ants. *Oecologia, 115,* 206-212.

Holway, D. A. (1998b). Effect of Argentine ant invasions on ground-dwelling arthropods in northern California riparian woodlands. *Oecologia, 116,* 252-258.

Holway, D. A., Suarez, A. V. & Case, T. J. (1998). Loss of intraspecific aggression in the success of a widespread invasive social insect. *Science, 282,* 949-952.

Holway, D. A. (1999) Competitive mechanism underlying the displacement of native ants by the invasive Argentine ant. *Ecology, 80,* 238-251.

Holway, D. A. & Case, T. J. (2001). Effects of colony-level variation on competitive ability in the invasive Argentine ant. *Animal Behaviour, 61,* 1181-1192.

Holway, D. A., Lach, L., Suarez, A. V., Tsutsui, N. D. & Case, T. J. (2002). The causes and consequences of ant invasions. *Annual Review of Ecology and Systematics, 33,* 181–233.

Howard, R. W. & Blomquist, G. J. (2005). Ecological, behavioral, andbiochemical aspects of insect hydrocarbons. *Annual Review of Entomology, 50,* 371-393.

Hulme, P. E. (2006). Beyond control: wider implications for the management of biological invasions. *Journal of Applied Ecology, 43,* 835-847.

Hulme, P. E. (2009). Trade, transport and trouble: managing invasive species pathways in an era of globalization. *Journal of Applied Ecology, 46,* 10-18.

Human, K. G. & Gordon, D. M. (1997). Effects of Argentine Ants on Invertebrate Biodiversity in Northern California. *Conservation Biology, 11,* 1242–1248.

Human, K. G. & Gordon, D. M. (1999). Behavioral interactions of the invasive Argentine ant with native ant species. *Insectes Sociaux, 46,* 159-163.

Huxel, G. R. (2000). The effect of the Argentine ant on the threatened valley elderberry longhorn beetle. *Biological Invasions,* 2, 81–85.

Ingram, K. K. & Gordon, D. M. (2003). Genetic analysis of dispersal dynamics in an invading population of Argentine ants. *Ecology, 84,* 2832-2842.

Jaquiéry, J., Vogel, V. & Keller, L. (2005). Multilevel genetic analyses of two supercolonies of the Argentine ant, *Linepithema humile*. *Molecular Ecology, 14,* 589-598.

Juliano, S. A. & Lounibos, L. P. (2005). Ecology of invasive mosquitoes: effects on resident species and on human health. *Ecology Letters, 8,* 558-574.

Keller, L., Passera, L. & Suzzoni, J.-P. (1989). Queen execution in the Argentine ant, *Iridomyrmex humilis*. *Physiological Entomology, 14,* 157-163.

Keller, L. & Ross, K. G. (1998). Selfish genes: a green beard in the red fire ant. *Nature, 394,* 573-575.

King, J. R., Tschinkel, W. R. & Ross, K. G. (2009). A case study of human exacerbation of the invasive species problem: transport and establishment of polygyne fire ants in Tallahassee, Florida, USA. *Biological Invasions, 11,* 373-377.

Klotz, J. H., Rust, M. K., Field, H. C., Greenberg, L. & Kupfer, K. (2008). Controlling Argentine ants in residential settings (Hymenoptera: Formicidae). *Sociobiology, 51,* 579-588.

Krushelnycky, P. D., Loope, L. L. & Reimer, N. J. (2005). The ecology, policy, and management of ants in Hawaii. *Proceedings of the Hawaiian Entomological Society, 37,* 1-25.

Krushelnycky, P. D. & Gillespie, R. G. (2008). Compositional and functional stability of arthropod communities in the face of ant invasions. *Ecological Applications, 18,* 1547-1562.

Laakkonen, J., Fisher, R. N. & Case, T. J. (2001). Effect of land cover, habitat fragmentation and ant colonies on the distribution and abundance of shrews in southern California. *Journal of Animal Ecology, 70,* 776–788.

Lach, L. (2003). Invasive ants: unwanted partners in ant–plant interactions? *Annals of the Missouri Botanical Garden, 90,* 91–108.

Lach, L. (2007). A mutualism with a native Membracid facilitates pollinator displacement by Argentine ants. *Ecology, 88,* 1994–2004.

Lach, L. (2008). Argentine ants displace floral arthropods in a biodiversity hotspot. *Diversity and Distributions, 14,* 281–290.

Lach, L. & Thomas, M. L. (2008). Invasive ants in Australia: documented and potential ecological consequences. *Australian Journal of Entomology, 47,* 275-288.

LeBrun, E. G., Tillberg, C. V., Suarez, A. V., Folgarait, P. J., Smith, C. R. & Holway, D. A. (2007). An experimental study of competition between fire ants and Argentine ants in their native range. *Ecology, 88,* 63-75.

Lester, P. J., Baring, C. W., Longson, C. G. & Hartley, S. (2003). Argentine and other ants (Hymenoptera: Formicidae) in New Zealand horticultural ecosystems: distribution, hemipteran hosts, and review. *New Zealand Entomologist, 26,* 79-89.

Leung, B., Lodge, D. M., Finnoff, D., Shogren, J. F., Lewis, M. A. & Lamberti, G. (2002). An ounce of prevention or a pound of cure: bioeconomic risk analysis of invasive species. *Proceedings of the Royal Society of London Series B Biological Sciences, 269,* 2407-2413.

Lewis, V. R., Merrill, L. D., Atkinson, T. H. & Wasbauer, J. S. (1992). Imported fire ants: potential risk to California. *California Agriculture, 46,* 29-31.

Liang, D. & Silverman, J. (2000). "You are what you eat": diet modifies cuticular hydrocarbons and nestmate recognition in the Argentine ant, *Linepithema humile. Naturwissenschaften, 87,* 412-416.

Liang, D., Blomquist, G. J. & Silverman, J. (2001). Hydrocarbon-released nestmate aggression in the Argentine ant, *Linepithema humile*, following encounters with insect prey. *Comparative Biochemistry and Physiology Part B, 129,* 871-882.

Lowe, S, Browne, M. & Boudlejas, S. (2000). 100 of the world's worst invasive alien species. *Aliens, 12,* 1–12.

Lubin, Y. D. (1984). Changes in the native fauna of the Galápagos Islands following invasion by the little red fire ant, *Wasmannia auropunctata. Biological Journal of the Linnean Society, 21,* 229-242.

Mack, R. N., Simberloff, D., Lonsdale, W. M., Evans, H., Clout, M. & Bazzaz, F. A. (2000). Biotic invasions: causes, epidemiology, global consequences, and control. *Ecological Applications, 10,* 689-710.

Markin, G. P. (1970a). The seasonal life cycle of the Argentine ant, *Iridomyrmex humilis* (Hymenoptera: Formicidae), in southern California. *Annals of the Entomological Society of America, 63,* 1238-1242.

Markin, G. P. (1970b). Foraging behavior of the Argentine ant in a California citrus grove. *Journal of Economic Entomology, 63,* 740-744.

Markin, G. P. & McCoy, C. W. (1968). The occurrence of a nematode, *Diploscapter lycostoma*, in the pharyngeal glands of the Argentine ant, *Iridomyrmex humilis*. *Annals of the Entomological Society of America, 61,* 505-509.

Martinez-Ferrer, M. T., Grafton-Cardwell, E. E. & Shorey, H. H. (2003). Disruption of parasitism of the California red scale (Homoptera: Diaspididae) by three ant species (Hymenoptera: Formicidae). *Biological Control, 26,* 279–286.

McGlynn, T. P. (1999). The worldwide transfer of ants: geographical distribution and ecological invasions. *Journal of Biogeography, 26,* 535-548.

Menke, S. B., Fisher, R. N., Jetz, W. & Holway, D. A. (2007) Biotic and abiotic controls of argentine ant invasion success at local and landscape scales. *Ecology, 88,* 3164-3173.

Menke, S. B., Holway, D. A., Fisher, R. N. & Jetz, W. (2009). Characterizing and predicting species distributions across environments and scales: Argentine ant occurrences in the eye of the beholder. *Global Ecology and Biogeography, 18,* 50–63.

Mgocheki, N. & Addison, P. (2009). Interference of ants (Hymenoptera: Formicidae) with biological control of the vine mealybug *Planococcus ficus* (Signoret) (Hemiptera: Pseudococcidae). *Biological Control, 49,* 180–185.

Mitchell, C. E. & Power, A. G. (2003). Release of invasive plants from fungal and viral pathogens. *Nature, 421,* 625-627.

Miyake, K., Kameyama, T., Sugiyama, T., Ito, F. (2002). Effect of Argentine ant invasions on Japanese ant fauna in Hiroshima Prefecture, western Japan: a preliminary report (Hymenoptera : Formicidae). *Sociobiology, 39,* 465-474.

Morrison, L. W., Porter, S. D., Daniels, E. & Korzukhin, M. D. (2004). Potential global range expansion of the invasive fire ant, *Solenopsis invicta*. *Biological Invasions, 6,* 183-191.

Nakamaru, M., Beppu, Y. & Tsuji, K. (2007). Does disturbance favor dispersal? An analysis of ant migration using the colony-based lattice model. *Journal of Theoretical Biology, 248,* 288-300.

Ness, J. H. & Bronstein, J. L. (2004). The effects of invasive ants on prospective ant mutualists. *Biological Invasions, 6,* 445–461.

Newell, W. & Rouge, B. (1909). Measures suggested against the Argentine ant as a household pest. *Journal of Economic Entomology, 2,* 324-332.

Newell, W. & Barber, T. C. (1913). The Argentine ant. *U. S. Department of Agriculture, Bureau of Entomology Bulletin, 122,* 1-98.

Nygard, J., Sanders, N. J. & Connor, E. F. (2008). The effects of the invasive Argentine ant ( *Linepithema humile* ) and the native ant *Prenolepis imparis* on the structure of insect herbivore communities on willow trees (*Salix lasiolepis* ). *Ecological Entomology , 33,* 789–795.

O'Dowd, D. J., Green, P. T. & Lake, P. S. (2003). Invasional meltdown on an oceanic island. *Ecology Letters, 6,* 812–817.

Okaue, M., Yamamoto, K., Touyama, Y., Kameyama, T., Terayama, M., Sugiyama, T., Murakami, K. & Ito, F. (2007). Distribution of the Argentine ant, *Linepithema humile*, along the Seto Inland Sea, western Japan: result of surveys in 2003-2005. *Entomological Science, 10,* 337-342.

Pascoe, A. (2002). Red imported fire ant response stood down. *Biosecurity, 45,* 7.

Passera, L., Keller, L. & Suzzoni, J.-P. (1988). Queen replacement in dequeened colonies of the Argentine ant *Iridomyrmex humilis* (Mayr). *Psyche, 95,* 59-65.

Passera, L. (1994). Characteristics of tramp species. In Williams, D. F. (Eds.), *Exotic ants: biology, impact, and control introduced species* (pp. 23-43). Westview Press, Boulder, Colorado.

Pedersen, J. S., Krieger, M. J. B., Vogel, V., Giraud, T. & Keller, L. (2006). Native supercolonies of unrelated individuals in the invasive Argentine ant. *Evolution, 60,* 782-791.

Pejchar, L. & Mooney, H. A. (2009). Invasive species, ecosystem services and human well-being. *Trends in Ecology and Evolution, 24,* 497-504.

Perrings, C., Williamson, M., Barbier, E. B., Delfino, D., Dalmazzone, S., Shogren, J., Simmons, P. & Watkinson, A. (2002). Biological invasion risks and the public good: an economic perspective. *Conservation Ecology, 6,* 1.

Phillips, P. A. & Sherk, C. J. (1991). To control mealybugs, stop honeydew-seeking ants. *California Agriculture, 45,* 26-28.

Pimentel, D., Zuniga, R. & Morrison, D. (2005). Update on the environmental and economic costs associated with alien-invasive species in the United States. *Ecological Economics, 52,* 273-288.

Pimm, S. L., Russell, G. J., Gittleman, J. L. & Brooks, T. M. (1995). The future of biodiversity. *Science, 269,* 347-350.

Pitt, J. P. W., Worner, S. P. & Suarez, A. V. (2009). Predicting Argentine ant spread over the heterogeneous landscape using a spatially explicit stochastic model. *Ecological Applications, 19,* 1176-1186.

Porter, S. D., Nogueira de Sá, L. A. & Morrison, L. W. (2004). Establishment and dispersal of the fire ant decapitating fly *Pseudacteon tricuspis* in North Florida. *Biological Control, 29,* 179-188.

Radchenko, A. (2005). Monographic revision of the ants (Hymenoptera: Formicidae) of North Korea. *Annales Zoologici, 55,* 127-221.

Reuter, M., Pedersen, J. S. & Keller, L. (2005). Loss of *Wolbachia* infection during colonisation in the invasive Argentine ant *Linepithema humile*. *Heredity, 94,* 364-369.

Rhoades, R. B., Stafford, C. T. & James Jr., F. K. (1971). Survey of fatal anaphylactic reactions to imported fire ant stings. *Journal of Allergy and Clinical Immunology, 84,* 159-162.

Ricciardi, A. & Rasmussen, J. B. (1998). Predicting the identity and impact of future biological invaders: a priority for aquatic resource management. *Canadian Journal of Fisheries and Aquatic Sciences, 55,* 1759-1765.

Rodriguez-Cabal, M., Stuble, K. L., Nuñez, M. A. & Sanders, N. (2009). Quantitative analysis of the effects of the exotic Argentine ant on seed-dispersal mutualisms. *Biology Letters, 5,* 499-502.

Roura-Pascual, N., Suarez, A. V., Gómez, C.,Pons, P., Touyama, Y., Wild, A. L. & Peterson, T. (2004). Geographical potential of Argentine ants (*Linepithema humile* Mayr) in the face of global climate change. *Proceedings of the Royal Society of London Series B Biological Sciences, 271,* 2527-2535.

Roura-Pascual, N., Suarez, A. V., McNyset, K., Gómez, C., Pons, P., Touyama, Y., Wild, A. L., Gascon, F. & Peterson, A. T. (2006). Niche differentiation and fine-scale projections for Argentine ants based on remotely sensed data. *Ecological Applications, 16,* 1832-1841.

Roura-Pascual, N., Brotons, L., Peterson, A. T. & Thuiller, W. (2009a). Consensual predictions of potential distributional areas for invasive species: a case study of Argentine ants in the Iberian Peninsula. *Biological Invasions, 11,* 1017-1031.

Roura-Pascual, N., Bas, J. M., Thuiller, W., Hui, Cang, Krug, R. M. & Brotons, L. (2009b). From introduction to equilibrium: reconstructing the invasive pathways of the Argentine ant in a Mediterranean region. *Global Change Biology, 15,* 2101-2115.

Rowles, A. D. & O'Dowd, D. J. (2007). Interference competition by Argentine ants displaces native ants: implications for biotic resistance to invasion. *Biological Invasions., 9,* 73-85.

Rowles, A. D. & O'Dowd, D. J. (2009a). Impacts of the invasive Argentine ant on native ants and other invertebrates in coastal scrub in south-eastern Australia. *Austral Ecology, 34,* 239-248.

Rowles, A. D. & O'Dowd, D. J. (2009b). New mutualism for old: indirect disruption and direct facilitation f seed dispersal following Agentine ant invasion. *Oecologia, 158,* 709-716.

Sagata, S. & Lester, P. J. (2009). Behavioural plasticity associated with propagule size, resources, and the invasion success of the Argentine ant *Linepithema humile*. *Journal of Applied Ecology, 46,* 19-27.

Sala, O. E., Chapin III, F. S., Armesto, J. J., Berlow, E., Bloomfield, J., Dirzo, R., Huber-Sanwald, E., Huenneke, L. F., Jackson, R. B., Kinzig, A., Leemans, R., David M. Lodge, D. M., Mooney, H. A., Oesterheld, M., Poff, N. L., Sykes, M. T., Walker, B. H., Walker, M. & Wall, D. H. (2000). Global Biodiversity Scenarios for the Year 2100. *Science, 287,* 1770-1774.

Silverman, J. & Brightwell, R. J. (2008). The Argentine ant: challenges in managing an invasive unicolonial pest. *Annual Review of Entomology, 53,* 231-252.

Simberloff, D., Parker, I. M. & Windle, P. N. (2005). Introduced species policy, management, and future research needs. *Frontiers in Ecology and the Environment, 3,* 12-20.

Skaife, S. H. (1955). The Argentine ant *Iridomyrmex humilis* Mayr. *Transactions of the Royal Society of South Africa, 34,* 355-377.

Smith, M. R. (1965). House-infesting ants of the eastern United States. *United States Department of Agriculture Technical Bulletin, 1326,* 1-105.

Sockman, K. W. (1997). Variation in life-history traits and nest-site selection affects risk of nest predation in the California gnatcatcher. *The Auk, 114,* 324-332.

Soeprono, A. M. & Rust, M. K. (2004). Strategies for controlling Argentine ants (Hymenoptera: Formicidae). *Sociobiology, 44,* 669-682.

Suarez, A. V., Tsutsui, N. D., Holway, D. A. & Case, T. J. (1999). Behavioral and genetic differentiation between native and introduced populations of the Argentine ant. *Biological Invasions, 1,* 43-53.

Suarez, A. V., Richmond, J. Q. & Case, T. J. (2000). Prey selection in horned lizards following the invasion of Argentine ants in southern California. *Ecological Applications, 10,* 711–725.

Suarez, A. V., Holway, D. A. & Case, T. J. (2001). Patterns of spread in biological invasions dominated by long-distance jump dispersal: Insights from Argentine ants. *Proceedings of the National Academy of Sciences of the United States of America, 98,* 1095-1100.

Suarez, A. V. & Case, T. J. (2002). Bottom-up effects on persistence of a specialist predator: ant invasions and horned lizards. *Ecological Applications, 12,* 291-298.

Suarez, A. V., Holway, D. A., Liang, D., Tsutsui, N. D. & Case, T. J. (2002). Spatiotemporal patterns of intraspecific aggression in the invasive Argentine ant. *Animal Behaviour, 64,* 697-708.

Suarez, A. V., Yeh, P. & Case, T. J. (2005). Impacts of Argentine ants on avian nesting success. *Insectes Sociaux, 52,* 378-382.

Suarez, A. V., Holway, D. A. & Ward, P. S. (2005). The role of opportunity in the unintentional introduction of nonnative ants. *Proceedings of the National Academy of Sciences of the United States of America, 102,* 17032–17035.

Suarez, A. V., Holway, D. A. & Tsutsui, N. D. (2008). Genetics and behavior of a colonizing species: the invasive Argentine ant. *The American Naturalist, 172,* 72-84.

Sugiyama, T. (2000). Invasion of Argentine ant, *Linepithema humile*, into Hiroshima Prefecture, Japan. *Japanese Journal of Applied Entomology and Zoology, 44,* 127-129.

Suhr, E. L., McKechnie, S. W. & O'Dowd, D. J. (2009). Genetic and behavioural evidence for a city-wide supercolony of the invasive Argentine ant *Linepithema humile* (Mayr) (Hymenoptera: Formicidae) in southeastern Australia. *Australian Journal of Entomology, 48,* 79-83.

Sunamura, E., Nishisue, K., Terayama, M. & Tatsuki, S. (2007). Invasion of four Argentine ant supercolonies into Kobe Port, Japan: their distributions and effects on indigenous ants (Hymenoptera: Formicidae). *Sociobiology, 50,* 659-674.

Sunamura, E., Hatsumi, S., Karino, S., Nishisue, K., Terayama, M., Kitade, O. & Tatsuki, S. (2009a). Four mutually incompatible Argentine ant supercolonies in Japan: inferring invasion history of introduced Argentine ants from their social structure. *Biological Invasions, 11,* 2329-2339.

Sunamura, E., Espadaler, X., Sakamoto, H., Suzuki, S., Terayama, M. & Tatsuki, S. (2009b). Intercontinental union of Argentine ants: behavioral relationships among introduced populations in Europe, North America, and Asia. *Insectes Sociaux, 56,* 143-147.

The Global Social Change Research Project. Basic guide to the world economic growth, 1970 to 2007. 2007. Available from: http://gsociology.icaap.org

Thomas, M. L., Payne-Makrisâ, C. M., Suarez, A. V., Tsutsui, N. D. & Holway, D. A. (2006). When supercolonies collide: territorial aggression in an invasive and unicolonial social insect. *Molecular Ecology, 15,* 4303-4315.

Tillberg, C. V., Holway, D. A., LeBrun, E. G. & Suarez, A. V. (2007). Trophic ecology of invasive Argentine ants in their native and introduced ranges. *Proceedings of the National Academy of Sciences of the United States of America, 104,* 20856-20861.

Torchin, M. E., Lafferty, K. D., Dobson, A. P., McKenzie, V. J. & Kuris, A. M. (2003). Introduced species and their missing parasites. *Nature, 421,* 628-630.

Torres, C. W., Brandt, M. & Tsutsui, N. D. (2007). The role of cuticular hydrocarbons as chemical cues for nestmate recognition in the invasive Argentine ant (*Linepithema humile*). *Insectes Sociaux, 54,* 329-333.

Touyama, Y., Ogata, K. & Sugiyama, T. (2003). The Argentine ant, *Linepithema humile*, in Japan: assessment of impact on species diversity of ant communities in urban environments. *Entomological Science, 6,* 57-62.

Touyama, Y., Ihara, Y. & Ito, F. (2008). Argentine ant infestation affects the abundance of the native myrmecophagic jumping spider *Siler cupreus* Simon in Japan. *Insectes Sociaux, 55,* 144-146.

Tsuji, K. & Tsuji, N. (1996). Evolution of life history strategies in ants: variation in queen number and mode of colony founding. *Oikos, 76,* 83-92.

Tsutsui, N. D., Suarez, A. V., Holway, D. A. & Case, T. J. (2000). Reduced genetic variation and the success of an invasive species. *Proceedings of the National Academy of Sciences of the United States of America, 97,* 5948-5953.

Tsutsui, N. D., Suarez, A. V., Holway, D.A. & Case, T. J. (2001). Relationships among native and introduced populations of the Argentine ant ( *Linepithema humile* ) and the source of introduced populations. *Molecular Ecology, 10,* 2151–2161.

Tsutsui, N. D., Suarez, A. V., Holway, D. A. & Case, T. J. (2003). Genetic diversity, asymmetrical aggression, and recognition in a widespread invasive species. *Proceedings of the National Academy of Sciences of the United States of America, 100,* 1078-1083.

Tsutsui, N. D., Kauppinen, S. N., Oyafuso, A. F. & Grosberg, R. K. (2003). The distribution and evolutionary history of *Wolbachia* infection in native and introduced populations of the invasive Argentine ant (*Linepithema humile*). *Molecular Ecology, 12,* 3057-3068.

Ugelvig, L. V., Drijfhout, F. P., Kronauer, D. J. C., Boomsma, J. J., Pedersen, J. S. & Cremer, S. (2008). The introduction history of invasive garden ants in Europe: integrating genetic, chemical and behavioural approaches. *BMC Biology, 6,* 11.

Vega, S. J. & Rust, M. K. (2001) The Argentine ant – a significant invasive species in agricultural, urban and natural environments. *Sociobiology, 37,* 3-25.

Vitousek, P. M. (1994). Beyond Global Warming: Ecology and Global Change. *Ecology, 75,* 1861-1876.

Vitouselk, P. M., D'Antonio, C. M., Loope, L. L. & Westbrooks, R. (1996). Biological invasions as global environmental change. *American Scientist, 84,* 468-478.

Vogel, V., Pedersen, J. S., d'Ettorre, P., Lehmann, L. & Keller, L. (2009). Dynamics and genetic structure of Argentine ant supercolonies in their native range. *Evolution, 63,* 1627-1639.

Ward, P. S. (1987). Distribution of the introduced Argentine ant (*Iridomyrmex humilis*) in natural habitats of the lower Sacramento Valley and its effects on the indigenous ant fauna. *Hilgardia, 55,* 1-16.

Ward, D. F., Harris, R. J. & Stanley, M. C. (2005). Human-mediated range expansion of Argentine ants *Linepithema humile* (Hymenoptera: Formicidae) in New Zealand. *Sociobiology, 45,* 401-407.

Ward, D. F., Beggs, J. R., Clout, M. N., Harris, R. J. & O'Connor, S. (2006). The diversity and origin of exotic ants arriving in New Zealand via human-mediated dispersal. *Diversity and Distributions, 12,* 601-609.

Walters, A. C. (2006). Invasion of Argentine ants (Hymenoptera: Formicidae) in south Australia: impacts on community composition and abundance of invertebrates in urban parklands. *Austral Ecology, 31,* 567-576.

Walters, A. C. & Mackay, D. A. (2005). Importance of large colony size for successful invasion by Argentine ants (Hymenoptera: Formicidae): evidence for biotic resistance by native ants. *Austral Ecology, 30,* 395-06.

Westphal, M. I., Browne, M., MacKinnon, K. & Noble, I. (2008). The link between international trade and the global distribution of invasive alien species. *Biological Invasions, 10,* 391-398.

Wetterer, J. K. & Porter, S. D. (2003) The little fire ant, *Wasmannia auropunctata*: distribution, impact and control. *Sociobiology, 42,* 1-41.

Wetterer, J. K. & Wetterer, A. L. (2006). A disjunct Argentine ant metacolony in Macaronesia and southwestern Europe. *Biological Invasions, 8,* 1123–1129.

Wetterer, J. K., Wild, A. L., Suarez, A. V., Roura-Pascual, N. & Espadaler, X. (2009). Worldwide spread of the Argentine ant, *Linepithema humile* (Hymenoptera: Formicidae). *Myrmecological News, 12,* 187-194.

Wilcove, D. S., Rothstein, D., Dubow, J., Phillips, A. & Losos, E. (1998). Quantifying threats to imperiled species in the United States. *BioScience, 48,* 607-615.

Wild, A. L. (2004). Taxonomy and distribution of the Argentine ant *Linepithema humile* (Hymenoptera: Formicidae). *Annals of the Entomological Society of America, 97,* 1204-1215.

Wild, A. L. (2007). Taxonomic revision of the ant genus *Linepithema* (Hymenoptera: Formicidae). *University of California Publications in Entomology, 126,* 1-159.

Williams, D. F., Oi, D. H. & Knue, G. J. (1999). Infection of red imported fire ant (Hymenoptera: Formicidae) colonies with the entomopathogen *Thelohania solenopsae* (Microsporidia: Thenohaniidae). *Journal of Economic Entomology, 92,* 831-836.

Williams, D. F., Oi, D. H., Porter, S. D., Pereira, R. M. & Briano, J. A. (2003). Biological control of imported fire ants. *American Entomologist, 49,* 150-163.

Witte, F., Goldschmidt, T., Wanink, J., van Oijen, M., Goudswaard, K., Witte-Maas, E. & Bouton, N. (1992). The destruction of an endemic species flock: quantitative data on the decline of the haplochromine cichlids of Lake Victoria. *Environmental Biology of Fishes, 34,* 1-28.

Xu, H., Ding, H., Li, M., Qiang, S., Guo, J., Han, Z., Huang, Z., Sun, H., He, S., Wu, H. & Wan, F. (2006). The distribution and economic losses of alien species invasion to China. *Biological Invasions, 8,* 1495-1500.

Yang, C. C., Shoemaker, D. D., Wu, W. J. & Shih, C. J. (2008). Population genetic structure of the red imported fire ant, *Solenopsis invicta*, in Taiwan. *Insectes Sociaux, 55,* 54-65.

Zhang, R., Li, Y., Liu, N. & Porter, S. D. (2007). An overview of the red imported fire ant (Hymenoptera: Formicidae) in mainland China. *Florida Entomologist, 90,* 723-731.

Zimmerman, E. C. (1941). Argentine ant in Hawaii. *Proceedings of the Hawaiian Entomological Society, 11,* 108.

In: Ant Colonies
Editor: Emily C. Sun
ISBN: 978-1-61122-023-0


*Chapter 5*

# ANT COLONY OPTIMIZATION USED IN NO WAVEFRONT SENSOR ADAPTIVE OPTICS SYSTEMS FOR SOLID-STATE LASERS

***Lizhi Dong,[1,2,3] Ping Yang,[1,2] Xiang Lei,[1,2,3] Wenjin Liu,[1,2,3] Hu Yan [1,2,3] and Bing Xu[1,2]***

[1]Laboratory on Adaptive Optics, Institute of Optics and Electronics, Chinese Academy of Sciences, Chengdu 610209, China
[2]Key Laboratory on Adaptive Optics, Chinese Academy of Sciences, Chengdu 610209, China
[3]Graduate School of Chinese Academy of Sciences, Beijing, 100084, China

## ABSTRACT

Adaptive optics is the technology for correcting the static and dynamic aberrations of optical systems. Traditional adaptive optics systems employ wavefront sensors to measure the phase aberrations in order to implement feedback controls. In recent years adaptive optics systems without wavefront sensors have been developed with the benefit of reduced complexity, cost, and size. These systems use some optimization algorithms to directly optimize the system performance metrics. We show that it is possible to compensate for phase aberrations with ant colony algorithm as the optimization algorithm in a no wavefront sensor adaptive optics system, which iteratively adjusts the control voltages of a deformable mirror to optimize the system performance metrics of the far-field intensity distribution of the laser beam. Encircled energy and Strehl ratio is used as the system performance metric. The effectiveness of this approach is analyzed numerically by use of a 37-element piezoelectric deformable mirror to correct simple and combined phase aberrations. Results demonstrate that this approach could effectively compensate for the phase distortions of laser beams and significantly improve beam qualities. A comparison indicates that this approach is much faster than a genetic algorithm while achieving almost the same beam quality.

# 1. INTRODUCTION

Adaptive optics (AO) is the technology for correcting random wavefront distortions in real time. The original AO systems were intended for correcting the turbulence of the atmosphere, freeing ground-based telescopes from the limitations imposed by the blurred atmosphere and ultimately enabling the full optical performance the telescopes can achieve [1]. Since its successful applications in astronomy, AO is now widely used in many different fields including medical and commercial industries, as the performance of all the optical systems in these fields are constrained by imperfections and aberrations in the beam path [2-4]. Traditional AO systems consist of three basic components: wavefront sensors (WFS) for measuring the phase aberrations, programmable optical elements such as deformable mirrors (DM) and spatial light modulators for correcting these aberrations, and wavefront controllers for generating control commands of the programmable elements to correct these phase aberrations. In recent years AO systems without wavefront sensors have been developed [5-9]. The reduction in complexity, cost, and size of the system is extremely beneficial, even though the absence of wavefront sensors makes them less efficient [2]. Most of these systems are implemented by direct optimization of a system performance metric based on certain optimization algorithms, such as hill-climbing [7], stochastic parallel gradient descent [5, 6], genetic algorithm [8] and simulated annealing algorithm [9]. These algorithms have all been proved effective in no wavefront sensor AO systems.

In this chapter we would introduce the application of ant colony algorithm in no wavefront sensor AO systems. Ant colony algorithm is a general-purpose heuristic algorithm that can be used to solve different combinatorial optimization problems, which is inspired by the behavior of real ants [10]. Ant colony algorithm has been successfully applied to a large number of difficult optimization problems including traveling salesman problems, quadratic assignment problems and scheduling problems, as well as to dynamic routing problems in telecommunication networks [11]. It has also been utilized to solve continues-space optimization problems [12].

The process of optimizing the system performance metric in a no wavefront sensor AO system is very similar to the problem of optimizing a function of multiple variables in the continues-space, thus it is reasonable to employ ant colony algorithm as the optimization algorithm of no wavefront sensor AO systems.

In solid-state laser systems, wavefront aberrations often result in great deteriorations of beam qualities. These aberrations are caused by many different factors, such as imperfections of optical components and pump-induced thermal effects including thermal lensing and thermally induced birefringence in the gain media [13, 14]. Many AO systems are developed to compensate for these aberrations in order to improve beam qualities [7, 8, 15]. Experiments have already shown that the phase aberrations of an Nd: YAG laser evolves very slowly, so convergence time is not quite important for such AO systems [16].

# 2. ANT COLONY ALGORITHM

Ant colony algorithm is inspired by the behavior of real ants, which are always able to find the shortest path between food sources and their nests. A moving ant seeking for food lays pheromone on the path it has covered. The intensity of the pheromone depends on the length of the path. The shorter the path is, the higher the trail intensity is. The next ant's tendency to choose a specific path is positively correlated to the intensity of trail. Thus the more ants following a certain trail, the more attractive that trail is to be followed. The final result of this positive feedback mechanism is that almost all the ants would choose the shortest path [10].

The detail of solving continues-space optimization problems using ant colony algorithm is described in Ref.12. It is modified by us to be utilized in no wavefront sensor AO systems as the control strategy. The flowchart of the control process is shown in Figure 1. In the beginning, it is necessary to define the range of an $n$-actuator DM's voltages $v_{jlower} \le v_j \le v_{jupper}$ ( $j$=1, 2, ... , $n$ ) to avoid damages to the DM, where $v_j$ is the $j$th actuator's voltage. After that the solution space is decomposed into grids. The grid nodes represent the voltages of actuators. Artificial ants move among these nodes and leave trails according to the metric of the route they have explored. The following ants choose their paths based on the intensity trail. When a certain amount of ants have finished their tour, there will be more pheromone on the nodes which are parts of a better path (evaluated by the performance metric of the AO system). Then the nodes with the most pheromone are found and the ants are constrained to move beside these nodes by reducing the range of allowed voltages. This process is repeated until the stopping criterion is met, resulting in nearly optimal system performance metric [12].

We use 20 ants in the following simulations. In the beginning of the optimization, the voltage of each actuator is divided into $N$ equal parts as:

$$dv_j = \frac{v_{jupper} - v_{jlower}}{N} (j=1, 2, \dots n). \tag{1}$$

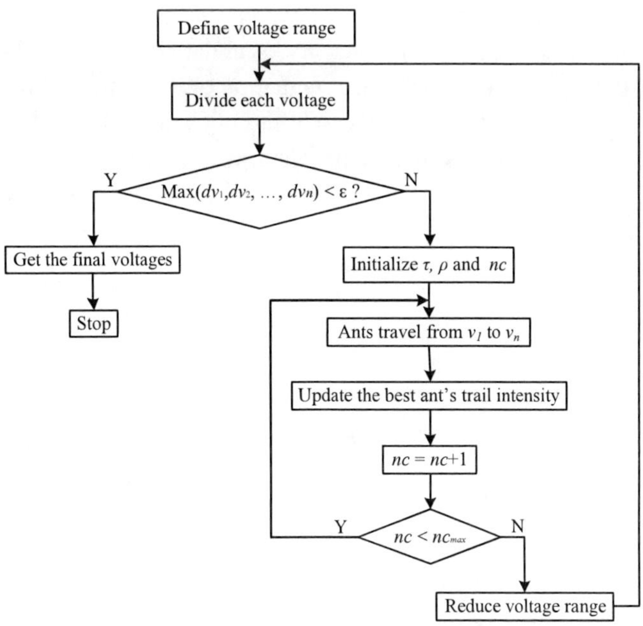


Figure 1. Flowchart of ant colony algorithm used in no wavefront sensor AO systems.

The *ith* node of the *jth* voltage is:

$$v_{ij} = v_{jlower} + dv_j \cdot i. \quad (2)$$

There are $N$+1 nodes for the voltage of each actuator, and $n(N+1)$ nodes in total for an $n$-actuator DM. We set $N$ to 10 in the simulations. Each element of the voltage vector $v$ is a single node of the corresponding voltage. The precision of the algorithm is determined by the parameter $\varepsilon$. Smaller $\varepsilon$ generally leads to higher beam quality but takes longer time. $\varepsilon$ should not exceed the precision of the DM actuator. When $max\ (dv_1, dv_2, \dots, dv_n) < \varepsilon$, the stopping criterion is met, and the final voltages are:

$$v_j^* = \frac{v_{jupper} + v_{jlower}}{2} \ (j=1, 2, \dots n). \quad (3)$$

The *kth* ant's transition probability from a node of $v_{j-1}$ to the *ith* node of $v_j$ is:

$$p_{ij}^k = \frac{\tau_{ij}}{\sum_{i=1}^{N} \tau_{ij}}, \quad (4)$$

where $\tau_{ij}$ is the trail intensity of the *ith* node of $v_j$. $\tau$ is initialized to $\tau_{\max}$ for all the nodes in the initialization step. The selection of the next node of the voltage vector is carried out using the roulette selection strategy, in which a node's chance to be chosen by an ant is proportional to the transition probability of the node.

We refer to the process that each ant has covered the tour from $v_1$ to $v_n$ as a cycle or a single iteration. After a cycle, the trail intensity is updated following the MAX-MIN Ant System (MMAS) strategy to avoid premature stagnation of the search. Only the best ant in the cycle is allowed to update the trail intensity, and the intensity is limited within a predefined range [17]. The best ant is the one whose path is most favorable (evaluated by the system performance metric of the AO system) and is preserved to the next cycle. The intensity of the best ant's trail is updated as [12]:

$$\tau_{ij}^{new} = (1-\rho) \cdot \tau_{ij}^{old} + \frac{J}{Q}, \quad (5)$$

where $\rho$ is a coefficient, $J$ is the performance metric of the best ant, and $Q$ is a constant. $\tau_{ij}^{new}$ is limited to $[\tau_{min}, \tau_{max}]$ given by:

$$\tau_{ij}^{new} = \begin{cases} \tau_{\min}, \tau_{ij}^{new} \le \tau_{\min} \\ \tau_{ij}^{new}, \tau_{\min} < \tau_{ij}^{new} \le \tau_{\max} \\ \tau_{\max}, \tau_{ij}^{new} > \tau_{\max} \end{cases} \quad (6)$$

$\rho$ is between 0 and 1 so that (1- $\rho$) represents the evaporation of trail between cycles. The optimization result of the algorithm is related to the value of $\rho$. Larger $\rho$ leads to higher convergence rate but may also cause premature stagnation, while smaller $\rho$ leads to lower convergence rate and lower probability of premature. A reasonable method is to set $\rho$ to a larger value in the beginning cycles to speed up the search and a lower value in the end to get better results. $\rho$ is updated after each cycle as:

$$\rho^{new} = \begin{cases} 0.95 \cdot \rho^{old} , & 0.95 \cdot \rho^{old} > \rho_{\min} \\ \rho_{\min} , & \text{otherwise} \end{cases} \tag{7}$$

The initial value of $\rho$ is set to 0.9. Strehl Ratio (SR) and encircled energy (EE) are among the most popular choices of the performance metric $J$ for no wavefront sensor AO systems. The definition of SR is:

$$SR = \frac{\max(I(x,y))}{\max(I_{dl}(x,y))}, \tag{8}$$

where $I_{dl}(x, y)$ is the diffraction-limited peak intensity in the far-field achievable without aberrations, while $I(x, y)$ is the actual peak intensity in the far-field. EE is defined as:

$$EE = \sum_{R} I(x,y), \tag{9}$$

where R is a user-defined region to collect the energy of the laser beam in the far-field. In the following simulations, R is set to the area within the first null of the diffraction-limited far-field intensity distribution. The value of $Q$ depends on the specific problem [12]. We set $Q$ to 0.1% of $I_{dl}(x, y)$ to keep $\tau_{ij}^{new}$ calculated using Eq.5 within a proper range compared to [$\tau_{min}$, $\tau_{max}$ ], so that $\tau_{ij}^{new}$ would not always be $\tau_{min}$ or $\tau_{max}$. Eq.6 ensures that the trail intensity of the nodes within a better path would be larger. The term $J/Q$ results in the maximum of $J$.

The next step is to find the maximum element in each column of the matrix $\tau$. The corresponding row index vector is ($m_1$, $m_2$, … , $m_n$). Then the range of each voltage is decreased to make the search space smaller. The range of voltages is updated as follows:

$$\begin{aligned} v_{jlower}^{new} &= v_{jlower}^{old} + (m_j - \Delta_{j1}) \cdot dv_j \quad (\mathrm{j}=1,2,\ldots,\mathrm{n}) \\ v_{jupper}^{new} &= v_{jlower}^{old} + (m_j + \Delta_{j2}) \cdot dv_j \quad (\mathrm{j}=1,2,\ldots,\mathrm{n}) \end{aligned}, \tag{10}$$

where

$$\begin{aligned} &\Delta_{j1} = m_j - 1,\ \Delta_{j2} = 2\Delta_0 + 1 - m_j, && m_j - \Delta_0 < 1 \\ &\Delta_{j1} = 2\Delta_0 + m_j - N,\ \Delta_{j2} = N - m_j, && m_j + \Delta_0 > N. \\ &\Delta_{j1} = \Delta_{j2} = \Delta_0, && otherwise \end{aligned} \tag{11}$$

The new range is $(2\Delta_0+1)/N$ times as before, and $\Delta_0$ is a constant set to 2 in the simulations. If all the voltages are within the same initial range $[v_{min}, v_{max}]$, the number of iterations would be:

$$n_{itr} = nc_{max} \cdot ns, \tag{12}$$

where $nc_{max}$ is the number of iterations between every two reductions of the voltage ranges, and $ns$ is the minimum integer that fulfills:

$$\frac{v_{max} - v_{min}}{N} \cdot \left(\frac{2\Delta_0 + 1}{N}\right)^{ns} < \varepsilon. \tag{13}$$

## 4. Simulations and Results

A functional diagram of the no wavefront sensor AO system used in the simulations is shown in Figure 2. The aberrated laser beam is corrected and reflected by the 37-actuator DM, and is then focused by a lens onto a digital camera. The computer processes the images grabbed from the digital camera and generates the control voltages of the DM based on the ant colony algorithm. In the following simulations, we assume the aberrations are static. The working wavelength of the AO system is 1064 nm.

Figure 3 shows the configuration of the 37-actuator piezoelectric deformable mirror used in the simulations. Each dot represents an actuator. This DM has a continuous faceplate with stacked PZT actuators [18], and its influence function describing the deformation when voltage is applied to a single actuator is:

$$V_i(x, y) = \exp[\ln \omega \cdot (\sqrt{(x - x_i)^2 + (y - y_i)^2} / d)^{\alpha}], \tag{14}$$

where $\omega$ is the coupling coefficient of the DM, $(x_i, y_i)$ is the position of the *ith* actuator, $\alpha$ is the exponent of Gaussian function, and $d$ is the distance between every two neighboring actuators. We set $\omega$ to 0.08 and $\alpha$ to 3 in the simulations. The shape of the central actuator's influence function is shown in Figure 4. The deformation of the DM's surface is:

$$\varphi(x, y) = \sum_{j=1}^{37} v_j V_j(x, y), \tag{15}$$

where $v_j$ is the voltage applied to the *jth* actuator.

The wavefront of the aberrated laser beam could be described by Zernike polynomials, which are orthogonal over the unit circle. Zernike polynomials are defined as [19]:

$$\left.\begin{aligned} Z_{even\ p} &= \sqrt{n+1}R_n^m(r)\sqrt{2}\cos m\theta \\ Z_{odd\ p} &= \sqrt{n+1}R_n^m(r)\sqrt{2}\sin m\theta \end{aligned}\right\} \quad m \neq 0 \quad , \qquad (16)$$

$$Z_p = \sqrt{n+1}R_n^0(r), \qquad m = 0$$

where

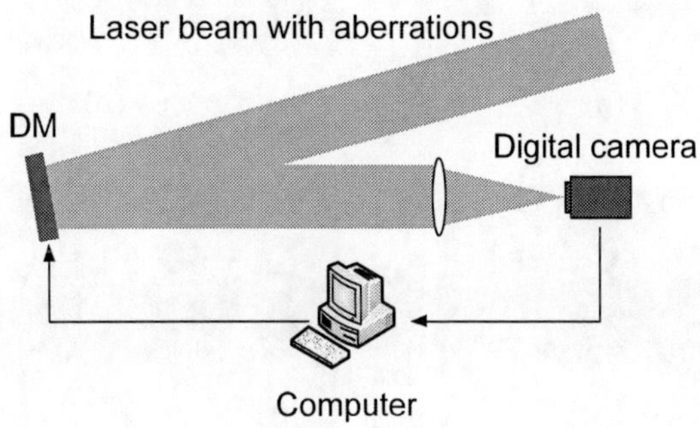


Figure 2. Model of the basic no wavefront sensor AO system

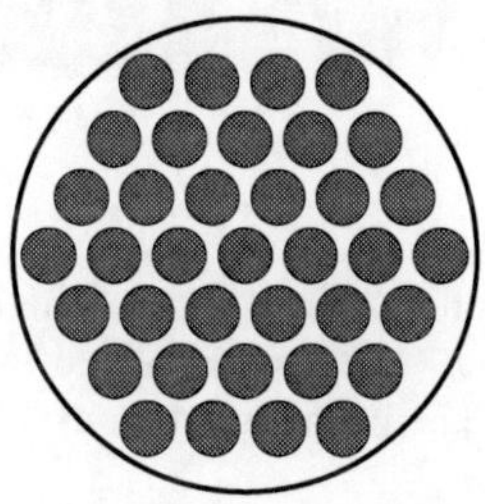

Figure 3. Configuration of the 37-actuator DM. Each dot represents an actuator

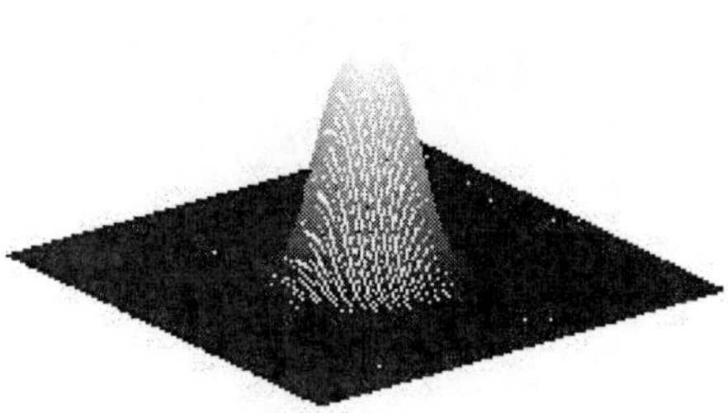

Figure 4. Influence function of the central actuator

$$R_n^m(r) = \sum_{s=0}^{(n-n)/2} \frac{(-1)^s (n-s)!}{s![(n+m)/2-s]![(n-m)/2-s]!} r^{n-2s}. \qquad (17)$$

The values of $n$ and $m$ are always integral and satisfy $m \leq n$, $n - |m| =$ even. The index $p$ is a mode ordering number and is a function of $n$ and $m$. We followed the ordering of the modes in Ref.19.

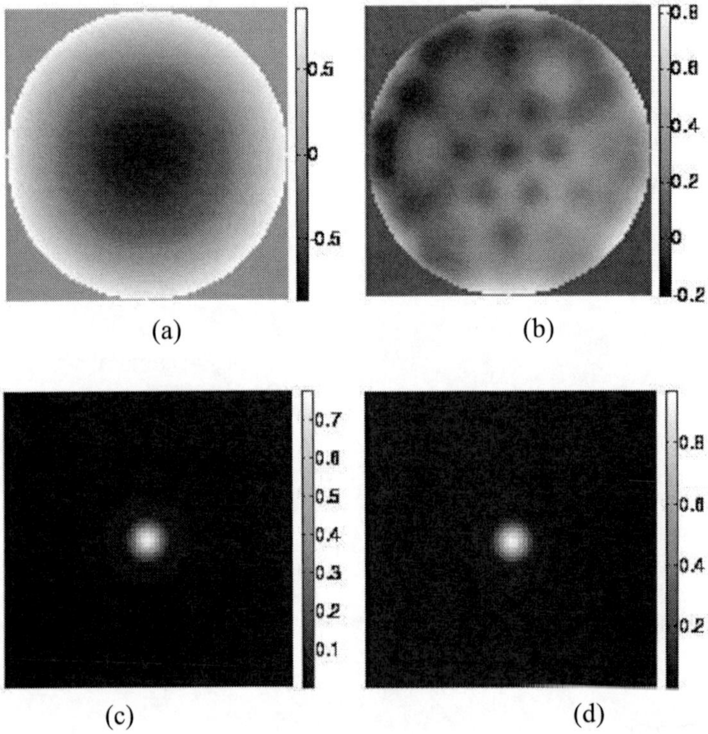


Figure 5. Result of correcting defocus. (a) Wavefront of the laser beam before correction in rad. RMS value is 0.51rad, and PV value is 1.76rad. (b) Wavefront of the laser beam after correction in rad. RMS value is 0.19rad, and PV value is 1.01rad. (c) The normalized far-field intensity distribution of the laser beam before correction. SR is 0.77. (d) The normalized far-field intensity distribution of the laser beam after correction. SR is 0.97

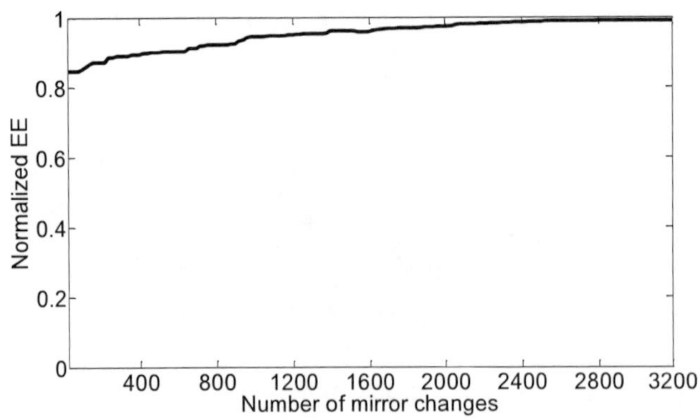


Figure 6. The optimization process of correcting defocus

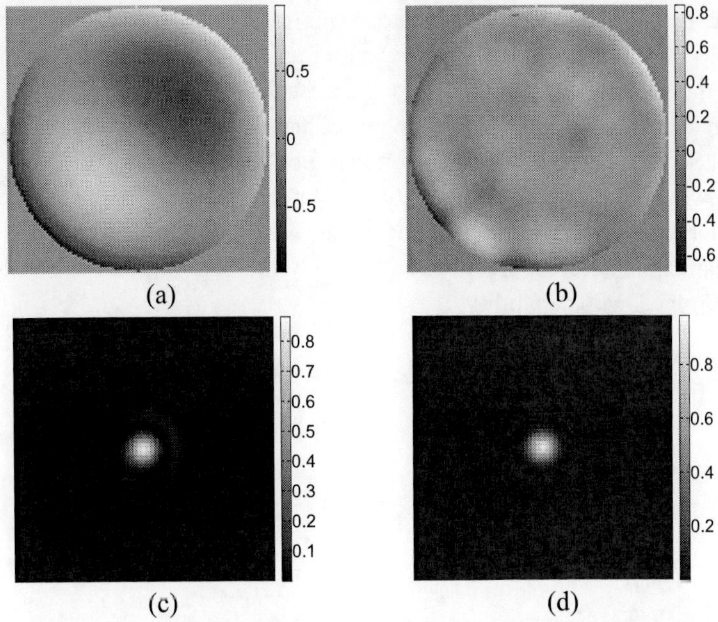


Figure 7. Result of correcting coma. (a) Wavefront of the laser beam before correction in rad. RMS value is 0.38rad, and PV value is 2.01rad. (b) Wavefront of the laser beam after correction in rad. RMS value of the wavefront is 0.13rad, and PV value is 1.57rad. (c) The normalized far-field intensity distribution of the laser beam before correction. SR is 0.88. (d) The normalized far-field intensity distribution of the laser beam after correction. SR is 0.98

We first added simple aberrations generated by Zernike polynomials to the beam, including tilt (expressed by $Z_2$ and $Z_3$), defocus (expressed by $Z_4$), astigmatism (expressed by $Z_5$ and $Z_6$) and coma (expressed by $Z_7$ and $Z_8$). The system performance metric is EE. SR is also employed to indicate the beam quality. Result of compensating for defocus is shown in Figure 5. Before correction, RMS value of the wavefront is 0.51rad, and peak to valley (PV) value is 1.76rad. SR of the far-field intensity distribution is 0.77. After correction, RMS value of the wavefront is 0.19rad, and PV value is 1.01rad. SR of the far-field intensity distribution is 0.97. The optimization process is illustrated in Figure 6 with a plot of normalized EE versus the number of mirror changes. Figure 7 depicts the result of correcting coma. Before correction, RMS value of the wavefront is 0.38rad, and PV value is 2.01rad. SR of the far-field intensity distribution is 0.88. After correction, RMS value of the wavefront is 0.13rad, and PV value is 1.57rad. SR of the far-field intensity distribution is 0.98. The optimization process is illustrated in Figure 8. These results clearly demonstrate that the AO system controlled by ant colony algorithm is able to effectively correct these simple aberrations.

More complicated phase aberrations generated by combining the first 65 Zernike polynomials were also added to the beam and corrected by the AO system. As is shown in Figure 9, after correction, the RMS value of the wavefront is reduced from 1.32rad to 0.13rad, the PV value is reduced from 5.71rad to 0.69rad, and the SR of the far-field intensity distribution of the beam is increased from 0.21 to 0.98. The convergence history is illustrated in Figure 10.

Using SR as the system performance metric $J$ in Eq. 5 has also been investigated. We found this approach often results in obvious tilt contained in the wavefront after correction and the position of the focal spot leaves the center of the camera obviously, no matter whether tilt is added to the initial aberrations or not. This can be explained as follows: the effect induced by tilt in the far-field is spot wandering from the center, while the intensity distribution of the spot almost remains the same as without tilt. As a result, the peak intensity of the far-field distribution does not change no matter how much tilt is contained in the wavefront, and SR remains the same. Thus it is impossible to identify tilt from the wavefront in this way. However, the region of calculating EE is set to an area in the center, and the value of EE is smaller when there is tilt existing in the wavefront and the focal spot leaves the center of the camera. Therefore EE could effectively indicate tilt, and tilt could be corrected as long as within the DM's capability.

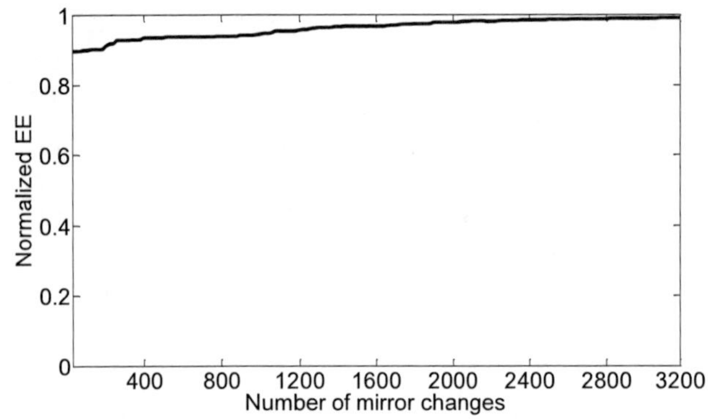


Figure 8. The optimization process of correcting coma

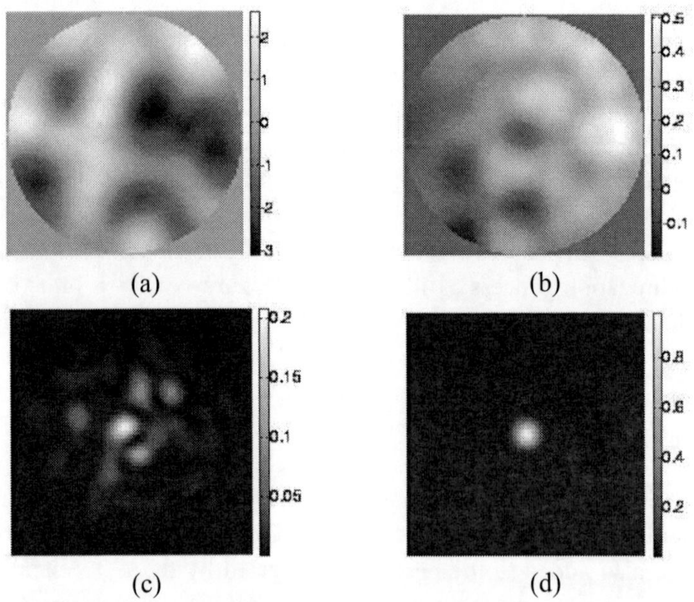


Figure 9. Result of correcting combined aberration. (a) Wavefront of the laser beam before correction in rad. RMS value of the wavefront is 1.32rad, and PV value is 5.71rad. (b) Wavefront of the laser beam after correction in rad. RMS value of the wavefront is 0.13rad, and PV value is 0.69rad. (c) The normalized far-field intensity distribution of the laser beam before correction. SR is 0.21. (d) The normalized far-field intensity distribution of the laser beam after correction. SR is 0.98

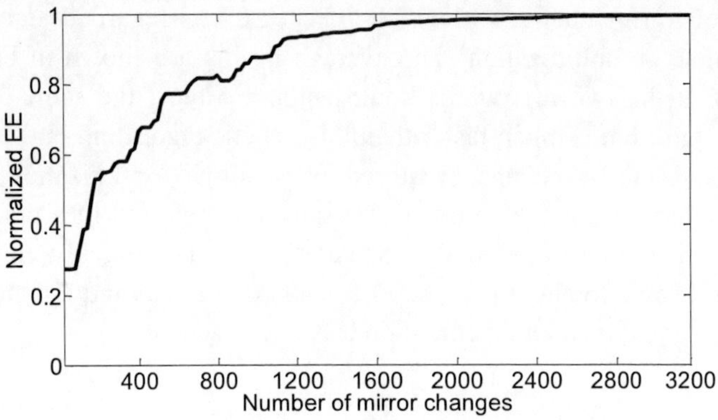


Figure 10. The optimization process of correcting combined aberrations

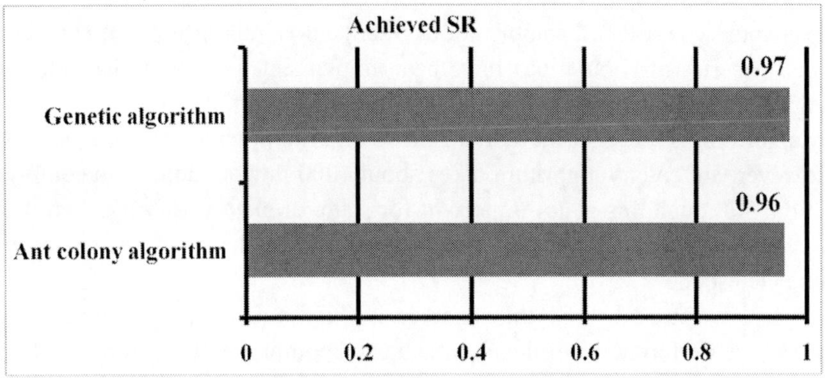


Figure 11. Average SR achieved with genetic algorithm and ant colony algorithm

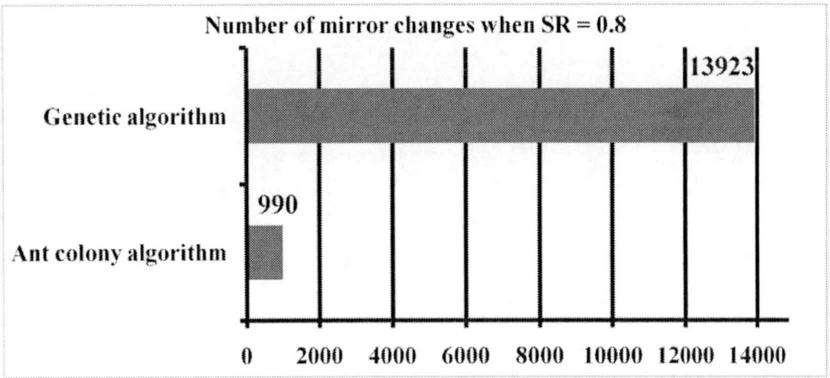


Figure 12. Average number of mirror changes when SR reaches 0.8 with genetic algorithm and ant colony algorithm

A comparison between ant colony algorithm and genetic algorithm which has also been used in compensating for the aberrations of solid-state lasers is made by adding the same phase aberrations and then correcting them with both algorithms. The coding strategy of genetic algorithm is real number encoding, and the crossover method is non-uniform arithmetical crossover [15]. Each algorithm is repeated 10 times. SR of the far-field intensity distribution after corrections is used to reflect the correction quality of the two algorithms, and the number of mirror changes when SR reaches 0.8 is regarded as a measure of time required to complete an optimization. The average results are shown in Figures 11 and 12, which indicates that the two algorithms could achieve almost the same correction quality, while ant colony algorithm is much faster than this genetic algorithm. However, there are still about one thousand mirror changes required by a single optimization with ant colony algorithm, thus high performance hardware systems are preferred in a practical system. For example, if the DM is able to respond to voltage commands quickly enough, with a high speed camera that is able to shoot over 1000 frames per second and a matching computer, a single optimization could be completed within less than a second.

## 5. Conclusion

In this chapter we present the applications of ant colony algorithm in no wavefront sensor AO systems. A series of simulations have been implemented to show that this algorithm is capable of correcting both simple and combined phase aberrations. We have also shown that ant colony algorithm is much faster than a genetic algorithm while achieving almost the same results. However, ant colony algorithm takes about 1000 mirror changes to complete a single compensation. Although this is not important for static or slowly varying aberrations, it may not be suitable for certain applications like atmosphere turbulence compensation required by ground-based telescopes.

The algorithm introduced in this chapter is only one implementation of ant colony algorithm, and the performance of the approach can be improved by optimizing the algorithm itself.

## References

[1] John. W. Hardy. *Adaptive Optics for Astronomical Telescopes*; Oxford University Press, 1998.

[2] Julie, A. Perreault; Allan Wirth. Proc. *SPIE.* 2005, *Vol.5903*, 590307.

[3] Austin Roorda, Fernando Romero-Borja, (2002). *William J. Donnelly III*; Hope Queener, Thomas Hebert, *Melanie Campbell. Opt. Express.*, *Vol.10*, 405-412.

[4] Benjamin Potsaid, Yves Bellouard, (2005). John T.Wen. *Opt. Express.*, *Vol.13*, 6504-6518.

[5] Vorontsov, M. A., Carhart, G. W. & Ricklin. J. C. (1997). *Opt. Lett.*, *Vol.22*, 907-909.

[6] Vorontsov, M. A. & Carhart, G. W. (2002). *Opt. Lett.*, *Vol. 27*, 2155-2157.

[7] Walter Lubeigt, Gareth Valentine, John Girkin, Erwin Bente, (2002). David Burns. *Opt. Express.*, *Vol.10*, 550-555.

[8] Ping Yang, Yuan Liu, Wei Yang, Mingwu Ao, Shejie Hu, Bing Xu, (2007). *Wenhan Jiang. Opt. Commun.*, *Vol.278*, 377-381.

[9] El-Agmy, R., Bulte, H., Greenaway, A. H., Reid, D. T. (2007). *Opt. Express.*, *Vol.13*, 6085-6091.

[10] Marco Dorigo, Vittorio Maniezzo, Alberto Colorni. (1996). *IEEE Transactions on Systems Man and Cybernetics-Part B:Cybernecits.*, 1996, Vol.26, 29-41.

[11] Marco Dorigo, Luca Maria Gambarella, Martin Middendorf, Thomas Stützle. (2002). *IEEE Transactions On Evolutionary Computation*, *Vol. 6*, 317-319.

[12] Shang Gao, Juan Zhong, Shujun Mo. (2003). *Microcomputer Development*, *Vol.13*, 21-22.

[13] Schmid, M., Graf, T. H., Weber, H. P. (2000). *J. Opt. Soc. Am. B.*, *Vol.17*, 1398-1404.

[14] Eduard Wyss, Thomas Graf, Heinz P. (2005). Weber. *IEEE J. Quantum Electr.*,*Vol. 41*, 671-676.

[15] Ping Yang, Yuan Liu, Mingwu Ao, Shijie Hu, Bing Xu. (2008). *Optics and Lasers in Engineering*, *Vol.46*, 517-521.

[16] Ping Yang, Shijie Hu, Xiaodong Yang, Shanqiu Chen, Wei Yang, Xiang Zhang, Bing Xu. (2005). *Proc. SPIE, Vol.6018*, 60180M.

[17] Thomas Stützle, Holger Hoos. (1997). *Proceedings of 1997 IEEE International Conference on Evolutionary Computation*, 309-314.

[18] Ping Yang, Mingwu, Ao, Yuan, Liu, Bing, Xu, Wenhan Jiang. (2007). *Opt. Express*, Vol.15, 17051-17062.

[19] Robert, J. & Noll. J. (1976 ). *Opt. Soc. Am.*, *Vol.66*, 207-211.

In: Ant Colonies
Editor: Emily C. Sun
ISBN: 978-1-61122-023-0


*Chapter 6*

# ANT COLONY OPTIMIZATION AGENTS AND PATH ROUTING: THE CASES OF CONSTRUCTION SCHEDULING AND URBAN WATER DISTRIBUTION PIPE NETWORKS

***S. Christodoulou and G. Ellinas***
University of Cyprus, Nicosia, Cyprus

**Abstract**

Ant Colony Optimization (ACO) is a population-based, artificial multi-agent, general-search technique for the solution of combinatorial problems with its roots based on the behavior of real-ant colonies. With its strong mathematical foundation and its simplicity of use, ACO provides an alternative method to routing optimizations with a wide range of applications. The chapter outlines ACO's mathematical background and describes a suggested possible implementation strategy for identifying shortest or longest paths in different types of networks. The ACO approach is initially applied to construction scheduling and resource-unconstrained network topologies, solving for the longest path in the network and utilized in performing critical-path calculations and evaluating a project's completion time. A second case study focuses on shortest-path calculations and on solving for minimum-impact paths in urban water distribution networks (UWDN) subjected to either unexpected or scheduled interruption of service. As with the scheduling paradigm, the application of ACO on piping networks provides the means to finding both shortest and longest paths between nodes of interest by imitating the natural selection processes utilized by real-life ants in search of the shortest path from an ant nest to a food source.

## 1. Introduction

Intelligent routing algorithms based on artificial agent techniques can be used for finding paths in a number of network topologies and different applications. The Ant Colony Optimization (ACO) approach, which is based on imitating the collective behavior of real-life ant colonies when in search for food, is one of such artificial agent techniques. In ACO, knowledge acquired by individual colony members separately as each ant traverses a possible path is processed and utilized by the colony in a collective manner to obtain the optimal path in the network. In software algorithmic implementations of the ACO method, ants are modeled as artificial agents while solutions to the path-traversal problem are found by considering the individual agents path-traversal experience and the importance of specific paths found in the network. Specifically, the individual agents' path-traversal experience is modeled by artificial pheromone trails which change dynamically during the simulation and while additional information specific to the problem being solved is utilized, such as the rate of accumulation of pheromone and the pheromone's relative importance to the construction of the optimal solution.

In this chapter the ACO method is applied to two different problems: (i) the scheduling of activities in resource-unconstrained projects (more specifically, in construction project scheduling problems), and (ii) the routing of pipes and water flow in water distribution networks.

The former ACO application restates the project-scheduling problem as a longest-path problem and solves it by use of ACO demonstrating how such problems which are typically solved utilizing the traditional Critical Path Method (CPM) algorithm can also be solved by the ACO metaheuristic. This is done by creating a directed acyclic graph corresponding to the underlying construction activity network, mapping resources, activities, relationships and durations to ACO ants, states, connections and arc lengths respectively in the ACO metaheuristic and utilizing the ACO technique to find the longest path in these graphs. It should be noted that in such problems, ACO is modified to search for longest instead of shortest paths in a network.

The second ACO application focuses on the the case of pipe and/or water-flow routing in urban water distribution systems (UWDS) showcasing how the ACO method's ability to search for shortest paths can be utilized in improving the design and operations of UWDS. As in the first case-study ACO application, unidirectional acyclic graphs are used to model real-life gravity-based water distribution networks and UWDS's water flow, operational state, pipes/valves and customers serviced are mapped as ACO ants, states, connections and cost function respectively. The ACO metaheuristic can then be employed to solve for the shortest path in these graphs. This approach can also be extended by considering different nodal states and ant types to solve for routes that allow for fast recovery of pipe failures, and for the efficient design and operation of UWDS (in terms of the better design of district metered areas 'DMA', and smaller variations in the operating pressure and the water flow).

The rest of the chapter is organized as follows: Section 2. provides the general framework of the ACO methodology and explains how a generic ACO optimization algorithm functions; Section 3. presents the first case study on construction scheduling and Section 4. presents the second case study on piping networks; Section 5. presents a comparison between ACO and other critical path methods and the chapter ends with Section 6. offering some concluding remarks on the examined ACO applications.

## 2. Ant Colony Optimization

Ant Colony Optimization is a population-based general search technique that can be used for the solution of difficult combinatorial problems [1]. ACO uses the knowledge-reinforcing mechanism used by real-life ants while traversing possible paths in search of

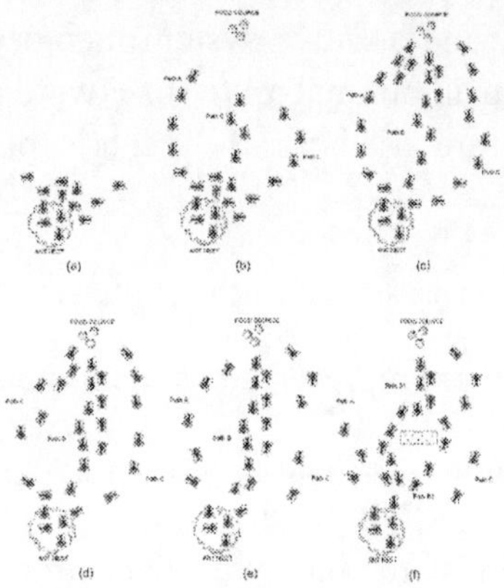

Figure 1. Basic ACO concepts: Pheromone laying and shortest path searching. (From [11], Figure 1. Copyright 2009 Elsevier. Used by permission of Elsevier.)

food, depositing a chemical substance (called *pheromone*) en-route and subsequently forming trails (*pheromone trails*) which can then be followed by other ants in the colony. Specifically, other ants tend to follow (with stronger tendency) the paths which are marked by higher pheromone concentrations and subsequently reinforce such paths with their own pheromone, thus making these paths more attractive for other ants to follow. Thus, the collective behavior is characterized by a reinforcing (positive) feedback loop where the probability with which each ant chooses the path to follow increases with the number of ants having chosen the same path in the preceding steps.

Figure 1 is used to illustrate this collective behavior. Initially, when a food source is introduced, the ant colony is characterized by random movement (Figure 1a). Over time, as some of the ant colony's members begin to sense the presence of the food source, they start to randomly move towards it, forming possible paths from the ant nest (source) to the food source (destination) (Figure 1b). As more time progresses, the path with the stronger pheromone concentration (Path $B$) tends to be the path of choice for successive ants (Figures 1c and 1d). This process continues to reinforce the path of choice while diminishing the importance of the other paths in the network (Figure 1e), finally, converging to the shortest path between source and destination. Figure 1f demonstrates that even when an obstacle is introduced on the selected path, the ants are able to quickly adapt dynamically, forming two sub-paths (paths $B_1$ and $B_2$) around the obstacle and continuing to move on the shortest path from source to destination.

## 2.1. The ACO Metaheuristic

Following the original work by Dorigo [1, 2], a number of ACO algorithms have been developed and tested on a variety of applications. Examples of such ACO-based algorithms include the original ACO method [1, 2, 3], the Ant Colony System (ACS) [3, 4], the Elitist Ant System [3], the Max-Min Ant System [5], the Rank-Based Ant System [6] and the Best-Worst Ant System [7]. The common framework for all ACO algorithms is the ACO metaheuristic [8, 9]. In this framework, artificial ants act as agents that have short-term individual memory helping them to identify available decision options when reaching a decision node (forward pass), and additive system memory when the agents' collective experience is combined to form an optimal route (backward pass).

The following definitions are used for the generic problem to be solved utilizing ACO [9]:

- The network's nodes are represented as the finite set $C = \{c_1, c_2, c_3, ..., c_N\}$.
- The states of the problem are represented as the finite set $x = \{x_i, x_j, ..., x_k, ...\}$.
- The states of the problem are defined in terms of sequences (relationships) over the elements of $C$, and the set of all possible sequences (paths) is denoted by $X$. This set represents the network's arcs (i.e., precedence relationships). A finite set of constraints in the system, $\Omega$, defines the feasible paths, $\bar{X}$ ($\bar{X} \subseteq X$).
- A set of feasible solutions, $S^*$, is given, with $S^*$ being a subset of $\bar{X}$ ($S^* \subseteq \bar{X}$). Additional constraints may be imposed on the feasible paths to obtain feasible solutions to a specific problem.
- A cost function $f(s, t)$ is associated with each candidate solution $s \in S^*$, and in some cases a separate cost function is defined and associated to states other than solutions. Cost functions can relate to a number of metrics such as financial cost, time, resources, delay penalties, etc.

As previously mentioned, the construction of the solution by the artificial ants is biased by the pheromone trails (which change at run-time), the heuristic information on the problem instance, and the ants' private memory. The generic behavior of the artificial ants is outlined as follows [9]:

- Ants build solutions by moving on the directed acyclic graph $G = (N, A)$, where $N$ is the set of nodes (representing components) in the network, and $A$ is the set of arcs (representing relationships) connecting the nodes. The problem constraints, $\Omega$, are taken into account during the ants' traversal of the network.
- A pheromone trail, $\tau$, and a heuristic value, $\eta$, are associated with the nodes and arcs of the network, allowing for the implementation of a long-term memory policy and the incorporation of problem-specific information about the ant search process, respectively.
- In order to find a path from the nest to the food source, each artificial ant, $k$, is assigned a start state, $x_s^k$, and one or more termination conditions, $e^k$. When an ant is at node $i$, it attempts to move to any node $j$ in the feasible solutions subset (immediate successors). If this is not possible, it might be allowed to move to any other node that it is not part of the immediate-successors subset. An ant's move to a successor node is determined by a stochastic decision rule and it is subject to a function of the locally pheromone and the connection's heuristic, the ant's memory, and the problem constraints. The path traversing procedure stops when at least one of the termination conditions is satisfied. The traversed path is then stored in the ant's memory ($M^k$).

- Once a solution is built, the ant retraces the same path backwards and updates the pheromone trails of the used components or connections.

Figure 2 is a flowchart representation of how the ACO algorithm operates.

## 3. Case Study 1: Resource-Unconstrained Construction Scheduling

In construction project management, problems such as project scheduling and resource allocation are of paramount importance to the success of the project, for they provide the means to efficiently manage both project time and project resources and therefore greatly contribute to the timely and cost-efficient completion of the project. An established deterministic technique for solving such problems is the Critical Path Method (CPM), which solves for longest (critical) paths in such network topologies. CPM exhaustively traverses an activity network utilizing forward and backward pass calculations and adding activity durations to path durations so as to arrive at the total duration for each network path and through that to the longest path in a network [10]. This procedure is well-documented in literature and briefly explained below.

The first calculation in CPM is a forward pass that unidirectionally (from start to end) computes the earliest each arc can be positioned within the network subject to the constraints imposed on the arc in terms of relationships with other arcs in the network. The forward pass results in the *EarlyStart* (ES) and *EarlyFinish* (EF) points for each arc, as well as the longest overall path in the network. The EF for each arc $i$ is computed as the ES of the arc plus the arc's length, whereas the ES for each arc $i$ is computed as the maximum of the EF of all direct predecessors to the arc:

$$EF_i = ES_i + l_i \tag{1}$$

$$ES_i = \max(EF_j)\ \forall j\ predecessor\ to\ i \tag{2}$$

The second calculation in CPM is a backward pass that unidirectionally (this time from end to start) computes the latest time the arc can be positioned within the network subject to the constraints imposed on the arc in terms of relationships with other arcs in the network. The backward pass results in the *LateFinish* (LF) and *LateStart* (LS) points for each arc. The LS for each arc $i$ is computed as the LF of the arc minus the arc's length, whereas the LF for each arc $i$ is computed as the minimum of the LS of all direct successors to the arc:

$$LS_i = LF_i - l_i \tag{3}$$

$$LF_i = \min(LS_j)\ \forall j\ successor\ to\ i \tag{4}$$

The difference in the start points ($LS-ES$) or in the finish points ($LF-EF$) of each arc is the *TotalFloat* (TF) of the arc, defining the available margin ("float") for variation from the arc's original state before such a variation impacts the overall length of the network. A smaller TF indicates an arc with higher importance ("criticality") in the network, since

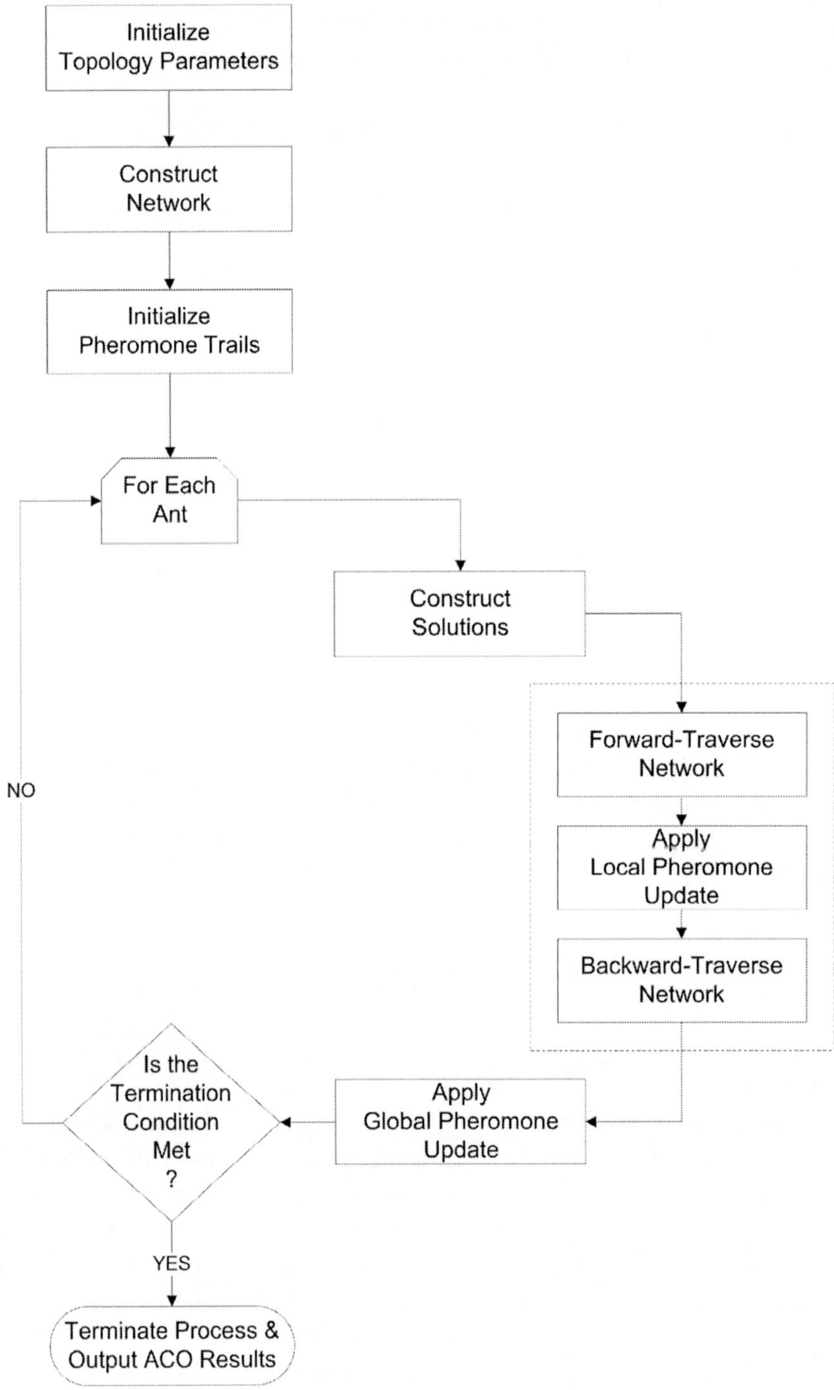


Figure 2. Flowchart of a generic ACO algorithm operation.
(From [11], Figure 2. Copyright 2009 Elsevier. Used by permission of Elsevier)

any modification to this arc's length and/or shift in time affects the overall condition of the network and its duration.

However, even though traditional techniques such as CPM have been widely utilized in construction management to solve project scheduling and resource allocation problems, they still exhibit limitations in their applicability [10, 11]. Some of these limitations are outlined below:

- CPM can not be used to identify the longest (or shortest) path from a node to any other node in the network.
- CPM can not account for resource-driven activity relationships, in which either a concurrent usage of resources is required or a substitute activity can be utilized. Even though CPM scheduling software can nowadays allow for inclusion of resources and costs in the critical path calculations, it does not enable activity-sequencing based on resource (rather than activity) relationships. Consider, for example, the case where we need to account for a situation in which an activity can start only when a resource from a predecessor activity is freed and then combined with a resource from another predecessor activity to enable the start of the successor activity without completion of the two predecessor activities. Traditional CPM falls short in addressing such situations.
- Traditional CPM algorithms are computationally inefficient and should resource-constrained scheduling be also considered then the algorithms become computationally complex. Exact solutions of the activity network can only be achieved by solving the underlying equations which represent the inter-relationships of the activities in the network. Such approaches utilize either linear algebra calculations, or linear programming, or network traversing. The first two approaches imply that the utilized solver is capable of handling a large number of equations and constraints, as well as handling optimization (the reader should note that in its most general form, the resource-constrained scheduling problem is NP-hard). The third approach implies that an exhaustive enumeration is needed of all possible network paths in the network and thus the associated set of forward and backward-pass calculations. Utilizing the third approach, solution is achieved by starting from the first activity and exhaustively identifying all possible paths (successive activities) until reaching the last activity, adding the duration of each link to the total duration of the identified path up to that point (*EarlyStart*, *EarlyFinish* dates) and then identifying the longest path in the network (forward pass). A reverse pass (same exhaustive procedure) is used to calculate the latest dates each activity can start and finish on, subject to keeping the project end-date fixed (as calculated during the forward pass phase). The combination of the two network passes provides the *TotalFloat* of each activity (*LateStart* – *EarlyStart*, or *LateFinish* – *EarlyFinish*) therefore the critical path and its activities (critical are the activities with *TotalFloat* = 0).

In order to improve on CPM's inefficiencies one could utilize intelligent path-traversing techniques so as to limit the solution space. The ACO metaheuristic is such an intelligent path-traversing method and can be used in solving both resource-unconstrained [11] and resource-constrained [10] scheduling problems. This is done by creating a directed acyclic graph corresponding to the construction activity network to be solved, and mapping resources, activities, relationships, and durations to ACO ants, states, connections and cost function respectively in the ACO metaheuristic. The ACO technique outlined below is then utilized to find the longest path in these graphs.

### 3.1. ACO-based Algorithm

A given construction network topology (project schedule) is defined by a graph $\mathcal{G} = (N,A)$, with $N$ being the set of nodes (activities) and $A$ being the set of arcs (activity relationships) connecting the subject nodes. The proposed ACO-based procedure for finding the critical path(s) between a set of chosen nodes $N_1$ (source) and $N_2$ (destination) can be summarized by the following steps [11]:

1. All network arcs are initiallized having a small amount of pheromone, $\tau_0$ . This value can be for example, the inverse line-distance between the nodes $N_1$ and $N_2$, or the inverse line-distance of each arc.

2. An artificial ant is launched from node $N_1$ and it traverses the network until it reaches either the end-node ($N_2$) or a dead end. When at a given node, the probability that the artificial ant will follow arc $i$ is given by:

$$p_i = \frac{\tau_i \eta_i^{\beta}}{\sum_i \tau_i \eta_i^{\beta}} \tag{5}$$

   where $\tau_i$ is the pheromone concentration on arc $i$, $\eta_i$ is an *a priori* available heuristic value for arc $i$, and $\beta_i$ is a parameter determining the relative influence of the heuristic information. The value of $\eta_i$ can be defined either as the inverse of the length of the arc, or the inverse of the length of the arc plus the line-distance between the subject node and $N_2$. It should be noted that previously visited arcs are excluded from the selection to enable the investigation of all possible arcs in the network and avoid preferential reinforcement of repeated arc traversals. The arc selection is further assisted by the consideration of a randomly generated number, $0 \leq q \leq 1$, which is compared to a predefined value, $q_0$, specific to the network topology. If $q \leq q_0$ then the arc with the highest value $p_i$ is selected. Otherwise, a random selection of an arc is used based on the distribution defined by the equation for $p_i$.

3. Upon selecting an arc, a local pheromone update rule is applied to update the level of pheromone concentration at the given arc. The updated pheromone level for arc $i$ is given by:

$$\tau_i = (1 - \rho)\,\tau_i + \rho\tau_0 \tag{6}$$

   where $\rho$ $(0 \leq \rho \leq 1)$ is the arc's level of pheromone evaporation. The goal of the local updating rule is to enable exploration of more path/route variations by making already traversed arcs less likely to be chosen again during the randomization of the arc selection process.

4. Steps (2) and (3) are repeated for all ants in the ant colony and the most successful ant (i.e., the one that traverses the optimum path) is used to globally update the network's pheromone trails. The global update rule is given by:

$$\tau_i = (1 - \alpha)\,\tau_i + \alpha\tau_L \tag{7}$$

where $\alpha$ is a network topology parameter ($0 \leq \alpha \leq 1$) whose value determines the level of evaporation of pheromone concentrations. Parameters $\rho$ and $\alpha$ help randomize the ACO process and in effect safeguard against memorization and premature convergence to a solution. The parameter $\tau_L$ has a value inversely proportional to the path length of the best solution in case of an arc visited by the best ant or zero for all other ants as shown by the equation below:

$$\tau_L = \begin{cases} 1/L_{best} & if\, arc\, i\, is\, visited\, during\, the\, best\, path\, tour \\ 0 & otherwise \end{cases} \tag{8}$$

The global update rule can be applied by either the "global-best" or the "iteration-best" ant. In the first case, the ant to perform the update is the one that obtained the best solution (found the longest path in the network) during the entire path traversing process. In the second case the update is performed by the ant reaching the best solution during each iteration of the algorithm.

5. Steps (2) - (4) are repeated for either a fixed number of iterations or until a predefined condition is met, and upon termination of the algorithm the pheromone trail in the graph is used to determine the solution. The arcs with highest pheromone concentration form the longest path in the network.

It should be noted that in the case of project scheduling the scope is to find the longest (and not the shortest) path in a network. Since ACO traditionally searches for shortest paths, a minor adjustment is made to the network topology in order to convert the problem from a longest-path search to a shortest-path search. This can be easily accomplished by operating on the negative values of the arcs' lengths and employing the traditional ACO method without any further modifications to it.

## 3.2. Construction Project Example

The aforementioned ACO algorithm was implemented [12] and applied on a case-study construction project. Figure 3 illustrates the construction network topology in study, representing the project schedule of 10 nodes and 17 arcs and assumed topology parameters $\beta = 1.0$, $\rho = 0.5$, $\alpha = 1.0$, $q_0 = 0.3$. The ant population for which a simulation is run is $n_{ants} = 50$. Three nodes in the network are defined as "ant nests" (i.e., nodes with no predecessors), six are regular (intermediate) nodes and one is a "food source" (i.e., a node with no successors). The generated network is a directed acyclic graph so as to emulate real-life

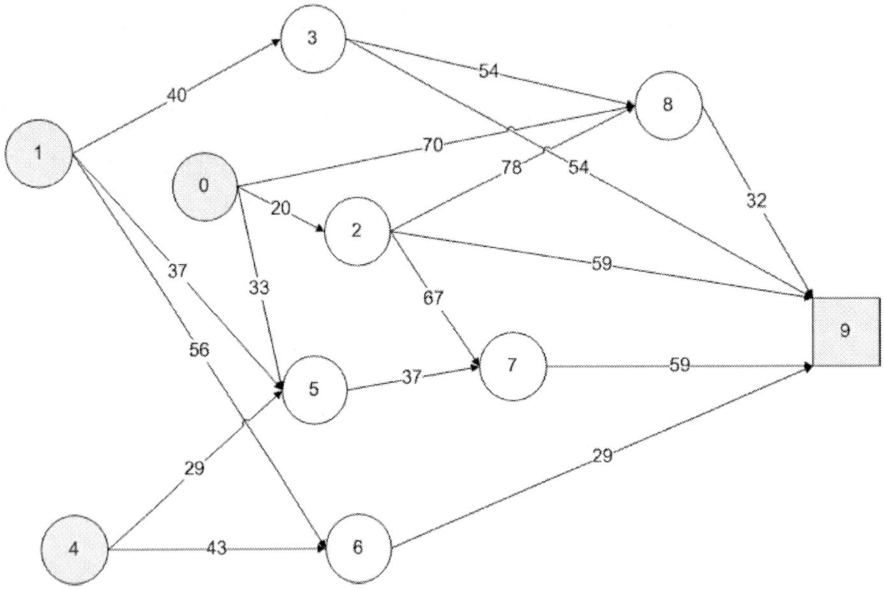


Figure 3. Case-study network topology.
(From [11], Figure 3. Copyright 2009 Elsevier. Used by permission of Elsevier)

construction networks. Furthermore, the network construction was based on an assumed maximum number of three successor connections per node, to simplify the calculations and subsequent verification by standard CPM procedures.

The ACO topology parameters ($q_0$, $\beta$, $\rho$, $\alpha$) are chosen based on a sensitivity analysis for ten other randomized topologies and on the observed rate and accuracy of convergence to an optimal solution [12]. In this case study, the value of $q_o$ in particular is kept low so as to allow for higher randomization in the arc-selection process (for a random number $q$, if $q \leq q_o$ then the arc with the highest value $p_i$ is selected).

The critical-path calculations on the topology of the case-study project network and the resulting *EarlyStart*, *EarlyFinish*, *LateStart*, *LateFinish* and *TotalFloat* values found using the traditional CPM procedure of forward and backward passes are tabulated in Table 1. As shown in Table 1, the CPM calculations result in identifying activities "1-3", "3-8" and "8-9" as critical (*TotalFloat* = 0), thus indicating a total project duration of 40+54+32 = 126 time-units.

### 3.2.1. The ACO Approach

In order to solve the same problem using the ACO algorithm, at first the arcs within the network are mapped with a pheromone level which is initialized to match the inverse of each arc's length. Then, every ant in the predefined ant population is processed through the network from the ant nest to the food source (ACO forward pass), and from there back to the ant nest (ACO backward pass). The process, even though having much in similarity with traditional CPM, is different than CPM in the level of intelligence built into it in relation to the selection of the arcs chosen for traversing the path from node to node. As explained previously, in the ACO procedure the choice of arcs that an ant will follow is stochastic.

**Table 1. Solution of the case-study network topology using the CPM approach. (From [11], Table 1. Copyright 2009 Elsevier. Used by permission of Elsevier.)**

| Start Node (1) | End Node (2) | Duration (3) | Successor Nodes (4) | Early Start (5) | Early Finish (6) | Late Start (7) | Late Finish (8) | Total Float (9) | Critical ? (10) |
|---|---|---|---|---|---|---|---|---|---|
| 0 | 2 | 20 | 7, 8, 9 | 0 | 20 | 15 | 35 | 15 | - |
| 0 | 5 | 33 | 7 | 0 | 33 | 45 | 78 | 45 | - |
| 0 | 8 | 70 | 9 | 0 | 70 | 24 | 94 | 24 | - |
| 1 | 3 | 40 | 8, 9 | 0 | 40 | 0 | 40 | 0 | Yes |
| 1 | 5 | 37 | 7 | 0 | 37 | 41 | 78 | 41 | - |
| 1 | 6 | 56 | 9 | 0 | 56 | 41 | 97 | 41 | - |
| 2 | 7 | 67 | 9 | 20 | 87 | 48 | 115 | 28 | - |
| 2 | 8 | 59 | 9 | 20 | 79 | 35 | 94 | 15 | - |
| 2 | 9 | 78 | - | 20 | 98 | 48 | 126 | 28 | - |
| 3 | 8 | 54 | 9 | 40 | 94 | 40 | 94 | 0 | Yes |
| 3 | 9 | 54 | - | 40 | 94 | 72 | 126 | 32 | - |
| 4 | 5 | 29 | 7 | 0 | 29 | 49 | 78 | 49 | - |
| 4 | 6 | 43 | 9 | 0 | 43 | 54 | 97 | 54 | - |
| 5 | 7 | 37 | 9 | 37 | 74 | 78 | 115 | 41 | - |
| 6 | 9 | 29 | - | 56 | 85 | 97 | 126 | 41 | - |
| 7 | 9 | 11 | - | 87 | 98 | 115 | 126 | 28 | - |
| 8 | 9 | 32 | - | 94 | 126 | 94 | 126 | 0 | Yes |

The choice is influenced by the pheromone levels ($\tau_i$) of each arc, by an a-priori defined network parameter ($\beta$), and by the importance assigned to the heuristic rule being used ($\eta_i$). The values of $\tau_i$, $\beta$ and $\eta_i$ are utilized by the ACO path-traversal algorithm to calculate the probability of selection for each candidate arc. A random number ($q$) is then generated and compared to the predefined value of $q_0$. If $q < q_0$ then the arc with the highest probability value is selected. The second time an ant reaches a node previously traversed, the previously traversed arc from that node will not be part of the subset of possible choices the ant has in terms of possible paths to follow. The goal in this exclusion is for the ACO algorithm to avoid memorization of previously found good solutions and thus improve on the algorithm's ability to find optimal solutions. This process is repeated for the entire ant population by use of the global pheromone update rule applied at the end of each ant run, with the algorithm eventually converging to the optimal path from the start to the end nodes.

It should be noted that the ACO algorithm through its iterative process arrives at the same solution as the traditional CPM algorithm. Even though different solution states are reached at the end of each "ant run", convergence to the correct solution is eventually achieved (in fewer than 10 iterations). Since the method is "intelligently" iterative (each successive iteration is stochastically dependent on previously acquired knowledge about the network topology) the critical path may change several times before converging to the correct solution (Figure 4).

Figure 5 shows the final results and these are also tabulated in Table 2. During each iteration ("ant-run") the algorithm generates the associated pheromone concentration levels for each arc and identifies the resulting longest path (thus the critical activities as shown in

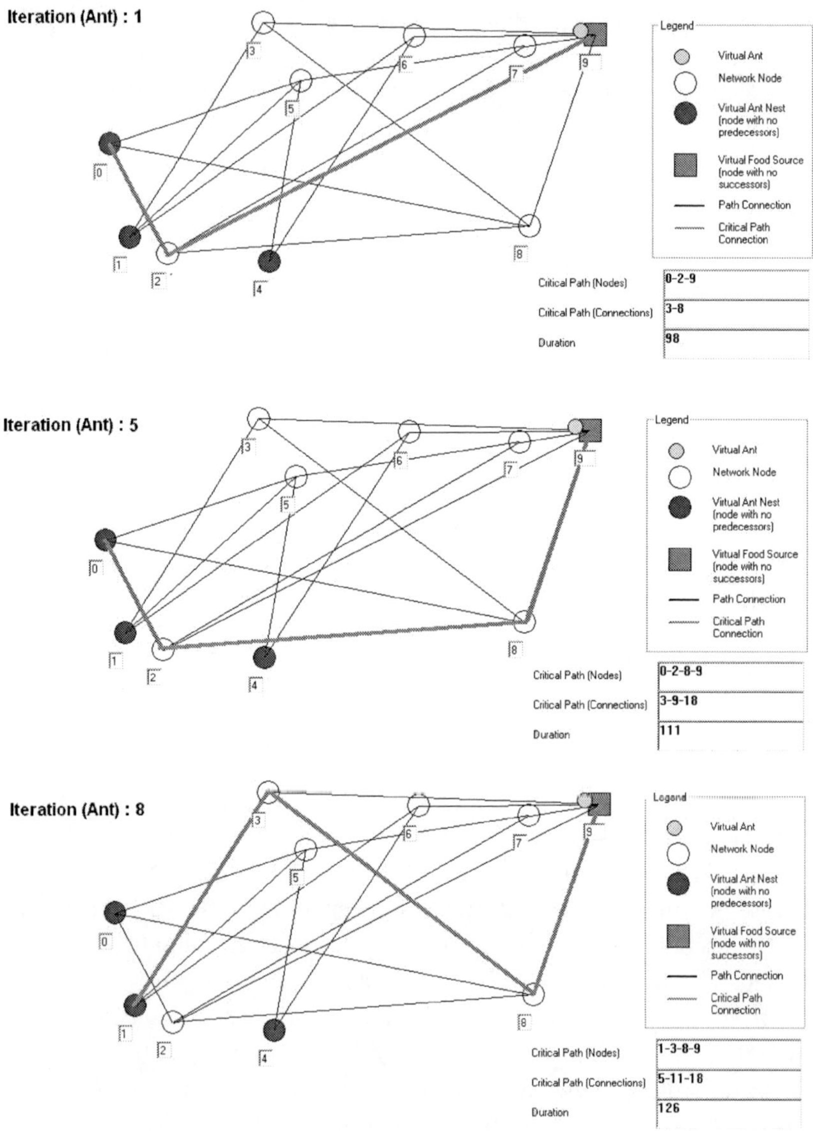


Figure 4. Snapshots of ACO solution states for different ant-runs.
(From [11], Figure 4. Copyright 2009 Elsevier. Used by permission of Elsevier.)

column "*Critical?*" in Table 2). For the specific example shown in this section, the ACO-based process converges to a solution that includes activities "0-2", "1-3", "1-6", "2-8", "3-8", "6-9" and "8-9" (high pheromone concentration). The algorithm then sifts through these activities to identify the longest continuous path from project-start to project-end and flags activities "1-3", "3-8" and "8-9" as critical, with a calculated critical path duration of 126 time-units (in agreement with the traditional CPM-based calculations).

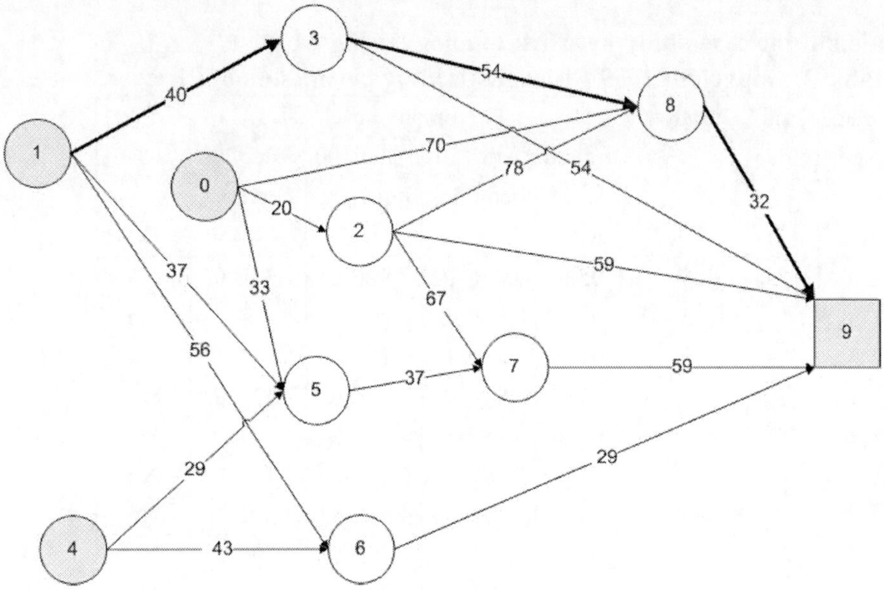


Figure 5. ACO solution of the case study network topology.
(From [10], Figure 5. Copyright American Society of Civil Engineers (ASCE). Used by permission of ASCE.)

# 4. Case Study 2: Routing of Piping Networks

The work presented in this section addresses the problem of quickly assessing node-to-node shortest or longest routes in a water piping network. In comparison to the first case study of finding the critical (i.e. longest) path in a project schedule, this second study is a reverse problem (shortest-path instead of longest path) but actually an application that is closer to the original scope of ACO for finding shortest paths between nodes of interest. The need to identify the longest and shortest paths to a desired location in a pipe network is important [13] given, for example, that at the time of an evaluation the water distribution system in study may be experiencing a failure at another location in the network. By solving the shortest-path problem the network manager can make intelligent decisions concerning the sequence of pipe segments (ACO arcs) and valves (ACO nodes) that need to be opened or closed to redirect the flow of water to the specific location (network node) at a minimum cost and time, as well as choosing the rerouting path that affects the smallest number of customers. Even though pipe rerouting is not an operation frequently performed since it is linked and/or necessitated by abnormal operational conditions (such as pipe failures), in countries and municipalities facing water scarcity problems and intermittent water supply such an operation of pipe rerouting is sometimes a daily event. In such cases, the pipe network managers are tasked with the search for minimal adverse impacts to the service provided to the public as a result of the rerouting.

**Table 2. Solution of the case-study network topology using ACO.**
**(From [11], Table 2. Copyright 2009 Elsevier. Used by permission of Elsevier.)**

| Activity :Nodes | Start Node | End Node | Duration | Pheromone Level | | | | Critical ? |
|---|---|---|---|---|---|---|---|---|
| | | | | Original | After 50 Iterations | After 100 Iterations | After 200 Iterations | |
| (1) | (2) | (3) | (4) | (5) | (6) | (7) | (8) | (9) |
| A: 0-2 | 0 | 2 | 20 | 0.0500 | 9.04E-04 | 7.82E-03 | 1.35E-02 | No |
| B: 0-5 | 0 | 5 | 33 | 0.0303 | 8.88E-16 | 7.89E-31 | 0 | No |
| C: 0-8 | 0 | 8 | 70 | 0.0143 | 1.26E-15 | 1.16E-30 | 0 | No |
| D: 1-3 | 1 | 3 | 40 | 0.0250 | 7.94E-03 | 8.08E-03 | 7.93E-03 | Yes |
| E: 1-5 | 1 | 5 | 37 | 0.0270 | 8.88E-16 | 7.89E-31 | 0 | No |
| F: 1-6 | 1 | 6 | 56 | 0.0179 | 5.59E-04 | 6.01E-04 | 2.79E-03 | No |
| G: 2-7 | 2 | 7 | 67 | 0.0149 | 5.07E-16 | 4.50E-31 | 0 | No |
| H: 2-8 | 2 | 8 | 59 | 0.0170 | 5.61E-03 | 5.59E-03 | 4.59E-03 | No |
| I: 2-9 | 2 | 9 | 78 | 0.0128 | 4.77E-16 | 4.23E-31 | 0 | No |
| J: 3-8 | 3 | 8 | 54 | 0.0185 | 7.94E-03 | 8.02E-03 | 7.93E-03 | Yes |
| K: 3-9 | 3 | 9 | 54 | 0.0185 | 1.73E-14 | 1.54E-29 | 0 | No |
| L: 4-5 | 4 | 5 | 29 | 0.0345 | 8.88E-16 | 7.89E-31 | 0 | No |
| M: 4-6 | 4 | 6 | 43 | 0.0233 | 8.88E-16 | 7.89E-31 | 0 | No |
| N: 5-7 | 5 | 7 | 37 | 0.0270 | 8.88E-16 | 7.89E-31 | 0 | No |
| O: 6-9 | 6 | 9 | 29 | 0.0345 | 1.08E-03 | 1.16E-03 | 5.39E-03 | No |
| P: 7-9 | 7 | 9 | 11 | 0.0909 | 6.42E-16 | 5.70E-31 | 0 | No |
| Q: 8-9 | 8 | 9 | 32 | 0.0313 | 1.56E-02 | 1.56E-02 | 1.42E-02 | Yes |

### 4.1. ACO-Based Algorithm

In the formulation that follows, the ACO method is developed using 'pipe length' as the metric to be minimized. However, the decision on how to traverse a water piping network could be based on any metric that the network manager values as the most important. Examples are: finding the shortest-path between nodes of interest, minimizing service disruption to end-users, minimizing number of valve operations required, etc. The general objective function to such problems is as follows:

$$\min \left[ \sum_{i,j \in p}^{n} (w_{ij} v_{ij}) \right] \tag{9}$$

$$s.t.\ p \in P_{st} \tag{10}$$

where $p$ is a path in the network and $P_{st}$ is the set of feasible paths in the network between the nodes of interest, $i$ and $j$ are a pipe's end-nodes, $n$ is the total number of pipe segments on a path, $v_{ij}$ is the metric being considered (e.g., length of a pipe), and

$w_{ij}$ is the weighing factor for $v_{ij}$. For example, when considering shorter paths on the basis of customers affected, a utilized pipe segment $v_{ij}$ may be chosen over a shorter pipe ($v_{kl} < v_{ij}$) simply because it is more important to have that segment on the operational path (i.e., $w_{ij}v_{ij} > w_{kl}v_{kl}$). This is the case of a pipe serving a hospital, or a pipe serving a high-value area, etc. In the event of pipe-length minimization the metric $v_{ij}$ is the length of the pipe ($l_{ij}$).

For these types of problems, an urban water distribution system is again modeled by a directed graph $G(N, A)$, with $N$ being the set of vertices (valves in this case) and $A$ being the set of arcs (water pipes). In this case, the ACO-based procedure for finding the shortest path(s) between a set of chosen nodes $N_1$ and $N_2$ follows the same steps as the process outlined above in Section 3.1.. It is important to note that since the desired optimization is on the shortest path of the network the calculations performed are on the negative values of the pipe lengths. This is necessitated by the fact that the aforementioned ACO algorithm maximizes the total distance between the start and end nodes. Therefore, for the calculation of the shortest distance an operation on the negative values of the pipe lengths is required, with the rest of the algorithm calculations kept unchanged.

Figure 6 shows a simple water piping network consisting of five arcs ('1' - '5') and four nodes ('a' - 'd') acting as valves. The subnet has one inflow (node 'a') and three outflows (nodes 'b', 'c' and 'd'), and the length of each pipe segment is assumed to be equal to its identification number (for example, the length of pipe '2' is 2 units, the length of pipe '3' is 3 units, etc.). As previously stated (Section 3.1.), all network arcs are initially mapped with a pheromone level defined as the inverse of their length. Then, every ant in the predefined ant population, traverses the network from an ant nest to the food source (ACO forward pass) and from there back to the ant nest (ACO backward pass).

Let us first consider the case in which water enters the network (inflow) from a source (node 'a') and unidirectionally traverses the network exiting from node 'd' (outflow). An artificial ant starting from node 'a', which is defined as an ant nest, faces the option of two possible arcs to follow next ('1' or '2'). The choice of which arc to follow is stochastic and is based on the pheromone levels ($\tau_i$) of each arc, the predefined network parameter $\beta$ and the importance assigned to the heuristic rule being used ($\eta_i$). Since the pheromone level ($\tau_i$) and the heuristic weight ($\eta_i$) of each arc were initialized as the inverse of the arc length and the inverse plus the arc length respectively then, the ant will choose the arc with the highest probability (in this case arc '1' with corresponding probability $p_1 = 0.615$) only if a random number ($q$) generated is less than a predefined value of $q_0$ for the network, and arc '2' otherwise. As the ant chooses an arc to move on to the next node in line, the pheromone level of the chosen arc is updated to reflect the ACO calculations and arc choice. At the next node this process is repeated until the ant reaches the destination (food source). Having reached the destination node (node 'd' in this case), the ant evaluates the path it traversed and should a better-than-previous solution is found (thus a shorter path) then the global update rule is applied to update the pheromone levels on all arcs (backward pass).

The second time an ant reaches node 'a', the previously traversed arc will not be part of the subset of possible choices the ant has in terms of possible paths to follow (so that the algorithm avoids memorization), and therefore a different path to the end-node will be considered as a possible solution. This process is repeated for the entire ant population with a global pheromone update rule applied at the end of each ant run, with the algorithm

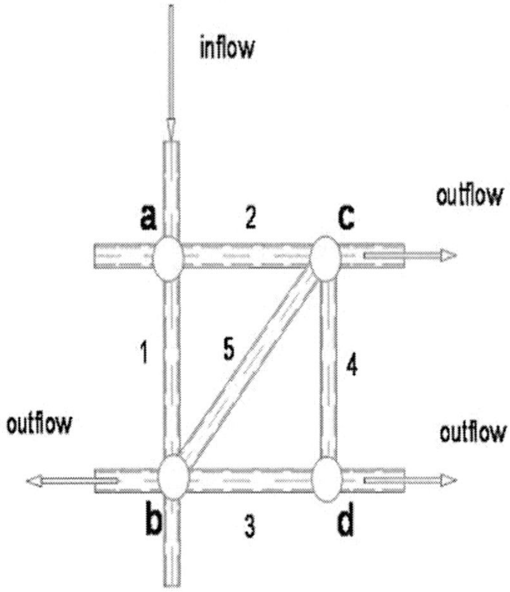


Figure 6. A Simple Piping Network.
(From [14], Figure 2. Copyright American Society of Civil Engineers (ASCE). Used by permission of ASCE.)

converging to the optimal path from the start to the end nodes.

## 4.2. A More Complicated Case Study

Let us now consider a slightly more complicated case, based on an urban pipe network topology as shown in Figure 7. The ACO algorithm was implemented by means of custom software [12] and the optimization performed is again on the shortest-path from one node (inflow) to another node (outflow).

The network topology in study (Figure 7) is a hypothetical simplified urban water distribution network that has 3 inputs (could be thought of as water reservoirs or inflow pipes), 6 main valves and 17 water distribution mains for a total length of 749 pipe-segments. The latter number is deduced by summing up the lengths of the arcs in the network (each arc length represents the number of pipe segments on that arc) and corresponds to the total pipe-length of the network.

In ACO terms, the case-study network has a topology of 10 nodes and 17 arcs and the ACO parameters are initialized as $C = 50$, $q_0 = 0.3$, $\rho = 0.5$, $\alpha = 0.5$, $\tau_{0i} = 1/l_i$, $\tau_{1i} = 1$, $\eta_i = l_i + 1/l_i$ and $\beta_1 = \beta_2 = ... = \beta_C = 1.0$. The values used are based on sensitivity analysis results from similar-size case studies reported by [12] and in which the performance of ACO topology parameters ($q_o$, $\beta$, $\rho$, $\alpha$, $C$) was examined against other network characteristics (the number of nodes and arcs in the network topology, and the number of "ant nests" (i.e., the number of possible start nodes in the network). It is also noted that the network in study is based on unidirectional nodal connections (an acyclic graph) so as to emulate real-life gravity-based water distribution networks. The corresponding graph of the network of Figure 7 is shown in Figure 8, which also includes the assumed node-to-node lengths of all pipe segments in the network. The reader should also note that the topology of the piping network in study (Figure 8) is identical to the scheduling network studied in Section 3. (Figure 3).

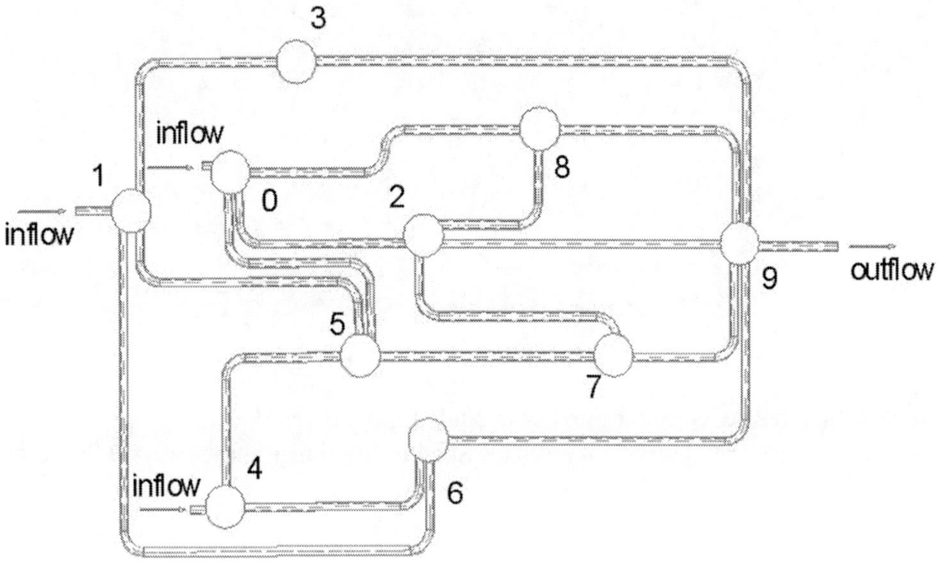


Figure 7. Two-dimensional topology of case-study piping network.
(From [14], Figure 3. Copyright American Society of Civil Engineers (ASCE). Used by permission of ASCE.)

This case study looks at the following problem: given that a pipe breaks at the outskirts of the network (e.g., just before one of nodes '0', '1', or '4'), what is the best way to reroute water flow so as to guarantee service at node '9'? Since 'service' is related to water flow and minimum acceptable water pressure at the node of interest, and since the pressure drop along a pipe ($\Delta p$) is linearly related to the pipe's length ($L$) then by use of Eq. 11, if the pipes are of equal diameter ($D$), of same material type, and with same volumetric flow rate ($Q$), the aforementioned problem becomes a node-to-node shortest-path problem that requires evaluation of all possible paths from start-nodes '0', '1' and '4' to end-node '9'. Factors $\rho$, $\lambda$ and $\xi$ in Eq. 11 are the fluid density, friction coefficient and minor-losses coefficient, respectively, for the pipes under investigation.

$$\Delta p = \frac{8\rho Q^2}{\pi^2 D^4}\left(\lambda\frac{L}{D} + \sum \xi\right) \tag{11}$$

The reader should note that the classical CPM approach (as described in Section 3.) can be modified to solve for any water piping network problem. The difference in this case is that instead of solving for critical paths (i.e., the longest path in a network) the solution sought is for shortest paths. A simple way to adjust CPM to solve for the shortest, instead of the longest, path is to perform all related backward calculations based on the minimum

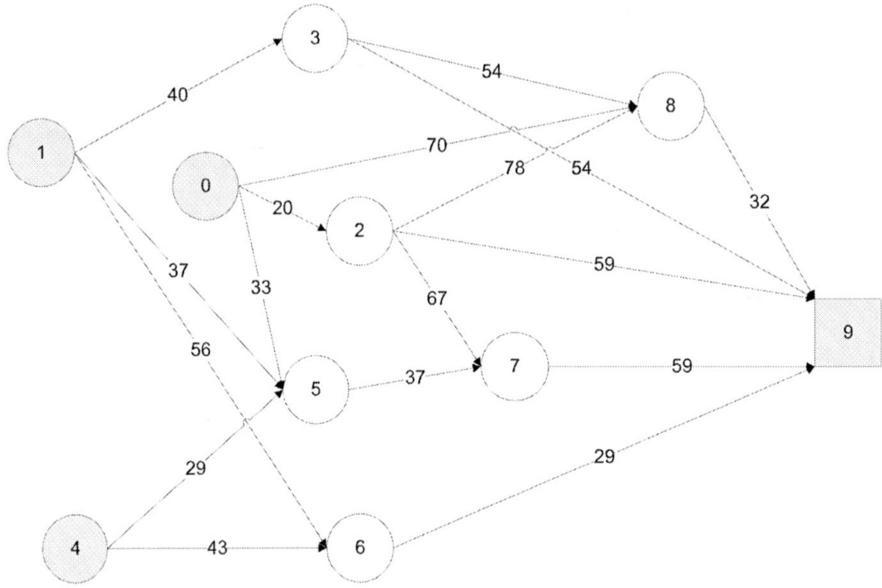


Figure 8. Annotated ACO topology of case-study piping network.
(From [14], Figure 4. Copyright American Society of Civil Engineers (ASCE). Used by permission of ASCE.)

value of *EarlyFinish* at each end-node during the forward pass calculations, and for the maximum value of the *LateStart* at each node during the backward pass calculations. In this case, the calculated ES, EF, LS, LF and TF values obtained by applying the Modified Critical Path Method (MCPM) [14] become as shown in Table 3. Furthermore, the MCPM values tabulated in Table 3 result in identifying activities '4-6' and '6-9' as critical (*TotalFloat* = 0) and thus resulting in a shortest-path length of 43+29=72 units.

#### 4.2.1. ACO-Based Solution

The ACO algorithm through its iterative stochastic process arrives at the same solution as the MCPM algorithm. Different snapshots of the ACO solution states for various ant runs are shown in Figure 9 and the final solution results are shown in Figure 10 and tabulated in Table 4. During each iteration ("ant-run" ) the algorithm generates the associated pheromone concentration levels for each arc, deduces the criticality of each connection and through that identifies the resulting shortest path (thus the critical pipe segments). The solution obtained by the ACO algorithm is tabulated in Table 4 as "FinalPheromone" values. The algorithm considers these values during the solution phase and decides which pipe segments on a continuous path are critical (column "On Shortest Path?" in Table 4).

The end-result (Table 4) is the convergence of the ACO-based process to segments '0-2', '1-6', '2-8', '4-6', '4-5', '5-7', '5-9', '6-9' and '7-9' as important (high pheromone concentration). The algorithm then sifts through these pipe segments to identify the shortest continuous path from network-start to network-end and flags activities '4-6' and '8-9' as critical, with a calculated shortest path length of 72 units (in agreement with the modified CPM-based calculations).

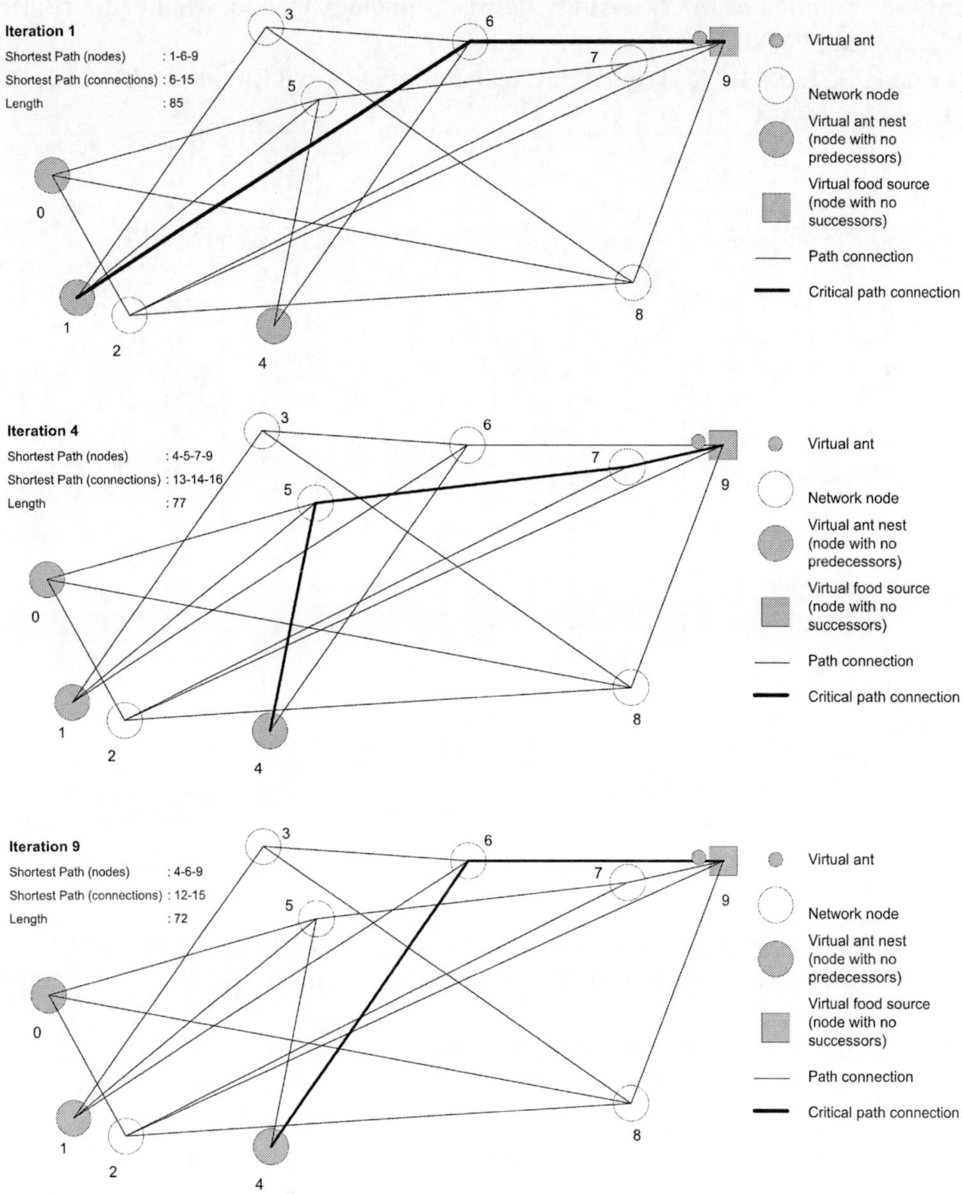


Figure 9. Snapshots of ACO solution states for various ant-runs.
(From [14], Figure 5. Copyright American Society of Civil Engineers (ASCE). Used by permission of ASCE.)

**Table 3. Solution of the case-study network topology using a Modified Critical Path Method (MCPM).**
**(From [14], Table 1. Copyright American Society of Civil Engineers (ASCE). Used by permission of ASCE.)**

| Start Node (1) | End Node (2) | Arc Length (3) | Successor Nodes (4) | Early Start (5) | Early Finish (6) | MCPM LS (7) | MCPM LF (8) | MCPM TF (9) | MCPM Critical ? (10) |
|---|---|---|---|---|---|---|---|---|---|
| 0 | 2 | 20 | 7, 8, 9 | 0 | 20 | -26 | - 6 | -26 | - |
| 0 | 5 | 33 | 7 | 0 | 33 | - 9 | 24 | -9 | - |
| 0 | 8 | 70 | 9 | 0 | 70 | -30 | 40 | -30 | - |
| 1 | 3 | 40 | 8, 9 | 0 | 40 | -22 | 18 | -22 | - |
| 1 | 5 | 37 | 7 | 0 | 37 | -13 | 24 | -13 | - |
| 1 | 6 | 56 | 9 | 0 | 56 | -13 | 43 | -13 | - |
| 2 | 7 | 67 | 9 | 20 | 87 | - 6 | 61 | -26 | - |
| 2 | 8 | 78 | - | 20 | 87 | - 6 | 72 | -15 | - |
| 2 | 9 | 59 | 9 | 20 | 79 | -19 | 40 | -39 | - |
| 3 | 8 | 54 | - | 40 | 94 | 18 | 72 | -22 | - |
| 3 | 9 | 54 | 9 | 40 | 94 | -14 | 40 | -54 | - |
| 4 | 5 | 29 | 7 | 0 | 29 | - 5 | 24 | - 5 | - |
| 4 | 6 | 43 | 9 | 0 | 43 | 0 | 43 | 0 | Yes |
| 5 | 7 | 37 | 9 | 33 | 70 | 24 | 61 | - 9 | - |
| 6 | 9 | 29 | - | 43 | 72 | 43 | 72 | 0 | Yes |
| 7 | 9 | 59 | - | 70 | 81 | 61 | 72 | - 9 | - |
| 8 | 9 | 32 | - | 70 | 102 | 40 | 72 | -30 | - |

# 5. Comparing ACO with other Path Search Techniques

As noted by Christodoulou and Ellinas ( [10], [11], [14]) when it comes to searching for shortest or longest network paths the ACO method compares favorably with traditional CPM and with other path search techniques, such as genetic algorithms (GAs) and particle swarm optimization (PSO) [15], [16], [17], [18].

As already noted, traditional CPM algorithms are iterative methods that have been proven to perform well, albeit with computational inefficiencies. The brute force iterative enumeration of all paths in the project network and the inability of CPM algorithms to perform arbitrary node-to-node calculations are among the most limiting features of the method. Further to quick convergence to the solution (through intelligent selection of arcs in its quest for optimal paths), though, the ACO method provides significant advantages over traditional CPM. These advantages stem from the graph-like nature of the ACO algorithm and the similarity between the ACO topology and real-life construction scheduling/water piping networks. This feature allows for quick adaptation of the ACO algorithm to network topologies with arcs and nodes, such as the aforementioned networks. Additionally, the problem of "the absence of activity start time flexibility" observed in CPM [15] is not present in the ACO algorithm. Activities can be designated "ant nests" and positioned in time at the planner's discretion without hindering implementation of ACO.

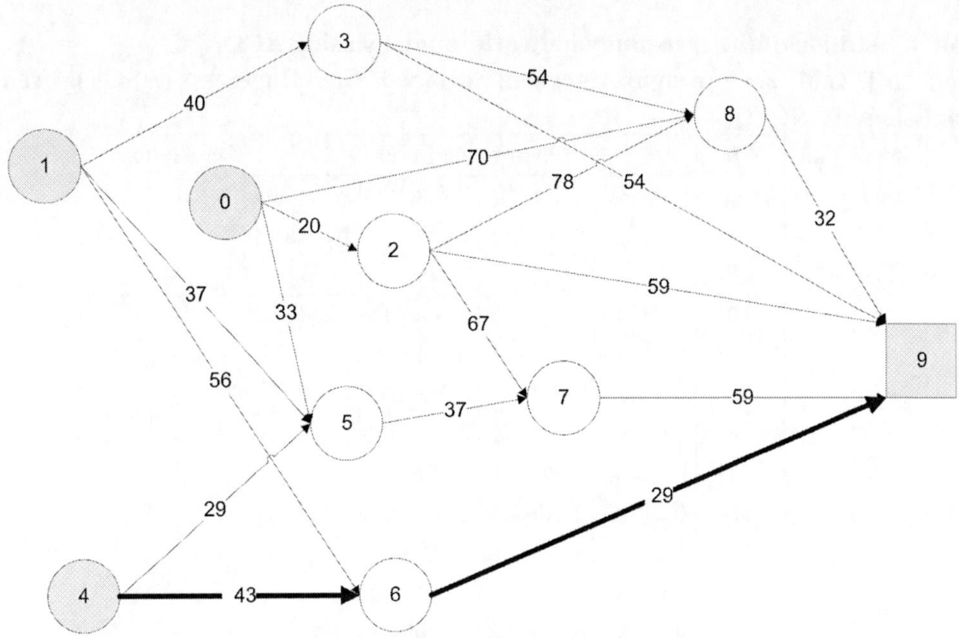


Figure 10. ACO solution of the case-study network topology.
(From [14], Figure 6. Copyright American Society of Civil Engineers (ASCE). Used by permission of ASCE.)

On the other hand, GA techniques behave similarly to ACO as they arrive at solutions by searching only a fraction of the total search space and which can be modified to incorporate additional objectives during optimization. In the work by Senouci and Eldin [17], for example, a GA is presented that incorporates precedence relationships, multiple crew strategies, total project cost minimization, and time-cost trade-off. GA techniques offer several improvements over CPM especially with reference to resource allocation and leveling in construction scheduling problems, since GAs can be used to search for near-optimum solutions by simultaneously considering both the resource allocation and the leveling aspects of resource-constrained scheduling problems [16]. Also both ACO and GA approaches possess features that make the methods suitable to large scale resource-constrained scheduling problems and parallel computing implementations.

Similarly, the case of PSO also shows many similarities with the underlying philosophy of the ACO approach, in the way the methods utilize both local and global knowledge during the solution-search process. Reported work on PSO [18] showed that the PSO algorithm had a slightly higher convergence rate than GA and a higher stability, while searching for optimum solutions. Furthermore, PSO is more robust than general analytical and heuristic methods, because it does not lead to combinatorial explosion or problem-dependent effectiveness [18]. However, when compared to ACO both GA and PSO have an additional level of complexity because of the need to transform the original project network into the data structure used by the methods (a structure that greatly deviates from the traditional CPM-like paradigm).

**Table 4. Solution of the case-study network topology using ACO.**
**(From [14], Table 2. Copyright American Society of Civil Engineers (ASCE). Used by permission of ASCE.)**

| Start Node (1) | End Node (2) | Arc Length (3) | Pheromone Level: Original (4) | After 50 Iterations (5) | After 100 Iterations (6) | After 200 Iterations (7) | On Shortest Path ? (8) |
|---|---|---|---|---|---|---|---|
| 0 | 2 | 20 | 0.05000 | 1.66E-15 | 1.43E-02 | 1.29E-02 | - |
| 0 | 5 | 33 | 0.03030 | 8.88E-15 | 0.00E+00 | 0 | - |
| 0 | 8 | 70 | 0.01429 | 3.69E-15 | 0.00E+00 | 0 | - |
| 1 | 3 | 40 | 0.02500 | 1.15E-15 | 0.00E+00 | 0 | - |
| 1 | 5 | 37 | 0.02703 | 8.88E-16 | 0.00E+00 | 0 | - |
| 1 | 6 | 56 | 0.01786 | 2.96E-15 | 2.51E-03 | 6.37E-04 | - |
| 2 | 7 | 67 | 0.01493 | 8.88E-16 | 0.00E+00 | 0 | - |
| 2 | 9 | 59 | 0.01282 | 4.55E-16 | 0.00E+00 | 0 | - |
| 2 | 8 | 78 | 0.01695 | 5.64E-03 | 4.85E-03 | 4.38E-03 | - |
| 3 | 8 | 54 | 0.01852 | 8.88E-16 | 0.00E+00 | 0 | - |
| 3 | 9 | 54 | 0.01852 | 9.70E-16 | 0.00E+00 | 0 | - |
| 4 | 5 | 29 | 0.03448 | 1.36E-04 | 3.37E-05 | 5.42E-03 | - |
| 4 | 6 | 43 | 0.02326 | 1.39E-02 | 1.39E-02 | 1.39E-02 | Yes |
| 5 | 7 | 37 | 0.02703 | 1.07E-04 | 2.64E-05 | 4.25E-03 | - |
| 6 | 9 | 29 | 0.03448 | 1.31E-02 | 7.08E-03 | 1.22E-02 | Yes |
| 7 | 9 | 59 | 0.09091 | 3.59E-04 | 8.89E-05 | 1.43E-02 | - |
| 8 | 9 | 32 | 0.03125 | 8.88E-16 | 0.00E+00 | 0 | - |

## 6. Conclusion

The ACO artificial agent seems to provide a powerful means to performing network optimization through shortest path calculations in piping networks and longest-path calculations in construction scheduling, since it is able to efficiently construct shortest/longest-path solutions in acyclic (unidirectional) network topologies. Despite the seemingly iterative approach of the ACO algorithm, the method exhibits quick convergence to the final solution (as shown in the examined case studies) and thus low computational time. ACO has a structure and representation that is very similar to traditional CPM networks and it is therefore easy to understand and implement on top of existing software tools, thus providing for a novel and efficient way to solve problems in construction scheduling and water piping networks.

In terms of construction scheduling, the ACO methodology can further be modified and extended to account for resource and cash flows, and node-to-node longest path calculations. The former can be achieved by considering the respective activity assignments and including them in the cost function of each arc. In such case, the calculations performed include not only activity durations but also activity costs and activity resources. In the event of resource-constrained scheduling, an added complexity is introduced to the problem which can be solved by simultaneously considering batches of artificial ants (equal to the maximum number of resources available to the planner, per time unit) instead of a single artificial ant at a time [10].

In the case study for piping networks, even though the ACO method was formulated based on pipe-length calculations, the underlying shortest-path framework can be applied to a number of other parameters, such as minimization of valves operated, minimization of customers affected, minimization of operating costs, etc., providing significant flexibility to the user [14]. The ACO methodology can further be modified and extended to account for reliability and level of service calculations, and node-to-node optimizations for real-life urban water distribution networks [14]. The former can be achieved by considering the probability of failure for each pipe segment and the number of customers serviced by each pipe path, and including these parameters in the utility function to be optimized. The latter can be achieved by setting the start node of the node-to-node sequence of interest as an "ant nest" and the end node as a "food source" and reconstructing the solution path (shortest path) while all other nodes are set as plain network nodes. To that effect, a more complicated case study network from an urban water distribution system, composed of tens of arcs and nodes and with a number of hypothetical path-search scenarios examined and solved by ACO is documented in [14].

# References

[1] Dorigo, M. (1991). Ant Colony Optimization - New Optimization Techniques in Engineering, by G. C. Onwubolu and B. V. Babu, Springer-Verlag Berlin Heidelberg, 101-117.

[2] Dorigo, M. (1992). Optimization, Learning and Natural Algorithms. Ph.D Thesis, Politecnico di Milano, Italy.

[3] Dorigo, M., Maniezzo, V. and Colorni, A. (1996). "Ant system: optimization by a colony of cooperating agents", *Systems, Man and Cybernetics, Part B, IEEE Transactions on*, 26(1):29–41.

[4] Dorigo, M. and Gambardella, L.M. (1997). "Ant Colony System: A Cooperative Learning Approach to the Traveling Salesman Problem", *IEEE Transactions on Evolutionary Computation* 1(1):53–66.

[5] Stützle, T. and Hoos, H.H. (2000). "MAX MIN Ant System", *Future Generation Computer Systems*, 16:889–914.

[6] Bullnheimer, B., Hartl, R.F. and Strauss, C. (1999). "A New Rank Based Version of the Ant System: A Computational Study", *Central European Journal for Operations Research and Economics*, 7(1):25–38.

[7] Cordón, O., Herrera, F., Fernández de Viana, I. and Moreno, L. (2000). *A New ACO Model Integrating Evolutionary Computation Concepts: The Best-Worst Ant System*

Proc. ANTS2000 From Ant Colonies to Artificial Ants: Second International Workshop on Ant Algorithms, Brussels, Belgium, 22–29, Sep. 7-9.

[8] Dorigo, M., Di Caro, G. and Gambardella, L.M. (1999). "Ant Algorithms for Discrete Optimization", *Artificial Life*, 5(2):37–172.

[9] Stützle, T. and Dorigo, M. (2002). The Ant Colony Optimization Metaheuristic: Algorithms, Applications, and Advances, F. Glover and G. Kochenberger (editors), Handbook of Metaheuristics, Kluwer Academic Publishers, Norwell, MA.

[10] Christodoulou, S. and Ellinas, G. (2010). "Scheduling Resource-Constrained Projects with Ant Colony Optimization Artificial Agents", *ASCE Journal of Computing in Civil Engineering*, 24(1):45–55.

[11] Christodoulou, S. (2009). "Construction Imitating Ants: Resource-Unconstrained Scheduling With Artificial Ants", *Elsevier Journal of Automation in Construction*, 18(3):285–293.

[12] Christodoulou, S. (2005). "Ant Colony Optimization in Construction Scheduling", Proc. *ASCE International Conference on Computing in Civil Engineering*, Cancun, Mexico, Jul. 12-15.

[13] Christodoulou, S., Deligianni, A., Aslani, P. and Agathokleous, A. (2009). "Risk-based asset management of water piping networks using neurofuzzy systems", *Computers, Environment and Urban Systems*, Elsevier, 33(2):138–149.

[14] Christodoulou, S. and Ellinas, G. (2010). "Pipe Network Routing Through Ant Colony Optimization", *ASCE Journal of Infrastructure Systems*, 16(2):149–159.

[15] Kim, K. and de la Garza, J.M. (2005). "Evaluation of the Resource-Constrained Critical Path Method Algorithms", *ASCE Journal of Construction Engineering and Management*, 131(5):522–532.

[16] Hegazy, T. (1999). "Optimization of Resource Allocation and Leveling Using Genetic Algorithms", *ASCE Journal of Construction Engineering and Management*, 125(3):167–175.

[17] Senouci, A.B. and Eldin, N.N. (2004). "Use of Genetic Algorithms in Resource Scheduling of Construction Projects", *ASCE Journal of Construction Engineering and Management*, 130(6):869–877.

[18] Zhang, H., Li, H. and Tam, C. (2006). "Permutation-Based Particle Swarm Optimization for Resource-Constrained Project Scheduling, *ASCE Journal of Computing in Civil Engineering*, 20(2):141–149.

In: Ant Colonies
Editor: Emily C. Sun
ISBN: 978-1-61122-023-0


*Chapter 7*

# KANTS: A SELF-ORGANIZED ANT SYSTEM FOR PATTERN CLUSTERING AND CLASSIFICATION

***A.M. Mora, C. Fernandes, J.J. Merelo****
Department of Architecture and Computer Technology
University of Granada, Spain

**Abstract**

In this chapter we introduce a new ant-based method, named KANTS, that takes advantage of the cooperative self-organization of Ant Colony Systems to create a naturally inspired clustering and pattern recognition method. The approach considers each data item as an ant, which moves inside a grid, changing the cells it goes through, in a fashion similar to Kohonen's Self-Organizing Maps. The resulting algorithm is conceptually more simple, takes less free parameters than other ant-based clustering algorithms. In order to test it, some of the well-known benchmark classification problems have been solved using our algorithm and some other methods. KANTS yields the best results after some parameter tuning. Moreover, some experiments have been performed to assess the algorithm as a data clustering tool, concluding that KANTS is in addition a very promising clustering method.

**Keywords:** Ant System, Ant Colony System, Ant-based Algorithm, Clustering, Classification, Pattern Recognition, Self-Organizing Maps.

## 1. Introduction

It has been observed in the nature that clustering is performed naturally by ants at least in two different ways. First, ant colonies recognize by odour other member of their colony (as mentioned by Labroche et al. in [13]) leading to a natural clustering of ants belonging to the same nest, which is a consequence of nurturing and also has some genetic support; second, ants do physically cluster their larvae and dead bodies, putting them in piles whose position and size is completely self-organizing, as described by [4]. Ant algorithms inspired

*Email address: {amorag,jmerelo}@geneura.ugr.es, cfernandes@laseeb.org

by these models such as those proposed by [1, 2, 13, 17] have been applied to clustering and classification. In general, these methods follow the second clustering behavior: data for training the clusters is represented as *dead bodies*, which ants have to pick up (with a certain probability, and following some rule) and drop (also following some rule), while at the same time dropping and following pheromones. This results in the introduction of a few artifacts in the method: while the number of *dead bodies* (data items) to sort is *natural*, grid size, number of ants, pheromone following behavior and the rest is not. This results in a certain amount of parameter tuning for obtaining good results, but in any case is farther away from natural inspiration.

In this chapter we present KohonAnts (KANTS), an Ant Colony System [5, 6] algorithm that merges the biologically inspired concepts in Kohonen's Self-Organizing Map (proposed and described in [11, 12]) and Chialvo et al. Ant Algorithm [3] (all of them will be introduced in next section). It is based in several new ideas. First, as in the above-mentioned Labroche et al. model, every ant represents a data item. Ants move in a grid dropping *vectorial* pheromones. The grid is filled with initially random vector pheromones (of the same dimension as the data), and every time an ant falls in a cell, it changes the pheromone following a method similar to that used in Kohonen Self-Organizing Map, making the cell pheromone closer to the data item stored in the ant itself.

Since ants move around in the grid, ant position and pheromone content co-adapt, so that eventually ants with similar data items are close together in the grid (a *nesting* behavior), and the grid itself contains vectors similar to those stored in the ants on top of them. The grid can then be used to classify in the same way as Kohonen's Self-Organizing Map (but with better results), while ants can be used to visually identify the position of the clusters.

The interesting part of this method is that self-organization comes through stigmergy: ants change their environment (pheromones stored on the grid), and that influences the behavior of the rest of the ants (that follow a path changed by their cluster-siblings). There are less non-natural parameters (grid size is one of them), and, finally, results obtained are quite competitive with other methods tested.

In this chapter, after presenting all concepts used in our method in Section 2., after it, we will describe the KohonAnts model itself in Section 3., followed by the experiments in Section 4.. Finally, we will conclude our description in Section 5. with a discussion of the obtained results and future lines of work.

## 2. Preliminary Concepts

Before describing KohonAnts, we would like to introduce the algorithms in which it is based on for the unfamiliar reader. First, Ant Colony Optimization algorithms are presented in Subsection 2.1., followed by Kohonen's Self-Organizing Map in Subsection 2.2.. Finally, Chialvo and Millonas' model is presented in Subsection 2.3..

### 2.1. ACO

The Ant Colony Optimization (ACO) is a meta-heuristic inspired by the behaviour of some species of ants that are able to find the shortest path from nest to food sources in a short time.

The method is based in the concept of *stigmergy*, that is, communication between agents using the environment, so every ant, while walking, deposits on the ground a substance called *pheromone* which other ants can smell. Every ant tends to follow strong concentrations of pheromone (it is evaporated after some time), which form a pheromone trail from nest to food source, so in intersections between several trails an ant moves with high probability following the highest pheromone level. This metaheuristic was introduced by Dorigo et al. [5,6] in 1991.

ACO algorithms take this behaviour as inspiration to solve combinatorial optimization problems, using a colony of 'artificial ants' which are computational agents that communicate each other using *pheromones*. The problem to be solved using ACO must be transformed into a graph with weighted edges. In every iteration, each ant builds a complete path (solution), by travelling through the graph. At the end of this construction (and in some versions, during it), each ant leaves a trail in the visited edges depending on the fitness of the solution it has found. This is a measure of desirability for that edge and it will be considered by the following ants. In order to guide its movement, each ant uses two kinds of information that will be combined: *pheromone trails*, which correspond to 'learnt information' changed during the algorithm run, denoted by $\tau$; and *heuristic knowledge*, which is a measure of the desirability of moving to the next node, based in previous knowledge about the problem (do not change during the algorithm run), denoted by $\eta$. The ants usually choose edges with better values in both properties, but sometimes they may 'explore' new zones in the graph because the algorithm has a stochastic component, that broadens the search space to regions not previously explored. Due to all these properties, all ants cooperate in order to find the best solution for the problem (the best path in the graph), resulting in an global emergent behaviour.

ACOs initially took two different shapes: Ant System (AS) and Ant Colony System (ACS). Nowadays there are lots of variants and new methods.

In the *Ant System* pheromone update is performed once all ants have built their solutions. There are two steps: first, all pheromone trails are reduced by a constant factor (evaporation), after this, every ant deposits an amount of pheromone in its path depending on the quality of its solution.

The building of solutions is strongly based in the *state transition rule*, since every ant uses it to decide which node $j$ is the next in the construction of a solution (path), when the ant is at the node $i$. This formula calculates the probability associated to every node in the neighbourhood of $i$, and is as follows:

$$P(i,j) = \begin{cases} \dfrac{\tau(i,j)^{\alpha} \cdot \eta(i,j)^{\beta}}{\sum\limits_{u \in N_i} \tau(i,u)^{\alpha} \cdot \eta(i,u)^{\beta}} & if\ j \in N_i \\ \\ 0 & otherwise \end{cases} \tag{1}$$

Where $\alpha$ and $\beta$ are weighting parameters to set the relative importance of pheromone and heuristic information respectively, and $N_i$ is the current feasible neighbourhood for the node $i$.

The pheromone updating is made at a global level by every ant, which retraces its solution path. It consists of an evaporation (left term) and a contribution (right term):

$$\tau^t(i,j) = (1-\rho)\cdot\tau^{t-1}(i,j) + \Delta\tau^{t-1}(i,j) \tag{2}$$

*t* marks the new pheromone value and *t-1* the old one. ρ in [0,1] is the common evaporation factor and Δτ is the amount of pheromone deposited depending on the quality of the solution.

The *Ant Colony System* (ACS) is similar to AS, but it uses a different state transition rule (called *pseudo-random proportional state transition rule* ):
If $(q \le q_0)$

$$j = \arg\max_{j\in N_i}\left\{\sum_{u\in N_i}\tau(i,u)^{\alpha}\cdot\eta(i,u)^{\beta}\right\} \tag{3}$$

Else

$$P(i,j) = \begin{cases} \dfrac{\tau(i,j)^{\alpha}\cdot\eta(i,j)^{\beta}}{\sum_{u\in N_i}\tau(i,u)^{\alpha}\cdot\eta(i,u)^{\beta}} & if\, j\in N_i \\ 0 & otherwise \end{cases} \tag{4}$$

Where $q$ is a random number in [0,1] and $q_0$ is a parameter which set the balance between exploration and exploitation. If $q < q_0$, the best node is chosen as next (exploitation), on the other hand one of the feasible neighbours is selected, considering different probabilities for each one (exploration). The rest of the parameters are the same as in Equation 1.

There is a *global pheromone updating*, which is only performed for the edges of the global best solution:

$$\begin{gathered} \forall(i,j)\ in\ S_{GlobalBest} \\ \tau^t(i,j) = (1-\rho)\cdot\tau^{t-1}(i,j) + \rho\cdot\Delta\tau(i,j)_{GlobalBest} \end{gathered} \tag{5}$$

There is also a *local pheromone updating*, which is performed by every ant, every time that a node *j* is added to the path which it is building. This formula is:

$$\tau^t(i,j) = (1-\varphi)\cdot\tau^{t-1}(i,j) + \varphi\cdot\tau_0 \tag{6}$$

Where φ in [0,1] is the local evaporation factor and $\tau_0$ is the initial amount of pheromone (it corresponds to a lower trail limit). This formula results in an additional exploration technique, because it makes the edges traversed by an ant less attractive to the following ants and helps to avoid that many ants follow the same path.

Any of them, but specially ACS, will have to be adapted to a particular problem, mainly through the heuristic functions, and possibly also by changing the number of colonies or pheromone arrays. In particular, those are possible ways of approaching multi-objective optimization problems, which will be introduced below.

## 2.2. SOM

The self organizing map (SOM) was introduced by Teuvo Kohonen in 1982 [12]. It is a non-supervised neural network that tries to imitate the self-organization done in the sensory cortex of the human brain, where neighbouring neurons are activated by similar stimulus. It is usually used as a clustering/classification tool or used to find unknown relationships between a set of variables that describe a problem. The main property of the SOM is that it makes a nonlinear projection from a high-dimensional data space (one dimension per variable) on a regular, low-dimensional (usually 2D) grid of neurons (see Figure 1).

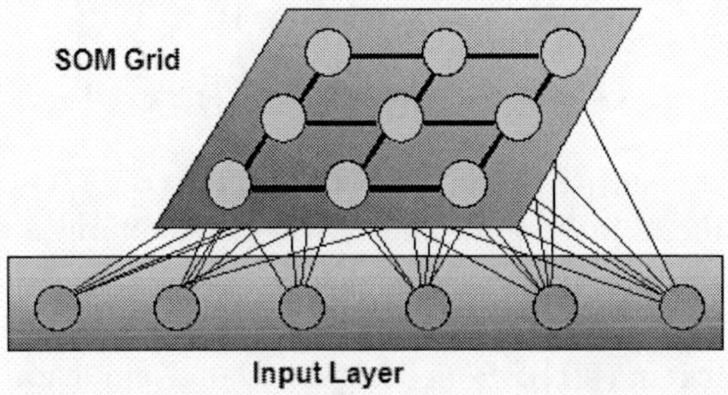


Figure 1. SOM Grid

Since this type of network is distributed in a plane (2-dimensional structure) it can be concluded that the projections preserve the topological relationships while simultaneously creating a dimensional reduction of the representation space (the transformation is made in a topologically ordered way).

The SOM processes a set of input vectors (samples or patterns), which are composed by variables (features) which typify each sample, and creates an output topological network where each neuron is associated also to a vector of variables (model vector) which is representative of a group of the input vectors. Note in Figure 1 that each neuron of the network is completely connected to all the nodes (each node is a sample) of the input layer. So, the network represents a feed-forward structure with only one computational layer formed by neurons or model vectors.

There are four main steps in the processing of the SOM. Excepting the first one, the others are repeated until a stop criteria is reached:

- **Initialization of model vectors**. Usually it is made by assigning small random values to their variables, but there are some other possibilities as an initialization using random input samples.
- **Competitive process**. For each input pattern $X$, all the neurons (model vectors) $W$ competes using a *similarity function* in order to identify the more similar or close to the sample vector. The more usual function is a distance measure (as Euclidean distance). The winner neuron is called the best matching unit (BMU).
- **Cooperative process**. The BMU determines the centre of a topological neighbourhood where those neurons inside it will be updated (the model vectors) to be even

more similar to the input pattern. There is a *neighbourhood function* used to determine the neurons to consider. If the lattice where the neurons are is rectangular or hexagonal, it is possible to consider as neighbourhood rectangles or hexagons with the BMU as centre. But it is more usual to use a Gaussian function to assure that the farther the neighbour neuron is, the smaller the updating to its associated vector is. In this process, the neurons inside a vicinity cooperate all of them to learn.

- **Learning process**. In this step the variables of the model vectors inside the neighbourhood are updated to be closer to those of the input vector. It means doing the neuron more similar to the sample. The *learning rule* used to update the vector ($W$) for every neuron $i$ in the neighbourhood of the BMU is:

$$W_i^t = W_i^{t-1} + \alpha^t \cdot N_{BMU}^t(i) \cdot (X - W_i^{t-1}) \quad (7)$$

  Where t is the current iteration of the whole process, $X$ is the input vector, $N_{BMU}$ is the neighbourhood function for the BMU, which returns a high value (in [0,1]) if the neuron $i$ is in the neighbourhood and close to the BMU (1 if $i = BMU$), and a small value in the other case (0 if $i$ is not located inside the neighbourhood). $\alpha$ is the *learning rate* (also in (0,1]). Both (neighbourhood and learning rate) depends on $t$, since it is usual to decrease the radius of the first one and the value of the second in order to make higher updating at the beginning of the process and almost none in the latter.

The consecutive application of Equation 7 and the update of the neighbourhood function, has the effect of 'moving' the model vectors, $W_j$, spatially from the winning neuron towards the input vector $X_i$. It is, the model vectors tend to follow the distribution of the input vectors. Consequently, the algorithm leads to a topological arrangement of the characteristic map of the input space, in the sense that adjacent neurons in the network tend to have similar weights vectors.

A SOM works as follows: there are 2 layers with the same number of neurons, the input layer and the output layer. Every set of data to study is introduced to the first one and transmitted directly to the second one where it is processed. In this process the SOM searches for the neuron (and its neighbourhood) which is more similar to the input data and makes them even more similar. So each neuron has a set of values (one for each variable), with random values at the beginning of the algorithm, and in every iteration it tries to minimize the distance (according to the measure of distance chosen) between every value of its set and the corresponding value of the nearest set of variables inside the data group which the SOM is studying. It uses a learning formula in every iteration that changes these values in order to make them closes. This updating involves not only the nearest neuron, but all the neurons in its neighbourhood defined using another function. This procedure is repeated a number of times fixed by the user. As a result, each neuron tends to occupy a spatial region so the whole neural network adjusts itself to the data space.

As a consequence, looking at the display of a SOM, it is possible to recognize some clusters as well as the metric-topological relations of the data items (vectors of variables of the problem) and the outstanding variables.

Although Kohonen's SOMs are not as accurate as other tools at the task of classification, they can be applied to many different types of data, yielding visualization of natural structures in the data and their relations, as well as the natural groupings that could be among them. In addition, SOM makes easy the estimation of the variables that have more influence on these groupings. Other statistical and soft computing tools can also be used for this purpose, but since Kohonen's SOMs offers a visual way of doing it, it is much more intuitive.

SOM is further processed using Ultsch method [19], the Unified distance matrix (U-matrix), which uses SOM's codevectors (vectors of variables of the problem) as data source and generates a matrix where each component is a distance measure between two adjacent neurons. It allows us to visualize any multi-variated dataset in a two-dimensional display, so we can detect topological relations among neurons and infer about the input data structure. High values in the U-matrix represent a frontier region between clusters, and low values represent a high degree of similarities among neurons on that region, clusters.

## 2.3. Ant System Model

In [3], Chialvo and Millonas presented a simple ant model where trails and networks of ant traffic emerge without impositions by any special boundary conditions, lattice topology, or additional behavioural rules. In this model, the state of an ant can be expressed by its position $r$ and orientation $\theta$. Since the response at a given time is assumed to be independent of the previous history of the individual, it is sufficient to specify a transition probability from one place and orientation $(r, \theta)$ to the next $(r^*, \theta^*)$ an instant later. In previous works [14,15] transition rules were derived and generalized from noisy response functions, which in turn were found to reproduce a number of experimental results with real ants. The response function can effectively be translated into a two-parameter transition rule between the cells by using the pheromone weighting function showed in Equation 8:

$$W(\sigma) = \left(1 + \frac{\delta}{1+\sigma\cdot\delta}\right)^{\beta} \tag{8}$$

This equation measures the relative probabilities of moving to a cell $r$ with pheromone density $\sigma(r)$. The parameter $\beta$ is associated with the osmotropotaxic sensitivity proposed in [21]. In practical terms, this parameter controls the degree of randomness with which each ant follows the gradient of pheromone: for low values of $\beta$, pheromone concentration does not greatly affect its choice, while high values cause it to follow pheromone gradient with more certainty, as proved in [3]. The sensory capacity $1/\delta$ describes the fact that each ant's ability to sense pheromone decreases somewhat at high concentrations. In addition to the former equation, there is a weighting factor $w(\Delta\theta)$, where $\Delta\theta$ is the change in direction at each time step, i.e. measures the magnitude of the difference in orientation. This weighting factor ensures that very sharp turns are much less likely than turns through smaller angles; thus each ant in the colony have a probabilistic bias in the forward direction. A discretization of the model is necessary in order to perform simulations and test some assumptions: Chialvo and Millonas created a square lattice where ants can move around, taking one step at every iteration. The decision (where to go) is made according to the pheromone concentration in all eight neighboring cells (Von Neumann neighborhood) and the weighting factor $w(\Delta\theta)$, using Equation 8, and computing the transition probabilities via Equation 9:

$$P_{ik} = \frac{W(\sigma_i)\cdot w(\Delta_i)}{\sum\limits_{j/k} W(\sigma_j)\cdot w(\Delta_j)} \tag{9}$$

This equation represents the transition probabilities on the lattice to go from cell $k$ to cell $i$ and notation $j/k$ indicates the sum over all the cells $j$ which are in the local (Von Neumann) neighborhood of $k$. $\Delta_i$ measures the magnitude of the difference in orientation for the previous direction at time $t-1$. As an additional condition, each individual leaves a constant amount $\eta$ of pheromone at the cell where it is located at every time step $t$. This pheromone decays at each time step at a rate $k$. Toroidal boundary conditions are imposed on the lattice to avoid boundary effects. Please note that there is no direct communication between the organisms but a type of indirect communication through the pheromone field. In fact, ants are not allowed to have any memory and the individual's spatial knowledge is restricted to local information about the whole colony pheromone density.

This model has been applied in many different works, for instance in [18], the authors adapted it by placing the ants 'over' a gray-scale image. So, they evolve reinforcing pheromone levels around pixels with different gray levels yielding pheromone maps that may be a suitable support for edge detection and image segmentation. This last model was improved in [7] by introducing a mechanism to eliminate and create ants along the evolution process, which means a self-regulated population size and it results faster and also more effective in creating pheromone trails around the edges of the images.

## 3. Self-Organizing Ants Model

The algorithm presented in this chapter is an ant algorithm with some common features with the Ant System of Chialvo et al., nevertheless it also includes some other features inspired by the Kohonen's SOM. It is called, for this reason, *KohonAnts* (or KANTS).

KANTS has been designed as a clustering and classification algorithm, so it is capable to group a set of input samples (training dataset) into clusters with similar features. In addition it behaves as a good classification algorithm. It works in a non-supervised (self-organizing) way, without considering the class of the input patterns during the process.

The main idea is to assign each input sample (which is a vector) to an ant, and put them into an habitat which is a toroidal $X \cdot Y$ grid. Then, they move around in the lattice changing the environment, which is a stigmergic mechanism. Every cell of the grid that constitutes the environment also contains a vector of the same dimension and range as the training set. The factor of change of the environment) depends on the values of the ant's vector, and, since every ant tends to move towards those zones in the grid which are more similar to themselves (to their associated vectors), ant position and pheromone content co-adapt. This means that eventually, ants with similar data items will be close together in the grid, and the grid itself will contain similar vectors to those stored in the ants on top of them.

Then, the grid can be used as a classification tool (in the same way as the resulting map after training using Kohonen's SOM), while ants will be grouped in clusters of similar individuals.

In the following paragraphs we present the most important features of the algorithm.

### 3.1. *Decide Where to Go* Rule

This is the most important function in the algorithm. It is used by every ant placed at cell $i$ to decide which is the next cell $j$ to move.

This function is based in Chialvo's Ants System pheromone weighting function and pseudo-random proportional rule of ACS, so it is:
If $(q \leq q_0)$

$$j = \arg\max_{j \in N_i} W(\sigma_{ij}) \tag{10}$$

Else

$$P_{ij} = \begin{cases} \dfrac{W(\sigma_{ij})}{\sum_{u \in N_i^t} W(\sigma_{iu})} & if\, j \in N_i^t \\ 0 & otherwise \end{cases} \tag{11}$$

In that rule, $q_0 \in [0,1]$ is the standard ACS parameter and $q$ is a random value in [0,1]. $N_i$ is the neighbourhood of the cell $i$, which is a function similar to the one used in SOM. It also has associated a *neighbourhood radius, nr* which diminish along the running, so the neighbourhood is different at every iteration $t$. This function returns '1' if the cell is included in the neighbourhood and '0' otherwise.

$\sigma$ is defined by the following equation:

$$\sigma_{ij} = \sqrt{(V_i(v) - CTR_j(v))^2} \qquad \forall v = 1..nvars \tag{12}$$

Where $V_i$ is the vector associated to the cell $i$ and $CTR_j$ is the centroid of a zone centered in the cell $j$. It is a vector where each value takes the arithmetic mean of the correspondent values of the vectors associated to the cells included within a *centroid radius, cr*. The formula is equivalent to calculate the Euclidean distance between the vector associated to the cell $i$ and the centroid vector for the cell $j$, both vectors have a number of variables $nvars$.

Finally, in the *decide where to go* rule, $W(\sigma)$ is the Ant System pheromone weighting function (Equation 8).

The rule works as follows: when an ant is building a solution path and is placed at one node $i$, a random number $q$ in [0,1] is generated, if $q \leq q_0$ the best neighbour $j$ is selected as the next node in the path (Equation 10). Otherwise, the algorithm decides which node is the next by using a roulette wheel considering $P_{ij}$ as probability for every feasible neighbour $j$ (Equation 11).

Notice that the second part of the rule (Equation 11) is similar to the transition probability defined by Chialvo et al. (Equation 9), but considering a weighting factor $w(\Delta\theta) = 1$, so, all the neighbour cells have the same probability in advance (before considering the $\sigma$ value).

In addition, there is an important factor to mark, which is that the ants are capable to move to cells far more than one hop from the cell where they are currently located. It means that they can 'jump' or 'fly' as some real-world ant species are able. This property is vanishing along the algorithm running because the neighbourhood radius is decreased until it takes a value of '1' (ants only move from one cell to a one hop distance neighbour).

## 3.2. The Updating Function

This process is usually performed in classical ant algorithms as a pheromone trail deposition. At every step, each ant $k$ updates the cell $i$ where is placed, using an updating formula similar to the learning function of SOMs (see Equation 7). Bearing in mind that every sample/ant and cell in the grid is a vector of *nvars* variables, the formula is as follows:

$$V_i^t(v) = V_i^{t-1}(v) + R \cdot [a_k(v) - V_i^{t-1}(v)] \quad \forall v = 1..nvars \tag{13}$$

Where $V_i$ is the vector associated to the cell $i$, $t$ is the current iteration, and $a_k$ is the vector associated to the ant $k$. $R$ is the reinforce of the update, which is described as:

$$R = \alpha \cdot (1 - \overline{D}(a_k, CTR_i)) \tag{14}$$

$\alpha$ is the learning rate factor typical in SOM (which is constant in this algorithm), $CTR_i$ is again the centroid of a zone centered in the cell $i$. Finally, $\overline{D}$ is the mean Euclidean distance between the ant's vector and the centroid vector. It is:

$$\overline{D} = \sum_{v=1}^{nvars} \frac{\sqrt{(a_k(v) - C_i(v))^2}}{nvars} \tag{15}$$

### 3.3. The Evaporation Function

As in all the ant algorithms, it is a very important process in which the environment reverts to its previous (or initial) state. This process is performed,for every cell $i$, once all the ants have moved and updated the environment in the current iteration.

$$V_i(v) = V_i(v) - \rho \cdot V_{i0}(v) \qquad \forall v = 1..nvars \tag{16}$$

Where $\rho$ is the usual evaporation factor and $V_{i0}$ is the initial vector associated to the cell $i$. It means that the function changes the values of the vector in order to be similar to the initial, which can be interpreted as an evaporation of the trails in the environment.

### 3.4. Pseudocode

The pseudocode of our model is presented in Algorithms 1 and 2. Here we consider each cell as a pair of coordinates, because the algorithm works using a grid.

**Algorithm 1** KANTS Algorithm

```
initialize_randomly_grid_vectors
place_randomly_ants_in_grid
for N_iterations do
   for each ant a at cell (x,y) do
      j = decide_where_to_go(a,(x,y))
   end for
   update_grid    // Using Equation 13
   evaporate_grid    // Using Equation 16
   update_neighbourhood_radio
end for
```

**Algorithm 2** Decide_Where_To_Go $(a,(i,j))$

```
for all cells (x,y) in neighbourhood of (i,j) do
    // Probability = Euclidean Distance to centroid
    σ_{ij,xy} = E_D((i,j),centroid((x,y)))
    compute W(σ_{ij,xy}) and P_{ij,xy}    // Using Equations 8 and 11
end for
// Ant Colony System/Ant System. Equations 10 and 11
q = random(0,1)
if q ≤ q_0 then
    // selected cell = the one with maximum probability
    (k,l) = MAX(P_{ij,xy})
else
    // selected cell = roulette_wheel
    (k,l) = roulette_wheel(P_{ij,xy})
end if
```

# 4. Experiments and Results

This section presents the data sets used to train and test KANTS algorithm (Subsection 4.1.), followed by the results obtained in clustering (Subsection 4.2.) and classification (Subsection 4.3.).

## 4.1. The Datasets

The datasets used to test and validate the model are some well-known real world databases:

- **IRIS**: contains data of 3 species of iris plant (Iris Setosa, Versicolor and Virginica), 50 samples of each one and 4 numerical attributes (the sepal and petal lengths and widths in cms.). The first class is linearly separable from the others while the other two are not.

- **GLASS**: contains data from different types of glasses studied in criminology. There are 6 classes, 214 samples (unevenly distributed in classes) and 9 numerical features related to the chemical composition of the glass. This database is difficult to classify (and depending on the algorithm, also difficult to cluster), since some classes are represented by just a few samples (3-10), and some other classes not being linearly separable.

- **PIMA**: this is the Pima Indians Diabetes database which contains data related to some patients (indians of that tribe) and a class lebel representing their diabetes diagnostic according to the world-wide health organization's criterion. There are 768 samples with 8 numerical features (medical data). Again, this is a hard to process database, because many samples of the two classes takes close values for the same variables.

In each of the three databases, we have consider 3 sets built by transforming the original into 3 disjoint sets of equal size. The original class distribution (before partitioning) is maintained within each set. Then we consider 3 pair of datasets 'training-test' by splitting the 3 previous into half size ones, they are named including the text *50tra-50tst*. In addition, 3 other pairs are created, but considering a distribution of 90% of samples for training and 10% for test. These sets are named including *90tra-10tst*.

## 4.2. Clustering

In [3], the authors performed a study on the distribution of ants with different configurations in the β-δ parameter space. Three types of behavior were observed when looking at the snapshots of the system after 1000 iterations: disorder, patches and trails.

The results obtained with their method follow theoretical prediction: a second order phase transition is observed, when a region of the parameter space which gives rise to disorder regimes "turns into" a region where trails are formed. Moving away from the order-disorder line, the system loses its ability to evolve lines/trails of ants and patches gradually appear. In addition, another experiment was conducted: the system was tuned to a region in the parameter space were trails emerge. After the traffic network was formed, β was decreased in order to tune the system bellow the transition line; then, the ants started executing random walks and left their previously formed trails. Once β was set again to the initial value, the ants self-organized again on a similar traffic network.

A similar test was performed with KANTS, but since Iris dataset was used (and due to it is not very complex), we have run the algorithm only a few iterations.

Parameters β and δ were varied, and the resulting ants' distribution after 100 iterations is depicted in Figure 2. Parameters α, *neighbourhood radius (nr)* and *centroid radius (cr)*, were set to 1, 1 and 3, respectively. From the figures it is not possible to distinguish three different types of behavior, as in Chialvo and Millonas' experiments with the original model, but it is clear that there is a transition line from a disordered state, where ants/data do not cluster, and a ordered state where cluster start to emerge. Further away from the transition line, the model's ability to form clusters gradually starts to decay (again). In the same way as in the original model, there is only a small region of the parameter space that gives rise to a self-organized behavior, but while Ant System forms trails, KANTS emerge clusters of ants that are actually data samples.

Considering this results, KANTS appear to be a promising tool for data clustering. With a simple mechanism and proper tuning of β and δ, data represented by (and behaving as) ants form clusters that are easily distinguishable in the grid. Even if some kind of local search is eventually necessary in order to tackle real-world problems, KANTS by now come forward as a core model where hybridization may be performed and the resulting algorithms applied to hard problems.

In Figure 3 an example of the ants evolution (movement during the run) in the grid is showed.

Looking at the snapshots of the grid at different iterations, it is possible to notice that every ant tends to move to a group of ants of the same class (they have similar values for the features). So, starting from a random initial configuration, in a few steps, the ants forms visible clusters.

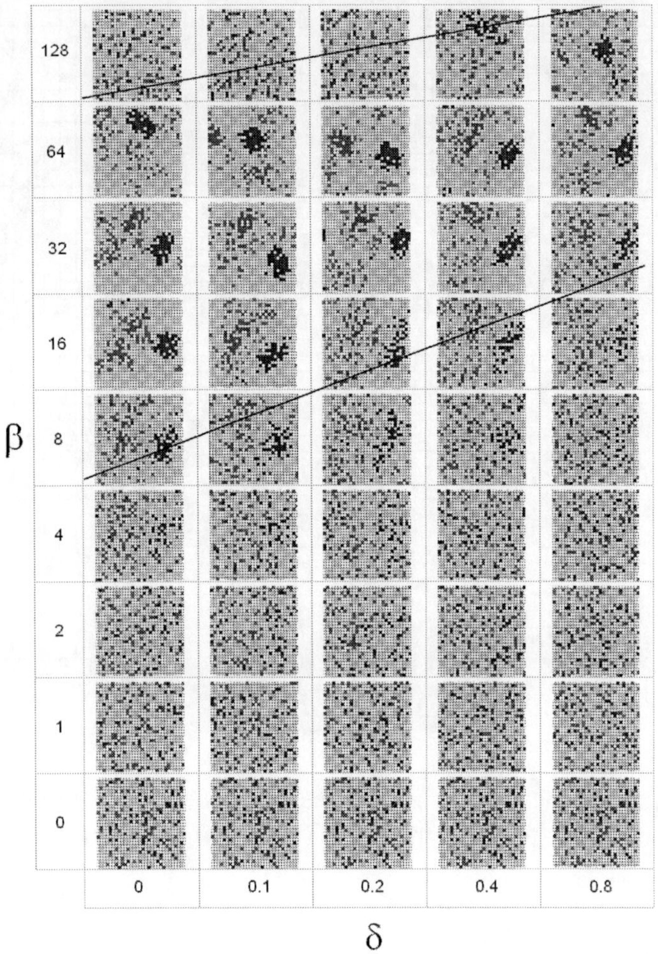


Figure 2. Snapshots of the ants in the system after 100 iterations for different β and δ values. The straight lines roughly delimit the region where clusters emerge.

### 4.3. Classification

In order to classify with KANTS, a parameter was introduced: the number of neighbours to compare with the test sample. This way, the algorithm searches for the $K$ nearest vectors in the grid (using the Euclidean distance) to the vector correspondent to the sample which it wants to classify. It assigns the class of the majority. It is similar to the one used in K-Nearest Neighbours (KNN) method (see [9] for details), but in this case it is used once the grid has been trained (with the training dataset) and many times the algorithm works well even considering $K = 1$. Ten runs were made for each pair of datasets (training and test). Results are presented in Table 1.

Results are compared with those yielded using some techniques. Two statistical methods: the traditional deterministic *KNN* and the *Linear Discriminant Analysis* (LDA) [10], which determines if an instance is of a class or not using linear classification based on the covariance matrix. In addition, we consider the results yielded by a Neural Network for

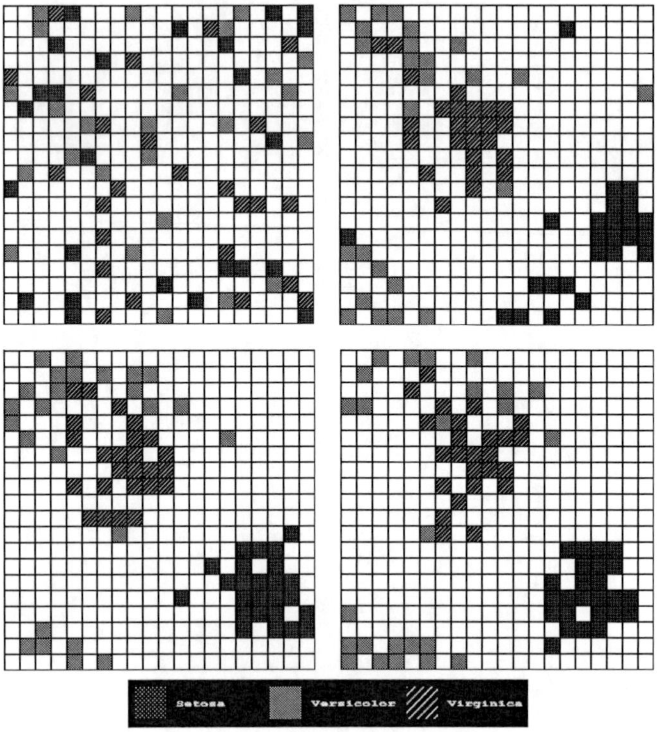


Figure 3. Evolution of position of ants in the grid for the IRIS problem. It shows the situation at the beginning (top-left), at step 50 (top-right) and 100 (bottom-left) and at step 150 (bottom-right).

classification (the *Multilayer perceptron for classification problems with Conjugate Gradient based training* (MLPCG) [16]), which is a typical back-propagation algorithm [20] where the weights are adjusted by using a method (for non-linear optimization) that is called conjugate gradient. All these algorithms have been applied using the Keel Project [1].

Results obtained by KANTS are always better when compared with the rest of the methods, even in the comparison with a traditional clustering and classification approach such as KNN and with the MLPCG method which also yields very good results. Glass and Pima datasets usually obtain a low classification rate (both are difficult databases as the LDA classifications show), while KANTS achieves in some cases a rate 10% higher than MLPCG and KNN.

In addition, it is important to comment that the running time of the algorithm is just a few seconds, depending on the dataset size: 8 seconds in Iris, 10 seconds in Glass and 20 seconds in Pima. The second best method (MLPCG) takes about 10 times more. All the experiments have been performed in a Pentium 1.6 GHz.

[1] http://www.keel.es/

**Table 1. Classification with Iris, Glass, Pima (6 different datasets each time).**

| IRIS | KANTS | | KNN | LDA | MLPCG | |
|---|---|---|---|---|---|---|
| Dataset | Best | Mean | Best | Best | Best | Mean |
| *50tra-50tst-Set1* | 98.67 | 98.00 ±0.67 | 97.30 | 97.00 | 97.00 | 95.00 ±2.22 |
| *50tra-50tst-Set2* | 98.67 | 97.60 ±0.53 | 96.00 | 99.00 | 95.00 | 93.00 ±1.06 |
| *50tra-50tst-Set3* | 100.00 | 98.80 ±0.40 | 94.60 | 97.00 | 96.00 | 94.00 ±0.80 |
| *90tra-10tst-Set1* | 100.00 | 100.00 ±0.00 | 100.00 | 100.00 | 100.00 | 99.00 ±2.10 |
| *90tra-10tst-Set2* | 100.00 | 99.33 ±2.00 | 93.33 | 100.00 | 100.00 | 100.00 ±0.00 |
| *90tra-10tst-Set3* | 100.00 | 100.00 ±0.00 | 93.33 | 100.00 | 100.00 | 100.00 ±0.00 |

| GLASS | KANTS | | KNN | LDA | MLPCG | |
|---|---|---|---|---|---|---|
| Dataset | Best | Mean | Best | Best | Best | Mean |
| *50tra-50tst-Set1* | 68.22 | 65.42 ±1.62 | 62.60 | 65.00 | 33.00 | 33.00 ±0.00 |
| *50tra-50tst-Set2* | 67.29 | 64.86 ±1.52 | 64.40 | 61.00 | 33.00 | 33.00 ±0.00 |
| *50tra-50tst-Set3* | 74.77 | 71.03 ±2.17 | 64.40 | 60.00 | 33.00 | 33.00 ±0.00 |
| *90tra-10tst-Set1* | 69.57 | 65.65 ±1.30 | 47.80 | 52.00 | 30.00 | 30.00 ±0.00 |
| *90tra-10tst-Set2* | 73.91 | 73.48 ±1.30 | 60.80 | 48.00 | 30.00 | 30.00 ±0.00 |
| *90tra-10tst-Set3* | 91.30 | 83.48 ±3.25 | 82.60 | 65.00 | 33.00 | 31.00 ±1.04 |

| PIMA | KANTS | | KNN | LDA | MLPCG | |
|---|---|---|---|---|---|---|
| Dataset | Best | Mean | Best | Best | Best | Mean |
| *50tra-50tst-Set1* | 75.52 | 74.32 ±0.61 | 70.03 | 78.00 | 76.00 | 70.00 ±2.02 |
| *50tra-50tst-Set2* | 77.34 | 76.61 ±0.58 | 71.80 | 77.00 | 73.00 | 71.00 ±1.61 |
| *50tra-50tst-Set3* | 77.60 | 75.13 ±0.85 | 72.90 | 77.00 | 77.00 | 72.00 ±2.61 |
| *90tra-10tst-Set1* | 83.12 | 80.52 ±1.42 | 64.90 | 76.00 | 75.00 | 67.00 ±3.08 |
| *90tra-10tst-Set2* | 79.22 | 75.32 ±1.42 | 73.60 | 77.00 | 79.00 | 75.00 ±2.12 |
| *90tra-10tst-Set3* | 84.42 | 80.65 ±2.05 | 70.10 | 77.00 | 81.00 | 77.00 ±2.79 |

# 5. Conclusion

This chapter presents KohonAnts, a new method for clustering and data classification, based on an hybridization of Ant Algorithms and Kohonen Self-Organizing Maps. The new model turns $n$-variable data samples into artificial ants that evolve in a 2D toroidal grid *paved* with $n$-dimensional vectors. Data/Ants act on the habitat vectors by pushing the values towards their own. In addition, ants are attracted by regions were the vector values are closer to their own data. In this way, similar ants tend to aggregate in common regions of the grid. There is indirect communication between ants through the grid (stigmergy) leading, with a proper setting of the model's parameters, to the emergence of data clusters. In addition, ants' actions (pheromone deposition) over the grid and pheromone evaporation creates a kind of cognitive field which has turned out be very effective for classification purposes.

It has been demonstrated that KANTS model is useful for clustering and classification tasks, yielding very good results in both kind of problems. The concept it is based on is quite simple and naturally inspired, but even so results obtained are quite good compared with traditional clustering methods (such as KNN). It is also a fast method, not needing a lot of computation time for obtaining the results mentioned above. As should be the spirit of publicly-funded research, we maintain all sources for the project as well as data used in experiments in the public repository ,
under a GPL license[2].

As future short-term lines of work, we will perform further tests on the algorithm, comparing it with more specific clustering and classification methods. We will also try to streamline ant movement rules, and compare among different options.

[2]It is only requested that this chapter (or another by the same authors) is referenced in published research.

In addition, a lot of enhancements are still possible in the original KANTS model presented in this chapter. A neighbourhood function may be considered, similar to the one used in Self-Organizing Maps for updating the environment in a radius. As in [7] and in [8], reproduction may improve speed and accurateness of the algorithm. Chialvo and Millonas probability equation (Equation 9) was not fully explored since weights $w(\Delta\theta)$ were set to 1. Finally, a stopping criteria is needed in order to avoid unnecessary iterations in the process.

Another line of work will be devoted to the test of KANTS in some other problems, applying it to real data clustering or classification (for instance Spanish companies data clustering or Sleep pattern classification), since it should be the final aim of these type of algorithms.

## References

[1] A. Abraham and V. Ramos. Web usage mining using artificial ant colony clustering and linear genetic programming. *Evolutionary Computation, 2003. CEC'03. The 2003 Congress on*, 2:1384–1391, 2003.

[2] E. Bonabeau, G. Theraulaz, V. Fourcassié, and J.L. Deneubourg. Phase-ordering kinetics of cemetery organization in ants. *Physical Review E*, 57(4):4568–4571, 1998.

[3] D. Chialvo and Mark Millonas. *The Biology and Technology of Intelligent Autonomous Agents*, volume 144 of *NATO ASI Series*, chapter How swarms build cognitive maps, pages 439–450. 1995.

[4] JL Deneubourg, S. Goss, N. Franks, A. Sendova-Franks, C. Detrain, and L. Chrétien. The dynamics of collective sorting robot-like ants and ant-like robots. *Proceedings of the first international conference on simulation of adaptive behavior on From animals to animats table of contents*, pages 356–363, 1991.

[5] M. Dorigo and G. Di Caro. The ant colony optimization meta-heuristic.

In D. Corne, M. Dorigo, and F. Glover, editors, *New Ideas in Optimization*, pages 11–32. McGraw-Hill, 1999.

[6] M. Dorigo and T. Stützle. The ant colony optimization metaheuristic: Algorithms, applications, and advances. In G.A. Kochenberger F. Glover, editor, *Handbook of Metaheuristics*, pages 251–285. Kluwer, 2002.

[7] Carlos Fernandes, Vitorino Ramos, and Agostinho C. Rosa. Self-regulated artificial ant colonies on digital image habitats. *International Journal of Lateral Computing*, 2(1):1–8, 2005.

[8] Carlos Fernandes, Vitorino Ramos, and Agostinho C. Rosa. Varying the population size of artificial foraging swarms on time varying landscapes. In W. Duch, J. Kacprzyk, E. Oja, and S. Zadrozny, editors, *15th International Conference on Artificial Neural Networks, ICANN2005*, volume 3696 of *LNCS*, pages 311–316. Springer-Verlag, 2005.

[9] Evelyn Fix and Jr J. L. Hodges. Discriminatory analysis: Nonparametric discrimination: Consistency properties. In *International Statistical Review*, volume 57, pages 238–247, September 1989.

[10] J. H. Friedman. Regularized discriminant analysis. *Journal of the American Statistical Association*, 84:165–175, 1989.

[11] Teuvo Kohonen. Representations of sensory information in self-organizing feature maps, and the relation of these maps to distributed memory networks. In R. M. J. Cotterill, editor, *Computer Simulation in Brain Science*, pages 12–25. Cambridge University Press, Cambridge, UK, 1988.

[12] Teuvo Kohonen. *The Self-Organizing Maps*. Springer, 2001.

[13] Nicolas Labroche, Nicolas Monmarché, and Gilles Venturini. Antclust: ant clustering and web usage mining. In *GECCO'03: Proceedings of the 2003 international conference on Genetic and evolutionary computation*, pages 25–36, Berlin, Heidelberg, 2003. Springer-Verlag.

[14] Mark Millonas. A connectionist-type model of self-organized foraging and emergent behavior in ant swarms. *Journal Theor. Biology*, (159):529, 1992.

[15] Mark Millonas. Swarms, phase transitions, and collective intelligence. In C.G. Langton, editor, *Artificial Life III*, volume XVII, pages 417–445, Massachussetts, 1994. Addison-Wesley Reading.

[16] F. Moller. A scaled conjugate gradient algorithm for fast supervised learning. *Neural Networks*, 6:525–533, 1990.

[17] V. Ramos and J. J. Merelo. Self-organized stigmergic document maps: Environment as a mechanism for context learning. In E. Alba, F. Fernández, J. A. Gómez, F. Herrera, J. I. Hidalgo, Juan-Julián Merelo-Guervós, and J. M. Sánchez, editors, *Actas primer congreso español algoritmos evolutivos, AEB ó2*, pages 284–293. Universidad de Extremadura, Febrero 2002.

[18] Vitorino Ramos and Fernando Almeida. Artificial ant colonies in digital image habitats - a mass behavior effect study on pattern recognition. In Marco Dorigo, Martin Middendorf, and Thomas Stüzle, editors, *ANTS'2000 - 2nd International Workshop on Ant Algorithms*, pages 113–116, Brussels, Belgium, 1994.

[19] S. Ultsch. Kohonen's self-organizing maps for exploratory data analysis. In *Proc. of the INNC'90*, pages 305–308, 2000.

[20] B. Widrow and M.A. Lehr. 30 years of adaptive neural networks: Peceptron, Madaline, and Backpropagation. In *Proceedings of the IEEE*, volume 78, pages 1415–1442, 1990.

[21] E.O. Wilson. *The Insect Societies*. Belknam Press, Cambridge, 1971.

In: Ant Colonies
Editor: Emily C. Sun
ISBN: 978-1-61122-023-0


*Chapter 8*

# A HYBRID SYSTEM BASED IN ANT COLONY AND PARACONSISTENT LOGIC

***Luiz Eduardo da Silva****
Alfenas Federal University, Brazil
***Germano Lambert-Torres***†
Itajuba Federal University, Brazil
***Ricardo Menezes Salgado***‡
Alfenas Federal University, Brazil
***Humberto César Brandão de Oliveira***§
Alfenas Federal University, Brazil

**Abstract**

The strategy of the swarm intelligence named Ant Colony has proved to be an interesting way to solve difficult combinatorial problems. In this strategy, the learning of ants is built through the trail of pheromones left by the each ant in the colony on the problem space. The ants iteratively using the pheromone level of the each path of the solution problem to decide which way to follow. The problem is that this decision is often uncertain or inconsistent. Classical logic can not handle this kind of decision problem. In this sense we use the non-classical logic, named Paraconsistent Logic for increasing the power of decision to the ants colony. This hybrid system based on Paraconsistent Logic and Ant Colony proves to be an interesting approach and has been statistically demonstrated in this work that the hybrid system provides a result equal to or greater in relation implementation of the $\mathcal{MAX} - \mathcal{MIN}$ Ant System (a classical Ant Colony Metaheuristic).

**Keywords**: Swarm Intelligence, Paraconsistent Logic, Ant Colony Metaheuristic, Hybrid Systems

*E-mail address: luizedu@bcc.unifal-mg.edu.br
†E-mail address: germano@unifei.edu.br
‡E-mail address: ricardo@bcc.unifal-mg.edu.br
§E-mail address: humberto@bcc.unifal-mg.edu.br

# 1. Introduction

The computer is currently used with intelligent systems to assist in problems of decision making. However, among these problems are those that cannot be solved in computers in the fullness of time. The number of tests that must be performed is so great that even the best of the computers known to man would take centuries to produce an optimal solution to the problem.

Failing to produce exact algorithms for these problems, stochastic algorithms have been increasingly used to produce, if not an optimal solution, at least a good solution to problems. Among the techniques used in artificial intelligence to find solutions to difficult problems in computing, there are bioinspired algorithms that simulate the operation of some human or nature mechanism in order to represent the intelligent process used by living organisms. Among the intelligent techniques used are artificial neural networks, genetic algorithms, genetic programming, the bunch of particles and colonies of ants.

The Artificial Intelligence technique called Ant Colony is a bioinspired system that simulates the process performed by ants of a colony in search of food. This technique is particularly suitable for combinatorial optimization problems. Combinatorial optimization is a field of applied mathematics that is based on the use of a set of algorithms and programming techniques used for solving optimization problems formulated on discrete sets. Ant colony uses a probability model for decision making during the process simulated in this Artificial Intelligence algorithm.

For decision making in the strategy of Ant Colony, it is only used a probability function. The uncertainty and inconsistency matters in decision-making of ants are not considered. Thus, in this chapter it is proposed a hybrid system of the strategy of ant colony with paraconsistent logic. Paraconsistent logic is a non-classical logic suitable for use in problems of vagueness, partial knowledge and inconsistencies. Paraconsistent logic is utilized along with the strategy of ant colony to aim at maximizing benefits and minimizing the inherent disadvantages of each strategy.

The result is a hybrid system, strongly linked, which behaves well or better than the best implemented strategy for ant colony. This chapter is organized as follows: In section 2. difficult computing problems and the strategies used are discussed, such as the metaheuristic of Ant Colony. In section 3. the concepts and foundations of non-classical logic, called Paraconsistent Logic, are presented in general description. It is also shown in this section an alternative to the implementing of paraconsistent logic that is used in this work. The hybrid of Paraconsistent Logic with the metaheuristic of Ant Colony is discussed in section 4., where some experimental results are also presented. This chapter is concluded in the section 5..

# 2. Ant Colony Optimization

The Ant Colony Optimization metaheuristic (ACO) is an intelligence strategy of swarms that seeks to reproduce the intelligent behavior of an ant colony with the intention of using it in solving combinatorial optimization problems.

Each ant individually, following simple rules, are capable of producing a viable solution to complex problems. The colony as a whole, through the indirect interaction of each independent agent, is able to construct complex patterns such as troubleshooting. This entire process is accomplished without central control, via a distributed computing system made by each individual agent, mediated by indirect communication through the modification of the environment.

Ants follow these rules of communication [20]:

- Ants deposit a chemical called pheromone, which can be perceived by other ants in the colony. The ants use the amount of pheromone to decide which way to go.
- Ants can only perceive the pheromone available locally, that is, the ant has to reach the site where the deposited information is left by other ants in the colony.

In the ACO metaheuristic, the ants construct solutions randomly, based on pheromone trails and on specific heuristic information of the problems. The use of trail pheromones to record the experience acquired by ants during problem solving makes the ACO metaheuristic different from traditional heuristics.

### 2.1. Combinatorial Optimization Problems

The combinatorial optimization problems, classified as NP-complete problems according to the theory of complexity of algorithms, aim at maximizing or minimizing a defined function on some finite domain. In general, it is easy to determine a possible solution to the problem of combinatorial optimization. Still, it is computationally impracticable to test all possible solutions to a given problem.

A typical example of combinatorial optimization problem is the traveling salesman problem [22], illustrated in Figure 1. This problem consists in determining a route of minimum length that passes through a number of cities (represented by the symbol 'x' in Figure 1) without repeating or leaving any city out. The problem can be represented by a graph $G = (V, A)$, in which the vertices $V$ represent cities and the edges $A$ represent all the roads connecting the cities. If we consider a fully connected graph, all cities are directly connected by a road. The traveling salesman problem corresponds to finding a Hamiltonian path in graph $G$ of minimum length. The Hamiltonian path is the closed path that encounters exactly once each $v = |V|$ vertices of $G$. The distance $d_{ij}$ between cities $i$ and $j$ is the value associated with each edge of $G$.

Whereas it is easy to find a viable solution to the traveling salesman problem, it is computationally impracticable to test all possible routes to find the optimal solution to the problem. The number of routes to be tested is around $n!$, where $n$ represents the number of cities in the problem.

This problem happens in real situations, such as the welding process of printed circuit boards, in which it is needed to determine the shortest path for the welding machine to connect all circuits on the board. The lower the trajectory of the welding machine, the faster the welding plate and therefore more plates may be welded in a time interval.

#### 2.1.1. Heuristic Algorithms

Failing to implement an algorithm that finds exact solutions in computationally impracticable time for optimization problems NP-complete, it explores some strategies that involve

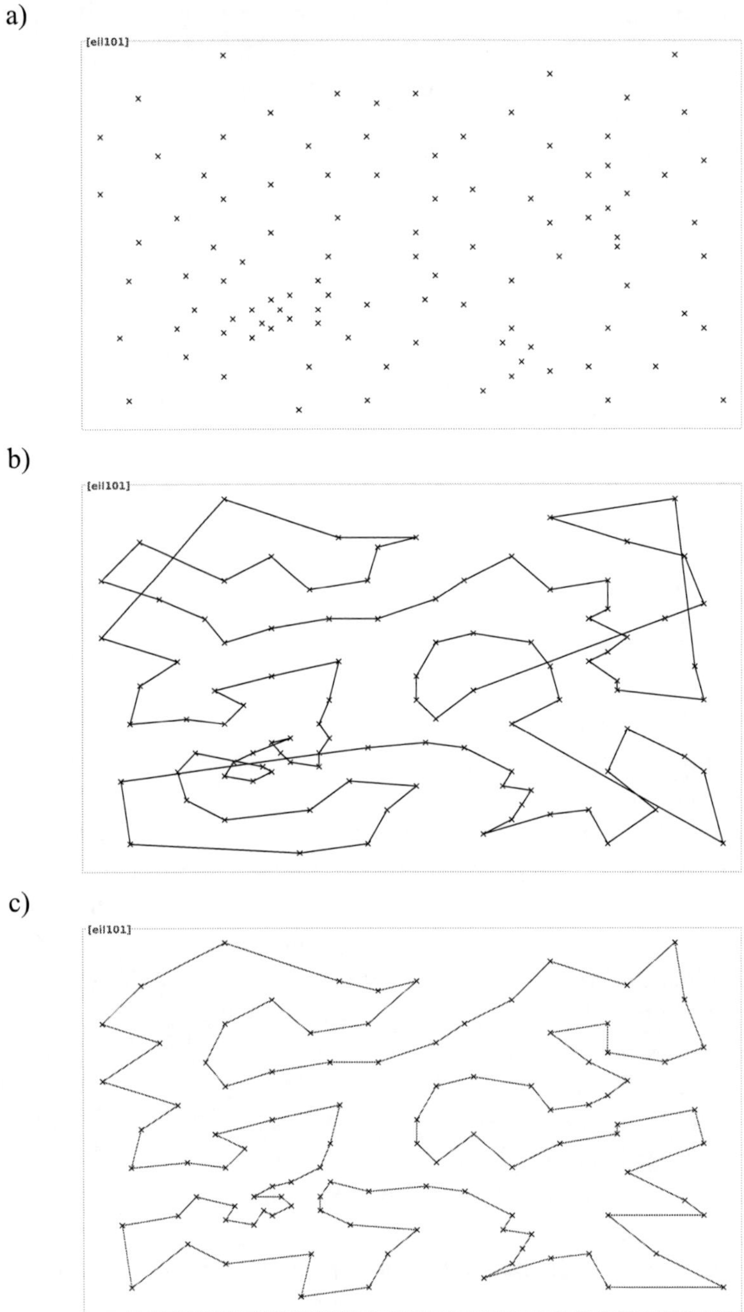


Figure 1. Implementation of the nearest neighbor algorithm on the instance eil101 of TSPLIB. a) Instance eil101 b) Solution found using the algorithm of the best neighbor c) Best known solution for instance eil101.

methods of integer programming, stochastic methods and approximation algorithms.

Among the approximation algorithms, it is possible to relate the methods of construction, the local search algorithms and metaheuristics. The construction methods deal with partial solutions, trying to extend these to obtain complete solutions. The local search methods promote modifications around complete solutions to the problem in order to improve them. The metaheuristics can combine aspects of the construction methods and local search to produce solutions to problems with reduced complexity compared to exact algorithms and providing, in general, viable and good quality solutions, but without guarantee of quality.

A simple constructive algorithm for solving the traveling salesman problem, for instance, is the one that, starting with any city, always choose the nearest city not yet visited until the original city is reached. This algorithm is known as tour construction heuristics of nearest neighbor (NN). An example of a solution to the problem called eil101, obtained from TSPLIB [1], is shown in Figure 1.

It can be observed in Figure 1 some distant connections between non-nearby cities, featuring bad solutions to this problem. In general, this strategy produces solutions quickly, but they are not of good quality.

### Metaheuristics

The metaheuristics comprise aspects of the construction methods and local search algorithms. The construction methods are used in metaheuristics in order to produce complete solutions to problems. The local search algorithms are employed in metaheuristics to improve the solutions found. The mechanisms for constructing solutions and improving found solutions are guided by a specific heuristic knowledge of each problem.

The Ant Colony Optimization metaheuristic (ACO) [18, 13],for example, is based on artificial ants that are procedures used to construct solutions of an optimization problem in a probabilistic way. Through this procedure, the ants interactively add components to the solution bearing in mind the experience accumulated by the colony, represented by the pheromone trails and heuristic information specific to the problem modeled.

This procedure allows the artificial ants build a wide variety of possible solutions to the problem. Moreover, the experience accumulated by the colony along with the heuristics of the problem can guide the algorithm to obtain good solutions. Thus, the ACO metaheuristic is an extension of the construction algorithm presented above. Thus, the ACO metaheuristic can be applied to any optimization problem for which it is possible to define a mechanism for building solutions.

## 2.2. Biological Inspiration

The ACO metaheuristic was inspired by experiments conducted by Deneubourg *et al.* [11] and Goss *et al.* [19], using a colony of Argentine ants. To perform this experiment, the researchers built an environment with only two possible paths connecting the nest to the power supply of the colony, as shown in 2.

[1]Traveling Salesman Problem Library [27]. http://comopt.ifi.uni-heidelberg.de/software/TSPLIB95/

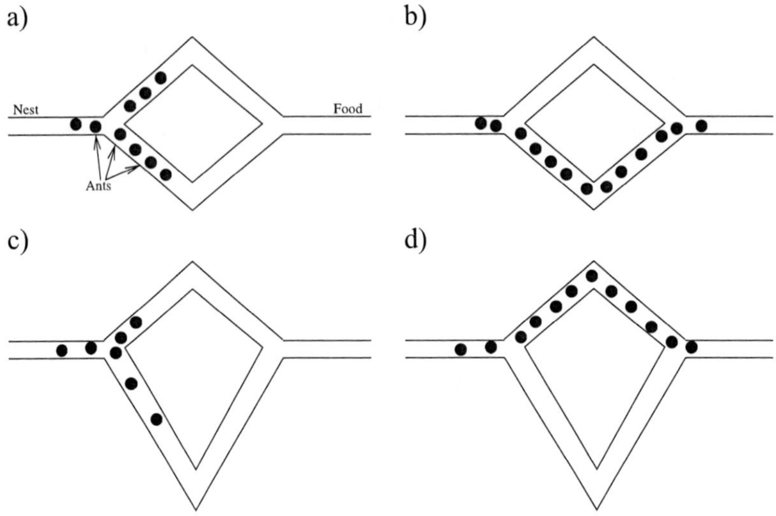


Figure 2. Actual experiment with Argentine ants a) initial situation with the bridges of the same length b) convergence of the ants for one of the paths c) same experiment with different bridge length d) choosing the best path by the ant colony.

In the work of Deneubourg *et al.* [11], both paths that connect the nest to a food source are the same length, as illustrated in Figures 2a and 2b. After an initial period in which the ants randomly experience the two paths, one of two bridges has a higher concentration of pheromone and shall be chosen by the majority of ants of the colony. The probability that ants chose the upper bridge and the lower bridge is 50 % in experiments. Goss *et al.* [19] considered a variation of the original experiment in which each path has a different length and for the ant to reach the food and then go back to the nest it has to choose between longer or shorter path, as illustrated in Figures 2c and 2d. The experimental observation was that after a transitional phase, most ants started to use the shortest path. One can also observe that the probability of the colony to select the shortest path increases when the difference in length of paths is greater.

The selection of the shortest path can be explained in terms of positive feedback and different lengths of the ways, and is accomplished through an indirect form of communication mediated by local modification of the environment by depositing pheromone on the paths. Argentine ants, when they go from nest to the food and vice versa, deposit pheromone. When they reach a decision point, as the intersection of the left or right bridge, they make a probabilistic decision based on the amount of pheromone that they perceive in the two arms. This behavior has an autocatalytic effect because the fact of choosing a path increases the probability that this path is chosen by the ant and again other ants in the future. In the beginning of the experiment, there is no pheromone on the paths, so the ants will go from nest to the food by choosing any of the paths with equal probability.

The ants that choose the shortest way get food first due to different lengths of paths. When they are on their way back, they make another decision. If the track they have been is the one with a greater amount of pheromone, it will be more likely to be chosen. During

```
1 ACOmetaheuristic() {
2    initialization();
3    while !terminationCondition() {
4       generateSolutions();
5       pheromoneUpdate();
6       [localSearch();]
7    }
8 }
```

Figure 3. Pseudo-code of algorithm for ACO metaheuristic.

this iterative process, the pheromone is deposited on the shortest path with a higher rate than the longer path, making it the shortest way more and more attractive until all ants start to use it.

## 2.3. Pseudo-code of the ACO Metaheuristic

From the experiment described in the section 2.2., Dorigo [12] suggested in his doctoral thesis an implementation of an algorithm that simulates the process of searching for food by a colony of ants. The algorithm originally proposed was used for solving the combinatorial optimization problem called the Traveling Salesman Problem. This original work prompted the development of several variations for the Ant Colony metaheuristic. The various activities carried out use instances of the traveling salesman problem as a benchmark for comparing the results obtained by the proposed algorithms.

The ACO metaheuristic can be summarized as follows: ant colony, asynchronously and concurrently, construct solutions to the problem modeled by defining paths in graph G that represents the problem. The choice of each ant is done through a probabilistic decision, taking into account the pheromone trail and heuristic information. During the construction process or after the ant has completed a course in graph G, ant colony can evaluate the solution that was built and thus deposit pheromone on the path to privilege the best solution found by the colony.

In a very simplified way, ACO metaheuristic can be presented through the pseudo-code in Figure 3. The routine called *initialization()*, line 2, comprises the operations to be performed at the beginning of the construction process. In this routine, the operations implemented comprise the setting up of structures to represent instances of the problem and the ant colony. The repetition (lines 3 to 7) defines the three fundamental operations performed in this algorithm until the routine *terminationCondition()* succeeds. The termination condition may be either the maximum time given to search, a maximum number of pre-established iterations or else until a quality parameter of the solution has been reached. The fundamental operations of the ACO metaheuristic are: a) *generateSolutions()*, line 4, which constructs a feasible solution for each ant of the colony; b) *pheromoneUpdate()*, line 5, which performs the update of statistics and structures used in implementing the metaheuristic, among them the structure that represents the pheromone rate on the path of solutions; c) *localSearch ()*, line 6, which performs some additional operation such as any

```
1 generateSoluctions() {
2   antInitialization();
3   while !getCompleteSolution() {
4     chooseNext();
5   }
6   calculateSolutionValue();
7 }
```

Figure 4. Pseudo-code of procedure for the construction of solutions of ant colony.

Local Search algorithms regarding each solution in order to improve it. This operation is optional, but can determine the quality and speed of convergence of metaheuristics towards a solution.

### 2.3.1. The Construction of Solutions by Ants

The original algorithm for the ACO metaheuristic was named AS (Ant System) [12], [16] and [17]. To use the AS, the problem to be solved must be modeled by a graph, where the vertices represent components of the problem and the edges determine the cost of the transition between the components of the problem. Each ant $k$, by moving in the graph, spreads pheromone in its path. The ant has a memory of the steps taken and the vertices already visited in order to avoid going through the same vertex more than once. When the ant is on vertex $i$, it chooses the next vertex $j$ using the probability function as Equation 1.

The routine of building solution (generateSolutions ()) of the ACO metaheuristic is represented in pseudo-code in Figure 4. This routine is performed asynchronously and concurrently by the ant colony. The ants are initialized (line 2 of Figure 4) and positioned in a random initial component of the problem. For the traveling salesman problem, each ant has its itinerary beginning with information on no visited city and each ant is randomly placed in a starting city.

The repetition of lines 3 to 5 in Figure 4 runs until all the ants in the colony obtain a complete solution to the problem. In the case of the traveling salesman problem, for example, the repetition ends after all the ants produce an itinerary passing by each city just once.

The choice of the next component of the solution of the problem is in routine *chooseNext()* (line 4 in Figure 4). This choice is made from the probability function defined in Equation 1.

$$p_{ij}^{k}(t) = \frac{[\tau_{ij}(t)]^{\alpha}[\eta_{ij}]^{\beta}}{\sum_{l \in N_i^k}[\tau_{il}(t)]^{\alpha}[\eta_{il}]^{\beta}} \qquad (1)$$

where:

- $k$ represents each ant in the colony.
- $\tau_{ij}(t)$ determines the amount of pheromone between vertices i and j at iteration t.

- $\eta_{ij}$ represents the heuristic function (specific for each problem).For the traveling salesman problem, for example, a good heuristic function can be given by the inverse of the distance between cities: $\eta_{ij} = \frac{1}{d_{ij}}$.
- $\alpha$ represents the importance of pheromone trail.
- $\beta$ represents the importance of heuristic information.
- $N_i^k$ represents the neighborhood not yet viewed from the vertex $i$.

After the ant colony build complete solutions, a score is assigned for each solution (line 6 of Figure 4).

### 2.3.2. Updating the Pheromone

To represent more closely the communication process used by the ant colony, it is assigned a mechanism of evaporation of pheromone in the solution space to the implementation of the ACO metaheuristic. Equation 2 shows how the evaporation process in the original ACO algorithm is.

$$\tau_{ij}(t+1) = (1-\rho)\tau_{ij}(t) + \sum_{k=1}^{m} \Delta\tau_{ij}^{k}(t) \tag{2}$$

where:

- $\tau_{ij}(t)$ determines the amount of pheromone at iteration t.
- $\rho$ represents the rate of pheromone evaporation at each iteration.
- $m$ is the amount of ant.

The evaporation rate $\rho$ is determined experimentally. The value cannot be very high to enable the convergence of solutions of the ants, nor very low to avoid premature convergence of sub-optimal solutions by ants in the colony.

### 2.3.3. Variations of the ACO Metaheuristic

Several variations of the original algorithm were developed in order to improve performance and achieve better results. Among the variations we have the algorithms as Elitist Ant System based on an elitist strategy [12], based on rank ($AS_{rank}$) [3], Ant Colony System ($ACS$) [15] and $\mathcal{MAX}-\mathcal{MIN}$ Ant System ($\mathcal{MM}$AS) [32], [14].

The variation based on elitist strategy is to reward the best solution built with an additional quantity of pheromone. The ASrank is somehow an elitist variant of the algorithm, where only one rank of the best solutions are allowed to update the pheromone trails, with a rate proportional to the quality of the solution. Moreover, the Ant Colony System, which introduced the possibility of updating local pheromone, besides the update performed at the end of the construction process.

Among the changes proposed, one of the most successful implementations of the ACO metaheuristic [14] is the algorithm called $\mathcal{MAX} - \mathcal{MIN}$ Ant System. The main innovations in this implementation are that only the best ant updates the pheromone trail and that the pheromone is limited by variables $\tau_{max}$ and $\tau_{min}$, that is, the pheromone cannot exceed the upper limit or the lower limit. The update of pheromone in this implementation is given by Equation 3.

$$\tau_{ij}(t+1) = [(1-\rho)\tau_{ij}(t) + \Delta\tau_{ij}^{best}]_{\tau_{min}}^{\tau_{max}} \tag{3}$$

Where:

- $\Delta\tau_{ij}^{best}$ represents the edges of the path built by the best ant in the colony.
- $[x]_{\tau_{min}}^{\tau_{max}}$ represents that the value $x$ is restricted to the interval $[\tau_{max}, \tau_{min}]$.

Values $\tau_{max}$ and $\tau_{min}$ can be defined empirically or by specific values of the problem. The best ant can be the best iteration ant or the best ant in general.

The next section presents the theoretical and practical foundations of Paraconsistent Logic, in order to present the necessary concepts for implementing the hybrid system capable of composing a swarm intelligence through the ACO metaheuristic related to the ability to reason with cases of inconsistency and uncertain knowledge, from Paraconsistent Logic.

## 3. Paraconsistent Logic

Paraconsistent logic is a non-classical logic, which can deal with situations of inconsistency, imprecision and partial knowledge in decision-making. Via paraconsistent logic it is possible to reason properly, dealing with the inconsistencies inherent in the real world situations.

This section presents a history of non-classical logics and, among them, paraconsistent logic and its interpretation methods considering its theoretical framework presented in the relevant papers of previous studies, as in [2], [7], [21], [23], [30] and [26]. From these interpretations, parallel applications are developed, which make processing of uncertain knowledge by translating these theoretical concepts into practical concepts.

### 3.1. Classical Logic

Classical logic is the basis and foundation of modern sciences. It was through the work of Aristotle (384-322 BC) in Macedonia that the classical Aristotelian logic began as we know it. Aristotle, in his work, established a set of rules for the conclusions that can be drawn from propositions about knowledge.

To establish connections between the propositions, a language in which these propositions can o nly be characterized as true or false was created.

In a formal way, we can describe the fundamental principles of classical logic as follows: Let us consider $p$ as any proposition and the symbols $=, \rightarrow, \neg, \wedge$ and $\vee$ representing respectively the operations of equality, implication, negation, conjunction and disjunction. Then we have:

1. $p = p$ (principle of equality), every proposition is identical to itself.

2. $p \rightarrow p$ (principle of propositional identity), every proposition implies itself.

3. $p \vee \neg p$ (principle of the excluded middle) of two contradictory propositions, one of them is true.

4. $\neg(p \vee \neg p)$ (principle of non-contradiction): of two contradictory propositions, one of them is false.

The formal language of classical logic, relying on these simple principles, has supported the development of logical thinking of humankind.

### 3.2. Non-classical Logic

Unfortunately, not all real-world situations can be classified as true or false. In certain situations, it is difficult or even impossible to establish the boundaries between the real and fake. These limits are often vague, uncertain, ambiguous or contradictory.

The new research in Artificial Intelligence (AI) [29] seeks to incorporate or simulate human intelligence or bioinspired intelligence in processes of decision making. To make decisions, it is not always possible to state precisely whether a proposition is true or false, as required by classical logic.

These new studies in AI propose other systems of decision making different from classical logic and that have foundations not as rigid as classical logic. To answer satisfactorily the situations in which classical logic is inappropriate, the non-classical logics were created. They are those which derogate from the principles of excluded middle and non-contradiction to allow uncertainties, ambiguities and contradictions in its grounds.

Among the various logics called non-classical logics there is the paraconsistent logic, which derogates from the principle of non-contradiction of classical logic and allows the processing of contradiction in their formulations.

### 3.3. History of Paraconsistent Logic

The Paraconsistent Logics had two precursors, the Russian A. N. Vasil'v and the Polish J. Lukasiewicz, in work unrelated in 1910. The two researchers have drawn attention to the fact that some principles of Aristotelian logic could be reviewed. However, their jobs are very limited for they refer only to review the principle of contradiction.

In fact, the first logician to formulate Propositional Paraconsistent Logic within the current standards of accuracy was the Polish logician S.Jskowski in 1948. Jskowski was prompted to work on his paraconsistent logic called Discursive Logic influenced by Lukasiewicz. However, he was limited solely to the development of a discursive propositional calculus, without extending it to higher-order logic, is that which has several quantifiers so that it can handle equality regardless of little rigidity.

The first logician to formulate a propositional calculations, quantificational calculations with or without equality, theories of descriptions and paraconsistent theories was Newton C. A. da Costa, Brazil, in the 50s, [7], [5], [4], [8] and [6].

The very logic of Jskowski was only developed from the 60s, when Da Costa and the Polish disciples of Jskowski, L. Dubikajtisand J. Kotas tried to enlarge the Discourse Propositional Calculus, being able to formulate discursive quantificational calculations of lower and higher order and theories of discourse sets; moreover, Da Costa and Kotas extended the basic idea of Jskowski which defined the discursive logic to any unary operator in any system, modal or not.

After these initial works, the Paraconsistent Logic evolved so much that today it would become difficult to follow the literature related to them throughout their length. For so many reasons, the Paraconsistent Logic has become a large field of research, at the most important centers of the world.

## 3.4. Foundations of Paraconsistent Logic

In general, we can define the paraconsistent logic as that which can substantiate inconsistent deductive systems, that is, those that admit the contradiction in theorems, but which are not trivial. Obviously, if a contradiction can be accepted according to these logics, then in them the traditional rule cannot be valid according to which a any formulated proposition can be inferred from any contradiction.

The statements demonstrated as true in a theory are called theorems. One theory is called trivial if all the sentences formulated in this theory are theorems. One theory is called consistent if among its theorems there is no theorem that is the negation of another theorem. If there is contradiction in a theory, this theory is called inconsistent.

Paraconsistent logic (parallel, to the side of consistency) is one that works with the fundamentals of inconsistent and not trivial theories. That is, paraconsistent logic is able to handle inconsistent information systems without the danger of trivialization.

The role of Paraconsistent Logic is to be a formal support for the existence of theories that relate to contradictions and inconsistencies of the real world. With regard to it, it is appropriate to mention Da Costa when he says "... we call inconsistency or contradiction any pair of propositions, one of which is the negation of the other. Paraconsistent Logic does not exclude the possibility that both propositions of a contradiction are true. It does not exclude the existence of real true contradictions, that is, contradictions whose components refer to the real world. We believe that a priori we cannot eliminate that possibility. Knowing if there are true contradictions in the real world is an empirical matter decidable only by means of Empirical Sciences" [7].

### Paraconsistent Logic Modeling Human Knowledge

A description of some portions of our reality can be inconsistent and it is common to encounter inconsistencies in daily life. To simplify the understanding of the proposal and the significance of Paraconsistent Logic, highlighting the importance of applying it in situations where classical logic is unable to generate good results, an example is presented.

*EXAMPLE*: at a condominium meeting to decide on a reform, the viewpoints of the dwellers are not always unanimous. If ever there was unanimity, it would facilitate greatly the decision of the apartment manager. Some want to reform, others do not, what generates contradictions. Others do not even have an opinion, what creates uncertainties. The detailed analysis of all opinions (contradictory, uncertain, against and in favor of the reform) may lead to other information to generate a decision to accept or not the reform of the building. The decision will be based on evidence provided by different opinions.

Paraconsistent Logic can model human behavior presented in these examples and thus be applied in control systems, because it presents itself more complete and adequate to handle real situations, with the possibility to deal with vagueness besides inconsistencies.

Considering that cases of inconsistencies are frequent, paraconsistent annotated logic is being widely accepted as a subject of research in development of projects for applications in various areas, mainly in Artificial Intelligence [28], [29] and computing in general. The results obtained in studies of the Paraconsistent Annotated Logic [2], [7], [21] and [1] show that it is fully viable the this logic in case of inconsistencies and that the results can interact either with the conventional logic, binary, or even with other types of non-classical logic, which makes it a strong tool for technical improvement in the field of digital electronics engineering.

### 3.4.1. Propositional Paraconsistent Annotated Logic $P_\tau$

A summary of the formal language that makes up the Propositional Paraconsistent Annotated Logic $P_\tau$ [9], [10] is presented so that it is possible to draw up an algorithm or the implementation of circuits that operate with the Paraconsistent Logic. The theory briefly presented here contains the main definitions and is enough so that one can apply the main concepts of Paraconsistent Logic and translate them through a practical algorithm and in electrical signals through electronic circuit. In [2], an extensive study of these logics is made, where the author demonstrates theorems the correctness and completeness for the calculations $Q_\tau$ (First-order Logic).

Paraconsistent Logic receives the following definition: Let $T$ be a theory based on a logic $L$, and suppose that the language of $L$ and $T$ contains a symbol for the negation. The theory $T$ is said to be inconsistent if it has contradictory theorems, that is, in case that one is the negation of the other; otherwise $T$ is said to be consistent. The theory $T$ is said to be trivial if all formulas of $L$ are theorems of $T$, otherwise T is called non-trivial. In the real world, the inconsistencies are important and cannot be neglected, because they are the information that brings important facts and sometimes completely changing the result of the analysis. The very existence of the inconsistency induces the system to promote searches looking for new and enlightening information with query other informants, to obtain a more real and credible conclusion. The main definitions of Propositional Paraconsistent Annotated Logic $P_\tau$ are briefly presented below.

Determining a finite lattice called Lattice of Truth Values, $\tau =< |\tau|, \leq >$, $\tau$ is lattice if:

1. $\forall x, x \leq x$ (reflexivity);
2. If $x \leq y$ and $y \leq x \Rightarrow x = y$ (anti-symmetric);
3. If $x \leq y$ and $y \leq z \Rightarrow x \leq y$ (transitivity);
4. $\forall x, y \in |\tau|$, there is a *supremum* of $x$ and $y$ denoted by $x^{\vee}y$;
5. $\forall x, y \in |\tau|$, there is a *infimum* of $x$ and $y$ denoted by $x^{\wedge}y$;

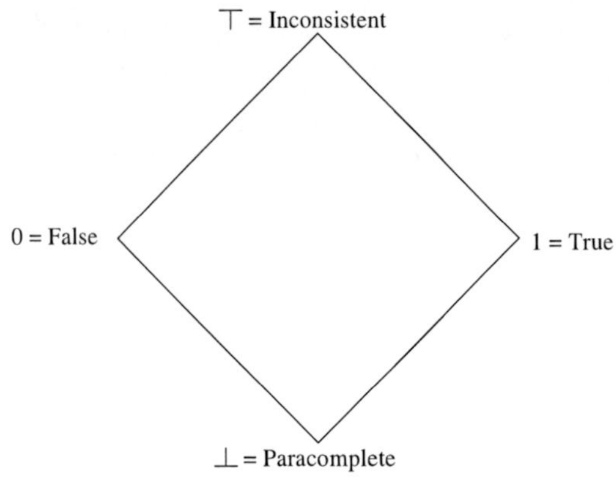


Figure 5. Finite lattice through the Hasse diagram.

The following symbols are associated with this lattice:

- $\perp \Rightarrow$ indicates the *minimum* of $\tau$;
- $\top \Rightarrow$ indicates the *maximum* of $\tau$;

Establishing an operator: $\sim |\tau| \Rightarrow |\tau|$ that intuitively means the negation logic operator of $P_\tau$, we have: $\sim (1) = 0; \sim (0) = 1; \sim (\perp) = \top; \sim (\top) = \perp$. The representation of a finite lattice is done usually via the Hasse diagram, according to Figure 5.

The $P_\tau$ language is composed of the following vocabulary:

1. Propositional variables: $p_1, p_2, p_3, \ldots, p_n, \ldots$
2. Connectives: $\neg$ (negation), $\wedge$ (conjunction or AND), $\vee$ (disjunction or OR) e $\rightarrow$ (implicaction);
3. Constants of annotation: $\mu, \lambda, \theta, \ldots$;
4. Auxiliary symbols: $(, ), \ldots$.

The $P_\tau$ formulas are defined by the following generalized inductive definition:

1. If $p$ is a propositional variable and $\lambda$ is a constant of annotation, then $p_\lambda$ is an atomic formula;
2. If $A$ ia a formula, then $\neg A$ is a formula;
3. if $A, B$ are formulas, then $A \wedge B$, $A \vee B$ and $A \rightarrow B$ are formulas;
4. An expression is a formula if and only if it is obtained by applying some of the previous rules.

The formula $\neg A$ is read as the negation of A.
The formula $A \wedge B$ is read as the conjunction of A and B.
The formula $A \vee B$ is read as the disjunction of A and B.
The formula $A \rightarrow B$ is read as the implication of B by A.

Intuitively, an atomic formula $p_\mu$ is read as: "I believe in the proposition $p$ with degree of belief at most $\mu$, or even $\mu(\leq \mu)$.

If $p$ is a propositional letter and $\mu \in |\tau|$ so far an atomic formula of the type $\neg^k p_\mu$ where $k > 0$, it is called a hyper-literal or simply literal. The other formulas are called complex formulas. The study of semantics of logic $P_\tau$ is briefly presented as follows. An interpretation on Annotated Logics $P_\tau$ is a function $I : P \rightarrow |\tau|$, where $P$ is the set of propositional variables. Every interpretation $I$ is associated with a valuation: $V_I : F \rightarrow 0, 1$ where $F$ is the set of all formulas. The valuation $V_I$ is defined inductively by:

1. If $p$ is a propositional letter, then:

$$V_I(p_\mu) = 1 \Longleftrightarrow I(p) \geq \mu$$
$$V_I(p_\mu) = 0 \Longleftrightarrow I(p) \geq \mu$$
$$V_I(\neg^k p_\mu) = V_I(\neg^{k-1} p_{\sim\mu}) \text{ onde, } k \geq 1$$

2. If $A$ and $B$ are any formulas, then:

$$V_I(A \rightarrow B) = 1 \Longleftrightarrow V_I(A) = 0 \text{ ou } V_I(B) = 1$$
$$V_I(A \wedge B) = 1 \Longleftrightarrow V_I(A) = 1 \text{ e } V_I(B) = 1$$
$$V_I(A \vee B) = 1 \Longleftrightarrow V_I(A) = 1 \text{ ou } V_I(B) = 1$$

A interpretation to $P_\tau, I : P \rightarrow |\tau|$ is inconsistent if there is $p \in P$ and $\mu \in |\tau|$ so that $V_I(p_\mu) = 1 = V_I(\neg p_\mu)$. A interpretation to $P_\tau, I : P \rightarrow |\tau|$ is trivial if there is $p \in P$ and $\mu \in |\tau|$ so that $V_I(p_\mu) = 0$. A interpretation to $P_\tau, I : P \rightarrow |\tau|$ is paraconsistent if it is inconsistent and non-trivial. Logic $P_\tau$ is said to be Paraconsistent if it accepts a paraconsistent interpretation.

### 3.4.2. Representation of Lattices of Annotated Paraconsistent Logic

Through an intuitive analysis of the Annotated Paraconsistent Logic, the atomic formula $p_\mu$ that is read as: I think of proposition $p$ with degree of belief at most $\mu$, or even $\mu(\leq \mu)$ considers the degree of belief as being one of the constants of annotation of lattice. This leads us to state that each degree of belief assigned to the proposition is a value that is contained in the set of values composed of the constants of annotation of lattice $\{\top, V, F, \bot\}$.

The annotations in this lattice are considered multi-valued and follow the rules determined by the Hasse diagram of Figure 5. The proposals are accompanied by notes that, in turn, assign the degree of belief corresponding to each propositional variable. Each propositional sentence, which by abuse of language is called proposition, is accompanied by a degree of belief that determines the connotation of truth or falsity of the formula.

- $p_\top$ = The note or degree of belief gives connotations of inconsistency to proposition $p$.

- $p_1$ = The note or degree of belief gives connotations of truth to proposition $p$.
- $P_0$ = The note or degree of belief gives connotations of falsity to proposition $p$.
- $p_\perp$ = The note or degree of belief gives connotations of uncertainty to proposition $p$.

For instance, a control system of a robot that is working with signals from two sensors, to do a job of putting a piece on a table, it must ensure that the table is in place. With the information and using the notations of Paraconsistent Annotated Logic, we have:

$p$ = The table is in place and $\mu$ = Degree of Belief;

The situations in the real world likely to happen would be:

- $p_\top$ = The table is and is not in the correct place (a sensor detects and the other does not).
- $p_1$ = The board is in place (the two sensors detect).
- $P_0$ = The table is not in the correct place (none of the sensors detect).
- $p_\perp$ = Nothing can be said - indefinable (the amplitudes of the signals from the two sensors are not enough for detection).

In case of inconsistency, the robot will seek information from another sensor that can be better located, move laterally or even make use of the data stored in its knowledge foundation that would act as decisive sign in the contradictions. In situations of truth and falsity, the action to be taken offers no discussion. When the situation is unclear, the action should be to increase the sensitivity of sensors such as cleaning the lens, focus, adjust of electrical power supply, etc.

In this example of application of Paraconsistent Annotated Logic, which uses the lattice, four situations were considered, of which two of them, inconsistency and uncertainty, are alien to the classical logic in the context that were employed. The Degrees of Belief, corresponding to the constant of annotation of the lattice are four and, as seen, their values were related to the four situations presented.

### 3.4.3. Paraconsistent Annotated Logic with Annotation of Two Values PAL2v

The Annotated Paraconsistent Logic presented so far brings annotation with a single component, where for every proposition, a single constant of annotation or degree of belief of the lattice is associated. In [7], a new proposal for bringing two lattice values in the annotation is presented. Application of Paraconsistent Annotated Logic with this lattice is a very interesting proposition from a practical viewpoint, because it allows greater control, more computational possibilities, resulting in a significant improvement in the performance of computer programs and control circuits that will be applied in systems. Annotations can be read as evidence and, therefore, when the circuit receives contradictory information these evidences have an important role in decision making.

Applying the evidential reasoning Paraconsistent Annotated Logic proposal, two values are now associated with a note of the lattice, calling this logic Paraconsistent Annotated Logic of Two Values - PAL2v. The first figure of note is the evidence which supports

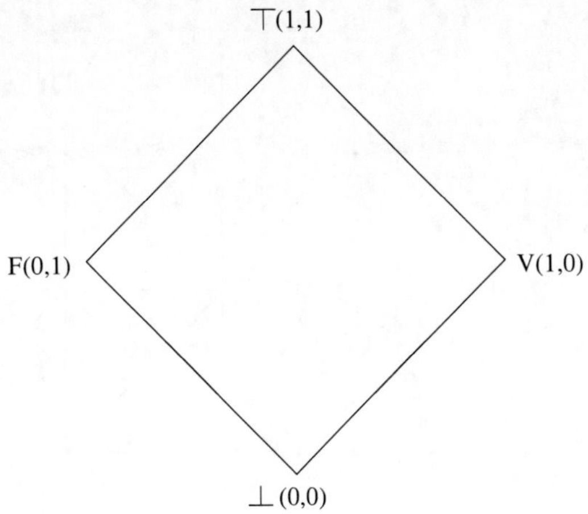


Figure 6. Diagram of Hasse - Lattice four of PAL2v.

the proposition p, and the second figure represents the evidence against the proposition p. Called Belief the favorable evidence and Disbelief the contrary evidence. The Degree of Belief is denoted by the letter $\mu_1$ and the Degree of Disbelief is denoted by the letter $\mu_2$. With these considerations, each constant of annotation of the lattice is now represented by the pair $(\mu_1, \mu_2)$. A Hasse lattice of annotation with two values is presented as figure 6.

The definitions for the annotations and for the $\sim$ operator is as follows. If $p$ is a basic formula and operator $\sim: |\tau| \rightarrow |\tau|$ is defined as $\sim [(\mu_1, \mu_2)] = (\mu_2, \mu_1)$ where $(\mu_1, \mu_2) \in \{x \in \Re | 0 \leq x \leq 1\}$, it is considered $(\mu_1, \mu_2)$ as an annotation $p$. The coordinates $\mu_1$ and $\mu_2$ can be read as the degree of belief assigned to $p$ and the degree of disbelief that is assigned to $p$, respectively. The values of the degrees of belief and disbelief are completely independent. Therefore, as a value does not depend absolutely on the other, any variation of value in the real closed interval can be between $0$ and $1$.

### 3.4.4. Another Interpretation of PAL2v

In [24], [25], it is used the concept of the Unitary Square of the Cartesian Plan (USCP) to formulate a new proposal for the interpretation of paraconsistent logic of two values PAL2v.

In this proposal for the paraconsistent logic of two values, an interpretation is a function $I : P \rightarrow |\tau|$ and that for every interpretation $I$ should join a valuation $V_I : F \rightarrow [0,1] \times [0,1]$, being $F$ the set of all formulas that can be viewed in USCP.

In USCP, the abscissa, with valid values in the real closed interval $[0,1]$, represents the degree of belief $\mu$ of a proposition and the coordinate axis, with values in the same interval $[0,1]$, represents the degree of disbelief $\lambda$ of the proposition. Figure 7 presents the notable points of USCP.

The segment $\overline{FV}$ of USCP is called *perfectly consistent line* (PCL) and the segment $\overline{\top\bot}$ is called *perfectly inconsistent line* (PIL), as illustrated in Figure 7a. In PCL, given the value of belief, disbelief is the value of its complement with respect to unity,

$$\mu + \lambda - 1 = 0$$

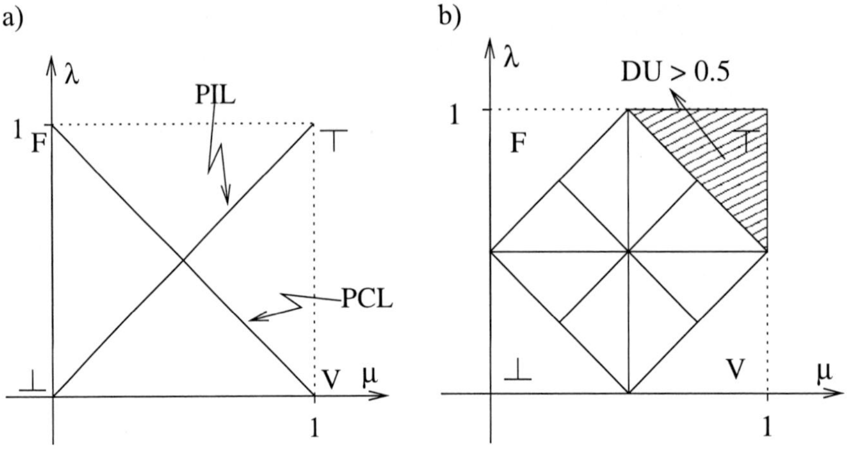


Figure 7. Unitary Square of the Cartesian Plan. a) Notable points and the perfectly inconsistent line, PIL, and the perfectly consistent line, PCL, of the USCP. b) Boundaries of areas in USCP with the inclusion of new notable points and identification of the region entirely inconsistent.

Likewise, in the PIL, for each belief value there is a disbelief one with the same intensity,

$$\mu - \lambda = 0$$

Given a pair $(\mu, \lambda)$ associated with a proposition, we define the *degree of uncertainty* (DU) by Equation 4 and *degree of certainty* (DC) by Equation 5.

$$DU = \mu + \lambda - 1 \tag{4}$$

$$DC = \mu - \lambda \tag{5}$$

Using equations of the DC and DU we can see that, as an ordered pair $(\mu, \lambda)$ of USCP detaches from the PIL toward the pair $(1, 0)$, there is an increase on the degree of certainty of the proposition associated, to reach its maximum value, which is $1$, located in $V$. Similarly, as an ordered pair $(\mu, \lambda)$ of USCP distances itself from the PIL toward the pair $(0, 1)$, there is an increased level of uncertainty associated with the proposition to reach its maximum value 1 located in $F$.

In [24], the inclusion of four more notable points in USCP is suggested. The point of coordinates (1, 0.5), called *quasi-true*, $qV$, the point of coordinates (0.5, 1), called *quasi-false*, $qF$, the point of coordinates (0, 0.5), called *quasi-non-true*, $q{\sim}V$ and the point of coordinates (0.5 ,0), called *quasi-non-false*, $q{\sim}F$, as illustrated in Figure 8. With the addition of points, the USCP is divided into new regions that receive names according to the proximity to the extreme points of the lattice. The regions of USCP are named as:

- $\top$: inconsistent
- $\perp$: paracomplete

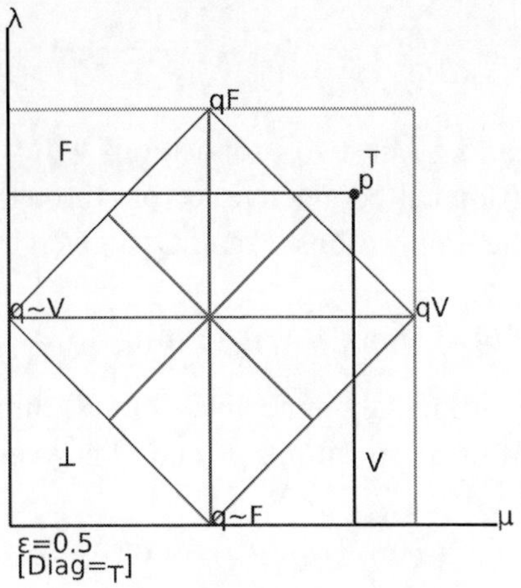


Figure 8. Example of identifying a point in the region $\top$ = inconsistent in USCP.

- $F$: false
- $V$: true
- $V \rightarrow qV$: true, tending to almost surely
- $\top \rightarrow qV$: inconsistent, tending to almost surely
- $F \rightarrow qF$: false, tending to almost false
- $\top \rightarrow qF$: inconsistent, tending to almost false
- $F \rightarrow q{\sim}V$: false, tending to almost non-true
- $\perp \rightarrow q{\sim}V$ paracomplete, tending to almost non-true
- $V \rightarrow q{\sim}F$: true, tending to almost non-false
- $\perp \rightarrow q{\sim}F$: paracomplete, tending to almost non-false

Intuitively, the regions in USCP represent the value associated with proposition $p_{\mu\lambda}$, given values of the degree of belief and disbelief of the proposition. The region $\top$, for example, is the region in USCP where $DU > 0.5$, as illustrated in Figure 7b.

As a proposition $p_{\mu\lambda}$, the value of paraconsistent logic associated with $p$ is determined by the region in USCP which point, whose coordinates are $p = (\mu, \lambda)$, is included. In Figure 8, for example, the values of $\mu$ and $\lambda$ are $0.85$ and $0.80$, respectively, and the logical value of $p$ is inconsistent ($\top$). The algorithm of Figure 9 shows how to obtain a diagnosis from the values of $\mu$ and $\lambda$ of any proposition $p$.

From this interpretation of paraconsistent logic of two variables, the logical operations of negation, conjunction and disjunction are defined. The operation of negation, for example, is obtained using the following formula. Given a proposition $P(\mu, \lambda)$, the denial of this interpretation of paraconsistent logic is as Equation 6.

$$\neg P(\mu, \lambda) = (1 - \mu, 1 - \lambda) \tag{6}$$

Let $P(\mu_P, \lambda_P)$ and $Q(\mu_Q, \lambda_Q)$ be two propositions with their degrees of belief and disbelief. The application of logical connective $\vee$ (or) through USCP and the degree of certainty and uncertainty of the propositions $P$ and $Q$ is given by Equation 7.

$$P \vee Q = (\max(\mu_P, \mu_Q), \min(\lambda_P, \lambda_Q)) \tag{7}$$

Similarly, the application of logical connective $\wedge$ (and) through USCP and the degree of certainty and uncertainty of the propositions $P$ and $Q$ is given by Equation 8.

$$P \wedge Q = (\min(\mu_P, \mu_Q), \max(\lambda_P, \lambda_Q)) \tag{8}$$

The algorithm of Figure 9 is applied to determine the paraconsistent logic state resulting from the application of each logical operator. The parameters of the diagnostic function of the algorithm are the *degree of belief* $\mu$ and the *degree of disbelief* $\lambda$. In the algorithm, the *degree of certainty* (DC) and *uncertainty* (DU) are calculated according to the equations Equation 5 and Equation 4. Values $C_1$, $C_2$, $C_3$ and $C_4$ and represent respectively the upper value of certainty control, lower value of certainty control, upper value of uncertainty control and lower value of uncertainty control. These figures are used under the conditions of the algorithm to identify regions related to each logical state.

The hybrid system presented in this chapter does not use logical operations. These issues are relevant to show that paraconsistent logic can extend the classical logic, that is, every possible formula in classical logic can be extended and interpreted using paraconsistent logic.

### 3.4.5. The Extent of the Paraconsistent Annotated Logic of Three Variables

In the study by Martins [24], an extension to the interpretation of paraconsistent annotated logic of two variables (PAL2v) is presented, adding to it another dimension to the lattice, called the *degree of specialization*. The idea is to consider the opinion of an expert in determining the logical value associated to the propositions. So, another axis is added to the Cartesian plane PAL2v, to obtain a cube analyzer, as illustrated in Figures 11, 12 and 13.

From the *experts*, it is expected a minimum of indecision, inconsistency and unawareness. Given a proposition to the expert, it is expected to reach a consistent and determined decision, according to classical logic. From the *neophytes*, any decision is admitted, given their inexperience. In the original work of Martins [24], it is considered an expert when $\varepsilon = 1$ and when $\varepsilon = 0$ we have a neophyte.

With the change in the degree of specialization, we have a deformation in the plan that identifies the various regions of the diagnosis of paraconsistent logic. For instance, for $\varepsilon = 0.25$ we have the cube and the regions of paraconsistent logic, as illustrated in Figure 11. The region *truth* and the region *false* are larger than the regions *inconsistent* and *paracomplete*. For $\varepsilon = 0.5$, we have the regions of the states of paraconsistent logic exactly like those of PAL2v. For $\varepsilon = 0.75$, *inconsistent* and *paracomplete* regions are larger than *true* and *false*.

```
diagnostic (μ, λ){
  dc ← μ − λ
  du ← (μ + λ) − 1
  c1 ← 0.5
  c2 ← −0.5
  c3 ← 0.5
  c4 ← −0.5
  if dc ≥ c1 return "V"
  if |dc| ≥ |c2| return "F"
  if du ≥ c3 return "⊤"
  if |du| ≥ |c4| return "⊥"
  if dc = 0 and du = 0 return "?"
  if dc ≥ 0 and dc < c1 and du ≥ 0 and du < c3 {
    if du < c3/c1 ∗ dc
      return "V → qV"
    return "⊤ → qV"
  }
  if dc > c2 and dc ≤ 0 and du ≥ 0 and du < c3 {
    if |du| < |c3/c2 ∗ dc|
      return "F → qF"
    return "⊤ → qF"
  }
  if dc > c2 and dc < 0 and du > c4 and du ≤ 0 {
    if |du| < |c4/c2 ∗ dc|
      return "F → q~V"
    return "⊥ → q~V"
  }
  if dc ≥ 0 and dc < c1 and du > c4 and du ≤ 0 {
    if du ≥ c4/c1 ∗ dc
      return "V → q~F"
    return "⊥ → q~F"
  }
}
```

Figure 9. Pseudo-code of the routine that makes the diagnosis using USCP. Given the value of the degree of belief $\mu$ and the value of the degree of disbelief $\lambda$, the routine returns to the corresponding paraconsistent logic state.

```
diagnostic (μ, λ, ε){
    dc ← μ − λ
    du ← (μ + λ) − 1
    c1 ← ε
    c2 ← −ε
    c3 ← 1 − ε
    c4 ← ε − 1
    (...)
}
```

Figure 10. Pseudo-code for diagnosis using USCP for PAL3v, considering the additional speciality parameter $\varepsilon$.

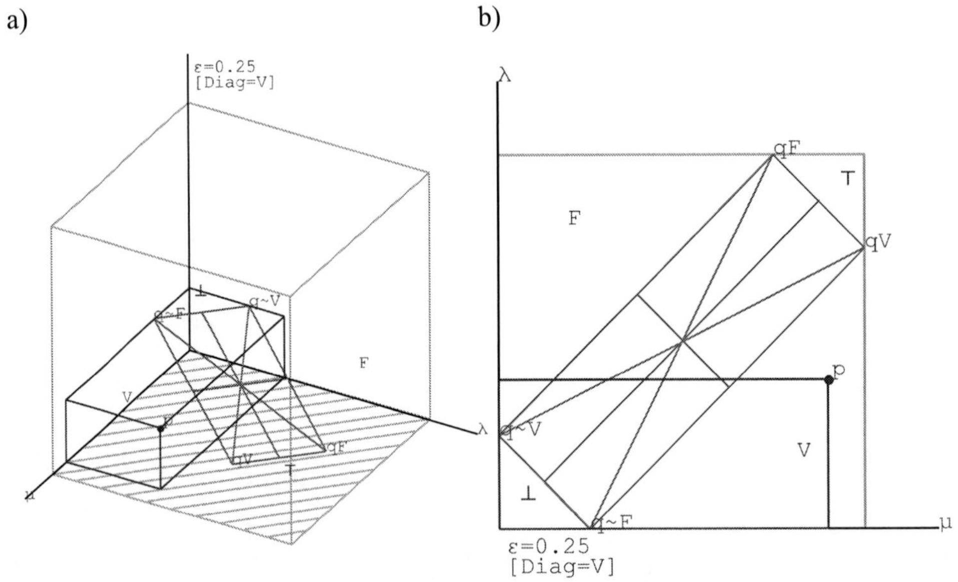


Figure 11. Cube of paraconsistent annotated logic analyzer of three variables. Determining the logical value for $\mu = 0.9$, $\lambda = 0.4$ and $\varepsilon = 0.25$. a) representation in the cube analyzer b) projection on the plan $\mu \times \lambda$.

The same value of the degree of belief and degree of disbelief of a proposition produces different resulting logic states, depending on the degree of specialization. Thus, for $\varepsilon = 0.25$, $\mu = 0.9$ and $\lambda = 0.4$, the resulting paraconsistent state is $V$, as shown in Figure 11. For $\varepsilon = 0.5$, $\mu = 0.9$ and $\lambda = 0.4$, the resulting paraconsistent state is still $V$, as illustrated in Figure 12, but with the result on the border of two different regions. For $\varepsilon = 0.75$, $\mu = 0.9$ e $\lambda = 0.4$, the resulting paraconsistent state is $\top$, Figure 13.

The algorithm of Figure 9 is easily adapted to consider an additional parameter of the degree of specialization. The changes in the algorithm are shown in Figure 10. Basically, the diagnostic function for PAL3v includes a new specialty parameter $\varepsilon$. This value is used to determine the values of superior and inferior control used to delimit the regions of the logical states. The new values are $C_1 \leftarrow \varepsilon$, $C_2 \leftarrow -\varepsilon$, $C_3 \leftarrow 1-\varepsilon$ and $C_4 \leftarrow \varepsilon - 1$. The other lines of the diagnostic algorithm remain the same.

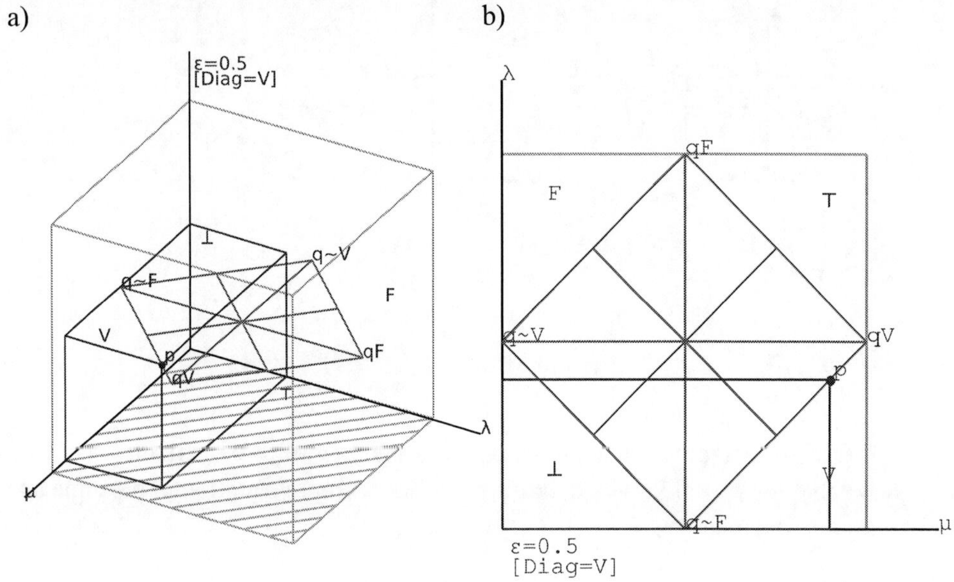


Figure 12. Cube of paraconsistent annotated logic analyzer of three variables. Determining the logical value for $\mu = 0.9$, $\lambda = 0.4$ and $\varepsilon = 0.50$. a) representation in the cube analyzer b) projection on the plan $\mu \times \lambda$.

After setting a value of specialty $\varepsilon$, we can use the same reasoning used for the application of logical operators of negation $\neg$, disjunction $\vee$ and conjunction $\wedge$, used to PAL2v, according to Equation 6, Equation 7 and Equation 8.

In this work, we symmetrically interpret the original work in order to capture the ant colony learning during the process of building solutions, as will be discussed in the next section.

## 4. Hybrid System = PAL + ACO

This section presents the hybrid system that makes up the Ant Colony metaheuristic with Paraconsistent Logic.The main purpose of the use of Paraconsistent Logic is to capture the learning from the ants during the process of construction of solutions. Thus, the original algorithm to construct ACO metaheuristic solutions, in Figure 4, is modified in line 4, the call of the routine that chooses the next neighbor. Instead of routine *chooseNext()* of the original algorithm, it is used routine *chooseNextParaconsistent(ε)* presented in pseudo-code in Figure 15. The process of decision-making of the ants in the colony, using paraconsistent logic, is determined by the equations Equation 9, Equation 10 and Equation 11.

$$x = \text{argmax}_{l \in N_i^k} [\tau_{il}]^{\alpha} [\eta_{il}]^{\beta} \tag{9}$$

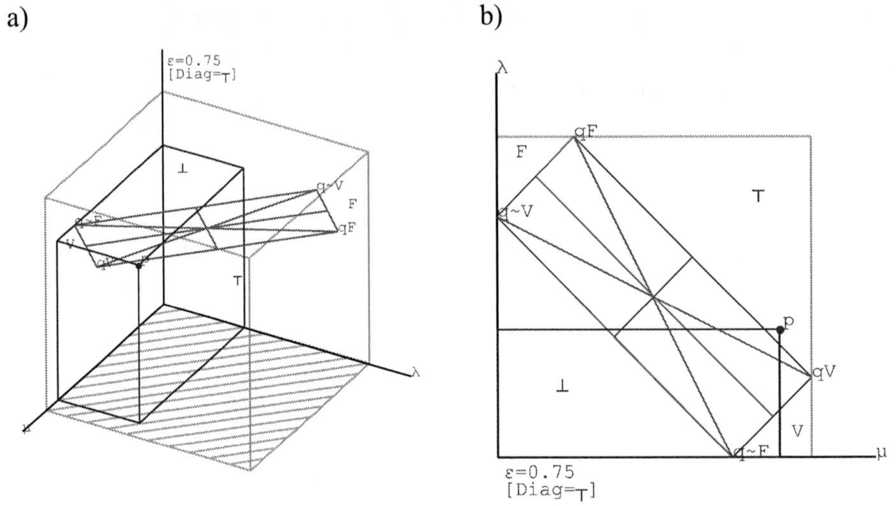


Figure 13. Cube of paraconsistent annotated logic analyzer of three variables. Determining the logical value for $\mu = 0.9$, $\lambda = 0.4$ and $\varepsilon = 0.75$. a) representation in the cube analyzer b) projection on the plan $\mu \times \lambda$.

where:

- *argmax* returns the neighbor whose $[\tau_{il}]^{\alpha}[\eta_{il}]^{\beta}$ is maximum
- $N_i^k$ s the neighborhood not yet visited from the vertex $i$

$$y = \text{argmin}_{l \in N_i^k} [\tau_{il}]^{\alpha}[\eta_{il}]^{\beta} \tag{10}$$

where:

- *argmin* returns the neighbor whose $[\tau_{il}]^{\alpha}[\eta_{il}]^{\beta}$ minimal

$$z = \text{argmax}_{l \in N_i^k - \{x\}} [\tau_{il}]^{\alpha}[\eta_{il}]^{\beta} \tag{11}$$

For decision making using PAL3v algorithm, each ant $k$ uses knowledge that is being built by the colony, represented by the product between pheromone $\tau$ and heuristic information $\eta$ in the problem. The degree of evidence favorable $\mu$ to the path with largest product $\tau \times \eta$ is adopted as $100\%$, $\mu = 1$. The degree of unfavorable evidence of this best neighbor is calculated as

$$\lambda = \frac{bestNeighbor - secondBestNeighbor}{bestNeighbor - worstNeighbor}$$

.

Where *bestNeighbor*, *worstNeighbor* and *secondBestNeighbor* are given by Equations 9, 10 and 11. Given a specialty, the corresponding paraconsistent state is calculated. If

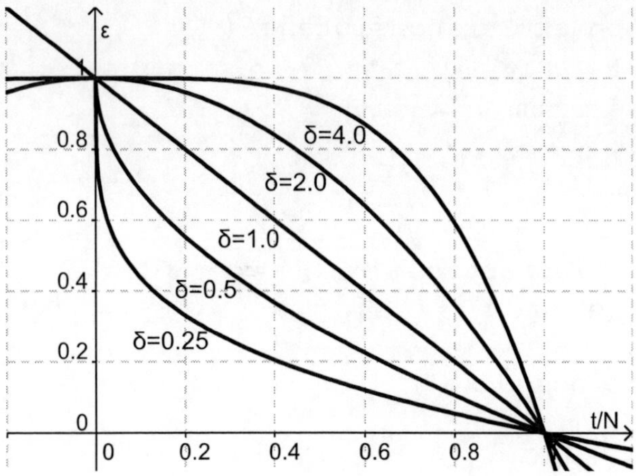


Figure 14. Graph of variation of specialty depending on the parameter $\delta$.

the resulting state is *totally true*, the best neighbor is decisively used in the solution being constructed. Otherwise, the algorithm of construction of solutions uses the routine *chooseNext()*, as the algorithm of the original ACO metaheuristic.

To consider the learning that is being done by the ant colony, the algorithm of Figure 15 has a parameter that determines the variation in the degree of specialization. The specialty $\varepsilon$ is a function of iterations and the parameter $\delta$, as defined in Equation 12. The smaller the iteration is, the most inexperienced the ant is to make decisions and the higher the iteration, the more expert the ant is.

$$\varepsilon = 1 - \left(\frac{t}{N}\right)^{\delta} \tag{12}$$

where:

- $t$, represents the current iteration.
- $N$, represents the maximum number of iterations, which determines the *termination-Condition()* of the ACO algorithm.
- $\delta$, determines how the variation of specialty during the iterations is.

Different values of $\delta$ produce variations in the specialty as illustrated in Figure 14. For $\delta = 1$, the change of specialty $\varepsilon$ is linear over the iterations, $t = 0$ we have $\varepsilon = 1$. For $t = N$ we have $\varepsilon = 0$. That is, at the end of the iterations, ants make decisions in a deterministic way, depending only on the pheromone trail created by the ant colony. For $\delta > 1$, the range of expertise is greater at the end of iterations. For $\delta > 0$ and $\delta < 1$ the range of expertise is lower at the end of iterations.

Ants begin the process of building solutions with no knowledge. In light of iterations, the ants are becoming more and more specialists, being able to decide deterministically which way to go, considering only the content of the pheromone trails. As discussed in [31], this proposal serves to regulate the convergence of the ant colony.

`chooseNextParaconsistent` $(\varepsilon)$ {<br>
  $x \leftarrow \text{argmax}_{l \in N_i^k} [\tau_{il}]^\alpha [\eta_{il}]^\beta$<br>
  $y \leftarrow \text{argmin}_{l \in N_i^k} [\tau_{il}]^\alpha [\eta_{il}]^\beta$<br>
  $z \leftarrow \text{argmax}_{l \in N_i^k - \{x\}} [\tau_{il}]^\alpha [\eta_{il}]^\beta$<br>
  $\mu \leftarrow 1.0$<br>
  $\lambda \leftarrow (x - z)/(x - y)$<br>
  `if diagnostic` $(\mu, \lambda, \varepsilon)$ = "$V$"<br>
    `return` $x$<br>
  `else`<br>
    `chooseNext()`<br>
}

Figure 15. Pseudo-code of procedure for choosing the next neighbor using paraconsistent logic for the algorithm of construction of solutions of the ACO.

The form, as is defined the integration of the ACO metaheuristic with the Paraconsistent Annotated Logic of Three Variables, allows the creation of hybrid systems with any variation of metaheuristic. The next section presents the implementation of the proposed algorithm to the variation of the metaheuristic called $\mathcal{MAX} - \mathcal{MIN}$ Ant System ($\mathcal{MM}$AS).

### 4.1. Experimental Results

To demonstrate the performance of the hybrid system of paraconsistent logic with Ant Colony metaheuristic, this section presents an implementation with the variation of ACO called $\mathcal{MAX} - \mathcal{MIN}$ Ant System. For the tests, the original implementation of the algorithm $\mathcal{MM}$AS and its hybrid with paraconsistent logic were applied to solve the traveling salesman problem (TSP). As already mentioned, this problem is an excellent benchmark for evaluating the ACO metaheuristic algorithms. The formal description of the problem of the TSP to the pheromone model of ACO can be found in [15].

In order to perform the tests, the standard $\mathcal{MM}$AS and $\mathcal{MM}$AS hybrid with paraconsistent logic have been used to solve the same instance of TSP, available in the repository TSPLIB [27], called 'tsp225.tsp'. For each algorithm, five experiments were performed with 2000 replicates per experiment, and these are divided into five attempts of 400 iterations, saving, among attempts, the best solution of all ants. The other parameters used by both techniques were: the number of ants used is the number of cities in the instance of the problem, in this case 225 ants, $\alpha = 1$, $\beta = 2$ and $\rho = 0.02$. According to [32], these parameters are good choices for the optimization problem of the traveling salesman. Besides, no operation of any of the local search algorithms was used.

As distance metric between the cities of the problem, we adopted the Euclidean distance to rounding. This was done because the optimum values of the pathways of such problems are available [27], being possible, then, an interesting analysis of those results with the ones found by both ACO strategies presented.

For hybrid $\mathcal{MM}$AS with paraconsistent logic, the variation of the convergence defined by the value of $\delta = 0.5$ was used, as illustrated in Figure 14.

Finally, for each of the models presented, five experiments were conducted with determined configurations, saving in each experiment the best solution found by ant colony.

The results presented in these experiments to the methodologies of the strategy of ACO, the standard $\mathcal{MMAS}$ and hybrid $\mathcal{MMAS}$ with paraconsistent logic are summarized in Table 1.

**Table 1. Results of strategies $\mathcal{MMAS}$ and paraconsistent $\mathcal{MMAS}$ for the instance of TSPLIB called 'TSP225'**

| Estratgia | 1 | 2 | 3 | 4 | 5 | Mdia | Desvio |
|---|---|---|---|---|---|---|---|
| $\mathcal{MMAS}$ | 4029 | 3999 | **3996** | 4094 | 4010 | 4025,6 | 40,36 |
| $\mathcal{MMAS}$ Parconsistente | 4008 | 4070 | **3975** | 4024 | 4031 | 4021,6 | 34,62 |

Table 1 shows the result of each test performed, the mean and standard deviation for the strategies of MMAS and paraconsistent MMAS. For the instance considered the optimal result is 3919. Figures 16a, 16b e 16c show the optimal outcome, the best result found by $\mathcal{MMAS}$ strategy and best results were found for paraconsistent $\mathcal{MMAS}$ strategy.

For Table 1, comparing the mean and standard deviation of both approaches, one can observe that the $\mathcal{MMAS}$ strategy of ACO with paraconsistent logic obtained better results than the original $\mathcal{MMAS}$ strategy. However, it is not possible to say that the average values are statistically different. Anyway, the proposed hybrid proves to be a unique variant of metaheuristic ant colony. There are some parameters to adjust as the way the variation of specialty defined by the parameter $\delta$, how to determine the degree of favorable $\mu$ and unfavorable $\lambda$ evidence used by ants in the colony during the process of decision making.

## 5. Conclusion

This chapter presents a variation of ant colony metaheuristic with a non-classical logic called Paraconsistent Logic. It is an extension of classical logic that allows to work with other logic states, besides the states true and false.

With the paraconsistent logic we can address more realistic problems of decision making involving uncertainty, partial knowledge and inconsistency. The ants of the optimization strategy called Ant Colony are faced with this kind of problem of inconsistency and indecision when builds solutions to problem. Paraconsistent Logic is built into the original algorithm of Ant Colony metaheuristic in order to try to capture the learning process conducted by the ants during the construction of solutions.

The proposed hybrid proves to be a viable variant for the ACO metaheuristic. New parameters need adjustment as determining the degree of belief, degree of disbelief and range of expertise to better capture the learning from the ants.

As future work, we intend to perform more tests and better adapt the proposed hybrid. The application of hybrid system in other optimization problems such as the problem of restoring electric power systems is still searched.

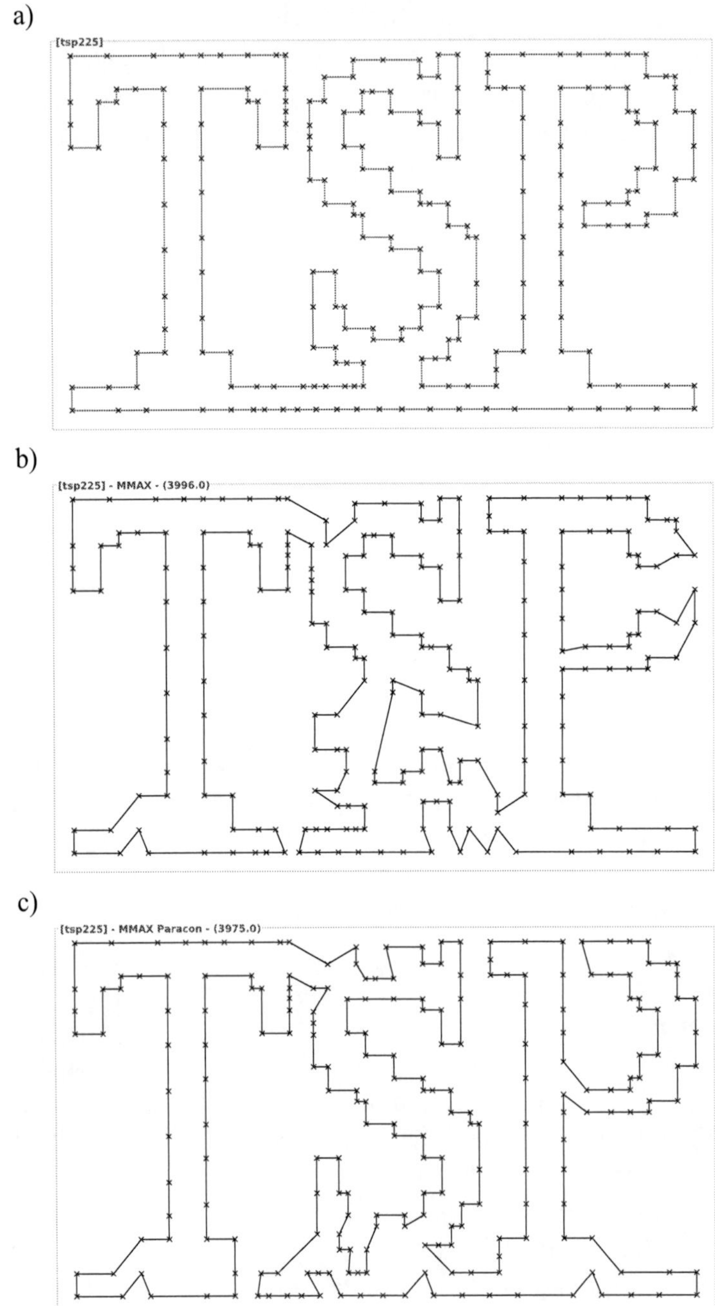


Figure 16. Implementation of strategies $\mathcal{MM}$AS and paraconsistent $\mathcal{MM}$AS in the instance of tsp225 of TSPLIB. a) optimal solution b) best solution found using the strategy $\mathcal{MM}$AS c) best solution found using the paraconsistent $\mathcal{MM}$AS strategy.

## References


[1] AAAI/Xerox Second Intl. Symp. on Knowledge Eng. *A Logic Programming System Based on a Six-Valued Logic*, Madri, Espanha, 1987.

[2] J. M. Abe. *Fundamentals of Annotated Logic*. PhD thesis, FFLCH/USP, SP, Brazil, 1992.

[3] B. Bullnheimer, R. F. Hartl, and C. Strauss. A new rank based version of the ant system: A computational study. *Central European Journal for Operations Research and Economics*, 7(1):25–38, 1999.

[4] N. C. A. Da Costa. On the theory of inconsistent formal systems. *Notre Dame Journal of Formal Logic*, **11**, 1974.

[5] N. C. A. Da Costa. *The Philosophic Importance of Paraconsistent Logic*, volume 11. Bol. Soc. Paranaense of Mathematic, 1990.

[6] N. C. A. Da Costa and J. M. Abe. *Lógica Paraconsistente Aplicada*. Editora Atlas, 1999.

[7] N. C. A. Da Costa, L. J. Hensche, and V. S. Subrahmanian. *Automatic Theorem Proving in Paraconsistent Logics: Theory and Implementation*, volume 3 of *Estudos Avançados, Coleção Documentos*. USP, SP, Brasil, 1990.

[8] N. C. A. Da Costa, V. S. Subrahmanian, and C. Vago. The paraconsistent logic p$\tau$. *Zeitschrift fur Mathematische Logik und Grundlagen der Mathematik*, **37**:139–148, 1991.

[9] J. I. Da Silva Filho. *Métodos de Aplicaçes da Lógica Paraconsistente Anotada com Dois Valores-LPA2v Com Construção de Algoritmo e Implementação de Circuitos Eletrônicos*. PhD thesis, EPUSP, São Paulo, 1999.

[10] J. I. Da Silva Filho, J. M. Abe, and G. Lambert-Torres. *Inteligência Artificial com as Redes de Análise Paraconsistente*. LTC, Rio de Janeiro, 2008.

[11] Deneubourg, S. Aron, S. Goss, and J. M. Pasteels. The self-organizing exploratory pattern of the argentine ant. *Journal of Insect Behavior*, **3**(2):159–168, March 1990.

[12] M. Dorigo. *Optimization, Learning and Natural Algorithms (in Italian)*. PhD thesis, Dipartimento di Elettronica, Politecnico di Milano, Milan, Italy, 1992.

[13] M. Dorigo, M. Birattari, and T. Stützle. Ant colony optimization: Artificial ants as a computational intelligence technique. *IEEE Computational Intelligence Magazine*, **1**(4):28–39, 2006.

[14] M. Dorigo, M. Birattari, and T. Stützle. Ant colony optimization. Artificial ants as a computational intelligence technique. Technical Report TR/IRIDIA/2006-023, IRIDIA, Université Libre de Bruxelles, Brussels, Belgium, 2006.

[15] M. Dorigo and L. M. Gambardella. Ant Colony System: A cooperative learning approach to the traveling salesman problem. *IEEE Transactions on Evolutionary Computation*, **1**(1):53–66, 1997.

[16] M. Dorigo, V. Maniezzo, and A. Colorni. Ant System: Optimization by a colony of cooperating agents. *IEEE Transactions on Systems, Man, and Cybernetics - Part B* , **26**(1):29–41, 1996.

[17] M. Dorigo and K. Socha. An introduction to ant colony optimization. Technical report, IRIDIA, Institut de Recherches Interdisciplinaires et de Développements en Intelligence Artificielle, Université Libre de Bruxelles, Belgium, April 2006.

[18] M. Dorigo and T. Stützle. The ant colony optimization metaheuristic: Algorithms, applications and advances. In Fred Glover and Gary Kochenberger, editors, *Handbook of Metaheuristics*, volume 57 of *International Series in Operations Research & Management Science*, chapter 9, pages 251–285. Kluwer Academic Publishers, Boston, MA, 2002.

[19] S. Goss, S. Aron, J. L. Deneubourg, and J. M. Pateels. Self-organized shortcuts in the argentine ant. *Naturwissenschaften*, **76**(76):579–581, December 1989.

[20] P. P. Grassé. La reconstruction du nit el les coordinations interindividuelles chez belliconsitermes natalensis et cubtermes sp. la théorie de la stigmergie: Essai d'interprétation du comportemente des termites constructeus. *Insectes Sociaus*, 6:41–81, 1959.

[21] IEEE Symposium on Logic Programming. *On the Semantics of Quantitative Logic Programs*, Washington DC, 1987. Computer Society Press.

[22] M. Jünger, G. Reinelt, and G. Rinaldi. *The Traveling Salesman Problem: a Bibliography*. Annotated Bibliography in Combinatorial Optimization, Willey, 1997.

[23] S.C. Kleene. *Introduction to Metamathematics*. Bibliotheca Mathematica. North-Holland, 1952.

[24] H. G. Martins. *The Four-Valued Annotated Paraconsistent Logic - 4vAPL Applied in a Case Based Reasoning System for Restoration of Electrical Substations* . PhD thesis, UNIFEI, Brazil, 2003.

[25] H. G. Martins, G. Lambert-Torres, and L. F. Pontin. *Annotated Paraconsistent Logic*. Ed. Communicar, 2007.

[26] J. Pearl. Belief networks revisited. *Artificial Intelligence*, **59**:49–56, 1993.

[27] G. Reinelt. Tsplib: A traveling salesman problem library, 1991.

[28] E. Rich and K. Knight. *Inteligência Artificial*. Makron Books, São Paulo, 2 edition, 1994.

[29] S. Russell and P. Norvig. *Inteligência Artificial*. Elsevier, Rio de Janeiro, 2 edition, 2004.

[30] SBC - Sociedade Brasileira de Computacao. *Representacao do Conhecimento Incerto*, Pernamburco, Brasil, 1996.

[31] L. E. Silva, H. G. Martins, M. P. Coutinho, G. Lambert-Torres, and L. E. B. Silva. The convergence control to the aco metaheuristic using annotated paraconsistent logic. In *ISICA2009*, Lectures Notes on Computer Science, pages 382–391, 2009.

[32] Thomas Stützle and Holger Hoos. Max min - ant system. *Future Generation Computer Systems*, **16**(8):889–914, 2000.

In: Ant Colonies
Editor: Emily C. Sun
ISBN: 978-1-61122-023-0


*Chapter 9*

# ANT COLONY OPTIMIZATION: A POWERFUL STRATEGY FOR BIOMARKER FEATURE SELECTION*

***Weixiang Zhao and Cristina E. Davis*†****
Department of Mechanical and Aerospace Engineering,
University of California, David, CA, USA

## ABSTRACT

As instrumentation develops in industry and science, we frequently generate multi-dimension data sets that may involve input from a large number of factors or variables. Many parameters of these instrument systems may not be directly related with the core function of the systems, and some factor may even lead to noise contamination of output signals. The potential obscuring effects of these variables on the data set can make it difficult to determine which parts of the instrument data are the most meaningful. Therefore, feature selection within data sets is becoming a core technique to detect pertinent factors or variable for system characterization. This not only reduces the data dimension but also provides pertinent information for system mechanism studies, and can ultimately yield information about the underlying instrumentation function.

Feature selection within data sets has been attempted using a variety of different methods, and some conventionally used methods include statistical analyses such as Student's t-test, the Fisher-ratio and analysis of variance (ANOVA); however, these methods may not always be feasible for nonlinear systems and non-classification problems. As an artificial intelligence method, genetic algorithm may provide a novel feature selection strategy to detect pertinent features for a variety of systems, even for those without clear mechanisms. And this type of biological inspired adaptive learning method has prompted other new approaches in feature selection, such as the ant colony algorithm (ACA) method.

---

* A version of this chapter was also published in *Applications of Swarm Intelligence,* edited by Louis P. Walters, published by Nova Science Publishers, Inc. It was submitted for appropriate modifications in an effort to encourage wider dissemination of research.

† Corresponding author: *cedavis@ucdavis.edu*

The ant colony algorithm that mimics the social behavior of ants is a typical swarm intelligence based optimization method, and this approach has increasingly been applied for system feature selection. This commentary will provide a short review of recent ACA based feature selection studies, compare the outcomes of these studies to other intelligent selection methods, and discuss the advantages and disadvantages of the ACA based feature selection method. Together this chapter will suggest promising directions for future research in this area.

## INTRODUCTION

As a key tool for chemical analysis, spectral instruments have been widely used for metabolomics and proteomics studies, especially as they relate to disease diagnostics [1, 2]. Aiming to provide direct information for biology and pathology studies, spectral instruments such as mass spectrometry and differential mobility spectrometry are able to measure analytes in human effluents with precision and specificity. These instruments also usually generate highly dimensional data in which putative biomarkers may be present along with much "background" information which is not pertinent to disease diagnostics. However, in many cases it can be very challenging to detect these potential "disease" biomarkers from the background spectral data. Therefore, a variety of strategies beyond that of traditional statistical analysis have been employed for biomarker detection in these complex data sets. Among these strategies, the optimization based feature selection methods have proven to be very successful, and even superior to conventional approaches such as those based on variance analysis and the Student's *t*-test. In fact, these new methods have shown the ability to discover biomarkers embedded in complex data such as nonlinear systems, and also they have been very useful in non-classification problems such as [3]. Recently a swarm intelligence based optimum searching approach called ant colony optimization has shown great power in detecting biomarkers from spectral data [4, 5]. To date, there have been only a few reports of the research in this emerging field, and this commentary will provide a short description of this biomarker identification approach, review current applications, discuss potential problems and limitations of the method, and suggest promising directions for future work in the field.

Mimicking group social behavior, the ant colony algorithm (ACA) is an optimization strategy [6-8]. In the physical real world, biological ants collaborate during their food searching process, and they do this by depositing pheromone on the paths they selected towards a food source. A pheromone is a chemical that triggers a collective response of other members in the colony, so a path with more pheromone deposited is more likely to be selected in the next searching step. Eventually, the entire ant colony will choose the same path that usually is the shortest path from their nest to food, and we observe this behavior as ants follow each other in remarkably close synched progression – even across the most uneven terrain.

We can take away some valuable concepts from this biological phenomenon, and the ACA utilizes the following four steps to perform a robust spectral biomarker searching process [4]: (1) "Pheromone amount initialization" in which the same amount of pheromone is given to each spectral signal (biomarker candidate); (2) "Solution selection" in which each artificial ant selects biomarkers based on a probability that is estimated from the pheromone on each feature; (3) "Solution score evaluation" in which a mathematical model is employed to evaluate the quality of selected features; and (4) "Pheromone amount updating" which consists of two parts: pheromone natural evaporation over iteration time and an increase that is proportional to the solution score (e.g. "better" features accumulate more pheromone). Ideally by repeating steps (2) – (4), all artificial ants will be convergent to the same set of features which theoretically represent the optimal biomarkers for a particular data set. Clearly, this is an adaptive objective driven biomarker detecting strategy. Through a user-defined objective function, we can detect putative biomarkers for both classification and quantitative estimation problems in both linear and nonlinear systems.

One of the more recent reports of ACA in the literature applied the method to detect the potential biomarkers for the diagnosis of ovarian cancer [4]. In this study, the mass spectral data of the sera from 162 ovarian cancer patients and 91 control healthy females were employed for biomarker detection. By identifying putative biomarkers within this data set, it may be possible in the future to automate high-throughput screening processes to example blood sera for markers of this or other diseases. To reduce the dimension of the original searching space, wavelet analysis was used to preprocess the original spectral data, and the ACA was then applied to select the distinguishable wavelet coefficients. The selected wavelet coefficients not only yielded a high diagnosis accuracy (98.8%) from an independent sample testing data set, but they also helped to locate the biomarkers in the original mass spectra for future pathology studies. Another successful application of ACA for spectral feature selection was the wavelength selection for Ultraviolet (UV) spectra and near infrared (NIR) spectra [5]. The results indicated that the predictive ability of the proposed model based on a small number of selected wavelengths were very often better than that obtained from the full spectra and the ACA helped to understand which part of spectra were more pertinent to the independent variable. The ACA based feature (biomarker) selection approaches were also conducted in the quantitative structure activity relationship (QSAR) modeling of drug anti-HIV-1 activities [3] and in the selection of the gene expression data for disease classification [9]. In these studies, ACA demonstrated its ability to search optimal feature sets. However, the application of ACA to spectral related biomarker detection is still in very initial stages and there are some potential obstacles that would need to be overcome in future research.

One challenge this method faces in the future is how to avoid including irrelevant and dispensable features in the final selected biomarker set. ACA is a searching program in which the evaluation of the quality for the selected features (biomarkers) depends on a user designed function, such as a pattern recognition model. It is likely that a function obtained through a robust machine learning process may generate an equally good output for two cases: (1) pertinent features versus (2) pertinent features accompanied with dispensable features, which would eventually result in the inclusion of extra dispensable features into the optimal feature set. One feasible way to solve this problem is to start the biomarker searching process with a very small feature number. For each feature number, the ACA search program could be executed for sufficient time to help ensure the optimal feature set is selected. It could then be possible to increase the feature number in an iterative process and re-apply the ACA program until there is no significant increase in the modeling accuracy. Alternatively, it may also be possible to integrate rough set theory into the ACA based feature selection process. The rough set theory is a mathematical method to deal with uncertainty and vagueness of decision systems and it has been applied successfully in many fields [10-13]. There have been some preliminary reports of integrating rough set theory with an ACA to detect the minimal set of features [14]. We can also attempt to prevent this problem by avoiding sophisticated and over-robust machine learning methods, as they are more likely to have the ability to eliminate possible disturbance from dispensable features included.

Convergence and searching speed are two additional key issues critical to the ACA algorithm. In other application fields of ACA, there have been some methods proposed to solve these two problems. First, parallelization is an efficient way to expedite an optimum searching process. Inherently ACA is a parallelizable search technique [15], but little research has been reported on this aspect. The reported results include a simple parallelization strategy without any interaction [16], an island model with ant colony trail information exchange [17], and a master-slave parallelization strategy [18]. Integrating ACA with other searching algorithms such as genetic algorithm is another promising direction [19]. The unique operators and properties of the genetic algorithm approach would be a vital force to keep ant colony member diversity and help ensure the convergence of the ACA searching processes. Designing a proper fitness function that can amplify the difference between various selected feature sets would also be a feasible method to expedite a searching process. For spectral data feature selection, digital signal processing (DSP) approaches can be another support to shorten the selection process time. For example, wavelet transformation was successfully applied to reduce the data dimension for the ACA based mass spectral feature selection [4, 20]. Auto-regression model and other DSP methods are also promising choices for spectral data dimension reduction [20]. We expect that these modified ACA approaches will benefit the biomarker feature selection for spectral data, and could bring the method into more widespread use as an effective biomarker selection and searching tool.

## CONCLUSION

ACA has demonstrated a positive effect on detecting biomarker features from the highly dimensional spectral data, showing its superiority to conventional feature selection strategies. The adaptive quality of the algorithm is an important virtue of this biomarker selection strategy, and partially accounts for its success. The application of ACA to spectral biomarker detection is still at the beginning stages of research, but the successful applications of ACA in other fields indicate a bright future of this method for high-level spectral data analysis in the chemical and biochemical fields – especially as they relate to metabolomics studies and disease diagnostics. New and creative modifications of the ACA will likely provide strong support and promising directions for a wide application of ACA use in spectral biomarker feature detection.

## ACKNOWLEDGMENTS

Partial support for the authors and this publication was made possible by Grant Number UL1 RR024146 from the National Center for Research for Resources, Gilead Sciences, Inc., California Citrus Research Board, and the Florida Citrus Production Research Advisory Council. The contents of this manuscript are solely the responsibility of the authors and do not necessarily represent the official views of the funding agencies.

## REFERENCES

[1] Petricoin, E. F., Ardekani, A. M., Hitt, B. A., Levine, P. J., Fusaro, V. A., Steinberg, S. M., Mills, G. B., Simone, C., Fishman, D. A., Kohn, E. C., Liotta, L. A. (2002). *Lancet, 359*, 572.

[2] Willingale, R., Jones, D. J. L., Lamb, J. H., Quinn, P., Farmer, P. B., Ng, L. L. (2006). *Proteomics*, *6*, 5903.

[3] Goodarzi, M., Freitas, M. P. & Jensen, R. (2009). *Chemometrics and Intelligent Laboratory Systems*, *98*, 123.

[4] Zhao, W. X., Davis, C. E. (2009). *Analytica Chimica Acta*, *651*, 15.

[5] Shamsipur, M., Zare-Shahabadi, V., Hemmateenejad, B., Akhond, M. (2006). *Journal of Chemometrics*, *20*, 146.

[6] Dorigo, M., Maniezzo, V. & Colorni, A. (1996). Ieee Transactions on Systems *Man and Cybernetics Part B-Cybernetics*, *26*, 29.

[7] Dorigo, M., Bonabeau, E., Theraulaz, G. (2000). Future Generation Computer Systems-the International *Journal of Grid Computing Theory Methods and Applications*, *16*, 851.

[8] Dorigo, M. & Blum, C. (2005). *Theoretical Computer Science*, *344*, 243.

[9] Robbins, K. R., Zhang, W., Bertrand, J. K. & Rekaya, R. (2007). *Mathematical Medicine and Biology-a Journal of the Ima*, *24*, 413.

[10] Thangavel, K. & Pethalakshmi, A. (2009). *Applied Soft Computing*, *9*, 1.

[11] Pawlak, Z., Skowron, A. (2007). *Information Sciences*, *177*, 3.

[12] Pawlak, Z. (2002). *Information Sciences*, *147*, 1.

[13] Pawlak, Z. (1982). *International Journal of Computer & Information Sciences*, *11*, 341.

[14] Ke, L. J., Feng, Z. R., Ren, Z. G. (2008). *Pattern Recognition Letters*, *29*, 1351.

[15] Randall, M. & Lewis, A. (2002). *Journal of Parallel and Distributed Computing*, *62*, 1421.

[16] Stutzle, T. (1998). Parallel Problem Solving from Nature - PPSN V. 5th International Conference. Proceedings|Parallel Problem Solving from Nature - PPSN V. 5th International Conference. *Proceedings*, *722*.

[17] Michel, R., Middendorf, M. (1998). Parallel Problem Solving from Nature - PPSN V. 5th International Conference. Proceedings|Parallel Problem Solving from Nature - PPSN V. 5th *International Conference. Proceedings*, *692*.

[18] Tsutsui, S. (2008). Parallel ant colony optimization for the quadratic assignment problems with symmetric multi processing, Ant Colony Optimization and Swarm Intelligence. 6th International Conference, *ANTS*, Springer-Verlag, Brussels, Belgium, *363*.

[19] Nemati, S., Basiri, M. E., Ghasem-Aghaee, N. & Aghdam, M. H. (2009). *Expert Systems with Applications*, *36*, 12086.

[20] Zhao, W. & Davis, C. E. (2009). *Chemometrics and Intelligent Laboratory Systems*, *96*, 252.

In: Ant Colonies
Editor: Emily C. Sun
ISBN: 978-1-61122-023-0


*Chapter 10*

# ANT COLONY OPTIMIZATION BASED MESSAGE AUTHENTICATION FOR WIRELESS NETWORKS*

***N. K. Sreelaja*†* and G. A. Vijayalakshmi Pai*#**
Department of Mathematics and Computer Applications,
PSG College of Technology, Coimbatore, India

## ABSTRACT

In recent days wireless communication plays a major role. The packets transmitted are vulnerable to Dos attacks caused by injecting forged packets. Authentication plays an important role in securing transfer of messages in wireless environment that are attractive to malicious attacks. In this chapter an Ant Colony Optimization (ACO) based method is proposed to reduce the computational and communication overhead while generating a mark for each packet. In this approach, the packets are represented in the form of a binary tree and are identified by a packet identifier ID. Each packet has a set of keys with which a mark is generated for the packet. The packets in a group are represented in the form of a truth table and a minimized boolean expression is obtained. The literals in the expression give the minimum number of keys for generating a mark. Sreelaja and Pai [5] proposed an Ant Colony Optimization based Boolean Expression Evolver (ABXE) algorithm to obtain a minimized Boolean expression. The ABXE algorithm is judiciously employed in the proposed work to efficiently generate marks for each packet. The literals in the product term of the Boolean expression represent the auxiliary keys to generate the marks for the packets using the root key. The receiver receives the packets and the root key is recovered using the auxiliary keys. The recovered roots help the receiver to classify received packets into disjoint sets and hence authentic packets and forged packets are placed separately. While the Merkle Tree packet filtering approach requires (n.log n) hashes to authenticate the packets, the proposed method requires only (log n) keys which serve to reduce the computational overhead. Also, the proposed approach calls for only

* A version of this chapter was also published in *Wireless Networks: Research, Technology and Applications,* edited by Jia Feng, published by Nova Science Publishers, Inc. It was submitted for appropriate modifications in an effort to encourage wider dissemination of research.

† Corresponding author: *sreelajank@gmail.com # paigav@mca.psgtech.ac.in

(log n) keys and n signatures to be sent to the receiver which serves to reduce its communication overhead. In comparison, the Merkle Tree packet filtering approach requires (n log n) hashes and n signatures to be sent to the receiver.

**Keywords:** Packet Filtering, Ant Colony Optimization, Minimized boolean expression, Message authentication

## 1. INTRODUCTION

In recent days wireless communication plays a major role. Wireless networks such as cellular communication is seeing an explosive growth due to increased usage. However, it is vulnerable to eavesdropping which poses a threat to security and privacy of the user. Thus cryptographic schemes are developed for protecting alphanumeric data transmitted between the users. Though the messages are encrypted and transmitted across the network, authentication plays a crucial role in transferring messages and each receiver should be able to ensure that the received packet comes from the real sender as it claims. The packets transmitted are vulnerable to Dos attacks caused by injecting forged packets. Authentication plays an important role in securing transfer of messages in wireless environment attractive to malicious attacks. Thus the packets transmitted include a mark generated by the sender and this is verified by the receiver. The message transmitted is divided into packets and the mark is attached to all the packets in the block to ensure message authentication.

Zhou et al [7], proposed a method of packet filtering using a Merkle tree approach. In this method a mark is generated for each packet before the packets are transmitted. A mark is generated for each packet and the receiver on receiving the packets checks whether it matches with that of the sender. The drawback is that the number of hash values given to the receiver to recover the root key from the mark generated in the packet depends on the number of packets in the group. Thus there is an increase in the communication overhead when the number of packets in the group is large.

This drawback can be overcome by reducing the computational and communication overhead by using a Boolean function minimization technique. This chapter discusses the application of Ant Colony Optimization (ACO) based approach to obtain a minimized Boolean expression and the literals of the minimized boolean expression is used to generate marks for the packets in the group to ensure message authentication in wireless networks. This approach reduces the number of keys used to generate marks for the packets in the group there by reducing the communication overhead.

Swarm intelligence is the emergent collective intelligence of groups of simple autonomous agents that models the collective behavior of social insects [6]. Here, an autonomous agent is a subsystem that interacts with its environment, which probably consists of other agents, but acts relatively independently from all other agents. The autonomous agent does not follow commands from a leader, or some global plan [1]. The characteristics of swarm are distributed and have no model of the environment. It senses the environment and has an ability to change environment. Ant system is an evolution from the swarm intelligence forming an evolutionary algorithm to solve optimization problems. Artificial Ants [4] have some characteristics which do not find counterparts with real ants. They live in a discrete world and the moves consist of transitions from one state to another. They have an internal state that contains the memory of the ant's past action. They deposit a particular amount of pheromone, which is a function of the quality of the solution found. The idea, loosely inspired by the behavior of real ants, is that of a parallel search based on local problem data and on a dynamic memory structure containing information on the quality of previously obtained result.

This work discusses an Ant Colony Optimization (ACO) based method of obtaining a minimized boolean expression to reduce the computational and communication overhead while generating a mark for each packet. In this approach, the packets are represented in the form of a binary tree and are identified by a packet identifier ID. Each packet has a set of keys with which a mark is generated for the packet. The packets in a group are represented in the form of a truth table and a minimized boolean expression is obtained. The literals in the expression give the minimum number of keys for generating a mark. Sreelaja and Pai [5] proposed an Ant Colony Optimization based Boolean Expression Evolver (ABXE) algorithm to obtain a minimized boolean expression. The ABXE algorithm is judiciously employed to efficiently generate marks for each packet.

## 2. Cellular Network System

Cellular communication is vulnerable to fraud and eavesdropping since it is carried out over the air interface. A cellular network [2] includes mobile stations (MSs), with wireless access to the public switched telephone network (PSTN). A base station (BS) serves the Mobile stations in the cellular network. The BS is fixed, and is connected to the mobile telephone switching office (MTSO), also known as the mobile switching center. A cluster of BS's is attached to an MTSO which is connected to the PSTN. Figure 1 illustrates a cellular network.

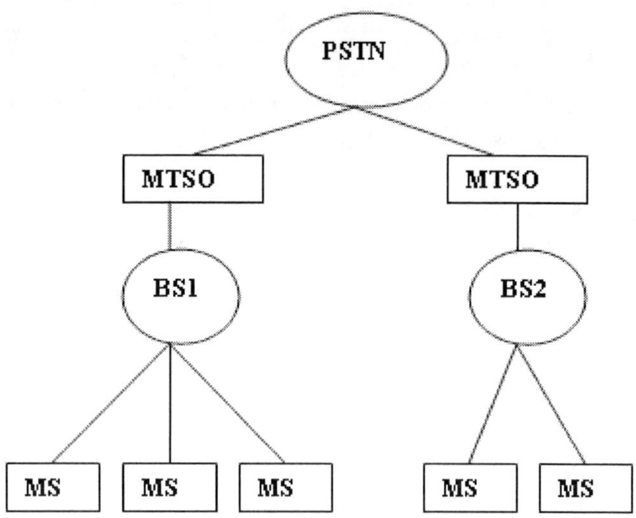


Figure 1. Model of a Cellular Network System

## 3. Ant Colony Optimization

A colony of ants denoting a set of computational concurrent and asynchronous agents moves through states of the problem corresponding to partial solutions of the problem to solve. They move by applying a stochastic local decision policy based on two parameters, called *trails* and *attractiveness*. By moving, each ant incrementally constructs a solution to the problem. When an ant completes a solution, or during the construction phase, the ant evaluates the solution and modifies the trail value on the components used in its solution. This pheromone information will direct the search of the future ants. Furthermore, an ACO algorithm includes two more mechanisms namely *trail evaporation* and optionally, *daemon actions*. Trail evaporation decreases all trail values over time, in order to avoid unlimited accumulation of trails over some component. Daemon actions can be used to implement centralized actions which cannot be performed by single ants, such as the invocation of a local optimization procedure, or the update of global information to be used to decide whether to bias the search process from a non-local perspective [8].

## 4. System Model and Key Distribution Scheme

The packets are represented in the form of a binary tree and are identified by a packet identifier ID. Each packet has a set of keys with which a mark is generated for the packet. The packets belonging to a group are represented as $\{P_1, P_2, P_3 \ldots P_N\}$ where $N=2^n$, $N$ denotes the total number of packets in the group and $n$ denotes the length of the binary string representing the packetid ($P_{ID}$) of each packet. The $P_{ID}$ of each packet P is written in binary form, as an n-bit ID $PID\ (P) = X_1X_2X_3 \ldots X_n$ where $X_i$ is either 0 or 1. The boolean membership function m*()* of the $P_{ID}$ is used to determine the existence of the packet in the group. A packet with $P_{ID}(X_1X_2 \ldots X_n)$ is in the group if $P(X_1X_2 \ldots X_n) = 1$ and is not in the group if $P(X_1X_2 \ldots X_n) = 0$.

Each packet in the group has a root key *SK* and a set of auxiliary keys $K_1K_2 \ldots K_n$, where $K_i$ takes the value $k_i$ if $X_i = 1$ and $k_i^{|}$ if $X_i = 0$. The auxiliary key pair corresponds to a bit in the PID. The Keys possessed by the packets in the group of size 4 is shown in Figure 2. The packets in the group are represented by square leaf nodes in the tree. The auxiliary keys are represented by round nodes in the system. A packet $P_2$ (UID 01) possesses the auxiliary keys $k_1$, $k_2$ in addition to the root key. The packets in a group are represented in the form of a truth table and a minimized boolean expression is obtained to find the minimum number of keys to generate mark for each packet. Table 1 shows the truth table representation of the packets in the group.

## 5. Mark Generation in Packets Using Ant Colony Optimization Based Boolean Function Minimization

A truth table denoting a boolean membership function represents the packets in the group with the packetid as the input and the output with a value of 1 represents the presence of the packet in the group and a value of 0 represents the absence of the packet in the group. An Ant

Colony optimization based approach of minimizing a Boolean expression is used for generating marks in the packet. The minimized boolean expression for the given truth table is obtained using ABXE algorithm. The literals in the minimized boolean expression represent the minimum number of auxiliary keys to generate marks for the packets in the group. The root key for the packet group is encrypted using the auxiliary keys denoted by the literals of the minimized boolean expression and a mark is generated for each packet in the group.

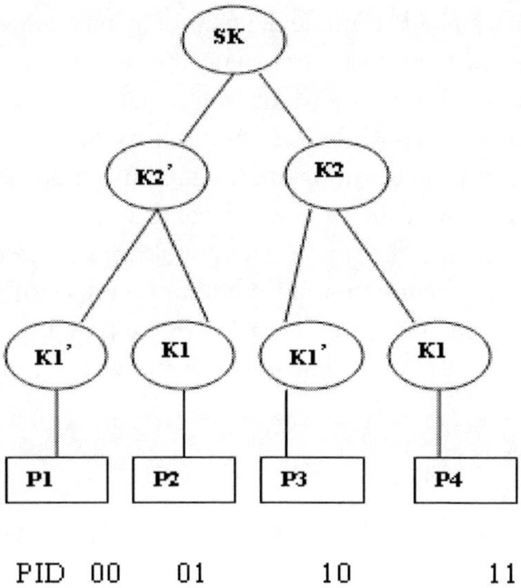


Figure 2. Key distribution for the packets in a group

**Table 1. Truth Table Representation of the packets in a group**

| Input ($K_2K_1$) | OUTPUT |
|---|---|
| 00 | 1 |
| 01 | 1 |
| 10 | 1 |
| 11 | 1 |

## 5.1. Model of an Ant System

The packets in a group are represented in the form of a truth table. An Ant System is used to determine the minimized boolean expression for a given input truth table. The ants in the system work together to obtain an optimal solution. Each ant agent moves to reach the solution by depositing pheromone. The Pheromones on the paths traveled by the ants serves as a means of communication between other ants. The pheromone deposition of each ant agent is a group of terms combined using an OR operator denoting the boolean expression. Each term is a literal or a series of literals combined using an AND operator. The energy value of the ant agent denotes its attractiveness towards the solution. The pheromone deposition of the ant agent denoting a boolean expression is evaluated to find its energy value. Each variable in the formula is replaced with its corresponding value from the truth table and the expression is evaluated and the output vector is found. The number of bits in the output vector of the boolean expression matching with that of the output of the given input truth table is the energy value of the ant agent.

Each ant agent has a tabu-list denoting its memory to store the pheromone deposition and its energy value. The pheromone deposition evaporates when the ant agent moves to the next trail and the ant agent updates its pheromone deposition by changing the terms. The ant agent compares the energy value of the current trail with that of the energy value of its previous trail and selects the pheromone deposition of the trail with a greater energy value so that some of the terms in the pheromone deposition can be used by the ant agent during pheromone updating. This would make the ant agent obtain the minimized boolean expression at a lesser number of trails. The ant agent with an energy value equal to the maximum number of packets in the group represents the minimized boolean expression. The literals in the minimized boolean expression represents the minimum number of keys to encrypt the root key using which a mark is generated for each packet in the group. The pheromone deposition, tabu-list, and energy monitoring help this novel Ant System (AS) to obtain an optimal solution.

## 6. ABXE Algorithm-Construction and Design

The ABXE algorithm is a novel approach for deriving minimized boolean expressions given the truth table as input. The algorithm, which is a swarm intelligence approach to the solution of the problem of minimizing boolean expressions, makes use of the Ant Colony Optimization wherein each ant agent changes the pheromone deposition to attain the minimized boolean expression and tabu-list maintenance keeps track of the energy value and pheromone deposition of the ant agent. The basic blocks of the Ant Colony Optimization approach applied to the problem are elaborated next.

### 6.1. Ant Agent Representation of the Boolean Expression

Each boolean expression expressed as an ant agent consists of terms at respective position denoting the pheromone deposition. Addition denotes the OR operation and multiplication denotes the AND operation in the boolean expression. The terms denoting the pheromone deposition of the ant agent is obtained by taking the combinations of the variables along with their complements. The combination of a variable and its complement is neglected. For a 3-variable case (D, E, F) the terms generated are shown in Figure 3. Each term contains either a literal or a series of literals related by AND operator. The terms are combined using an OR operator. Figure 4 illustrates the ant agent representing the terms at each position for a two variable case. For instance, in a two variable case the ant agent with a pheromone deposition {3, 4} denotes the terms at positions 3 and 4. Thus the terms $x_2$ *and* $x_2^{|}$ at the corresponding positions for a two variable case is combined using an OR operator. Thus the pheromone deposition {3, 4} denotes the boolean expression $x_2+x_2^{|}$.

The maximum number of terms in the ant agent depends on the size of the packet group. The number of terms grows exponentially with the input size. It is shown that for a function of n variables the maximum number of terms for the ant agent is $3^n - 1$. In general, the number of terms for an n-variable expression and therefore the number of positions for an ant agent is given as

$$nC_1 .2^1 + nC_2 .2^2 + ..nC_n .2^n \tag{1}$$

$$= \sum_{i=1}^{n} (nC_i).2^i \tag{2}$$

$$= 3^n - 1 \tag{3}$$

The computation of terms for each variable is done using a divide and conquer technique thereby reducing the exponential timing for term generation. The terms are computed and stored as a static table. The ant agent retrieves the terms for the pheromone deposition at each position and computes the energy level.

| **1-Variable Terms** | **2-Variable Terms** | **3-Variable Terms** |
|---|---|---|
| $D, D^{\vert}$<br>$E, E^{\vert}$<br>$F, F^{\vert}$ | $DE, D^{\vert}E, DE^{\vert}$<br>$D^{\vert}E^{\vert}, D^{\vert}F^{\vert}, D^{\vert}F$<br>$DF, DF^{\vert}, E^{\vert}F^{\vert}$<br>$E^{\vert}F, EF, EF^{\vert}$ | $D^{\vert}E^{\vert}F^{\vert}, D^{\vert}E^{\vert}F,$<br>$D^{\vert}EF^{\vert}, D^{\vert}EF,$<br>$DEF^{\vert}, DEF,$<br>$DE^{\vert}F^{\vert}, DE^{\vert}F$ |

Figure 3. Terms Generated for a 3-Variable Case

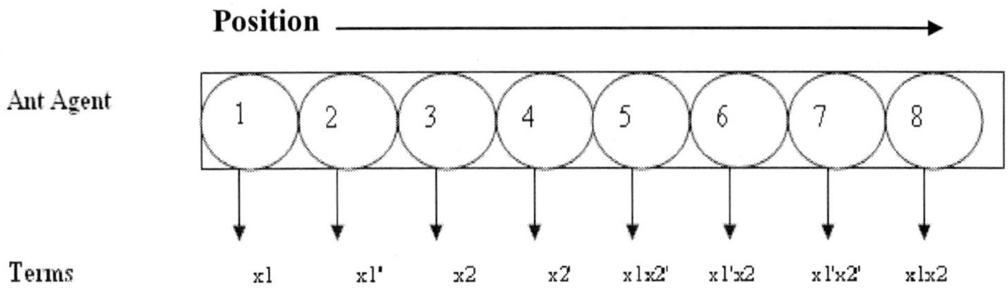


Figure 4. Representation of an Ant agent for a 2-Variable case

## Assignment of Energy Value

The attractiveness of the ant agent towards the solution is denoted by the energy value. Energy value is a measure of how well a desired behavior is performed by an ant agent. Each of the boolean expression encoded and represented as an ant agent is considered as a potential problem solution. For instance the ant agent {3, 4} represents the boolean expression *x2+x2'*. Each variable in the formula is replaced with its corresponding value from the truth table and the expression is evaluated. The energy value of an ant agent is given by the number of bits in its output vector matching with that of the bits in the truth table output vector. Let $A_i$ be the ant agent where the truth table output vector and the Ant agent's output vectors are given in Equations (4) and (5). Energy value is calculated using Equation (6).

$$T = (t_1, t_2, t_3, t_4), t_i = 0 \; or \; 1 \tag{4}$$

$$Output(A_i) = (o_i^{(1)}, o_i^{(2)}, o_i^{(3)}, o_i^{(4)}), o_i^{(j)} = 0 \; or \; 1$$

(j th bit of the output vector of i th ant agent, j = 1, 2, 3, 4) (5)

$$Energy(A_i) = count(t_j = o_i^{(j)}) \tag{6}$$

where count $(w_k = z_k)$ is a function that counts the number of instances where $w_k$ and $z_k$ are equal. The pheromone deposition of an ant agent having the energy value equal to the maximum number of packets in the group corresponds to the minimized boolean expression.

## Computation of Energy Value for a Large Number of Packets in a Group

The truth table representing the packets in the group is partitioned and a divide and conquer technique is used to find the energy value of each ant agent for a very large number of packets in a group. The energy value of an ant agent is computed for each partitioned truth table and added to give the total energy value.

## 6.4. Algorithm: Ant Colony Optimized Boolean Expression Evolver

Figure 5 illustrates the pseudo-code of the ABXE algorithm

```
Procedure ABXE ()
K=0;
Choose Ant agents with terms at random positions denoting
      Pheromone deposition;
Evaluate the energy value of each ant agent Ai according to the
energy function
        energy (Ai)=count (tj=Oi(j));
Repeat
Update the Pheromone deposition by changing
the terms and compute the energy of the ant agent;
Select the pheromone deposition of the ant agent with
 energy (ant agent in current trial)>=energy(ant
     agent in previous trial);
  Return (ant agent with energy value=maximum number of
          packets in a group);
        Until (energy= maximum number of packets in a group);
end ABXE;
```

Figure 5. ABXE Algorithm Pseudocode

### 6.4. Algorithm: Ant Colony Optimized Boolean Expression Evolver

Figure 5 illustrates the pseudo-code of the ABXE algorithm

## 7. Experimental Results

The experimental results are discussed for maximum of 4 packets in a group. The packets in a group are represented as a truth table. Table 2 shows the truth table representation for the packets in the group. The problem is in two binary variables $K_2$, K1 where the minimized boolean expression is to be found using ABXE algorithm. The binary vector from 00 to 11 is taken as the input. The key distribution for the packets in the group is given in Figure 6. The Square nodes represent the packets in the group. The round nodes represent the keys possessed by the packets. The minimized boolean expression for the truth table is obtained by using an Ant Colony Optimization approach.

**Table 2. Truth Table Representation of the packets attached to a group**

| Input ($K_2K_1$) | OUTPUT |
|---|---|
| 00 | 1 |
| 01 | 1 |
| 10 | 1 |
| 11 | 1 |

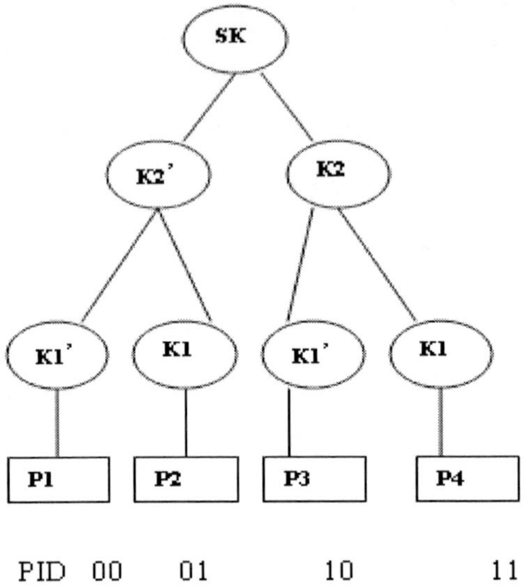


Figure 6. Key distribution of packets in the group

In the ACO based approach the ant agent moves to find the solution by depositing pheromone. The pheromone deposition denotes the boolean expression. The energy value of the ant agent gives its attractiveness towards the solution. Each ant agent has terms denoting the pheromone deposition. For instance, the first ant agent has the terms at positions 1 and 5. Thus the pheromone deposition of the ant agent 1 is *k*1+*k1 k2'*. Each variable in the formula is replaced with its corresponding value from the truth table and the expression is evaluated and the energy value is obtained. Thus the energy value of the first ant agent is 2. The pheromone deposition along with the energy value is stored in the tabu list of the corresponding ant agent. The ant agent changes its pheromone deposition by choosing the term at positions 1,3 and the energy value is calculated. Since this energy value is greater than that of the previous trail, the tabu list is updated with this value. The process is repeated until any one of the ant agent obtains an energy value equal to the maximum number of packets in the group. Table 3 shows the trails in which each ant agent finds the minimized boolean expression for several packets in a group. In the given example the first ant agent has an energy value equal to the maximum number of packets in the group. Hence the pheromone deposition of the ant agent at positions 3, 4 represents the minimized boolean expression $k_2+k_2'$.

The literals in the product term represents the auxiliary keys $k_2'$ and $k_2$. The auxiliary keys are used to encrypt the root key SK of the packet group to generate a mark for the packets in the group. The keys used for generating mark of the packet P1, P2 are $k_2'$ *and* P3, P4 is $k_2$ respectively. The keys generate a mark for each packet using the root key SK. The root key *SK* is encrypted using the corresponding auxiliary keys of the packets and a mark is generated for the packets in the group. The mark for the packet P1 and P2 is generated by encrypting the root key using $\{SK\}_{k2'}$ and the mark for packets P3 and P4 are generated using $\{SK\}_{k2}$ respectively. The receiver receives the packets and the root is recovered using the auxiliary keys. The recovered roots help the receiver to classify received packets into disjoint sets and hence authentic packets and forged packets are placed separately. This helps the receiver to get only authenticate messages from the sender.

Figure 7 shows the pheromone deposition of ant agent 4 having an energy value 1048576 in the 4th trail corresponds to the minimized boolean expression to obtain the keys for generating marks for the packets in the group of size 1048576. Figure 8 shows the time taken by the ant agent to obtain a minimized boolean expression for the packets in the group to generate marks for the packets in the group.

**Table 3. Sample Trails leading to the minimization of a Boolean expression**

| Ant Agent | I Trail | Energy | Tabu-List | II Trail | Energy | Tabu-List | III Trail | Energy | Tabu-List |
|---|---|---|---|---|---|---|---|---|---|
| 1 | {1,5} | 2 | {1,5}-2 | {1,3} | 3 | {1,3}-3 | {3,4} | 4 | {3,4}-4 |
| 2 | {3,5} | 3 | {3,5}-3 | {3,5,8} | 3 | {3,5,8}-3 | {5,8} | 2 | {3,5,8}-3 |
| 3 | {3,7} | 3 | {3,7}-3 | {3,5} | 3 | {3,5}-3 | {3} | 2 | {3,5}-3 |
| 4 | {2,5} | 3 | {2,5}-3 | {5} | 1 | {2,5}-3 | {5,6} | 2 | {2,5}-3 |

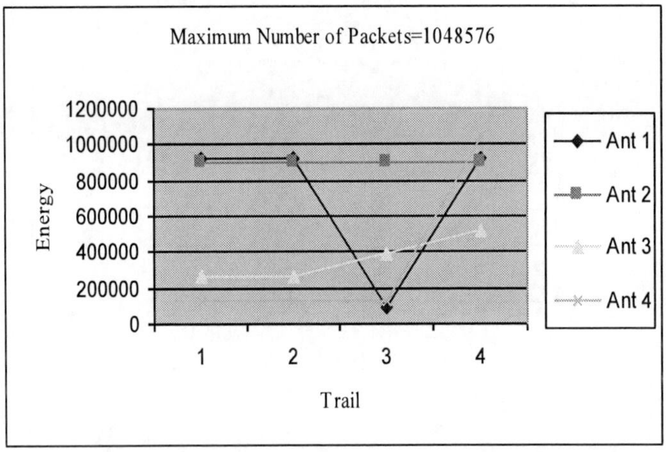


Figure 7. Ant Agent obtaining minimized boolean expression to generate marks for packets

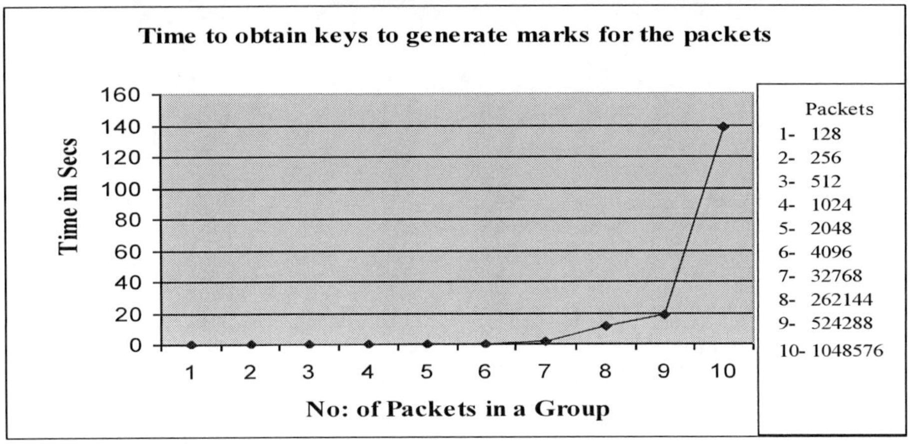


Figure 8. Time taken by the ant agent to obtain keys to generate marks for various number of packets

# 8. Comparison with Existing Methods

## 8.1. Merkle Tree Approach

Zhou et al.,[7] proposed a method of packet filtering using a Merkle tree approach. In this approach a Merkle Tree [3] is used to generate marks for the packets in the group. Figure 9 shows an example of a binary tree for 8 packets in a group. Each leaf is a hash of one packet. Each internal node is the hash value for both its left and right children. A mark is constructed for each packet in the group as a set of siblings of the nodes along the path from the packet to the root. In this example the mark of the packet $P_2$ is $\{H_2,H_{3,4},H_{5,8}\}$.The root is recovered by the receiver as $H_{1,8}$=(( $H_{3,4}$,(H($P_2$), $H_2$)), $H_{5,8}$).Thus to construct a mark for the packets the hash value for the packets along the path from the packet to the root is used. Thus nlogn hashes are required to generate marks for the packets. The number of hash values of the packets to be given to the receiver to recover the root value is 8 in this case.

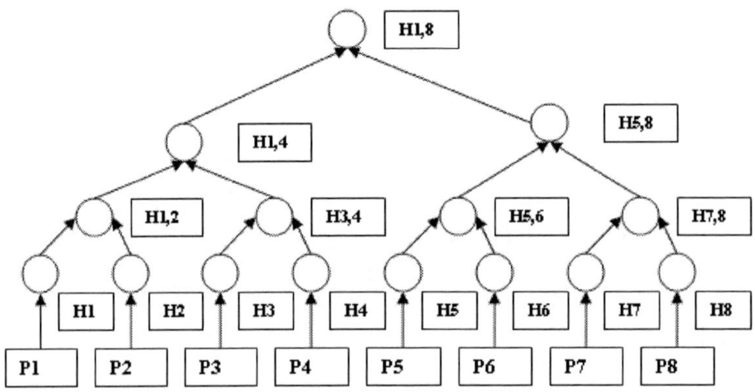


Figure 9. Binary Tree for 8 packets in a group

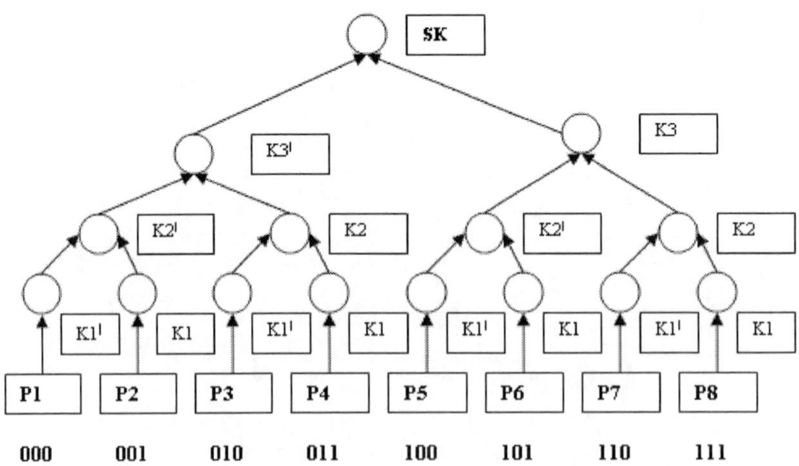


Figure 10. Key distribution for 8 packets in a group

**Table 4. Comparison between ACO based Message authentication and Merkle tree approach**

| | Merkle tree Packet Filtering Approach | ACO based Message Authentication |
|---|---|---|
| Computational Overhead | This approach requires n log n hashes to authenticate the packets. | This approach requires log n keys to generate marks to authenticate the packets. |
| Communication Overhead | The communication overhead is n signatures and n log n hashes sent to the receiver. | The communication overhead in this approach is n signatures and log n keys sent to the receiver. |

## 8.2. ACO Based Message Authentication

In this approach a binary tree is constructed for the packets in the group and a minimized boolean expression is obtained. The literals in the minimized boolean expression denote the keys used to generate marks for the packets in the group. Consider the binary tree for 8 packets in a group as shown in Figure 10. The minimized boolean expression obtained using ACO approach for the binary tree is $k_2+k_2'$. These auxiliary keys encrypt the root key to generate marks for the packets in the group. The mark of the packet $P_2$ is generated as $\{SK\}_{k2'}$. Thus only one key is used to generate the mark for the packet $P_2$. Thus in this approach log n keys are used to generate marks for the packets in the group. The receiver receives the auxiliary keys and recovers the root. Thus 2 auxiliary keys and 1 root key must be given to the receiver to recover the root value which is less when compared to Merkle tree approach.

Table 4 shows a comparison between ACO based message authentication and Merkle tree approach.

# 9. CONCLUSION

An efficient scheme involving minimized boolean expressions using Ant Colony Optimization based approach for packet filtering has been proposed. The ABXE algorithm evolves minimized boolean expressions to find the minimum number of keys needed to generate marks for each packet in the group. A divide and conquer technique is employed to find the minimized boolean expression for groups having large number of packets.

The ABXE algorithm overcomes the drawbacks of the Merkle tree approach by reducing the number of values to be transmitted by the sender for verifying the messages received. This method reduces the communication overhead and also the computational overhead for generating marks in the packet.

## ACKNOWLEDGMENT

The authors express their sincere thanks to the All India Council for Technical Education, New Delhi, INDIA for supporting this research under the Research Promotion Scheme (F.No 8023/BOR/RPS-104/2006-07).

## REFERENCES

[1] Flake, G. *The Computational Beauty of Nature*, Cambridge, MA: MIT Press, 1999.

[2] Jingyuan Zhang, Ivan Stojmenovic, *Cellular Networks*, University of Alabama, University of Ottawa, Canada.

[3] Merkle, R. "Protocols for Public Key cryptosystems", *Proc.IEEE Symposium Security and Privacy,* Apr 1980.

[4] Padhy, NP. Artificial Intelligence and Intelligent Systems, Oxford University press, 2005.

[5] Sreelaja, NK; Vijayalakshmi Pai, GA. Group Rekeying in Cellular Networks using Swarm Intelligence based Boolean expression minimization", *International Journal of Computer Standards and Interfaces*, 2008, (Communicated).

[6] Yang, Liu & Kevin, M. Passino, *Swarm Intelligence: Literature Overview,* Dept. of Electrical Engineering, The Ohio State University, 2015 Neil Ave, Columbus, OH 43210, March 30, 2000.

[7] Yun, Zhou & Yuguang, Fang, "Multimedia Broadcast Authentication based on Batch Signature", *IEEE Communications Magazine*, August 2007, Vol.45, No: 8, 72-77.

[8] Vittorio, Maniezzo; Luca Maria, Gambardella & Fabio de Luigi. "*Ant Colony Optimization*", *http://www.idsia.ch/~luca/aco2004.pdf.*

# INDEX

## C

## D



## E

## F



## G



## H

## I



## J



## K



## L

## M



## N

## O



## P

## Q



## R



## S